There is no question that the sporting activity of young animals is a rehearsal for the serious business of adult life. Kittens that pounce on whirling leaves will eventually pounce on running mice in precisely the same way. Puppies that wrestle with each other will eventually fight in earnest for mates or territory.

And so it is with human beings, whose kinship to other animals is far closer than our self-love pretends.

Human beings compete with each other in deadly combat often enough, but there are periods of time when the immediate necessity for such combat does not arise. At those times, pseudo-combats are arranged.

Of all the ancients, the Greeks took their games most seriously. It started simply enough with a day's worth of foot-races but grew steadily more complex until the Olympic Games came to last several days.

In our own day, passions are most intimately aroused by team sports, in which groups of highly trained combatants meet to play football, baseball, basketball, or soccer.

The association of crime and sport makes us uneasy. We have therefore assembled a dozen and a half tales in which such associations exist, and hope you will enjoy the incongruity of combining sport and crime.

THE SPORT OF CRIME

LYNX BOOKS
New York

THE SPORT OF CRIME

ISBN: 1-55802-248-1

First Printing/January 1989

This is a work of fiction. Names, characters, places, and incidents are either the product of the authors' imagination or are used fictitiously. Any resemblance to actual events, locales, or persons, living or dead, is entirely coincidental.

Copyright © 1989 by Nightfall, Inc. and Carol-Lynn Rössel Waugh and Martin H. Greenberg
All rights reserved. No part of this book may be reproduced or transmitted in any form or by any means electronic or mechanical, including by photocopying, by recording, or by any information storage and retrieval system, without the express written permission of the Publisher, except where permitted by law. For information, contact Lynx Communications, Inc.

This book is published by Lynx Books, a division of Lynx Communications, Inc., 41 Madison Avenue, New York, New York, 10010. The name "Lynx" together with the logotype consisting of a stylized head of a lynx is a trademark of Lynx Communications, Inc.

Printed in the United States of America

0 9 8 7 6 5 4 3 2 1

Acknowledgments

Isaac Asimov—Copyright © 1980 by Nightfall, Inc. From *Ellery Queen's Mystery Magazine*. Reprinted by permission of the author.

Jon Breen—Copyright © 1971 by Jon L. Breen; first published in *Ellery Queen's Mystery Magazine*. Reprinted by permission of the author.

Anthony Boucher—Copyright 1943 by Little, Brown, Inc. Reprinted by permission of Curtis Brown, Ltd.

Leo R. Ellis—Copyright © 1966 by H.S.D. Publications, Inc. From *Alfred Hitchcock's Mystery Magazine*. Reprinted by permission of Larry Sternig Literary Agency.

David Ely—Copyright © 1964 by David Ely. From *Ellery Queen's Mystery Magazine*. Reprinted by permission of Roberta Pryor, Inc.

Joyce Harrington—Copyright © 1976 by Joyce Harrington. From *Ellery Queen's Mystery Magazine*. Reprinted by permission of the author and her agents, the Scott Meredith Literary Agency, Inc., 845 Third Avenue, New York, NY 10022.

Clark Howard—Copyright © 1982 by Clark Howard. From *Alfred Hitchcock's Mystery Magazine*. Reprinted by permission of the author.

John Lutz—Copyright © 1978 by John Lutz. From *Ellery Queen's Mystery Magazine*. Reprinted by permission of the author.

Ed McBain—Copyright © 1962 by Ed McBain. Reprinted by permission of John Farquharson Ltd.

John D. MacDonald—Copyright 1950; renewed 1978 by John D. MacDonald. Reprinted by permission of George Diskant Associates, Inc.

Stuart Palmer—Copyright 1942 by Little, Brown, Inc. Reprinted by permission of the agents for the author's Estate, the Scott Meredith Literary Agency, Inc., 845 Third Avenue, New York, NY 10022.

Ellery Queen—Copyright 1939 by Ellery Queen; renewed 1967 by Ellery Queen. Reprinted by permission of the agents for the author's Estate, the Scott Meredith Literary Agency, Inc., 845 Third Avenue, New York, NY 10022.

Jack Ritchie—Copyright © 1982 by Davis Publications, Inc. From *Alfred Hitchcock's Mystery Magazine*. Reprinted by permission of Larry Sternig Literary Agency.

Rex Stout—"This Won't Kill You," from *Three Men Out* by Rex Stout. Copyright 1952 by Rex Stout, renewed 1980, 1981 by Pola Stout, Barbara Selleck and Rebecca Bradbury. All Rights Reserved. Reprinted by permission of Viking Penguin, Inc.

Julian Symons—Copyright © 1961 by Julian Symons. Reproduced by permission of Curtis Brown Ltd., London, on behalf of Julian Symons.

Walter Tevis—Copyright © 1956 by *Playboy Magazine*. Copyright renewed 1984 by *Playboy Magazine* and assigned to the Walter Tevis Copyright Trust. Originally appeared in *Playboy Magazine*. Reprinted by permission of Susan Schulman Literary Agency, Inc.

Wodehouse—Copyright 1927 by P. G. Wodehouse; renewed 1955. Reprinted by permission of the Scott Meredith Literary Agency, Inc., 845 Third Avenue, New York, NY 10022.

Contents

Introduction	ix
Isaac Asimov, **The Man Who Pretended to Like Baseball**	1
Jon L. Breen, **Diamond Dick**	19
Robert Barr, **A Game of Chess**	30
Anthony Boucher, **Coffin Corner**	45
Leo R. Ellis, **The Great Rodeo Fix**	61
David Ely, **The Sailing Club**	75
Joyce Harrington, **The Season Ticket Holder**	89
Clark Howard, **The Last Downhill**	104
John Lutz, **The Other Runner**	120
Ed McBain, **Storm**	132
John D. MacDonald, **Dead on the Pin**	193
Arthur Morrison, **The Affair of the "Avalanche Bicycle and Tyre Co., Limited"**	201

Stuart Palmer, **Tomorrow's Murder**	227
Ellery Queen, **Trojan Horse**	243
Jack Ritchie, **The Return of Cardula**	265
Rex Stout, **This Won't Kill You**	275
Julian Symons, **Murder on the Race Course**	321
Walter S. Tevis, **The Hustler**	345
P.G. Wodehouse, **Without the Option**	361

Introduction

Sport

ISAAC ASIMOV

Sport is older than humanity. We see it in non-human animals that are sufficiently intelligent for their actions to be interpreted in human terms.

Kittens will pursue a piece of string with great assiduity and will attack their mother's twitching tail. Puppies will wrestle with each other and engage in mock combat. Even grown dogs will pant eagerly as they wait for their masters to begin the game of fetch-the-stick. (Grown cats, however, scorn any form of activity that doesn't have as its immediate end either sex or food.)

There is no question that the sporting activity of young animals is a rehearsal for the serious business of adult life. Kittens that pounce on whirling leaves will eventually pounce on running mice in precisely the same way. Puppies that wrestle with each other will eventually fight in earnest for mates or territory.

And so it is with human beings, whose kinship to other animals is far closer than our self-love pretends.

Human beings compete with each other in deadly combat often enough, but there are periods of time when the immediate necessity for such combat does not arise. At those times, partly to feel excitement and partly to keep in trim, pseudo-combats are arranged.

The oldest detailed account of organized sport is to be found in the 23rd book of *The Iliad*, where the funeral games in honor of the dead Patroklos are described. Both chariot races and foot-races take place and are fiercely contested (as they should be for they are activities of prime importance in the warfare of the time—whether for hot pursuit or rapid retreat.) There was also boxing, wrestling, spear-throwing and so on.

Of all the ancients, the Greeks took their games most seriously. Beginning in 776 B.C. (according to tradition) quadrennial games were celebrated at the town of Olympia in southwestern Greece (hence the "Olympian" or "Olympic" games). It started simply enough with a day's worth of foot-races but grew steadily more complex until the Olympic Games came to last several days, to be open to all Greek-speaking peoples, and to involve a wide variety of competitions (including even intellectual ones such as the judging of poetry and dramas).

So important were the Olympic Games that they were considered one of the three factors that united the thousand independent cities of Greece into a single culture (the other two being the Greek language and the Homeric poems). Indeed, so important were they that at the time of the Games, even war was suspended and contestants from enemy cities met in peace upon the playing fields.

The games continued for nearly twelve hundred years till they were brought to an end in 393 by the Christian authorities who considered them a pagan festival. In 1896, they began again, and were opened to all the world and not only to those who spoke Greek—though a less hopeful fact is that in modern times, the games are suspended to allow wars to continue, rather than vice versa.

In all cultures, organized competition has played an

important role—from relatively peaceful strivings for victory in dancing, singing, or running, to pseudo-combats that could, on occasion, be maiming or even fatal. Needless to say, excitement was heightened by the fact that spectators would involve themselves deeply in the outcome, if not by actual participation, then by the exercise of local partisanship in the form of cheering, wagering, and disputatious after-the-fact arguments.

In our own day, passions are most intimately aroused by team sports, in which groups of highly trained combatants meet to play football, baseball, basketball, or soccer. The teams represent colleges, or towns, or even nations so that local pride and national patriotism are involved and, on occasion, produce riots among the spectators. (Nevertheless, if we look upon such sports cold-bloodedly, as a way of sublimating passions in a relatively harmless fashion, we must conclude that the very worst soccer riot is preferable to even a small military battle.)

If sports are to be exciting confrontations (whether they are as intellectual as a game of chess or as crudely physical as a boxing match; and whether they are fought out one-to-one as in a singles tennis match, or eleven-to-eleven as in a football game) every effort must be made to make the competition as even as possible. There is little excitement in any sport in which one side is so overwhelmingly superior that the outcome is never in doubt and in which a decision is reached almost at once.

Different ways of making competitions more even are used (the imposition of handicaps springs immediately to mind), but by far the most important method is that of setting up rigid rules designed to eliminate unfair practices, and of the use of referees or umpires whose job it is to interpret the rules and see that they are duly enforced.

So important are the rules that the concept of "sportsmanlike behavior" has come to be looked upon as a form of integrity. Despite the intensity with which victory is sought, there remains a belief in the importance of "playing the game." The defeated party is supposed

to congratulate the victor, and being a "good sport" is
a term of high praise. In fact, to be perceived as having
won by cheating robs a victory of all its value, and pun-
ishment for breaking the rules is far more severe in sport
than it is, for instance, in politics or business.

It follows, then, that the association of crime and sport
(while in no way unthinkable, when we consider the
manner in which competitions are sometimes "fixed"
for the benefit of professional gamblers) makes us uneasy
indeed. Even when the association is tangential we feel
that purity is violated and are shocked.

We have therefore gathered together a dozen and a half
tales in which such associations exist, sometimes intimately, as in Rex Stout's tale of murder in a baseball
clubhouse, to something as unimportant as my own story,
in which baseball offers a casual means of passing a message in what seems to be some form of illegal activity.

We hope, then, you will enjoy the incongruity of combining sport and crime.

THE SPORT OF CRIME

The Man Who Pretended to Like Baseball

ISAAC ASIMOV

The hits and outs of baseball did not, as a rule, disturb the equanimity (or lack of it) of a Black Widowers banquet. None of the Black Widowers was a sportsman in the ordinary sense of the word, although Mario Gonzalo was known to bet on the horses on occasion.

Over the rack of lamb, however, Thomas Trumbull brushed at his crisply waved white hair and said, "I've lost all interest in baseball. Once they started shifting franchises, they broke up the kind of loyalties you inherited from your father. I was a New York Giants fan when I was a young man, as was my father before me. The San Francisco Giants are strangers to me, and as for the Mets, well, they're just not the same."

"There are still the New York Yankees," said Geoffrey Avalon, deftly cutting meat away from bone and bending his dark eyebrows in concentration on the task, "and in my own town we still have the Phillies, though we lost the Athletics."

"Chicago still has both its teams," said Mario Gonzalo, "and there are the Cleveland Indians, the Cincinnati Reds, the St. Louis—"

"It's not the same," said Trumbull. "Even if I were to switch to the Yankees, half of the teams they play are teams that Lou Gehrig and Bill Dickey never heard of. And now you have each league in two divisions, with playoffs before the World Series, which becomes almost anticlimactic, and a batting average of .290 marks a slugger. Hell, I remember when you needed .350 if you were to stand a chance at cleanup position."

Emmanuel Rubin listened with the quiet dignity he considered suitable to his position as host—at least, until his guest turned to him and said, "Is Trumbull a baseball buff, Manny?"

At that, Rubin reverted to his natural role and snorted loudly. His sparse beard bristled. "Who, Tom? He may watch a baseball game or two on TV, but that's about it. He thinks a double is two jiggers of Scotch."

Gonzalo said, "Come on, Manny, you think a pitcher holds milk."

Rubin stared at him fixedly through his thick-lensed spectacles, and then said, "It so happens I played a season of semi-pro baseball as shortstop in the late 1930's."

"And a shorter stop—" began Gonzalo, then stopped and reddened.

Rubin's guest grinned. Though Rubin was only five inches above the five-foot mark, the guest fell three inches short of that. He said, "I'd be an even shorter stop if I played."

Gonzalo, with a visible attempt to regain his poise, said, "You're harder to pitch to when you're less than average height, Mr. Just. There's that."

"You're heavily underestimated in other ways, too, which is convenient at times," agreed Just. "And, as a matter of fact, I'm not much of a baseball buff myself. I

The Man Who Pretended to Like Baseball

doubt if I could tell a baseball from a golf ball in a dim light."

Darius Just looked up sharply at this point. "Waiter," he said, "if you don't mind, I'll have milk rather than coffee."

James Drake, waiting expectantly for his own coffee, said, "Is that just a momentary aberration, Mr. Just, or don't you drink coffee?"

"Don't drink it," said Just. "Or smoke, or drink alcohol. My mother explained it all to me very carefully. If I drank my milk and avoided bad habits, I would grow up to be big and strong; so I did—and I didn't. At least, not big. I'm strong enough. It's all very un-American, I suppose, not liking baseball. At least you can fake liking baseball, though that can get you in trouble, too—here's the milk. How did that get there?"

Gonzalo smiled. "That's our Henry. Noiseless and efficient."

Just sipped his milk contentedly. His facial features were small but alive and his eyes seemed restlessly aware of everything in the room. His shoulders were broad, as though they had been made for a taller man, and he carried himself like an athlete.

Drake sat over his coffee, quiet and thoughtful, but when Rubin clattered his water glass with his spoon, the quiet ended. Drake's hand was raised and he said, "Manny, may I do the honors?"

"If you wish." Rubin turned to his guest. "Jim is one of the more reserved Black Widowers, Darius, so you can't expect his grilling to be a searching one. In fact, the only reason he's volunteering is that he's written a book himself and he wants to rub shoulders with another writer."

Just's eyes twinkled with interest. "What kind of book, Mr. Drake?"

"Pop science," said Drake, "but the questions go the other way.—Henry, since Mr. Just doesn't drink, could you substitute ginger ale for the brandy. I don't want him to be at a disadvantage."

"Certainly, Dr. Drake," murmured Henry, that miracle of waiters, "if Mr. Just would like that. With all due respect, however, it does not seem to me that Mr. Just is easily placed at a disadvantage."

"We'll see," said Drake. "Mr. Just, how do you justify your existence?"

Just laughed. "It justifies itself to me now and then when it fills me with gladness. As far as justification to the rest of the world is concerned, that can go hang.— With all due respect, as Henry would say."

"Perhaps," said Drake, "the world will go hang even without your permission. For the duration of this evening, however, you must justify your existence to *us* by answering our questions. Now, I have been involved with the Black Widowers for more than half of a reasonably lengthy existence and I can smell out remarks that are worth elaboration. You said that you could get in trouble if you faked the liking of baseball. I suspect you did once, and I would like to hear about it."

Just looked surprised, and Rubin said, staring at his brandy, "I warned you, Darius."

"You know the story, do you, Manny?" said Drake.

"I know there is one, but I don't know the details," said Rubin. "I warned Darius we'd have it out of him."

Just picked up the caricature that Mario Gonzalo had drawn of him. There was a face-splitting grin on it and arms with prodigious biceps were lifting weights.

"I'm not a weightlifter," he said.

"It doesn't matter," said Gonzalo. "That is how I see you."

"Weightlifting," said Just, "slows you. The successful attack depends entirely on speed."

"You're not being speedy answering my question," said Drake, lighting a cigarette.

"There *is* a story," said Just.

"Good," said Drake.

"But it's an unsatisfactory one. I can't supply any rationale, any explanation—"

"Better and better. Please begin."

"Very well," said Just—

The Man Who Pretended to Like Baseball

* * *

I like to walk. It's an excellent way of keeping in condition, and one night I had made my goal the new apartment of a friend I hadn't seen in a while. I was to be there at 9 P.M., and it was a moderately long walk by night, but I don't much fear the hazards of city streets in the dark, though I admit I do not seek out particularly dangerous neighborhoods.

However, I was early, and a few blocks from my destination I stopped at a bar. As I said, I don't drink, but I'm not an absolute fanatic about it and I will, on rare occasions, drink a Bloody Mary.

There was a baseball game on the TV when I entered, but the sound was turned low, which suited me. There weren't many people present, which also suited me. Two men sat at a table against the wall, and a woman on a stool at the bar.

I took the stool next but one to the woman, and glanced at her briefly after I ordered my drink. She was reasonably pretty, reasonably shapely, and entirely interesting. Pretty and shapely are all right—what's not to like?—but interesting goes beyond that and it can't be easily described. It's different for each person, and she was interesting in my frame of reference.

Among my abstentions, women are not included. I even speculated briefly if it were absolutely necessary that I keep my appointment with my friend, who suffered under the disadvantage, in the circumstances, of being male.

I caught her eye just long enough before looking away. Timing is everything, and I am not without experience. Then I looked up at the TV and watched for a while. You don't want to seem too eager.

She spoke. I was rather surprised. I won't deny I have a way with women, despite my lack of height, but my charm doesn't usually work *that* quickly. She said, "You seem to understand the game." It was just make-talk. She couldn't possibly know my relationship with baseball from my glazed-eye stare at the TV set.

I turned, smiled, and said, "Second nature. I live and breathe it."

It was a flat lie, but if a woman leads, you go along with the lead.

She said, rather earnestly, "You really understand it?" She was looking into my eyes as though she expected to read the answer on my retina.

I continued to follow and said, "Dear, there isn't a move in the game I can't read the motivations of. Every toss of the ball, every crack of the bat, every stance of the fielder, is a note in a symphony I can hear in my head." After all, I'm a writer: I can lay it on.

She looked puzzled. She looked at me doubtfully, then, briefly, at the men at the table. I glanced in their direction, too. They didn't seem interested—until I noticed their eyes in the wall mirror. They were watching our reflection.

I looked at her again and it was like a kaleidoscope shifting and suddenly making sense. She wasn't looking for a pickup, she was scared. It was in her breathing rate and in the tension of her hands.

And she thought I was there to help her. She was expecting someone and she had spoken to me with that in mind. What I answered was close enough—by accident—to make her think I might be the man, but not close enough for her to be sure of it.

I said, "I'm leaving soon. Do you want to come along?" It sounded like a pickup, but I was offering to protect her if that was what she wanted. What would happen afterward—well, who could tell?

She looked at me unenthusiastically. I knew the look. It said: you're five-foot-two; how can *you* help me?

It's a chronic underestimate that plays into my hands. Whatever I do is so much more than they expect that it assumes enormous proportions. I'm the beneficiary of a low base-line.

I smiled. I looked in the direction of the two men at the table, let my smile widen, and said, "Don't worry."

There were containers of cocktail amenities just behind the bar where she sat. She reached over for the

The Man Who Pretended to Like Baseball

maraschino cherries, took a handful, and twisted the stems off; then one by one she flicked them broodingly toward me, keeping her eyes fixed on mine.

I didn't know what her game was. Perhaps she was just considering whether to take a chance on me and this was a nervous habit she always indulged in when at a bar. But I always say: Play along.

I had caught four and wondered how many she would flick at me, and when the barman would come over to rescue his supply; then my attention shifted.

One of the men who had been seated was now between the woman and myself, and was smiling at me without humor. I had been unaware of his coming. I was caught like an amateur, and the kaleidoscope suddenly shifted again. That's the trouble with kaleidoscopes—they keep shifting.

Sure the woman was afraid. She wasn't afraid of the men at the table. She was afraid of *me*. She didn't think I was a possible rescuer; she thought I was a possible spoiler. So she kept my attention riveted while one of her friends got in under my guard—and I had let it happen.

I shifted my attention to the man now, minutes after I should have done so. He had a moon face, dull eyes, and a heavy hand. That heavy hand, his right one, rested on my left hand on the bar, pinning it down.

He said, "I think you're annoying the lady, chum."

He underestimated me, too.

You see, I've never been any taller than I am now. When I was young I was, in point of fact, smaller and slighter. When I was 19, I would have had to gain five pounds to be a 96-pound weakling.

The result you can guess. The chivalry and sportsmanship of young people are such that I was regularly beaten up, to the cheers of the multitude. I did not find it inspiring.

From 19 on, therefore, I subscribed to build-yourself-up courses. I struggled with chest expanders. I took boxing lessons at the Y. Bit by bit I've studied every one of the martial arts. It didn't make me any taller, not one-half inch, but I grew wider and thicker and stronger. Unless I run into a brigade, or a gun, I don't get beaten up anymore.

So the fact that my left arm was pinned did not bother me. I said, "Friend, I don't like having a man hold my hand, so I think I will have to ask you to remove it." I had my own right hand at eye-level, palm up, something that might have seemed a gesture of supplication.

He showed his teeth and said, "Don't ask anything, pal. *I'll* ask."

He had his chance. You must understand that I don't fight to kill, but I do fight to maim. I'm not interested in breaking a hold; I want to be sure there won't be another one.

My hand flashed across between us. Speed is of the essence, gentlemen, and my nails scraped sideways across his throat en route, as the arc of my hand brought its edge down on his wrist. *Hard!*

I doubt that I broke his wrist that time, but it would be days, perhaps weeks, before he would be able to use that hand on someone else as he had on me. My hand was free in a moment. The beauty of the stroke, however, was that he could not concentrate on the smashed wrist. His throat had to be burning and he had to be able to feel the stickiness of blood there. It was just a superficial wound, literally a scratch, but it probably frightened him more than the pain in his wrist did.

He doubled up, his left hand on his throat, his right arm dangling. He was moaning.

It was all over quickly, but time was running out. The second man was approaching, so was the bartender, and a newcomer was in the doorway. He was large and wide and I was in no doubt that he was a member of the charming group I had run into.

The risks were piling up and the fun flattening out, so I walked out rapidly—right past the big fellow, who didn't react quickly enough, but stood there, confused and wondering, for the five seconds I needed to push past and out.

Somehow I didn't think they'd report the incident to

the police. Nor did I think I'd be followed, but I waited for a while to see. I was on a street with row houses, each with its flight of steps leading to the main door well above street level. I stepped into one of the yards and into the shadow near the grille-work door at the basement level of a house that had no lights showing.

No one came out of the barroom. They weren't after me. They weren't sure who I was and they still couldn't believe that anyone as short as I am could be dangerous. It was the providential underestimate that has done so well for me countless times.

So I moved briskly along on my original errand, listening for the sound of footsteps behind me or the shifting of shadows cast by the street lights.

I wasn't early any longer and I arrived on the corner where my friend's apartment house was located without any need for further delay. The green light glimmered and I crossed the street, and then found matters were not as straightforward as I had believed.

The apartment house was not an only child but was a member of a large family of identical siblings. I had never visited the complex before and I wasn't sure in which building I was to find my friend. There seemed no directory, no kiosk with a friendly information guide. There seemed the usual assumption underlying everything in New York that if you weren't born with the knowledge of how to locate your destination, you had no business having one.

The individual buildings each had its number displayed, but discreetly—in a whisper. Nor were they illuminated except by the glint of the street lights, so finding the right building was an adventure.

One tends to wander at random at first, trying to get one's bearings. Eventually I found a small sign with an arrow directing me into an inner courtyard with the promise that the number I wanted was actually to be found there.

Another moment and I would have plunged in when I remembered that I was, or just conceivably might be, a marked man. I looked back in the direction from which I had come.

I was spared the confusion of crowds. Even though it was not long after 9 P.M., the street bore the emptiness characteristic of night in any American city of the Universal Automobile Age. There were automobiles, to be sure, in an unending stream, but up the street I had walked I could see only three people in the glow of the street lights—two men and a woman.

I could not see faces, or details of clothing, for though I have 20/20 vision I see no better than that. However, one of the men was tall and large and his outline was irresistibly reminiscent of the man in the doorway whom I had dodged past in leaving the bar.

They had been waiting for him, of course, and now they had emerged. They would probably have come out sooner, I thought, but there had been the necessity of taking care of the one I had injured and, I supposed, they had left him behind.

Nor, I gathered, were they coming in search of me. Even from a distance I could tell their attention was not on something external to the group, as though they were searching for someone. Attention was entirely internal. Each of the two men was on the side of the woman and they were hurrying her along. It seemed to me that she was reluctant to move, that she held back, that she was being urged forward.

And once again the kaleidoscope shifted. She was a woman in distress after all. She had thought I was her rescuer and I had left her cold—and still in distress.

I ran across the avenue against the lights, dodging cars, and racing toward them. Don't get me wrong. I am not averse to defending myself; I rather enjoy it as anyone would enjoy something he does well. Just the same I am not an unreasoning hero. I do not seek out a battle for no reason. I am all for justice, purity, and righteousness, but who's to say which side, if either, in any quarrel represents those virtues.

A personal angle is something else, and in this case I had been asked for help and I had failed.

The Man Who Pretended to Like Baseball

Oh, I admit I had honestly decided the woman was not on my side and had needed no help, but I hadn't stayed to find out. It was that large man I was ducking, and I had to wipe that out.

At least that's what I decided in hot blood. If I'd had time to think, or to let the spasm of outrage wear off, I might have just visited my friend. Maybe I would have called the police from a street phone without leaving my name and *then* visited my friend.

But it *was* hot blood, and I ran toward trouble, weighing the odds very skimpily.

They were no longer on the street, but I had seen which gate they had entered, and they had not gone up the steps. I chased into the front yard after them and seized the grille-work door that led to the basement apartment. It came open but there was a wooden door beyond that did not. The window blinds were down but there was a dim light behind them.

I banged at the wooden door furiously but there was no answer. If I had to break it down, I would be at a disadvantage. Strength, speed, and skill are not as good at breaking down a door as sheer mass is, and mass I do not have.

I banged again and then kicked at the knob. If it were the wrong apartment, it was breaking and entry, which is what it also was if it were the right apartment. The door trembled at my kick, but held. I was about to try again, wondering if some neighbor had decided to get sufficiently involved to call the police—when the door opened. It was the large man—which meant it was the right apartment.

I backed away. He said, "You seem uncomfortably anxious to get in, sir." He had a rather delicate tenor voice and the tone of an educated man.

I said, "You have a woman here. I want to see her."

"We do not have a woman here. She has us here. This is her apartment and we are here by her invitation."

"I want to see her."

"Very well, then, come in and meet her." He stepped back.

I waited, weighing the risks—or I tried to, at any rate; but an unexpected blow from behind sent me staggering forward. The large man seized my arm and the door closed behind me.

Clearly, the second man had gone one floor upward, come out the main door, down the stairs, and behind me. I should have been aware of him, but I wasn't. I fall short of superman standards frequently.

The large man led me into a living room. It was dimly lit. He said, "As you see, sir—our hostess."

She was there. It was the woman from the bar but this time the kaleidoscope stayed put. The look she gave me was unmistakable. She saw me as a rescuer who had failed her.

"Now," said the large man, "we have been polite to you although you treated my friend in the bar cruelly. We have merely asked you in when we might have hurt you. In response, will you tell us who you are and what you are doing here?"

He was right. The smaller man did not have to push me in. He might easily have knocked me out, or done worse. I presume, though, that they were puzzled by me. They didn't know my part in it and they wanted to find out.

I looked about quickly. The smaller man remained behind me, moving as I did. The large man, who must have weighed 250 pounds, with little of it actually fat, remained quietly in front of me. Despite what happened in the bar, they still weren't afraid of me. It was, once again, the advantage of small size.

I said, "This young woman and I have a date. We'll leave and you two can continue to make yourself at home here."

He said, "That is no answer, sir."

He nodded and out of the corner of my eye I saw the smaller man move out. I lifted my arms to shoulder level as he seized me about the chest. There was no use allowing my arms to be pinned if I could avoid it. The smaller man held tightly, but it would have taken more strength than he had at his disposal to break my ribs. I waited for the correct positioning and I hoped the large man would give it to me.

He said, "I do need an answer, sir, and if I do not get one very quickly, I will have to hurt you."

He came closer, one hand raised to slap.

What followed took less time than it takes to explain, but it went something like this. My arms went up and back, and around the smaller man's head to make sure I had a firm backing, and then my feet went up.

My left shoe aimed at the groin of the large gentleman and the man doesn't live who won't flinch from that. The large man's hips jerked backward and his head automatically bent downward and encountered the heel of my right shoe moving upward. It's not an easy maneuver, but I've practiced it many times.

As soon as my heel made contact, I tightened my arm grip and tossed my head backward. My head and that of the smaller man made hard contact and I didn't enjoy it at all, but the back of my head was not as sensitive as the nose of the man behind me.

From the woman's point of view, I imagine, there could be no clear vision of what had happened. One moment I seemed helplessly immobilized and then, after a flash of movement, I was free, while both of my assailants were howling.

The smaller man was on the floor with one hand over his face. I stamped on one ankle hard to discourage him from attempting to get up. No, it was not Marquis of Queensberry rules, but there were no referees around.

I then turned to face the larger man. He brought his hands away from his face. I had caught him on the cheekbone and he was bleeding freely. I was hoping he had no fight left in him, but he did. With one eye rapidly puffing shut, he came screaming toward me in a blind rage.

I was in no danger from his mad rush as long as I could twist away, but once he got a grip on me in his present mood I would be in serious trouble. I backed away, twisted. I backed away, twisted again. I waited for a chance to hit him again on the same spot.

Unfortunately I was in a strange room. I backed away, twisted, and fell heavily over a hassock. He was on me, his knee on my thighs, his hands on my throat, and there was no way I could weaken that grasp in time.

I could hear the loud thunk even through the blood roaring in my ears and the large man fell heavily on me—but his grip on my throat had loosened. I wriggled out from below with the greatest difficulty though the woman did her best to lift him.

She said, "I had to wait for him to stop moving." There was a candleholder lying near him, a heavy wrought-iron piece.

I remained on the floor, trying to catch my breath. I gasped out, "Have you killed him?"

"I wouldn't care if I did," she said, indifferently, "but he's still breathing."

She wasn't exactly your helpless heroine. It was her apartment, so she knew where to find the clothesline, and she was tying both of them at the wrists and ankles very efficiently. The smaller man screamed when she tightened the ropes at his ankle, but she didn't turn a hair.

She said, "Why the hell did you mess up the response in the bar when I asked you about baseball? And why the hell didn't you bring people with you? I admit you're a pint-sized dynamo, but couldn't you have brought *one* backup?"

Well, I didn't really expect gratitude, but—

I said, "Lady, I don't know what you're talking about. I don't know about the baseball bit, and I don't go about in squadrons."

She looked at me sharply. "Don't move. I'm making a phone call."

"The police?"

"After a fashion."

She went into the other room to call. For privacy, I suppose. She trusted me to stay where I was and do nothing. Or thought me stupid enough to do so. I didn't mind. I wasn't through resting.

When she came back she said, "You're not one of us. What *was* that remark about baseball?"

I said, "I don't know who us is, but I'm not one of anybody. My remark about baseball was a remark. What else?"

She said, "Then how—you had better leave. There's no need for you to be mixed up in this. I'll take care of everything. Get out and walk some distance before you hail a taxi. If a car pulls up at this building while you're within earshot, don't turn around and for God's sake don't turn back."

She was pushing and I was out in the yard when she said, "But at least you knew what I was telling you in the bar. I am glad you were about and waiting."

At last gratitude! I said, "Lady, I don't know what—" but the door was closed behind me.

I made it over very quickly to my friend's apartment. He said nothing about my being an hour late or being a little the worse for wear, and I said nothing about what had happened.

And what did happen was nothing. I never heard a thing. No repercussions. And that's why it's an unsatisfactory story. I don't know who the people were, what they were doing, what it was all about. I don't know whether I was helping the good guys or the bad guys, or whether there were any good guys involved. I may have bumped into two competing bands of terrorists playing against each other.

But that's the story about my faking a knowledge of baseball . . .

When Just was finished, a flat and rather unpleasant silence hung over the room, a silence that seemed to emphasize that for the first time in living memory a guest had told a rather long story without ever having been interrupted.

Finally Trumbull heaved a weary sigh and said, "I trust you won't be offended, Mr. Just, if I tell you that I think you are pulling our leg. You've invented a very dramatic story for our benefit, and you've entertained us—me, at least—but I can't accept it."

Just shrugged; he didn't seem offended. "I've embroidered it a little, polished it up a bit—I'm a writer, after all—but it's true enough."

Avalon cleared his throat. "Mr. Just, Tom Trumbull is sometimes hasty in coming to conclusions but in this case I am forced to agree with him. As you say, you're a writer. I'm sorry to say I have read none of your works but I imagine you write what are called hard-boiled detective stories."

"As a matter of fact, I don't," said Just, with composure. "I have written four novels that are, I hope, realistic, but are not unduly violent."

"It's a fact, Geoff," said Rubin, grinning.

Gonzalo said, "Do *you* believe him, Manny?"

Rubin shrugged. "I've never found Darius to be a liar, and I know *something* happened, but it's hard for a writer to resist the temptation to fictionalize for effect. Forgive me, Darius, but I wouldn't swear to how much of it was true."

Just sighed. "Well, just for the record, is there anyone here who believes I told you what actually happened?"

The Black Widowers sat in an embarrassed silence, and then there was a soft cough from the direction of the sideboard.

"I hesitate to intrude, gentlemen," said Henry, "but despite the over-romantic nature of the story, it seems to me there is a very good chance it is true."

"A chance?" said Just, smiling. "Thank you, waiter."

"Don't underestimate the waiter," said Trumbull. "If he thinks there is a chance the story is true, I'm prepared to revise my opinion.—What's your reasoning, Henry?"

"If the story were fiction, Mr. Trumbull, it would be neatly tied up. This one has an interesting loose end which, if it makes sense, cannot be accidental.—Mr. Just, at the end of the story you told us the woman remarked at her relief that you knew what she was telling you in the bar. What had she told you?"

Just said, "This *is* a loose end, because she didn't tell

The Man Who Pretended to Like Baseball 17

me a damn thing. I could easily make something up, if I weren't telling the truth."

"Or you could let it remain loose now," said Halsted, "for the sake of verisimilitude."

Henry said, "And yet if your story is accurate, she may indeed have told you something, and the fact that you don't know what she told you is evidence of its truth."

"You speak in riddles, Henry," said Just.

Henry said, "You did not, in your story, mention precise locations—neither the location of the bar nor of the apartment complex in which your friend lives. There are a number of such apartment complexes in Manhattan."

"I know," interposed Rubin. "I live in one of them."

"Yours, Mr. Rubin," said Henry, "is on West End Avenue. I suspect that the apartment complex of Mr. Just's friend is over on First Avenue."

Just looked astonished. "It *is*. But how did you know that?"

Henry said, "Consider the opening scene of your story. The woman at the bar knew she was in the hands of her enemies and would not be allowed to leave except under escort. The two men in the bar were merely waiting for their large confederate. They would then take her to her apartment for reasons of their own. The woman thought you were one of her group, felt you could do nothing in the bar, but wanted you on the spot, near her apartment, with reinforcements.

"She therefore flicked maraschino cherries at you—an apparently harmless and, possibly, flirtatious gesture, though even that roused the suspicions of the two men in the bar."

Just said, "What of that?"

Henry said, "She had to work with what she could find. The cherries were small spheres—little balls—and she threw you four, one at a time. You had claimed to be a baseball fanatic. She threw you four balls, and in baseball parlance four balls—that is, four pitches outside the strike zone—means the batter may advance to first base. More colloquially, he 'walks to first.' That's what she was telling you, and you, quite without understanding this, did indeed walk to First Avenue for reasons of your own."

Just looked stupefied. "I never thought of that."

"It's because you didn't and yet incorporated the incident into the account," said Henry, "that I think your story is true."

Diamond Dick

JON L. BREEN

Disrespect for constituted authority is nothing new, my friends. Why, it's an American tradition. I should know that this is true better than anybody, because I've been a baseball umpire for twenty-five years. I'm Ed Gorgon. Maybe you've seen me on TV.

It's an interesting job, and I like it fine, frustration and all. That's why I was so anxious not to lose it after that incident in New Hopton last season. I had to make like a detective and clear my good name. Of course, umpiring and detective work have a good deal in common anyway, though I won't be led off on that tangent just now.

Two background facts you should know: first, I am a Southerner, born and brought up in Montgomery, Alabama; and second, about a year ago I gave an interview to a newspaper sportswriter, something an umpire should be careful not to do too often, especially when the writer is a hostile Yankee (no relation to the ball team). I was quoted out of context in his story in such a way that I came out sounding like a racist, something I am not. Like everybody else I'm subjected to some prejudices, but I can keep my conscious mind policed, even if I lack control over what's under the surface; and I can tell you sincerely that I do my best to treat all men alike.

That's the background. We take you now, as they say on the news, to beautiful New Hopton Stadium. It's the top of the ninth inning and the New Hopton Grizzlies (they're one of the new expansion teams you probably have trouble keeping track of) are leading Chicago 6–3. Their scoreboard (one of the fanciest in the Major Leagues) has deserted its commercial announcements (DON'T MISS BAT NIGHT A WEEK FROM SATURDAY) and group announcements (WELCOME TO THE NEW HOPTON ELKS CLUB) and taken up cheerleading—a frenzy of GO-GO and CHARGE! and that sort of thing. It's a small crowd but on edge. New Hopton isn't winning many, and they can smell a victory.

I'm working behind home plate. Joey Gilbert, the Grizzlies' starting pitcher, a tall skinny kid only a couple of years out of college, is struggling. He's given up a hit and a walk in the top of the ninth and has nobody out. He and his catcher, Ben Butcher, have been on me all night. According to Gilbert, he's never thrown a ball outside the strike zone since his Little League days.

A pinch hitter comes to bat for Chicago—a little Cuban fellow in a clean uniform and freshly shined shoes. He crouches over the plate, making a very small strike zone for Gilbert to aim at. The first pitch is a little high and I call it a ball.

The catcher Butcher grunts. "Damn midget. Didn't you use to work for Bill Veeck?" In Veeck's days as a baseball owner he hired a midget with the idea of sending him up to bat in bases-loaded situations, figuring he'd walk every time. However, this ploy was promptly outlawed.

Although Butcher apparently agrees the last one was a ball, Gilbert still glares at me, as though from habit.

The next pitch appears to hit the dirt and bounces back to the screen, the two runners advancing to third and second. The batter says to me, "It hit my foot."

"Let's see the ball," I say, and the catcher tosses it to me. I take a look and tell the batter, "Take your base."

Poor persecuted Joey Gilbert lets out a roar on the mound, and Butcher tears off his catcher's mask and stamps his foot like a kid in a tantrum. "That didn't touch him! It must have bounced a foot away from him!"

I show him the ball. "Shoe polish," I tell him.

Another red face has joined us in the meantime. Kelly Drummond, the Grizzlies' manager, is not about to listen to my explanation. I allow him his usual ranting time and then threaten to kick him out of the game. When he's pacified I show him the evidence on the ball. The shoe-polish bit is nothing new, of course. There was that incident in the 1969 World Series, you may recall.

Drummond decides he'd rather talk to his pitcher than be banished to the clubhouse, so he goes out and holds a conference on the mound. Butcher and Gilbert and Vic Bilben, their shortstop and field captain, exchange a few remarks. Gilbert, red-faced, starts to stomp around when Drummond signals the bullpen he wants his right-handed relief pitcher. The little red golf cart appears from behind the bullpen fence out in right field, and Mickey Fogarty is revealed as the passenger, keeping his right arm in the sleeve of his jacket during the ride around the track.

The crowd cheers. In New Hopton, like no other town, they actually enjoy seeing their starting pitcher chased, because Mickey Fogarty is the one bright spot on the dim Grizzlies' scene and they love to see him get in. He pitches an inning or two in about half their games—a busy kid.

Fogarty, a short stocky fellow in contrast to the skinny giant he's replacing, strolls confidently to the mound. Gilbert tosses him the ball and sulks his way off to a round of applause from the small crowd. Drummond follows him off, giving me an evil glare on his way.

Fogarty gets oohs and aahs on his warmup pitches. He

really throws some smoke. To heighten the effect, he has thick glasses, like Ryne Duren used to wear. This often scares batters into thinking he can't see where's he's throwing; but unlike Duren, Fogarty has great control. Not much finesse, but with his arm he doesn't need it. In a few years, when the smoke he throws is only a smolder, he'd better develop an extra pitch, I say to myself.

The next Chicago batter comes up. The first pitch blazes down the middle and I call it a strike. He doesn't get the bat off his shoulder. The second pitch is the same story.

The hitter turns to me and says, "That one sounded high." Butcher laughs, but it's an old joke.

The next one is low and outside. With two strikes on the hitter, Fogarty doesn't want to throw anything too good. The batter swings weakly at the next pitch, and there's one out.

The next hitter is Chicago's current version of "the Mighty Casey," a real long-ball slugger. He takes hard swings at the first two whether he can see them or not, and if he'd made contact I'm sure the ball would have carried into the next county. With two strikes on the hitter, Fogarty throws his nickel slider (a full-value slider is what we used to call a nickel curve) and the batter looks at it for strike three. I get another dirty look.

Now instead of no outs with the bases full, there are two down and the crowd is going crazy. They should. Fogarty has two strikeouts on only seven pitches.

The next hitter doesn't go down that easy. With a count of three balls and two strikes, he fouls off six straight pitches in shades of Richie Ashburn. The next one he swings at and misses, however, to end the ball game.

The scoreboard operator spells out YIPPEE on the message board. I think what a real clever fellow he is and then start looking forward to getting back to the hotel. It's been a long evening. Before I can get off the field, though, Drummond is giving me a few more well-chosen words about what I think is a very cut-and-dried play, but it's Drummond's frustration talking, not his mind.

Two A.M. back at the hotel. I am a very sound sleeper and I don't know how many times the phone by my bed rings before I answer it. It's the night clerk saying apologetically, "I'm very sorry to disturb you, Mr. Gorgon, but there's a gentleman here who wants to see you. He says it's urgent."

"What's his name?"

"Marvin Beal."

I groan. That damn Yankee reporter who brought me so much misery. "I won't see him."

"He says it's a matter of life and death, Mr. Gorgon."

I doubt it very much, but who can go back to sleep after a pronouncement like that? I wearily agree to see him.

Beal is a brave fellow, I must admit. He's a little guy about the size of a steeplechase jockey, and I stand six-three and have been told I look every bit as mean as is appropriate for an umpire in the Majors. Besides which I have reason to be very mad at him. Still, an umpire taking a swing at a newspaperman wouldn't sit any better with the Commissioner than a player doing the same thing. Remember the Bo Belinsky incident a few years back? Or more recently, Denny McLain and his ice-water?

"Make it quick," I tell him.

"I can, Ed. One question: have you ever been a member of the Ku Klux Klan?"

I do a fast burn, like Edgar Kennedy at triple speed. "No, and I didn't let you come up here at two in the morning for an interview! Now what's so blamed important?"

"Take it easy, Ed," he says. "I want to help you. If you have a background in the Klan, it's best you reveal it now to me. I can have the story on the street by the time the police have even finished questioning you. Of course, it may mean you have to take up a new line of work, but still—"

"What the hell are you talkin' about?" I roar at him.

"I suppose I ought to let you in on what happened. That is, if you don't know already."

I don't answer. Just glare. But my murderous glare is not as effective on him as it is on ballplayers. This scribe seems mighty sure of himself.

"About an hour after the game tonight, Ed, there was a murder out at the stadium. Al Burlington. Do you know him?"

I can't place the name immediately, though I know I've heard it before.

"He's the guy that runs the scoreboard out at the stadium."

I nod. "I know him. A very slick and sneaky-looking guy. Moonlights at the stadium. Also works as a private detective. Not a very pleasant character."

"That's him. But his most lucrative vocation was neither private detective work nor scoreboard operating. He was a blackmailer."

"Oh? Do the police know this?"

"They'll be figuring it out very shortly, if they don't. Burlington was shot to death tonight in his booth at the stadium."

"Why was he still there so late after the game?"

"The cops figure he may have arranged to meet somebody."

"And do they know who shot him?"

"Not yet, but they'll be putting two and two together pretty fast. Now, Ed, I don't want you to think I'm accusing you of anything—"

"Me?"

"Yes. I'm not saying you shot him, but I have reason to think you'll be suspected."

"Why?" I'm holding my temper tight.

"Well, Burlington spent all his waking hours getting dirt on people. He got the job running the scoreboard, in my opinion, because he had something on Colonel Foley, the Grizzlies' owner."

"What?"

"Haven't found out yet, Ed, but I'll keep trying. Anyhow, if it were to come out that you were a KKK member, even if it were years ago, it might seriously jeopardize your career as an umpire, wouldn't it? Racial tensions being what they are?"

"We're back to the Klan again, are we? Look, Beal, I am not now and never have been one of the white-sheet set. I don't hold with their activities. And the only reason my racial attitudes have even been called into question is that damn story you wrote, quoting me out of context! And anyway, what's the Klan got to do with this?"

"Before Burlington died he left a message on the message board. He spelled out three letters: KKK."

"I see."

"The police have theorized that if the killer took the quickest route from Burlington's booth to the parking lot, he wouldn't even see the message board as he left, so he wouldn't know the incriminating message, if that's what it is, was there. And even if he did, there wouldn't be much he could do about it. So there it stood, way up over the field in giant letters, for the cops to see."

"Wouldn't the security guards have been some help in telling who left the stadium?"

"Bill Thomas, the watchman in that area, got hit over the head and was out for a few minutes. He's the one who found the body, but he doesn't have any idea who hit him."

"You seem to know the whole story, Beal. How do you guys get on top of things so fast?"

"Professional secret."

"With such a talent for gathering facts I wish you'd get out of the habit of writing fiction."

Beal grins. I can't get him mad. "I ought to resent such remarks, Ed."

"You would, if they weren't true. But if Burlington were as prolific a blackmailer as you say, there ought to be plenty of suspects. Right?"

"Sure, Ed. But there's that dying message—KKK."

"Points straight to me, huh?" I'm getting madder and madder. "Look, you sniveling yellow journalist! I'm not a Klansman and never was and for that reason there can't be any evidence against me. But I bet you could make it look that way, couldn't you, spelling it out just short of libel in your damn scandal sheet? Wouldn't surprise me if you were in partnership with Burlington in his blackmail racket."

He protests, still unruffled. "I just want to help, Ed."

I give him the thumb, the way I would to an irate manager who's gone too far. "Get outa here, little man!"

He does, but I don't go back to bed. I know the police will be coming soon, and they do.

Once it seemed that the cops were Irish. Now I'd swear they're mostly Latin-American. Sergeant Rojas is a chunky little guy, just at the minimum height for a policeman I suppose, and he has the kind of penetrating eyes that would unnerve me if I had anything to hide. His English is perfect (that is, better than mine) but a slight shading of inflection underlines his ethnic background.

He asks me when I left the stadium and establishes that I have no alibi except for a twenty-minute period when I was having a late snack with the other umps. Rojas is just a guy doing his job, so when he brings up the same interpretation of KKK, probably planted in his head by my good buddy Marvin Beal, I don't get mad at him. I'm sure he can be reasoned with.

We go over the KKK jump, and I am relieved to see he regards Beal's version of it about as silly as I do. Still, I realize he'd see it in a new light if he found any evidence that I ever *had* been a Klansman; but, of course, there isn't any to find.

"How well did you know Burlington, Mr. Gorgon?"

"Only casually. I'll have to admit I was ignorant of his blackmailing exploits until Marvin Beal filled me in earlier tonight."

Rojas makes a face at the mention of Beal. "I'm glad to have that *hombre* out of my hair, Mr. Gorgon, except I'm worried about what he might be nosing into while I'm not watching him."

"I know what you mean. Sergeant, I've been thinking

about this whole thing—thinking to save my own hide, to be perfectly truthful. That Beal would do anything to throw mud on me. I think he has a 'thing' about Southerners."

Rojas smiles tightly. "I know about prejudices, Mr. Gorgon."

"Anyway, I've come up with a possible line of inquiry for you to follow. It could be a dead end, but maybe not."

"Let's have it."

"Have you seen that book came out last year by Jim Bouton, called *Ball Four*?"

"I've heard of it. Didn't sit too well with the Commissioner's office, did it?"

"There's some stuff in there about ballplayers who cheat on their wives while they're on the road. Most people don't like to think the lads who participate in our National Pastime even *know* about sex and such unsavory matters. But such things do go on.

"It's a two-way street, though. There are baseball wives who have been known to indulge in extracurricular activities of their own while the husbands are away. Now if one such baseball wife was playing around with this unpleasant Burlington fellow, and the husband found out about it, that would be a motive for murder, wouldn't it?"

"Might."

"Now, Sergeant Rojas, I'm going to give you the name of a lady you might like to have a talk with. She's been known as the Mrs. Round Heels of New Hopton in local baseball circles for some time now, and supposedly her husband has been blissfully unaware of it. But you never know when the last to know might find out, do you?"

Sergeant Rojas nods. "I'll talk to the lady. It's just a possibility, but it's worth a try."

Then I explain to the sergeant why I think it might be more than just a possibility, and I give him the lady's name.

Sergeant Rojas is a fast worker. Later that same day an arrest is made in the murder of Al Burlington. I'm sitting in my hotel room two hours before game time, wondering what it'll be like in New Hopton Stadium that evening. The atmosphere is going to be pretty gloomy, I figure, and the team and what few curious spectators show up are going to be in a state of shock.

The phone rings.

"Hello."

"Ed, this is Marvin Beal," he says, like an old friend.

"Oh."

"Ed, Sergeant Rojas mentioned your name at the press conference today. Said you gave him the lead that broke the Burlington case."

"That's nice of him, but he did all the work."

Silence.

"You expect me to tell you all about it, don't you, Beal? You damn presumptuous Yankee. After all you've done to me in the past!"

"Ed, I'm coming to you with my hat in my hand. Let bygones be bygones."

"Okay, Beal, I'll meet the press in the lobby of this hotel in half an hour and tell all of you. No exclusives."

Umpires shouldn't give interviews too often, but now I've got half a dozen reporters with pencils poised, so at least one of them ought to get it right.

"I shouldn't have to figure this one out for a bunch of sportswriters. Every real baseball fan knows the meaning of the three letters Burlington put up on the message board. Those three letters combined with certain other facts that Sergeant Rojas probably has told you about—and if he hasn't I won't either—led me to a simple hypothesis. Sergeant Rojas investigated that hypothesis and bagged the murderer. Excuse me, he bagged the suspect, who is innocent till proved guilty."

"He confessed," says one of the assembled scribes.

"I still say suspect, and be sure you quote me right.

"As you should all know—no, scratch that out. I'm beyond expecting a sportswriter to know anything. In the official scoring of a baseball game, a strikeout is represented by the letter K. So three strikeouts in a row read KKK. And an hour before Burlington was shot, a pitcher for the Grizzlies accomplished the feat of striking out three men in a row. So the letters KKK did not refer to a night-riding organization from my part of the country but were simply a handy abbreviation for Mickey Fogarty—and how any baseball writer could miss that is beyond me!''

A Game of Chess

ROBERT BARR

Here follows a rough translation of the letter which Henri Drumont wrote in Boukrah, two days before his death, to his uncle, Count Ferrand in Paris. It explains the incidents which led up to the situation hereinafter to be described.

My Dear Uncle,

You will have gathered from former letters of mine, that, when one gets east of Buda Pest, official corruption becomes rampant to an extent hardly believable in the West. Goodness knows, things are bad enough in Paris, but Paris official life is comparatively clean when brought into contrast with Boukrah. I was well aware before I left France that much money would have to be secretly spent if we were to secure the concession for lighting Boukrah

A Game of Chess

with electricity, but I was unprepared for the exactions that were actually levied upon me. It must be admitted that the officials are rapacious enough, but once bought, they remain bought, or, at least, such has been my experience of them.

There are, however, a horde of hangers-on, who seem even more insatiable than the governing body of the town, and the worst of these is one Schwikoff, editor of the leading paper here, the *Boukrah Gazette*, which is merely a daily blackmailing sheet. He has every qualification needed by an editor of a paper in Eastern Europe, which may be summed up by saying that he is demoniacally expert with the rapier, and a dead shot with a pistol. He has said time and again that his scurrilous paper could wreck our scheme, and I believe there is some truth in his assertion. Be that as it may, I have paid him at different times large sums of money, but each payment seems but the precursor of a more outrageous demand. At last I was compelled to refuse further contributions to his banking account, and the young man smiled, saying he hoped my decision was not final, for, if it was, I should regret it. Although Schwikoff did not know it, I had the concession signed and completed at that moment, which document I sent to you yesterday morning. I expected Schwikoff would be very angry when he learned of this, but such did not appear to be the case.

He met me last night in the smoking room of the Imperial Club, and shook hands with great apparent cordiality, laughing over his discomfiture, and assuring me that I was one of the shrewdest businessmen he had ever met. I was glad to see him take it in this way, and later in the evening when he asked me to have a game of chess with him, I accepted his invitation, thinking it better for the company that he should be a friend, if he were so disposed.

We had not progressed far with the game, when he suddenly accused me of making a move I had no right to make. I endeavored to explain, but he sprang up in an assumed rage and dashed a glass of wine in my face. The room was crowded with officers and gentlemen. I know you may think me foolish for having sent my seconds to such a man as Schwikoff, who is a well-known blackmailer, but, nevertheless, he comes of a good family, and I, who have served in the French Army, and am of your blood, could not accept tamely such an insult. If what I hear of his skill as a swordsman is true, I enter the contest well aware that I am outclassed, for I fear I have neglected the training of my right arm in my recent pursuit of scientific knowledge. Whatever may be the outcome, I have the satisfaction of knowing that the task given me has been accomplished. Our company has now the right to establish its plant and lay its wires in Boukrah, and the people here have such an eastern delight in all that is brilliant and glittering, that I feel certain our project will be a financial success.

Schwikoff and I will meet about the time you receive this letter, or, perhaps, a little earlier, for we fight at daybreak, with rapiers, in the large room of the Fencing School of Arms in this place.

Accept, my dear uncle, the assurance of my most affectionate consideration.—Your unworthy nephew,
Henri

The old man's hand trembled as he laid down the letter after reading it, and glanced up at the clock. It was the morning of the duel, and daylight came earlier at Boukrah than at Paris.

Count Ferrand was a member of an old French family that had been impoverished by the Revolution. Since then, the Ferrand family had lived poorly enough until the Count, as a young man, had turned his attention toward science, and now, in his old age, he was supposed to possess fabulous wealth, and was known to be the head of one of the largest electric manufacturing companies in the environs of Paris. No one at the works was aware that the young man, Henri Drumont, who was

A Game of Chess

given employ in the manufactory after he had served his time in the army, was the nephew of the old Count, for the head of the company believed that the young man would come to a more accurate knowledge of the business if he had to take the rough with the smooth, and learn his trade from the bottom upwards.

The glance at the clock told the old Count that the duel, whatever its result, had taken place. So there was nothing to be done but await tidings. It was the manager of the works who brought them in.

"I am sorry to inform you, sir," he said, "that the young man, Henri Drumont, whom we sent to Boukrah, was killed this morning in a duel. His assistant telegraphs for instructions. The young man has no relatives here that I know of, so I suppose it would be as well to have him buried where he died."

The manager had no suspicion that he was telling his chief of the death of his heir.

"The body is to be brought back to France," said the Count quietly.

And it was done. Later, when the question arose of the action to be taken regarding the concession received from Boukrah, the Count astonished the directors by announcing that, as the concession was an important one, he himself would take the journey to Boukrah, and remain there until the electric plant, already forwarded, was in position, and a suitable local manager found.

The Count took the Orient Express from Paris, and, arriving in Boukrah, applied himself with an energy hardly to be expected from one of his years, to the completion of the work which was to supply the city with electricity.

Count Ferrand refused himself to all callers until the electric plant was in operation, and the interior of the building he had bought, completed to his satisfaction. Then, practically the first man admitted to his private office was Schwikoff, editor of the *Boukrah Gazette*. He had sent in his card with a request, written in passable French, for information regarding the electrical installation, which would be of interest, he said, to the readers of the *Gazette*. Thus Schwikoff was admitted to the presence of Count Ferrand, whose nephew he had killed, but the journalist, of course, knew nothing of the relationship between the two men, and thought, perhaps, he had done the courteous old gentleman a favor, in removing from the path of his advancement the young man who had been in the position now held by this gray-haired veteran.

The ancient noble received his visitor with scrupulous courtesy, and the blackmailer, glancing at his hard, inscrutable face, lined with experience, thought that here, perhaps, he had a more difficult victim to bleed than the free-handed young fellow whom he had so deferentially removed from existence, adhering strictly to the rules of the game, himself acquitted of all guilt by the law of his country, and the custom of his city, passing unscathed into his customary walk of life, free to rapier the next man who offended him. Count Ferrand said politely that he was ready to impart all the information in his possession for the purposes of publication. The young man smiled and shrugged his shoulders slightly.

"To tell you the truth, sir, at once and bluntly, I do not come so much for the purpose of questioning you regarding your business, as with the object of making some arrangement concerning the Press, with which I have the great honor to be connected. You may be aware, sir, that much of the success of your company will depend on the attitude of the Press toward you. I thought, perhaps, you might be able to suggest some method by which all difficulties would be smoothed away; a method that would result in our mutual advantage."

"I shall not pretend to misunderstand you," replied the Count, "but I was led to believe that large sums had already been disbursed, and that the difficulties, as you term them, had already been removed."

"So far as I am concerned," returned the blackmailer, "the sums paid to me were comparatively trivial, and I was led to hope that when the company came into active operation, as, thanks to your energy, is now the case, it would deal more liberally with me."

The Count in silence glanced at some papers he took from a pigeonhole, then made a few notes on the pad before him. At last he spoke.

"Am I right in stating that an amount exceeding ten thousand francs was paid to you by my predecessor, in order that the influence of your paper might be assured?"

Schwikoff again shrugged his shoulders.

"It may have been something like that," he said carelessly. "I do not keep my account of these matters."

"It is a large sum," persisted Ferrand.

"Oh! a respectable sum; but still you must remember what you got for it. You have the right to bleed for ever all the inhabitants of Boukrah."

"And that gives you the right to bleed us?"

"Oh! if you like to put it that way, yes. We give you *quid pro quo* by standing up for you when complaints of your exactions are made."

"Precisely. But I am a businessman, and would like to see where I am going. You would oblige me, then, by stating a definite sum, which would be received by you in satisfaction of all demands."

"Well, in that case, I think twenty thousand francs would be a moderate amount."

"I cannot say that moderation is the most striking feature of your proposal," said the Count drily, "still we shall not trouble about that, if you will be reasonable in the matter of payment. I propose to pay you in installments of a thousand francs a month."

"That would take nearly two years," objected Schwikoff. "Life is uncertain. Heaven only knows where we shall be two years from now."

"Most true; or even a day hence. Still, we have spent a great deal of money on this establishment, and our income has not yet begun; therefore, on behalf of the company, I must insist on easy payments. I am willing, however, to make it two thousand francs a month, but beyond that I should not care to go without communicating with Paris."

"Oh, well," swaggered Schwikoff, with the air of a

man making great concessions, "I suppose we may call that satisfactory, if you make the first payment now."

"I do not keep such a sum in my office, and besides, I wish to impose further terms. It is not my intention to make an arrangement with any but the leading paper of this place, which I understand the *Gazette* to be."

"A laudable intention. The *Gazette* is the only paper that has any influence in Boukrah."

"Very well; then I must ask you, for your own sake as for mine, to keep this matter a strict secret; even to deny that you receive a subsidy, if the question should come up."

"Oh, certainly, certainly."

"You will come for payment, which will be in gold, after office hours, on the first of each month. I shall be here alone to receive you. I should prefer that you came in by the back way, where your entrance will be unseen, and so we shall avoid comment, because, when I refuse the others, I should not care for them to know that one of their fellows has had an advantage over them. I shall take the money from the bank before it closes. What hour, therefore, after six o'clock will be most convenient to you?"

"That is immaterial—seven, eight, or nine, or even later, if you like."

"Eight o'clock will do; by that time everyone will have left the building but myself. I do not care for late hours, even if they occur but once a month. At eight o'clock precisely you will find the door at the back ajar. Come in without announcement, so that we may not be taken by surprise. The door is self-locking, and you will find me here with the money. Now, that I may be able to obtain the gold in time, I must bid you adieu."

At eight o'clock precisely Count Ferrand, standing in the passage, saw the back door shoved open and Schwikoff enter, closing it behind him.

"I hope I have not kept you waiting," said Schwikoff.

"Your promptitude is exceptional," said the other politely. "As a businessman, I must confess I like punctuality. I have left the money in the upper room. Will you have the goodness to follow me?"

They mounted four pairs of stairs, all lighted by incandescent lamps. Entering a passageway on the upper floor, the Count closed the big door behind him; then opening another door, they came to a large oblong room, occupying nearly the whole of the top story, brilliantly lighted by an electric lustre depending from the ceiling.

"This is my experimenting laboratory," said the old man as he closed the second door behind him.

It was certainly a remarkable room, entirely without windows. On the wall, at the right hand near the entrance, were numerous switches in shining brass and copper and steel.

From the door onward were perhaps ten feet of ordinary flooring, then across the whole width of the room extended a gigantic chessboard, the squares yellow and gray, made alternately of copper and steel; beyond that again was another ten feet of plain flooring, which supported a desk and some chairs. Schwikoff's eyes glittered as he saw a pile of gold on the desk. Near the desk was a huge open fireplace, constructed like no fireplace Schwikoff had ever seen before. The center, where the grate should have been, was occupied by what looked like a great earthenware bathtub, some six or seven feet long. "That," said the electrician, noticing the other's glance at it, "is an electric furnace of my own invention, probably the largest electric furnace in the world. I am convinced there is a great future before carbide of calcium, and I am carrying on some experiments drifting toward the perfection of the electric crucible."

"Carbide of calcium?" echoed Schwikoff. "I never heard of it."

"Perhaps it would not interest you, but it is curious from the fact that it is a rival of the electric light, and yet only through the aid of electricity is carbide of calcium made commercially possible."

"Electricity creates its own rival, you mean; most interesting I am sure. And is this a chessboard let into the floor?"

"Yes, another of my inventions. I am a devotee of chess."

"So am I."

"Then we shall have to have a game together. You don't object to high stakes, I hope?"

"Oh, no, if I have the money."

"Ah, well, we must have a game with stakes high enough to make the contest interesting."

"Where are your chessmen? They must be huge."

"Yes, this board was arranged so that living chessmen might play on it. You see, the alternate squares are of copper, the others of steel. That black line which surrounds each square is hard rubber, which does not allow the electricity to pass from one square to another."

"You use electricity, then, in playing."

"Oh, electricity is the motive power of the game; I will explain it all to you presently; meanwhile, would you oblige me by counting the gold on the desk? I think you will find there exactly two thousand francs."

The old man led the way across the metal chessboard. He proffered a chair to Schwikoff, who sat down before the desk.

Count Ferrand took the remaining chair, carried it over the metal platform, and sat down near the switch, having thus the huge chessboard between him and his guest. He turned the lever from one polished knob to another; the transit caused a wicked, vivid flash to illuminate the room with the venomous glitter of blue lightning. Schwikoff gave a momentary start at the crackle and the blinding light. Then he continued his counting in silence. At last he looked up and said, "This amount is quite correct."

"Please do not move from your chair," commanded the Count. "I warn you that the chessboard is now a broad belt of death between you and me. On every disc the current is turned, and a man stepping anywhere on the board will receive into his body two thousand volts, killing him instantly as with a stroke of lightning, which, indeed, it is."

"Is this a practical joke?" asked Schwikoff, turning a

little pale about the lips, sitting still, as he had been ordered to do.

"It is practical enough, and no joke, as you will learn when you know more about it. You see this circle of twenty-four knobs at my hand, with each knob of which, alternately, this lever communicates when I turn it."

As the Count spoke he moved the lever, which went crackling past a semi-circle of knobs, emitting savage gleams of steel-like fire as it touched each metal projection.

"From each of these knobs," explained the Count, as if he were giving a scientific lecture, "electricity is turned on to a certain combination of squares before you. When I began speaking, the whole board was electrified; now, a man might walk across that board, and his chances of reaching this side alive would be as three to one."

Schwikoff sprang suddenly to his feet, terror in his face, and seemed about to make a dash for it. The old man pushed the lever back into its former position.

"I want you to understand," said the Count suavely, "that upon any movement on your part, I shall instantly electrify the whole board. And please remember that, although I can make the chessboard as safe as the floor, a push on this lever and the metal becomes a belt of destruction. You must keep a cool head on your shoulders, Mr. Schwikoff, otherwise you have no chance for your life."

Schwikoff, standing there, stealthily drew a revolver from his hip pocket. The Count continued in even tones:

"I see you are armed, and I know you are an accurate marksman. You may easily shoot me dead as I sit here. I have thought that all out in the moments I have given to the consideration of this business. On my desk downstairs is a letter to the manager, saying that I am called suddenly to Paris, and that I shall not return for a month. I ask him to go on with the work, and tell him on no account to allow anyone to enter this room. You might shout till you were hoarse, but none outside would hear you. The walls and ceiling and floor have been deadened so effectively that we are practically in a silent, closed box. There is no exit except up through the chimney, but if you look at the crucible to which I called your attention you will see that it is now white hot, so there is no escape that way. You will, therefore, be imprisoned here until you starve to death, or until despair causes you to commit suicide by stepping on the electrified floor."

"I can shatter your switchboard from here with bullets."

"Try it," said the old man calmly. "The destruction of the switchboard merely means that the electricity comes permanently on the floor. If you shatter the switchboard, it will then be out of my power to release you, even if I wished to do so, without going downstairs and turning off the electricity at the main. I assure you that all these things have had my most earnest consideration, and while it is possible that something may have been overlooked, it is hardly probable that you, in your now excited state of mind, will chance upon that omission."

Schwikoff sank back in his chair.

"Why do you wish to murder me?" he asked. "You may retain your money, if that is what you want, and I shall keep quiet about you in the paper."

"Oh, I care nothing for the money nor the paper."

"Is it because I killed your predecessor?"

"My predecessor was my nephew and my heir. Through his duel with you, I am now a childless old man, whose riches are but an incumbrance to him, and yet those riches would buy me freedom were I to assassinate you in broad daylight in the street. Are you willing now to listen to the terms I propose to you?"

"Yes."

"Very good. Throw your pistol into the corner of the room beside me; its possession will do you no good."

After a moment's hesitation, Schwikoff flung his pistol across the metal floor into the corner. The old man turned the lever to still another knob.

"Now," he said, "you have a chance of life again; thirty-two of the squares are electrified, and thirty-two

A Game of Chess

are harmless. Stand, I beg of you, on the square which belongs to the Black King.''

"And meet my death."

"Not on that square, I assure you. It is perfectly safe."

But the young man made no movement to comply. "I ask you to explain your intention."

"You shall play the most sinister game of chess you have ever engaged in; Death will be your opponent. You shall have the right to the movements of the King—one square in any direction that you choose. You will never be in a position in which you have not the choice of at least two squares upon which you can step with impunity; in fact, you shall have at each move the choice of eight squares on which to set your foot, and as a general thing, four of those will mean safety, and the other four death, although sometimes the odds will be more heavily against you, and sometimes more strongly in your favor. If you reach this side unscathed, you are then at liberty to go, while if you touch one of the electric squares, your death will be instantaneous. Then I shall turn off the current again, with the result that for a few moments there will be thick, black smoke from the chimney, and a handful of white ashes in the crucible."

"And you run no danger."

"No more than you did when you stood up against my nephew, having previously unjustly insulted him."

"The duel was carried out according to the laws of the code."

"The laws of my code are more generous. You have a chance for your life. My nephew had no such favor shown to him; he was doomed from the beginning, and you knew it."

"He had been an officer in the French Army."

"He allowed his sword arm to get out of practice, which was wrong, of course, and he suffered for it. However, we are not discussing him; it is your fate that is in question. I give you now two minutes in which to take your stand on the King's square."

"And if I refuse?"

"If you refuse, I turn the electricity on the whole

board, and then I leave you. I will tear up the letter which is on my desk below, return here in the morning, give the alarm, say you broke in to robe me of the gold which is beside you on the desk, and give you in charge of the authorities, a disgraced man."

"But what if I tell the truth?"

"You would not be believed, and I have pleasure in knowing that I have money enough to place you in prison for the rest of your life. The chances are, however, that, with the electricity fully turned on, this building will be burned down before morning. I fear my insulation is not perfect enough to withstand so strong a current. In fact, now that the thought has suggested itself to me, fire seems a good solution to the difficulty. I shall arrange the wires on leaving so that a conflagration will break out within an hour after my departure, and, I can assure you, you will not be rescued by the firemen when they understand their danger from live wires in a building from which, I will tell them, it is impossible to cut off the electricity. Now, sir, you have two minutes."

Schwikoff stood still while Ferrand counted the seconds left to him; finally, as the time was about to expire, he stepped on the King's square, and stood there, swaying slightly, drops of perspiration gathering on his brow.

"*Brava!*" cried the Count, "you see, as I told you, it is perfectly safe. I give you two minutes to make your next move."

Schwikoff, with white lips, stepped diagonally to the square of the Queen's Pawn, and stood there, breathing hard, but unharmed.

"Two minutes to make the next move," said the old man, in the unimpassioned tones of a judge.

"No, no!" shouted Schwikoff excitedly, "I made my last move at once; I have nearly four minutes. I am not to be hurried; I must keep my head cool. I have, as you see, superb control over myself."

His voice had now risen to a scream, and his open hand drew the perspiration down from his brow over his face, streaking it grimly.

"I am calm!" he shrieked, his knees knocking together, "but this is no game of chess; it is murder. In a game of chess I could take all the time I wanted in considering a move."

"True, true!" said the old man suavely, leaning back in his chair, although his hand never left the black handle of the lever. "You are in the right. I apologize for my infringement of the laws of chess; take all the time you wish, we have the night before us."

Schwikoff stood there long in the ominous silence, a silence interrupted now and then by a startling crackle from the direction of the glowing electric furnace. The air seemed charged with electricity and almost unbreathable. The time given him, so far from being an advantage, disintegrated his nerve, and as he looked fearfully over the metal chessboard the copper squares seemed to be glowing red hot, and the dangerous illusion that the steel squares were cool and safe became uppermost in his mind.

He curbed with difficulty his desire to plunge, and stood balancing himself on his left foot, cautiously approaching the steel square with his right toe. As the boot neared the steel square, Schwikoff felt a strange thrill pass through his body. He drew back his foot quickly with a yell of terror, and stood, his body inclining now to the right, now to the left, like a tall tree hesitating before its fall. To save himself he crouched.

"Mercy! Mercy!" he cried. "I have been punished enough. I killed the man, but his death was sudden, and not fiendish torture like this. I have been punished enough."

"Not so," said the old man. "An eye for an eye."

All self-control abandoned the victim. From his crouching position he sprang like a tiger. Almost before his out-stretched hands touched the polished metal his body straightened and stiffened with a jerk, and as he fell, with a hissing sound, dead on the chessboard, the old man turned the lever free from the fatal knob. There was no compassion in his hard face for the executed man, but instead his eyes glittered with the scientific fervor of research. He rose, turned the body over with his foot, drew off one of the boots, and tore from the inside a thin sole of cork.

"Just as I thought," he murmured. "Oh, the irony of ignorance! There existed, after all, the one condition I had not provided for. I knew he was protected the moment he stepped upon the second square, and, if his courage had not deserted him, he could have walked unharmed across the board, as the just, in medieval times, passed through the ordeal of the red-hot plowshares."

Coffin Corner
ANTHONY BOUCHER

The young man stood tall and straight, but his voice was rising shakily with his emotion.

"So you can see, Father, why I've got to learn the answer. They look at the record and what do they see? I was arrested once for murder. Sure, I was released, never tried, but that murder is still on the books as unsolved. And until I'm completely in the clear I'd hate to bet on my chances for an air commission."

"He's right, Father," the older man put in. He was old only by comparison with the dark youth beside him. In fact, he was in his early thirties, as tall and well-built as the boy, and at the moment even more anxious. "Before now it didn't matter so much that the mess never got cleared up. No one who knew Jim ever seriously suspected him. But these Government investigators . . . they don't know him."

"It isn't pride, Father," the boy went on. "Being a buck private would be O.K. with me. But I'm a good flier, and I'd be more use to my country up there. I can't let an unsolved murder stand between me and a Jap carrier."

"I understand," the priest said. "But what can I do? If the police have failed . . ."

"We thought . . ." the boy began. "Well, you might maybe—"

"We aren't used to crime," the older man explained. "Private detectives and that sort of thing scare us. We thought you might know who was honest and capable. I guess it's just that every graduate of this university, Father, always leaves it thinking that you can answer any problem."

"I'm afraid," the priest smiled, "I'm better on economic or theological problems than I am on murder. I really don't know . . ." He paused, and the smile deepened. "Just a minute. 'Economic problems' reminds me: do you know the Sisters of Martha of Bethany?"

The older man nodded. "They do good work."

"They've asked me to lend them one of my economics professors to give a brief lecture course on inflation. Through their baby clinic and such works they have so much contact with the New Rich that Mother Flanner thought it would be a good idea to have some formal grounding in their problems."

The two laymen exchanged looks of puzzlement. "But what . . . ?"

"I know it's hardly Christian to request favors in return for favors. But in exchange for my economist, Jim, I'm going to try to get the answer to your problem."

The young man gaped. "From a nun?"

Father Pearson smiled. "You don't know this nun, Jim. Want to come with me?"

Jim Echeverri frowned. "I couldn't. I mean I'd feel so . . . Going up to a nun and saying, 'Sister, will you sleuth for me . . . ?' "

"You will though, Bob? Good. Between us I think we

can tell her the whole story. And I hope, Jim, that she'll keep you flying."

Father Hubert Pearson, S.J., explained his inspiration to Bob Cassidy as they waited in the convent of Martha of Bethany. The early spring air was crisp, but sun brightened the adobe walls of the patio.

"I've met this Sister Ursula only casually, but I've heard a great deal about her. Her father was a quite noted chief of police someplace in Iowa. She had planned to be a policewoman until illness cheated her hopes of passing the physical standards.

"She took the veil, recovered her health, and became a most vigorous and useful nun, forgetting her early ambitions until she happened to be a witness in a curious, complex murder case, and startled the police in charge by solving it for them. Since then, I hear, she's been an unofficial adviser to one police lieutenant in several other cases."

"Sounds astonishing," Cassidy commented.

But there was nothing astonishing in the appearance of Sister Mary Ursula, O.M.B., when she came into the patio to greet them. She seemed—no, not just like any other nun, but like the ideal of a nun such as you conceive but do not always find. Quiet, simple, human, with the unobtrusive but intense inner glow of the devotional life.

The preliminary business was soon dispatched. The nun seemed surprised to receive the Rector of Bellarmine University in person on such a matter, but accepted the honor gratefully, and efficiently hit on the most convenient arrangement for the lecture course.

She did not seem surprised when Father Pearson hesitantly suggested a *quid pro quo*. "I must confess, Father, that I have been waiting for that ever since I wondered why you had come yourself. But where can we nuns help you when your own fine university staff fails?"

"We have a problem . . ." Cassidy began, and balked.

"I sense," said Sister Ursula, "that this is going to

be a long story. Please go ahead. And smoke if you wish."

"Thank you." Father Pearson lit a cigarette. "I doubt if Mr. Cassidy's name means anything to you."

The nun's eyes lit up as she turned to the layman. "You aren't . . . you couldn't be Coffin Corner Cassidy?"

He nodded, embarrassed.

"Heavens! Could I ever forget that Big Game ten years ago? Bellarmine trailing 14-13 with less than a minute to play. Bellarmine's ball on the midfield stripe, fourth down and twelve to go. And you produced a fifty-yard punt that went out of bounds within the one-yard line and set the stage for Wozzeck's blocked kick and the safety that gave Bellarmine the game 15-14. Mr. Cassidy, you're wonderful."

Father Pearson grinned. "I told you she was amazing, Bob."

"We heard it," she confessed, "on the radio. We almost sang a *Te Deum* afterwards. You have several loyal Bellarmine fans here. And tell me, do they still keep your old jersey framed in glass in the trophy room?"

The priest answered for the bashful hero. "Yes, Cassidy's 29 is as historic to us as Grange's 77 is to Illinois. No one's ever worn the number since, in honor of the most highly educated toe in Western football annals."

"It wasn't anything so wonderful," Cassidy protested. "Coach Leary and I just happened to realize why the game's called football."

"And what's become of you, Mr. Cassidy? That sounds odd; but I mean, you never turned professional or went to Hollywood or . . ."

"I'm the Southern California manager of the Interstate Kitchenware Corporation—nothing romantic, but much more secure and restful than Hollywood or pro football. But what we came about, Sister . . ."

"I'm sorry. But meeting heroes in the flesh is distracting. To get back to your problem . . . ?"

"I was thinking," said Father Pearson, "of another connection in which you might have heard Bob's name recently. But I think I had better save that for its proper place in the story."

"If you are a Bellarmine fan, Sister, you don't need to be told what the annual Bellarmine-Santa Juana game means. There are three great Big Games in West Coast football: Cal–Stanford, St. Mary's–Santa Clara, and ours; and each means the total demoralization of the university and its community for at least a week beforehand. Nothing is conceivably so important to students as winning one of those Big Games.

"Whether that's good or bad, I won't attempt to decide. Sometimes, as rector, I feel obliged to protest against overemphasis; at other times I think it's a healthy release of emotions—emotions that are now channeled into something bigger than any game. And approving or protesting, I have not missed a Big Game since I took office.

"That was last fall. We played up North at Santa Juana, and I went along. Bob here is a fixture of Big Games—they wouldn't seem right without him on the bench—so he made the trip too.

"We went up on the Daylight Limited Friday to give the boys a good night's rest. And especially we wanted a good rest for Jim Echeverri. You may have been following his career? He's the greatest kicker we've had since Coffin Corner Cassidy, and a fine boy to . . . besides. I almost—forgive me—said *to boot*!

"The team's attack that year was patterned along the punt-and-pray system, and Echeverri's punts, like those of a Cassidy or a Tipton, were not only a defensive but an offensive weapon. He was essential to the team; and that is essential to the story.

"Do you know the town of Santa Juana? It's a small community whose chief industries are fruit orchards, vineyards, and the university. I spent a pleasant evening with brothers on the faculty, admiring as always the local wine, and after mass next morning worked a little in the library. While I was finishing lunch and preparing to leave for the stadium, a phone call came for me.

"It was from our coach Shawn Leary. I have never heard such frantic emotion in that harsh voice, not even in the dressing room between halves when Bellarmine was trailing by three touchdowns. It was hard to figure out what he was trying to tell me, but I finally managed to decipher that he was at the stadium with all the team—save Echeverri. Jim had gone out for a walk that morning and failed to return. Leary had finally been driven to phone the police, who said sure, they knew where Echeverri was. He was being held on suspicion of murder.

"I couldn't believe it. I thought I must be misinterpreting him. But there was no misinterpreting the terrible urgency of his appeal. Jim and his captors, the police had said, were still at the scene of the crime. I agreed to meet Leary there in the fewest minutes possible.

"The scene of the crime turned out to be a night club called The Purple Porker, and there is nothing so dankly desolate as a night club in the daytime. A uniformed officer was polite to my cloth but anxious to hustle me away until I explained who I was. Then he was eager to admit me.

" 'You fix it so's they turn Echeverri loose, Father,' he urged. 'We can lick your boys any day, but if Echeverri ain't playing it won't look so good. You fix it, Father.'

"Coach Leary arrived at almost the same time as I, and Bob Cassidy with him. The three of us were shown back to the elevator. And as the elevator boy opened the door, his eyes popped wide and he screeched (with several expletives which you will pardon my not repeating), 'Them's the other two!'

"The officer's eyes hardened and said, 'Tell that to the sergeant, bud. And be sure of it.'

"Leary and Cassidy looked at each other with surprise and an apprehension that I did not understand. When he reached the tower room, the boy followed us out of the car and announced to another uniformed officer, 'Tell the sarge I brung him the other two.'

"Sergeant Hanlon was more than glad to see us. He beamed sarcastically and said, 'So you two boys was

Coffin Corner 51

here before. And you had to come back for another gander, huh? Well, we'll show you— Oh, excuse me, Father.'

"I took advantage of my position. 'Please, Sergeant, before you begin accusing us of something, can't you tell us what the situation is?'

"He began to apologize and—but I can tell the story better in synopsis than by trying to reproduce my difficulties in drawing it out of the sergeant.

"In short, this tower room belonged to Pat Michaelis, the biggest gambler in Santa Juana. He owned The Purple Porker. Its second story was a gambling establishment, and the tower was his private office. It could be reached only by the one-car elevator.

"Around twelve-thirty the elevator boy had brought Jim Echeverri up there. Jim stayed perhaps three minutes. When he rang to come down again, he looked so worried and shaken that the boy grew suspicious. He crossed the hall to the office and found Michaelis dead at his desk. He had been shot through the chest with his own automatic.

"The boy took Jim downstairs, turned him over to some of Michaelis's men, and called the police. The men weren't necessary. Jim was too dazed to say or do anything. And before long Sergeant Hanlon had decided to hold him for murder.

"There was no possibility of suicide. As the sergeant explained it, there were no powder marks on the wound, no prints on the gun, and no something-or-other specks on the dead man's bare hands.

"Michaelis was definitely alive at eleven-thirty, when he was seen by several of his henchmen downstairs in the bar. In the following hour, the elevator boy took only three men, aside from Jim, to the tower room. Two of them he didn't know. One of those, he said, had the proper credentials, and the other had too threatening a right to disregard. The third was a small-time local racketeer named Rolfe Chasen, and more usually known simply as 'The Beak.'

"The two unknowns had come first, so Sergeant Hanlon decided to disregard them. He was left with the choice of The Beak and Jim. Jim claimed that he had found Michaelis dead. The Beak, pulled in by a dragnet, at first refused to talk without a lawyer, then, seeing the sergeant's growing suspicion of Jim, said that Michaelis was alive when he left him.

"Later The Beak was to swear that he had found Michaelis's corpse. Obviously he wanted his relations with the Law to be as brief and pleasant as possible; his testimony is valueless.

"Two things made the sergeant elect Jim as chief suspect. One was the motive which the elevator boy supplied; more of that later. The other was the fact that Michaelis had been playing cribbage when he died.

"I can still see that office as Sergeant Hanlon showed it to me. The body had been removed, but I could imagine it slumped over that incredibly clear desk. It had been a fetish of Michaelis's, I learned, to have his desk top completely clear of all pencils, papers, and such; he believed that the large blank space gave him a psychological advantage over the man on the other side.

"There was nothing at all on the desk but playing cards, flecked with blood. A pack of cards at Michaelis's right with a five of diamonds turned up under them, four cards face down in front of him, four at his opponent's place, and four more at his left. It was unmistakably the arrangement for cribbage.

"Sergeant Hanlon turned over the hand of the gambler's last adversary. 'Some luck!' he grunted. 'You play cribbage?' The blood spots made the pips hard to read, but I saw what he meant. The hand was the fives of clubs, hearts, and spades, and the jack of diamonds. With the five of diamonds for a turn-up, that made the highest hand possible in cribbage, something as fabulous as thirteen spades at bridge.

"I turned over Michaelis's hand. It was random and poor: ace, four, seven, nine of mixed suits, only two points with the turn-up. Michaelis's luck was all bad that day.

"Now it was common Santa Juana gossip, the sergeant

explains, that Michaelis liked cribbage, nonprofessionally. 'It ain't no sucker's game,' he used to say. It was also common knowledge that The Beak never touched cards; dice and the wheel were his sports. And Jim admitted that he played a fair hand of cribbage.

"That, with the motive, was enough for Sergeant Hanlon. If we had not arrived when we did, Jim would have been on his way to the station for booking.

"All this I learned over the constant protestations of Coach Leary. It was nearly time for the kick-off. He'd given instructions to his assistant Trig Madison; the boys could make out all right without him, but not without Jim Echeverri. He wanted Echeverri, as vociferously as ever a rooting section wanted a touchdown, and Bob Cassidy and I were almost equally demanding.

"But Bob and the coach were in the unfortunate position of being suspects themselves since the elevator boy had identified them as his two first passengers, and had to give an account of why they had come.

"Bob's explanation was simple: he had forgotten to place an intended bet on the game before leaving the South. A politician friend in Santa Juana had recommended him to Michaelis and given him a card to insure his entree.

"Coach Leary's was even simpler: He had heard that one of Michaelis's boys had been hanging around the team. He was afraid of an attempted fix and had come here to put the fear of the Lord into the gambler. He had succeeded too, he thought.

"At last the sergeant took us in to see Jim. I would hardly have known that handsome Basque. His face was drawn and white, and the gleam was gone from his black eyes.

" 'Cheer up, Jim,' I told him. 'They'll never be able to fasten a charge like this on you.'

" 'It isn't that, Father,' he protested. 'But they're holding me. I'm going to miss the Big Game . . .'

"I tried to quiet him and finally got his story. He had motive enough, poor fellow. It might never have come out save for the elevator boy, who had brought Michaelis a bottle of whiskey the night before and found him at his desk, dealing out solitaire with his habitual deadly monotony, and listening to Jim Echeverri threatening to kill him.

"Now Jim explained. It was what Coach Leary had sensed, an attempted fix. Michaelis had something on him, and was trying to blackmail him into muffling those deadly punts. If Echeverri played a bad game, the odds were all in favor of Santa Juana.

"I never learned till much later what that 'something' was. A cousin of Echeverri's was in this country illegally. She was one of the Catholic Basque Loyalists who suffered so cruelly during the civil war, and if exposed she would be sent back to Spain and doubtless to a firing squad. Through what underworld and underground connections Michaelis had learned this, I never knew; but the girl is safe now . . . if safety is the word for carrying on counterespionage for the Mexican government against Falangist agents.

"Jim had slipped out the night before, after a threatening note from Michaelis, and had the bitter quarrel with him which the elevator boy overheard. It was a painful problem in loyalties. Last night he had ended by consenting to betray his team rather than his cousin and her ideals of democracy. In the morning he was all confused again. He came back to try to talk Michaelis out of it, even with some vague idea of beating him out of it.

"He found the corpse. His problem was solved, but he was plunged into the midst of another. If he reported the murder, he would be held first as a witness, then, when the boy talked, as a suspect. And he had to be at the stadium. He couldn't miss the Big Game, now that he was free to play it honestly.

"When Jim had reached this point in his story, Shawn Leary let out a yell of pure rage. He had been the first to hear the radio switched on in the next room and words, 'They're coming out on the field now, the Bellarmine Bearcats in their green-and-gold-striped jerseys . . .'

"Murder wasn't going to keep those Santa Juana policemen from hearing the Big Game.

" 'Give him a parole or something for just three hours,' Leary pleaded. 'Just let him play this game. I'll bring him back to you myself.'

" 'Let me go,' Jim urged, 'and I'll sign anything you want. What is this, a new kind of third degree?'

"I put in a word too, offering my own standing and my word of honor as pledge for Jim's return. But Sergeant Hanlon was adamant. It seemed as though nothing could prevent him from taking Jim to the station then and there.

"It took Bob here to save the situation. You see, there was nothing the sergeant could do but release Jim after Bob had confessed to the murder."

Father Pearson paused. "I think the rest of this is Bob's story. But it is clear so far? Any questions, Sister?"

Sister Ursula took her astonished eyes from Coffin Corner Cassidy, who had confessed a murder. "Yes. About that cribbage arrangement. You said that the gambler's own hand was bad, only two. Is that usual? How do scores run in cribbage?"

The priest suppressed any curiosity as to the question. "Anywhere from zero to twenty-nine. An average passably good hand would be from eight to sixteen."

"And all that was on the desk was the cards arranged for cribbage?"

"Yes."

Sister Ursula's face was not happy. "Tell me," she said after a moment's reflection, "this Michaelis—was he well-versed in football, or simply interested in scores and odds as a gambler?"

Father Pearson looked to Cassidy. "Bob?"

"Very well-versed, I'd say. He wasn't only a gambler; he was a Santa Juana rooter. He could tell you the score of every Big Game in the past twenty years and who stood out on what plays."

Sister Ursula nodded, frowning. "Thank you."

"Then if that's all, Sister, perhaps Bob should take up the—"

"Just a minute, Father. Reverend Mother was saying

yesterday that she wanted to see you about something. Perhaps you could talk to her while Mr. Cassidy tells me the story that you must know by heart."

"Fine, Sister. Do a good job on it, Bob."

Cassidy cleared his throat several times. At last he said, "There isn't much to the rest of it, Sister. Have you got any ideas yet? You've got to help us clear Jim."

"I believe he's well worth it, Mr. Cassidy, and I shall certainly try. I do have an idea . . . but I'd like to hear the rest of your story first."

"Well, as Father said, there wasn't anything the sergeant could do then but book me, while Father and Coach took Jim off to the stadium. I think they all guessed right away why I confessed.

"The sergeant wanted a full statement, but I persuaded him to let me hear the game first. It wasn't hard; he was on tenterhooks to hear it himself. So we sat there in the station and heard one of the greatest of all Big Games.

"Maybe you remember it, Sister. Jim went in there full of fire, and in the first quarter he dropped one in coffin corner that resulted in a touchdown when a blocked kick sailed into Cyrovich's arms. But after that, something happened to him. He told me later it reminded him of me in that game you were talking about and he got to thinking about me in jail and he sort of went to pieces. A little later one of his punts made only five yards net from scrimmage, and Santa Juana took over on the twenty and marched straight for a touchdown.

"After that Coach Leary pulled him out for a while. You remember the end of the game, though: 13–7 in their favor, and Cyrovich finally gets away to the races for forty yards and a touchdown. Thirteen–thirteen, and Jim sent in to boot the extra point. The strain on him by then was something terrific. And the kick was blocked.

"But Jim got hold of himself at the last minute, grabbed the ball, and ran it over to make it 14–13.

"It was a great game. And just as the announcer was saying it had been one, Sergeant Hanlon switched off the radio and said, 'Now, you son—' I beg your pardon, Sister—'now tell me how you killed him.'

" 'Killed who?' I said. And that was that.

"Not that I got off easy. I'd insulted the police of Santa Juana, and they were out to teach me a lesson. I won't go into all that. I could show you scars . . .

"They found a motive for me. Jim had told me his dilemma and I'd saved him from it. The Beak switched his story so it seemed I must've done it. It was bad enough so that my lawyer advised to reserve my defense and stand trial.

"When I did, it was a cinch. We produced witnesses that established I couldn't possibly have seen or heard from Jim between his visit to Michaelis and mine. We got in The Beak's first story—stricken out as hearsay but still having its effect on the jury. And I took the stand myself and told just why I'd confessed so that a fine boy could play a great game.

"That jury darned near gave me a medal.

"The police were all for going back to their first suspect. But the D.A.'s office weren't going to be made fools of again; they wouldn't ask for an indictment without a perfect case. By then the trail was cold, and the police finally gave up. I think that's all the story, Sister. But now—"

"Now," said Sister Ursula, "Jim Echeverri wants a commission. Don't look so surprised, Mr. Cassidy. That's no wonderful deduction. In times like this, that's the most likely reason why it should suddenly be imperative to clear him of this lingering suspicion. And you want me to tell you who is guilty?"

"I want you to tell us how to prove it. It's pretty obvious who did it. Michaelis was alive when I saw him, so it couldn't be Coach. I'm acquitted, and we all believe Jim's story. It must have been The Beak. But to prove that . . ."

Sister Ursula did not look at Cassidy. "Must it?" She chose her words carefully. "You've fallen into a common snare on your reasoning there, all of you. You assume that there are only four possible answers, and eliminate three of those. But isn't there a fifth?"

"Father explained it couldn't have been suicide. If only it could . . ."

"What evidence gives you that limitation of four suspects? What evidence almost sent Jim to trial? Who had the best opportunity of all and yet was so little noticed that Father did not even mention his name?"

Cassidy looked suddenly stricken. "Good Lord! I never thought of him. The elevator boy!"

Sister Ursula nodded.

"But no, he couldn't be." His words came fast and urgent. "It isn't possible. He had no motive. There's no reason why he—"

The nun smiled ruefully. "The Beak is dead, isn't he?"

"Yes. Got into the sugar-hijacking racket and was shot a few weeks ago. But how did you know that?"

Sister Ursula's voice was low and earnest. "It was a lucky guess. . . . Am I equally lucky in guessing that you haven't been to Communion since the Big Game?"

There was a long silence in the sunny patio. At last Cassidy said tonelessly, "How did you know?"

"I didn't think you would receive the sacrament under that burden of guilt any more than you would try to shift the murder onto a living man."

"I've been acquitted, you know," he said quietly.

"I know. That makes Jim's problem more difficult."

"But how—what—"

"Let's start with the cribbage game. There was one thing glaringly wrong. On the desk was nothing but the piles of cards. I don't play cribbage myself, but I do know that it is always scored on a cribbage board. In an emergency, paper and pencil might do; but they were also absent.

"Therefore it was not a cribbage game. Then what was it? Because there was no mention of fingerprints on the cards, which could so easily have established which of the four was present, I knew they must have borne only Michaelis's prints. The cards, as Father described them, were bloodstained on both sides. Then they were laid out after the shooting, or they would have been stained on only one side.

"Michaelis was shot through the chest. He could have lived a short while after such a wound. There was nothing on his desk with which to leave a message, and when he tried to get up he would find the exertion too much for him. He had only his habitual solitaire deck so he laid out an imaginary cribbage game, and for his adversary's hand he arranged the cards that positively identified him.

"Father said that that hand was the highest possible in cribbage. He also said that cribbage scores ran from zero to twenty-nine. That was the rarest of hands, as striking and distinctive as thirteen spades: the twenty-nine hand."

"And I never noticed that," Cassidy groaned. "Never thought of it"

"Twenty-nine is the number of your immortal jersey. If a man had just been visited by Red Grange and then announced, 'Seventy-seven has done thus and so to me,' his meaning would be clear enough. And Michaelis was well-versed in football history."

"I didn't mean to," Cassidy said. He kept his face turned away. "When I went to lay my bet he warned me the game was fixed: he thought he was doing me a favor because of my friend the politician. I got mad and called him out for it. He was feeling so damned proud of himself for how he'd sewed up Jim. Finally I took a sock at the cocky little rat and he pulled his gun. I got it away from him and then all of a sudden I saw how to solve Jim's problem . . .

"I don't even remember pulling the trigger. I just remember wiping the gun and leaving it there and getting the hell out. Thank God that damned elevator boy didn't spot anything wrong with me."

Sister Ursula showed no reaction to the profanity. "Do you?" she asked gently.

"Do I what?"

"Do you thank God that you went unspotted?"

"No," Cassidy said after a long silence. "Because I

didn't go unspotted. I mean, I'm spotted inside me. I'm not clear. But if I'd stood trial honestly on the truth instead of the farce that cleared me . . ."

He broke off and lit a cigarette. After a long draw, he said, "It's up to you, Sister. I urged Father to reopen this closed case because I hoped we might clear Jim by shifting the blame onto that dead racketeer. But you saw through that. All right, Sister; you've solved it. Now solve your solution. What can I do? I can't clear Jim by confessing; they'd laugh at me because they couldn't try me."

"You can confess," she said, "to God. You can ask Him for grace and guidance. And you can confess to the officers examining Jim's record."

"They won't believe me."

"I think they will if your statement is supported by the priest who gave you absolution. One doesn't joke about murder in the confessional."

Cassidy tossed away his cigarette and straightened up. He looked ten years younger and ready for another fifty-yard punt. "Sister," he said, "if my prayers are worth anything at all, you'll never stay long in purgatory."

Sister Ursula laughed softly. "I might resent the implication that I'd be there indefinitely without you."

When Father Pearson came back, she said simply, "Father, I think Mr. Cassidy wants to talk to you alone."

The nun walked out of the patio, leaving the murderer with the priest.

(1943)

The Great Rodeo Fix

LEO R. ELLIS

The Spook traveled light. He arrived in Higginston by freight truck, unencumbered by social security, draft, or credit cards. He peered out of the rear opening and shot a cautious look around. This action came partly from habit, but made the more necessary this time by having misjudged the state of intoxication of a drunk in the last town. The lush had come out of his alcoholic daze with the Spook's hand in his pocket. The guy was still screaming loudly for the cops when the Spook had swung aboard the truck.

The Spook, a shrimp of a man, had a sallow, drawn complexion and not enough hair to fill a good-sized paint brush. He hopped down, dusted off a too-tight suit, and tilted his hat a few degrees off his left eyebrow before he fingered the only object in his pockets, a rabbit's foot.

The charm seemed to work with a suddenness that

surprised even the Spook. He saw a county fair was in progress here in Higginston, and the Spook worked on the percentage theory: If given a crowd with spending money, a percentage of it should end up in his pocket.

He caught another ride to the fairgrounds and approached the turnstile with an air of confidence. "Member of the working press," he said grandly. Before the gateman could recover, the Spook had slithered through the turnstile and had lost himself in the crowd.

He avoided the livestock barns and exhibits, and headed for the amusement area. At a refreshment stand he paused to sniff the sizzling meat patties on a grill.

The man in the stand pointed a spatula in the Spook's direction. "You want a job working the counter, Mac?"

The Spook reacted as though the man had slapped him across the face. He drew himself up to his five feet four inch height. "Drop dead," he said haughtily and strode on.

He traveled the length of the noisy, teeming midway, rubbing the charm constantly, but the rabbit's foot failed to turn a mark. The grandstand loomed ahead and another turnstile blocked his way.

A moment later a workman staggered by, burdened with an armload of cartons. The Spook deftly removed the top carton. "Let me give you a hand, buster," he said and fell in step behind the workman. Beyond the turnstile, the Spook tossed the carton to the ground, then went on, behind the back of the grandstand. He was mechanically rubbing the rabbit's foot, when suddenly he stopped, and his thin nose quivered as he sniffed the air. His brain had received a signal; the good luck charm grew hot in his hand.

Then he saw his target—a huge, young man in a cowboy hat and boots. The mark had his back turned.

The Spook had often regretted he had never spent the time necessary to develop the skill of a professional dip. He seldom tried to hoist a sober man's poke, but the top of the leather that peeked out of the hip pocket begged to be lifted. The wallet seemed to be trying to wriggle out, so it could drop into the Spook's hand.

The Great Rodeo Fix

He sidled over. He had the wallet out of the Levi's, when suddenly he was lifted off his feet and held dangling by the scruff of his neck. The Spook stared fearfully into the freckled face of a youthful grizzly bear, shuddered as he strove to find some way to prevent having to listen to the sound of his own bones being snapped. He desperately waved the wallet. "I found this on the ground," he gasped. "I was trying to shove it back into your pocket."

The giant stared at the wallet with blank eyes. A slow grin spread across his broad face, and he lowered the Spook gently to the ground. "Gosh, thanks," he said in a squeaky drawl. "That was right nice of you, mister."

"It was nothing," the Spook said as he straightened his coat. He eyed the wallet. "Of course if you want to reward an act of honesty and integ—"

The young man turned red. "I'd sure like to give you a reward, mister." He spread open the wallet and displayed the empty interior. "Of course you didn't know it was empty," he added quickly.

The Spook gave his rabbit's foot a reproachful pinch.

"My name's Courtney Philmore," the young man said, and pointed to the arena beyond the fence. "I was watching the rodeo. Came into town to compete, but met up with a couple of card sharks last night. They took my entry money, so all I can do now is watch."

"I'm sorry," the Spook said, but he was more sorry that he hadn't found Courtney before the card sharks. The way things had broken so far, maybe it would pay to let his luck get adjusted before he made another try. He climbed up on the fence. The Spook had never seen a rodeo before, and he glumly watched the action for a few minutes. "What's the point in chasing those midget cows around?" he growled.

"That's the calf roping event," Courtney said. "The man who ropes and ties his calf in the best time wins the big money."

The Spook turned. "You talking about cash money?"

"Sure, a rodeo like this one is big business."

The Spook suddenly developed a new interest in the

rodeo game. The calf roping event ended, but a new attraction was ready to come on. A gate flew open and a cowboy came out on top of something that resembled a bundle of bedsprings wrapped up in horsehide. The bronc leaped, spun, and twisted in front of the chute.

"They ought to train that dog better before they break him out of the gate," the Spook said. "He ain't going to win any races with a start like that."

"This is the saddle bronc event," Courtney said with a choke in his voice. "That's what I was going to enter. Maybe I'm not too good, but I sure wanted to try my luck at a big time rodeo."

The Spook watched the bronc put his rider into orbit. "Yeah? What do they pay you to put on an act like that?"

"Nothing; you pay your entry fee, then if you make high points on the go-around, you win day money. If you pile up the most points for the three-day meet, you win the average, or the big money. Of course you've got to stay in the saddle until the whistle blows, or you draw a goose egg. Day money runs about five hundred dollars here," Courtney added.

The mention of five hundred triggered a switch that sent the Spook's brain into gear. "The odds don't sound right. How do they rig the fix in this rodeo racket?"

The blank look the Spook had come to expect spread over the young cowboy's face. "The fix?"

"The gimmick, the hook, the deal. How do they rig this bronc riding game so the right party walks off with the loot?"

The bewildered expression remained. "It's on the level. If I ride better than the other guys, I win the money."

"What a crummy way to run a racket." It was hard for the Spook to believe that anything where five hundred bucks hung in the balance could be on the level. Some smart operator would have figured a way to skim the cream; name the sport and somebody had put the fix on it at some time.

But this was a countrified deal, a hick game. Maybe the smart boys had overlooked the rodeo. The Spook

The Great Rodeo Fix

began to get excited when he realized he might have stumbled into virgin territory. "I've hung around the bullring racetracks," he said. "I know a dope that will slow a horse down to a walk. One shot of that stuff in a horse, and anybody could ride him."

"Gosh, you don't want to slow a bronc down. The judges score points on the horse, and the rider. If your bronc doesn't buck, you don't get enough points to win."

"Just an idea, there's other angles." The Spook had been working angles all his life; this would be just a case of coming up with the right approach. "Maybe we could work it like a wrestling match," he said.

Courtney shoved back his hat and scratched his head. "I don't think you could talk a bronc into throwing a ride."

"Okay, okay." The Spook went back through his list, sifting out the gimmicks he had worked in the past. Then he thought of all the tricks he had ever heard of; but none of them would work here. He'd have to come up with a brand new angle. "I don't suppose we could tie your ankles together under the horse," he said hopefully.

"Nope, if you don't spur the horse in the shoulders on the first jump out of the chute, you're disqualified."

The Spook watched the third rider in a row hit the dirt before the ten-second whistle blew. It all boiled down to one simple fact; if he could figure out a way to keep Courtney in the saddle until the whistle blew, he'd have heavy odds running his way. "I'll figure out some way to have you riding tomorrow," he said.

Courtney didn't look too hopeful. "I don't have any entry fee."

"I'll worry about that once I get this other thing worked out. I'm not putting up any money to enter until I'm sure we're going to win." He studied Courtney. "In the meantime, I've got to do something with you. C'mon with me."

The Spook led the young cowboy back to the refreshment stand, where he finally managed to talk the owner into giving Courtney a job behind the counter.

"No," the owner said, after the Spook had made a

demand. "I'm not going to give you an advance on the kid's wages, and I'm not paying a fee because you found me a counterman. Now beat it before I get sore."

The Spook shrugged and turned to Courtney. "How much jingling money you got?" He accepted the fifty-cent piece and put it into his pocket. "You won't need this. I'll meet you outside the front gate at closing time. And don't let this character try to pay you off in hamburgers," he warned.

The Spook left the fairgrounds, and near the bus stop he saw a small crowd. He moved in, drawn like a fly to a honeypot. From the center of the crowd he heard the smooth, liquid voice of a man he recognized as Oily Parker. The Spook shoved his way in to the front row, where he watched the round man working behind a table.

The Spook had shilled for Oily a couple of times in the past. He had been the delighted user of a razor hone, and on another occasion he had delivered a testimonial on the efficiency of a multi-purpose vegetable peeler. Now he hoped the pitchman might see fit to use his services again for a couple of bucks.

The immaculate, white-haired Oily Parker held a small bottle aloft. His eyes slid across the faces, and as they paused on the Spook, he gave a slight shake of his head.

"Of the many marvels of the atomic age, this, my friends, has proved to be of the greatest value to you and me," Oily said, shaking the bottle. "This formula was developed behind locked doors, stamped Top Secret, and now lies guarded in a Pentagon vault. This is the miracle substance that holds the metal skin to our missiles as they zoom through space."

So Oily is pushing glue, the Spook thought. He looked over the crowd, but didn't move. Oily would have broken his leg if the Spook had tried to work the tip.

Oily spoke softly, in a persuasive voice. "Now you no longer need to throw broken articles away. Grip-Hold will mend them better than new." He picked up one of the several mended articles lying on the table. "As you can see, this hammer handle has been sawed in half, and then joined together with a single drop of Grip-Hold."

He tossed the piece of wood to a man. "Inspect the joint, friend. Test it any way you see fit, try to break the tenacious grip."

While the spectator pounded the hammer handle on the ground, the Spook let his mind wander back to his own problem. He still hadn't figured a way to rig the bronc riding event.

"Grip-Hold will adhere any one substance to another—glass to metal, wood to metal, cloth to leather. Once this miracle fluid has been applied, and the surfaces pressed together, no force can separate them again."

The Spook heard the pitch with his conscious mind, while his subconscious mind still worked on his problem. Suddenly the two minds synchronized. He wanted a way to keep Courtney stuck in the saddle; Oily Parker claimed he had a product that would stick anything.

"It is my personal guarantee that Grip-Hold will mend anything but a broken heart, and will hold everything but a wayward spouse."

The Spook waited impatiently while Oily sold a few bottles of his merchandise, then moved in when the pitchman began to fold up his table. "Hi, there, Oily old pal," the Spook said.

The pitchman didn't look up. "If it's a touch, I'm stony, Spook."

The Spook laughed loudly. "That's rich, Oily. Why would I be looking for money, when I'm sitting on top of the greatest thing since the Brink holdup?"

The pitchman placed the last of the articles in his kit. "I pay a fat fee to operate in this town. But if the local law sees you talking to me, they'll revoke my license."

"Ha, ha, you're a kick, Oily. Say, is that Grip-Hold any good? I mean, will it really stick stuff together?"

Oily snapped his kit closed. "It's a good product, and it will cost you one buck a copy, cash, the same as anyone else."

"But look, Oily," the Spook wheedled, "I figured that since we could be partners in this thing—"

Oily regarded him with a cold, pale eye. "I'd consider

that arrangement on a par with holding hands with a guy sitting in the electric chair." The pitchman placed the folded table under his arm and reached for his kit.

The Spook grabbed his arm. "Look, Oily, let me have a few bottles of that Grip-Hold. I'll give you a hundred clams tomorrow night, sure. I swear I will."

Oily faced the Spook with a cherubic smile on his round face. "Give me your hand on that, Spook. But cut it off at the wrist first—I'll need it for security."

The Spook took the same bus into town, then tailed Oily to his hotel. He blew the last of the fifty cents on a hot dog and coffee, then went out and found a lumberyard. He slipped in, took off one shoe and sock, and filled the foot of the sock from a sand bin.

Two hours later, Oily Parker appeared in the hotel dining room, and while the Spook ate his heart out in a doorway across the street, the pitchman devoured his way through a huge dinner. After several cups of coffee, Oily picked up his table and kit and left the hotel.

Two figures moved down the darkened street. The fat man in front waddled easily, while the short, thin figure behind him sneaked closer at every step. The first man stepped off the curb at an alleyway. The second man moved in fast. A sand-filled sock swung through the air and came down with a thud on the fat man's head.

Oily staggered, and started to slump as the Spook shoved him into the alley. "This is what you get for not trusting me," he said as he kneeled and unfastened the catch on the kit. He scooped out the bottles and stuffed them into his pockets. Then he turned his attention to the unconscious man.

Oily had lied to him; the pitchman wasn't broke, he had a thin roll and some loose change.

The Spook slipped out of the alley and hugged the shadows as he hurried away.

When the fair closed down that evening, the Spook met Courtney outside the gate. He relieved the young man of his wages. "Get a good night's sleep," he said. "You're going to ride one of those broncs tomorrow."

The Great Rodeo Fix 69

Courtney gazed with new admiration in his eyes. "Gosh, you're terrific, Mr. Spook."

"Yes," the Spook said, tipping his hat. "I agree."

After a good night's sleep in a second-rate hotel, the Spook ate breakfast and returned to the fairgrounds. He found Courtney waiting, with stable straw still stuck to his clothes. The Spook regarded his new charge with a critical eye. "Maybe I should have you do some road work first, to get into shape."

"I don't need road work, Mr. Spook. Bronc riders do their job sitting down."

"Maybe you're right." The Spook rubbed his hands together. "Well, the first thing I'll do as your manager is to get you signed up for the main event. Where do I find the matchmaker?"

After Courtney had pointed out the rodeo office, the Spook entered and demanded that the rodeo secretary issue Courtney a permit to ride, on credit. The secretary flatly refused. The Spook threatened to withdraw his boy, but finally peeled off some bills from Oily's roll. He accepted the numbered square of cloth that Courtney would wear on his back, and glared across the counter. "I'm going to buy this two-bit operation," he shouted, "and the first thing I'll do is fire you."

Courtney had waited for the Spook beside a barn. The young cowboy proudly pointed to a saddle he had borrowed. "And I've got my chaps, too," he announced.

The Spook watched as Courtney buckled on the heavy, plastic chaps, then inspected the open rear, where the seat of the Levi's was left available, but was partially concealed by the bat wings on either side.

He nodded with satisfaction and pulled out one of Oily's bottles. "Here's our little gold mine. Now you listen and I'll give you the pitch."

Courtney's eyes widened as he listened. "Gosh, that sounds good all right, Mr. Spook. But I don't know whether using glue would be legal."

"Legal, smeegal," the Spook snapped. He saw the stubborn expression on Courtney's face and changed his tone. "Look, kid," he said, "fighters tape their hands inside their gloves, don't they?"

"I reckon they do."

"Sure, and football players wear shoulder pads and helmets. Baseball players put spikes on their shoes. That's no different than smearing glue on the seat of your pants. All the stuff they do is to give them the advantage. It's the same way with us—it swings the odds our way."

"If you say it's all right, Mr. Spook. But I'm wondering what the rodeo officials are going to say when they find out."

"They're not going to find out," the Spook said quickly. "If all the other riders start using Grip-Hold, then you'll never get to be the Mickey Mantle of the rodeo racket."

"Yeah, I guess you're right. Okay, I'll keep it a secret."

Shortly after noon the broncs were drawn, and the pairings posted on the bulletin board. Courtney had drawn a bronc called Destruction. The Spook made some inquiries. He learned Destruction was considered a top bucking horse, guaranteed to put on a good show for the judges. He also tried to get a morning line on his boy, but nobody had ever heard of Courtney Philmore.

The Spook spent a full hour driving home the invincibility of Grip-Hold. He wanted to make sure his boy had plenty of assurance when he hit the arena. "There's only one hitch," the Spook admitted to Courtney. "This Grip-Hold is expensive, and I had a tough time getting a few bottles. I don't know how we'll get any more. Hard to find, too."

Courtney looked worried. "Gosh, that's bad."

"Yeah, but maybe something will turn up."

The Spook found that Courtney would be the last rider out of the chute. He waited until the saddle bronc event was half over before he dragged Courtney behind a truck. "Bend over," he commanded. When the young man obeyed, the Spook poured a bottle of Grip-Hold over the tightly stretched Levi's.

Courtney sprang upright. "Hey, that stuff's cold."

The Great Rodeo Fix

"Quit fooling around," the Spook said angrily, and shoved Courtney down. He applied two more bottles, then smeared the mess around with a wooden paddle. "Okay, get down to the chute, and into the saddle before that glue dries."

The young cowboy took off in a spraddle-legged duckwalk, with the bat wings of the chaps flapping out on either side.

The Spook walked in a tight circle. He took out his rabbit's foot, blew on it, rubbed it behind his ear, and jammed it back into his pocket. He began to pace again.

When the bullhorn on the pole announced the last rider in the saddle bronc event, the Spook rushed over, climbed up, and perched on the top rail of the fence.

"Courtney Philmore, coming out of chute four on Destruction," the horn bellowed.

The gate swung open. A hammerhead chestnut horse exploded out of the opening. The bronc hit the ground and flew high again, this time in a rainbow arch. Destruction made three fast spins, then went into a series of bone-jolting porpoise leaps across the arena.

The Spook clutched his good luck charm with one hand while he held the other over his eyes.

Courtney stayed in the saddle. He swung his legs. He rode the bronc—not with grace, but more in the manner of an overmatched club fighter hanging on for the final bell.

The whistle blew. The Spook peeked out through his fingers. He saw his boy still in the saddle and knew his gimmick had worked; at least he hadn't crapped out.

The horn blared out the news that the judges had awarded Courtney Philmore one hundred and seventy-two points for his ride. This meant nothing to the Spook, but moments later the voice announced that the one hundred and seventy-two points made Courtney Philmore high point rider for the day.

The Spook clutched the board to keep from falling. "I won," he croaked. "I copped me a five hundred dollar payoff."

"Congratulations," a smooth voice said from behind him.

The Spook looked down, saw Oily Parker, and dropped to the ground. Oily wouldn't start anything here, and the Spook knew the pitchman had too much professional pride to finger him for the cops. The knowledge made the little man cocky. He stuck out his chest. "You're talking to a big time operator," he said. "I tried to cut you in on the action, but you were too smart to buy any, remember?"

"I remember very well." The billikin face remained impassive as Oily touched the back of his head. "A funny thing happened to me on my way to the fairgrounds last night. I got sapped."

"You don't say," the Spook said with elaborate concern. "How terrible."

"Yes, the culprit took my bankroll and the bottles out of my kit." Oily placed a cigarette between his lips, flicked a lighter, and touched the flame to the tip. "At first I couldn't figure why anyone would take my stock," he said, blowing out a cloud of smoke. "Then I remembered a certain grubby little character who had been desperate to get his hands on a few bottles of Grip-Hold."

"You can't prove anything."

"I can to my own satisfaction," Oily said in an amiable voice. "When I had the deal figured, I kept my eye on that little character today."

"Okay, so you know," the Spook blustered. "What do you think you can do about it?"

The pitchman flicked an ash from his cigarette. "Only a fool would believe that you could stick a man in a saddle with glue."

"It worked," the Spook yelled. He pointed over the fence. "You saw it yourself. That horse couldn't buck my boy off."

"Grip-Hold didn't keep him in the saddle, psychology did. Your boy is gullible, which is another way of saying he is even more stupid than you are. He thought he was stuck in the saddle, so he stayed stuck. You drew to

The Great Rodeo Fix 73

luck," Oily went on. "Destruction was the class of the field. That bronc piled up the points your boy missed."

"Okay, maybe Grip-Hold didn't work. As long as the big ape thinks it will, we're in free."

"I wouldn't count on that," Oily said, smiling. "Someday your boy is going to get smart enough to wonder how he can slide out of the saddle, once the whistle has blown." The pitchman shook his head. "I'm afraid you've got a one-shot deal here, Spook. You'd better hang on tight to your money."

The Spook watched Oily Parker waddle off, with mixed feelings. If the pitchman was right, he'd have to drop Courtney. But the Spook felt he had made a good haul, five hundred clams, and it was all his; nobody else was going to take a nick out of this money. He'd collect the prize and blow town, only this time not in a freight truck.

The rodeo officials proved to be as tough about handing over the prize money as they had been about extending credit. They would pay only the rider—no Courtney, no cash. When the Spook got belligerent, they kicked him out, with the order not to return.

The Spook hated to let his money pass through a middleman's hands, but now he was forced to look up Courtney.

The young cowboy looked worried as the Spook approached. "I can't get my pants off," he said. "They're stuck on."

"I'll work that out later." The Spook pushed Courtney toward the rodeo office. "Get the money and bring it to me. I'll wait for you at the front gate."

Courtney walked off, stiff-legged and shaking his head in wonderment. "Gosh, that Grip-Hold is terrific stuff, all right."

The Spook had no idea how long it would take the rodeo officials to make the payoff, but it seemed he had paced for an hour. He wasn't worried that his boy had given him the slip; the Spook had stopped that possibility by covering the only exit. Besides, Courtney was too honest and dumb to think of a smart deal like that. The boy was a born sucker.

Courtney appeared through the crowd, his freckled face wreathed in a grin. The Spook rushed forward, holding out his hand. "The five hundred," he said hoarsely.

The young man continued to grin, but he made no move toward his pocket. "I can't get over what terrific stuff that Grip-Hold is."

"You said that before." The Spook wiggled his fingers impatiently. "Gimme."

"Gosh, it will mend everything but a broken heart, and hold anything but a wayward spouse."

A cold, chilling fear clutched the Spook's chest. "Where did you hear that?" he demanded.

"The man who gave me this said that," and Courtney reached into his pocket.

The Spook grabbed the sheet of paper and read the handwriting with a growing dread.

To Whom it may concern:
  For considerations paid, Courtney Philmore has been granted exclusive rights for Grip-Hold in the state of Oklahoma. It is further agreed that he can purchase unlimited quantities of the product for the wholesale price of one dollar a bottle.

"You don't have to worry anymore, Mr. Spook," Courtney said happily. "Now we can get all the Grip-Hold we need to make me champ."

The Spook sobbed as he read the final lines, which grew blurred and dim through his tears.

For the sum of five hundred dollars paid, in cash, I hereby relinquish all claims for damages, injuries, wounded feelings, and loss of bankroll and merchandise.

                                    Signed,
                                    Oily J. Parker

The Sailing Club

DAVID ELY

Of all the important social clubs in the city, the most exclusive was also the most casual and the least known to outsiders. This was a small group of venerable origin but without formal organization. Indeed, it was without a name, although it was generally referred to as the Sailing Club, for its sole apparent activity was a short sailing cruise each summer. There were no meetings, no banquets, no other functions—in fact, no club building existed, so that it was difficult even to classify it as a club.

Nevertheless, the Sailing Club represented the zenith of a successful businessman's social ambitions, for its handful of members included the most influential men in the city, and many a top executive would have traded all his other hard-won attainments for an opportunity to join. Even those who had no interest in sailing would willingly have sweated through long practice hours to learn, if the

Club had beckoned. Few were invited, however. The Club held its membership to the minimum necessary for the operation of its schooner, and not until death or debility created a vacancy was a new man admitted.

Who were the members of this select group? It was almost impossible to be absolutely certain. For one thing, since the Club had no legal existence, the members did not list it in their *Who's Who* paragraphs or in any other catalogue of their honors. Furthermore, they appeared reluctant to discuss it in public. At luncheons or parties, for example, the Club might be mentioned, but those who brought up the name did not seem to be members, and as for those distinguished gentlemen who carefully refrained at such times from commenting on the subject—who could tell? They might be members, or they might deliberately be assuming an air of significant detachment in hopes of being mistaken for members.

Naturally, the hint of secrecy which was thus attached to the Sailing Club made it all the more desirable in the eyes of the rising business leaders who yearned for the day when they might be tapped for membership. They realized that the goal was remote and their chances not too likely, but each still treasured in his heart the hope that in time this greatest of all distinctions would reward a lifetime of struggle and success.

One of these executives, a man named John Goforth, could without immodesty consider himself unusually eligible for the Club. He was, first of all, a brilliant success in the business world. Although he was not yet fifty, he was president of a dynamic corporation which had become preeminent in several fields through a series of mergers he himself had expertly negotiated. Each year, under his ambitious direction, the corporation expanded into new areas, snapping up less nimble competitors and spurring the others into furious battles for survival.

Early in his career Goforth had been cautious, even anxious, but year by year his confidence had increased, so that now he welcomed new responsibilities, just as he welcomed the recurrent business crises where one serious mistake in judgment might cause a large enterprise

The Sailing Club

to founder and to sink. His quick rise had not dulled this sense of excitement, but rather had sharpened it. More and more, he put routine matters into the hands of subordinates, while he zestfully attacked those problems that forced from him the fullest measure of daring and skill. He found himself not merely successful, but powerful, a man whose passage through the halls of a club left a wake of murmurs, admiring and envious.

This was the life he loved, and his mastery of it was his chief claim to recognition by the most influential social group of all, the Sailing Club. There was another factor which he thought might count in his favor: his lifelong attachment to the sea and to sailing.

As a boy, he had stood in fascination at the ocean's edge, staring out beyond the breakers to the distant sails, sometimes imagining himself to be the captain of a great ship; at those times, the toy bucket in his hand had become a long spyglass, or a pirate's cutlass, and the strip of reed that fluttered from his fingers had been transformed into a gallant pennant, or a black and wicked skull-and-bones.

At the age of ten, he had been taught to sail at his family's summer place on the shore; later, he was allowed to take his father's boat out alone—and later still, when he was almost of college age, he was chosen for the crew of one of the yacht club entries in the big regatta. By that time, he had come to regard the sea as a resourceful antagonist in a struggle all the more absorbing because of the danger, and a danger that was far from theoretical, for every summer at least one venturesome sailor would be lost forever, far from land, and even a sizable boat might fail to return from some holiday excursion.

Now, in his middle years, John Goforth knew the sea as something more than an invigorating physical challenge. It was that still, but he recognized that it was also an inexhaustible source of renewal for him. The harsh sting of blown spray was a climate in which he thrived, and the erratic thrusts of strength that swayed his little boat evoked a passionate response of answering strength within himself. In those moments—like the supreme moments of business crisis—he felt almost godlike, limitless, as he shared the ocean's solitude, its fierce and fitful communion with the wind, the sun, and the sky.

As time passed, membership in the Sailing Club became the single remaining honor which Goforth coveted but did not have. He told himself: not a member—no, not yet! But of course he realized that this prize would not necessarily fall to him at all, despite his most strenuous efforts to seize it. He sought to put the matter out of his mind; then, failing that, he decided to learn more about the Club, to satisfy his curiosity, at least.

It was no easy task. But he was a resourceful and determined man, and before long he had obtained a fairly accurate idea of the real membership of the Sailing Club. All these men were prominent in business or financial circles, but Goforth found it strange that they seemed to lack any other common characteristic of background or attainments. Most were university men, but a few were not. There was, similarly, a variety of ethnic strains represented among them. Some were foreign-born, even, and one or two were still foreign citizens. Moreover, while some members had a long association with sailing, others seemed to have no interest whatever in the sea.

Yet just as Goforth was prepared to shrug away the matter and conclude that there was no unifying element among the members of the Sailing Club, he became aware of some subtle element that resisted analysis. Did it actually exist, or did he merely imagine it? He studied the features of the supposed Club members more closely. They were casual, yes, and somewhat aloof—even bored, it seemed. And yet there was something else, something buried: a kind of suppressed exhilaration that winked out briefly, at odd moments, as though they shared some monumental private joke.

As his perplexing survey of the Club members continued, Goforth became conscious of a quite different sensation. He could not be sure, but he began to suspect that while he was quietly inspecting them, they in turn were examining him.

The Sailing Club

The most suggestive indication was his recent friendship with an older man named Marshall, who was almost certainly a Club member. Marshall, the chairman of a giant corporation, had taken the lead in their acquaintanceship, which had developed to the point where they lunched together at least once a week. Their conversation was ordinary enough—of business matters, usually, and sometimes of sailing, for both were ardent seamen—but each time, Goforth had a stronger impression that he was undergoing some delicate kind of interrogation which was connected with the Sailing Club.

He sought to subdue his excitement. But he often found that his palms were moist, and as he wiped them he disciplined his nervousness, telling himself angrily that he was reacting like a college freshman being examined by the president of some desirable fraternity.

At first he tried to moderate his personality, as well. He sensed that his aggressive attitude toward his work, for example, was not in harmony with the blasé manner of the Club members. He attempted a show of nonchalance, of indifference—and all at once he became annoyed. He had nothing to be ashamed of. Why should he try to imitate what was false to his nature? He was *not* bored or indifferent, he was *not* disengaged from the competitive battle of life, and he would not pretend otherwise. The Club could elect him or not, as it chose.

At his next session with Marshall he went out of his way to make clear how fully he enjoyed the daily combat of business. He spoke, in fact, more emphatically than he had intended to, for he was irritated by what seemed to be the other man's ironic amusement.

Once Marshall broke in, wryly, "So you really find the press of business life to be thoroughly satisfying and exciting?"

"Yes, I do," said Goforth. He repressed the desire to add, "And don't you, too?" He decided that if the Sailing Club was nothing but a refuge for burned-out men, bored by life and by themselves, then he wanted no part of it.

At the same time he was disturbed by the thought that

he had failed. The Sailing Club might be a worthless objective for a man of his temperament—still he did not like to feel that it might be beyond his grasp.

After he had parted none too cordially from Marshall, he paced along the narrow streets toward the harbor, hoping that the ocean winds would blow away his discontent. As he reached the water's edge, he saw a customs launch bounce by across the widening wake of a huge liner. A veil of spray blew softly toward him. Greedily he awaited the familiar reassurance of its bitter scent. But when it came, it was not quite what he had expected.

He frowned out at the water. No, it was not at all the same.

That winter Goforth became ill for the first time in years. It was influenza, and not a serious case, but the convalescent period stretched on and on, and before he was well enough to do any work, it was spring.

His troubles dated from that illness, he decided; not business troubles, for he had a fine executive staff, and the company did not suffer. The troubles were within himself.

First, he went through a mild depression (the doctors had of course cautioned him of this as an aftereffect), and then an uncharacteristic lassitude, broken by intermittent self-doubts. He noted, for example, that his executive vice-president was doing a good job of filling in the presidency—and then subsequently realized that this fact had no particular meaning for him. He became uneasy. He should have felt impatient to get back in harness, to show them that old Goforth still was on top.

But he had felt no emotion. It was this that disturbed him. Was it simply a delayed result of illness, or was it some inevitable process of aging which the illness had accelerated?

He tested himself grimly. He made an analysis of a stock program proposal worked out by one of the economists. He did a masterly job; he knew it himself, with a rush of familiar pride. In its way, his study was as good as anything he had ever done. No, he was not growing feeble—not yet. The malaise that possessed him was something else, undoubtedly not permanent.

That summer he spent with his family at their place on the shore. He did not feel up to sailing; he watched others sail as he lay on the beach, and was again mildly surprised by his reaction. He did not envy them at all.

In the fall he was back at his desk, in full charge once more. But he was careful to follow the advice of the doctors and the urgings of his wife, and kept his schedule light. He avoided the rush-hour trains by going to work late and leaving early, and two or three times a month he remained at home, resting.

He knew that he once would have chafed impatiently at such a regimen, but now he thought it sensible and had no sensation of loss. As always, he passed the routine problems down to his staff; but now, it seemed, so many things appeared routine that there was not much left on his desk.

The shock came late in winter, when he realized that he had actually turned over to his staff a question of vital importance. It had been well handled, true enough, and he had kept in touch with its progress, but he should have attended to it personally. Why hadn't he? Was he going through some kind of metamorphosis that would end by his becoming a semiactive Chairman of the Board? Perhaps he should consider early retirement . . .

It was in his new condition of uncertainty that he had another encounter with Marshall, this time at a private university club to which they both belonged. Marshall offered to stand him a drink, and commented that he seemed to have recovered splendidly from his illness.

Goforth glanced at him, suspecting irony. He felt fully Marshall's age now, and looked, he thought, even older. But he accepted the drink, and they began to talk.

As they chatted, it occurred to him that he had nothing to lose by speaking frankly of his present perplexities. Marshall *was* older, in point of fact; possibly the man could offer some advice.

And so Goforth spoke of his illness, his slow convalescence, his disinclination to resume his old working place, even his unthinkable transfer of responsibility to his staff—and strangest of all, his own feeling that it did not really matter, none of it.

Marshall listened attentively, nodding his head in quiet understanding, as if he had heard scores of similar accounts.

At length Goforth's voice trailed off. He glanced at Marshall in mild embarrassment.

"So," said Marshall calmly, "you don't find business life so exciting anymore?"

Goforth stirred in irritation at this echo of their previous conversation. "No," he replied, shortly.

Marshall gave him a sharp, amused look. He seemed almost triumphant, and Goforth was sorry he had spoken at all.

Then Marshall leaned forward and said, "What would you say to an invitation to join the Sailing Club?"

Goforth stared at him. "Are you serious?"

"Quite so."

It was Goforth's turn to be amused. "You know, if you'd suggested this two years ago, I'd have jumped at the chance. But now—"

"Yes?" Marshall seemed not at all taken aback.

"But now, it seems of little importance. No offense, mind you."

"I completely understand."

"To put it with absolute frankness, I don't honestly care."

Marshall smiled. "Excellent!" he declared. "That's precisely what makes you eligible!" He winked at Goforth in a conspiratorial way. "We're all of that frame of mind, my friend. We're all suffering from that same disease—"

"But I'm well now."

Marshall chuckled. "So the doctors may say. But you know otherwise, eh?" He laughed. "The only cure, my friend, is to cast your lot with fellow sufferers—the Sailing Club!"

He continued with the same heartiness to speak of the

Club. Most of it Goforth already had heard. There were sixteen members, enough to provide the entire crew for the Club's schooner during its annual summer cruise. One of the sixteen had recently died, and Goforth would be nominated immediately to fill the vacancy; one word of assent from him would be enough to assure his election.

Goforth listened politely; but he had reservations. Marshall did not say exactly what the Club did on its cruises, and Goforth moodily assumed it was not worth mentioning. Probably the members simply drank too much and sang old college songs—hardly an enviable prospect.

Marshall interrupted his musing. "I promise you one thing," he said, more seriously. "You won't be bored."

There was a peculiar intensity in the way he spoke; Goforth wondered at it, then gave up and shrugged. Why not? He sighed and smiled. "All right. Of course. I'm honored, Marshall."

The cruise was scheduled to begin on the last day of July. The evening before, Goforth was driven by Marshall far out along the shore to the estate of another member, who kept the schooner at his private dock. By the time they arrived, all the others were there, and Goforth was duly introduced as the new crewman.

He knew them already, either as acquaintances or by reputation. They included men so eminent that they were better known than the companies or banking houses they headed. There were a few less prominent, but none below Goforth's own rank, and certainly none was in any sense obscure. He was glad to note that all of them had fought their way through the hard competitive years, just as he had done, and then in the course of the evening he slowly came to realize a further fact—that not one of these men had achieved any major triumph in recent years.

He took some comfort from this. If he had fallen into a strange lassitude, then so perhaps had they. Marshall had evidently been right. He was among "fellow sufferers." This thought cheered him, and he moved more easily from group to group, chatting with as much self-possession as if he had been a member of the Club for years.

He had already been told that the ship was in full readiness and that the group was to sail before dawn, and so he was not surprised when the host, a gigantic old man named Teacher, suggested at nine o'clock that they all retire.

"Has the new member signed on?" someone inquired.

"Not yet," said Teacher. He beckoned to Goforth with one huge hairless hand. "This way, my friend," he said.

He led Goforth into an adjoining room, with several of the others following, and after unlocking a wall safe, withdrew a large black volume so worn with age that bits of the binding flaked off in his fingers.

He laid it on a table, thumbed through its pages, and at length called Goforth over and handed him a pen. Goforth noticed the old man had covered the top portion of the page with a blank sheet of paper; all that showed beneath were signatures, those of the other members.

"Sign the articles, seaman," said Teacher gruffly, in imitation of an old-time sea captain.

Goforth grinned and bent over the page, although at the same time he felt a constitutional reluctance to sign something he could not first examine. He glanced at the faces surrounding him. A voice in the background said, "You can read the whole thing, if you like—after the cruise."

There was nothing to do but sign, so he signed boldly, with a flourish, and then turned to shake the hands thrust out to him. "Well done!" someone exclaimed. They all crowded around then to initial his signature as witnesses, and Teacher insisted that they toast the new member with brandy, which they did cheerfully enough, and then went off to bed.

Goforth told himself that the ceremony had been a juvenile bit of foolishness, but somehow it had warmed him with the feeling of fellowship.

The Sailing Club

His sense of well-being persisted the next morning when in the predawn darkness he was awakened and hurriedly got dressed to join the others for breakfast.

It was still dark when they went down to the ship, each man carrying his sea bag. As he climbed aboard, Goforth was just able to make out the name painted in white letters on the bow: *Freedom IV*.

Since he was experienced, he was assigned a deck hand's job, and as he worked alongside the others to ready sails for hoisting, he sensed a marked change in their attitude.

The Club had its reputation for being casual, and certainly the night before, the members had seemed relaxed to the point of indolence; but there was a difference now. Each man carried out his tasks swiftly, in dead seriousness and without wasted motion, so that in a short time the *Freedom IV* was skimming eastward along the Sound toward the heart of the red rising sun.

Goforth was surprised and pleased. There was seamanship and discipline and sober purpose on this ship, and he gladly discarded his earlier notion that they would wallow about with no program beyond liquor and cards.

With satisfaction, he made a leisurely tour of the ship. Everything was smart and sharp, on deck and below, in the sleeping quarters and galley. Teacher, who seemed to be the captain, had a small cabin forward and it, too, was a model of neatness.

Goforth poked his head inside to admire it further. Teacher was not there, but in a moment the old man stepped through a narrow door on the opposite bulkhead, leading to some compartment below, followed by two other members. They greeted Goforth pleasantly, but closed and locked the door behind them, and did not offer to show him the compartment. He, for his part, refrained from asking, but later in the day he inspected the deck above it and saw that what had seemed earlier to be merely a somewhat unorthodox arrangement of crisscross deck planking was actually a hatchway, cleverly concealed.

He crouched and ran his fingers along the hidden edges

of the hatch, then glanced up guiltily to meet Marshall's eyes. Marshall seemed amused, but all he said was, "Ready for chow?"

In the next few days Goforth occasionally wondered what the forward compartment contained. Then he all but forgot about it, for his enjoyment of the voyage was too deep-felt to permit even the smallest question to trouble him. He was more content now than he had been in many months. It was not because he was sailing again, but rather, he believed, because he was actively sharing with others like himself a vigorous and demanding experience. It seemed, indeed, that they formed a little corporation there on the *Freedom IV*—and what a corporation! Even the member who occupied the lowly post of cook's helper was a man accustomed to deal in terms of millions.

Yes, what a crew it was! Now Goforth began to understand the suppressed excitement he had long ago detected as a subtle mark identifying members of the Sailing Club. Theirs was no ordinary cruise, but a grand exercise of seamanship, as if they had decided to pit their collective will against the force and cunning of the ocean, to retrieve through a challenge to that most brutal of antagonists the sense of daring which they once had found in their work . . .

They were searching for something. For a week they sailed a zigzag course, always out of sight of land, but Goforth had not the faintest notion of their whereabouts, nor did he judge that it would be proper for him to inquire. Were they pursuing a storm to provide them with some ultimate test with the sea? He could not be sure. And yet he was quite willing to wait, for there was happiness enough in each waking moment aboard the *Freedom IV*.

On the eighth day he perceived an abrupt change. There was an almost tangible mood of expectancy among the members, a quickening of pace and movement, a tightening of smiles and laughter that reminded him oddly of the atmosphere in a corporation board room, when

The Sailing Club 87

the final crisis of some serious negotiation approaches. He guessed that some word had been passed among the crew, save for himself, the neophyte.

The men were tense, but it was the invigorating tensity of trained athletes waiting in confidence for a test worthy of their skills. The mood was infectious; without having any idea of what lay ahead, Goforth began to share the exhilaration and to scan the horizon eagerly.

For what? He did not care now. Whatever it might be, he felt an elemental stirring of pride and strength and knew that he would meet whatever ultimate trial impended with all the nerve and daring that his life had stamped into his being.

The *Freedom IV* changed course and plunged due east toward a haze that lay beneath heavier clouds. Goforth thought perhaps the storm lay that way and keenly watched for its signs. There were none, but he took some heart at the sight of another yacht coming toward them, and hopefully imagined that it was retreating from the combat which the *Freedom IV* seemed so ardently to seek.

He studied the sky. The clouds drifted aimlessly, then broke apart for a moment to disclose a regular expanse of blue. He sighed as he saw it, and glanced around at the other crewmen to share his feeling of frustration.

But there was no disappointment on those faces. Instead, the mood of tension seemed heightened to an almost unbearable degree. The men stood strained and stiff, their features set rigidly, their eyes quick and piercing as they stared across the water.

Goforth searched their faces desperately for comprehension, and as it slowly came to him—when at last he *knew*—he felt the revelation grip him physically with a wild penetrating excitement.

He *knew*, and so he watched with fierce absorption but without surprise as the forward hatch swung open to permit what was below to rise to the surface of the deck, and watched still more intently as the crew leaped smartly forward to prepare it with the speed born of long hours of practice.

He stood aside then, for he knew he would need training, too, before he could learn his part; but after the first shot from the sleek little cannon had smashed a great hole in the side of the other yacht, he sprang forward as readily as the others to seize the rifles which were being passed around. And as the *Freedom IV* swooped swiftly in toward the floundering survivors, his cries of delight were mixed with those of his comrades, and their weapons cracked out sharply, gaily, across the wild echoing sea.

The Season Ticket Holder
JOYCE HARRINGTON

The stadium sat like a huge frosted doughnut on the rim of the river. Mrs. Stella Crump, trotting resentfully beside her husband, wished that a giant hand would swoop out of the overhanging clouds and dunk it into the coffee-colored water. Instead, a strong gust of wind swept across the walkway, disarranging Mrs. Crump's carefully tinted and lacquered hair. The pennants on top of the stadium snapped and fluttered. Mrs. Crump shrieked and stopped in her tracks to tie a purple scarf over her ruined hairdo. Mr. Owen Crump waited impatiently, while the crowd surged around them, eager to reach their seats before the final recorded strains of the national anthem died away.

"Hurry up, Stella! Why don't you wear that nice red hat I got for you?"

"Because I hate red and that hat looks like a squashed soup-bowl."

"Come on, Stella. We've already missed the starting lineup."

"What difference does it make? They all look alike to me. Wait a minute. I've got something in my shoe." Mrs. Crump limped to the side of the walkway, methodically removed one shoe, shook it out, felt gingerly inside it, and replaced it on her foot.

The crowd had thinned out and a roar sounded from inside the stadium. An amplified mumble could be heard making an announcement. Owen Crump took his wife's arm and hauled her at a half-run toward the stadium gates.

"Not so fast, Owen," she whimpered, "I've got a pain in my side. I want to stop at the ladies' room. Wait for me."

By the time they reached their seats, the opposing team had two men on and their most powerful batter was approaching the plate. Owen Crump began hastily filling in his score card, while Stella ostentatiously pulled out her knitting, a complicated mass of cables and popcorns, and began furiously clacking her needles.

The count was three and two, and the batter had just popped a foul into the stands behind home plate.

Stella said, "I'm thirsty. I'd like a soda."

Owen, leaning forward in his seat and ready to groan in dismay if the batter connected, muttered, "In a minute, Stella."

"I'm thirsty *now*, Owen. The least you can do after dragging me out here is get me something to drink. I don't think that's too much to ask for. I'd go myself, but I've still got that pain in my side."

"All right. All right. Here." He handed her the score card. "Keep track of what happens." As Owen rose from his seat, the umpire signaled ball four, and the players walked. The bases were loaded, with no outs.

Stella peered down at the field through her bifocals, shook her head scornfully, and stuffed the score card into the bottom of her knitting bag. Owen raced up the stairs toward the refreshment counter, staring over his shoulder as he went.

As the crowd in the stadium tensely awaited the next batter, Stella settled back in her seat to knit and rehearse her grievances. Bad enough, she thought, that we used to have to see every weekend game. But now that Owen had retired, he'd bought season tickets. This year he intended to see every home game. And Stella would see them too. Oh, she could stay home, tend to her knitting, visit their daughter and the grandchildren. But where was the fun in that when Owen would be here at the stadium enjoying himself without her?

The umpire called ball one.

Stella completed an intricate cable and her needles worked rapidly toward the next pattern. No. If Stella didn't go to the ball games, Owen would take some crony and they would drink too much beer and eat those filthy hot dogs, and he would come home flushed and overexcited and more than slightly drunk. This way, at least, she could keep an eye on him and make sure he didn't overdo things. He was just like a little boy. Stella smiled grimly and considered herself extremely noble for sacrificing her summer afternoons and evenings.

The batter swung and missed but Stella was oblivious.

It wasn't as if she didn't have better things to do. Stella's thoughts strayed over all the better things she could be doing. They all involved Owen's money and Francis X. Lafferty. Dear, sensitive, handsome, refined, perceptive Francis.

Stella had met Francis X. Lafferty almost a year ago when he'd come to address the Garden Club on the subject of "Flowers of Contentment." Someone at the speaker's bureau had got their signals mixed. Francis X. Lafferty knew nothing of gardening, but his talk was well received all the same. It was inspirational without being embarrassing. Mr. Lafferty's melodious voice caressed the ears of his listeners, and no one felt obliged to rush off and do good works, or be kind to animals, lose weight, or stop drinking sherry. The ladies loved Francis X. Lafferty and flocked to buy copies of his slim, privately printed book. Stella smiled again, this time fondly, wishing that she could help dear Francis in his desire to travel across the country, indeed around the world, spreading his message. Preferably with Stella at his side.

Down on the field, the pitcher threw an inside curve and was rewarded with a called strike, but Stella was miles away, touring the great cities of the world and witnessing the peace and contentment that dear Francis would bring to troubled hearts everywhere.

It was inevitable that Stella would compare Francis X. Lafferty and Owen Crump. There was no comparison. While the stands grew restless and erupted in cries of encouragement to the pitcher, Stella knitted on and totted up a mental ledger. On the one side, dear Francis, although far from the first blush of youth, was young at heart. He viewed the world with enthusiasm and made all dreams seem possible. Owen had for forty years viewed life from the confines of the paper-box factory whose finances he had guided and guarded until the day of his retirement. Paper boxes had been good to Owen, but the years of poring over balance sheets and operating statements had left him bald, stoop-shouldered, and paunchy. Dear Francis stood straight and slim and silver-maned, and had a most imposing presence on the speaker's platform. Owen shambled and told coarse jokes in mixed company. On the other hand, Owen had been clever about investments while dear Francis, through his devotion to his mission, had admittedly neglected the crasser side of life's potential. It was a problem.

Stella looked up from her knitting as a sharp crack split the expectant air and the crowd went wild. Dimly, she saw a small white object fly through the air and land in an outstretched glove.

"Here's your drink. What happened?" Owen plumped himself down beside her.

"I don't know. Somebody caught a ball. That fellow over there, I think it was." Stella gestured vaguely toward the outfield.

"Where's my score card?"

"Oh, dear. Did I have it? I must have dropped it."

Stella bent to look under the seats. "Not there. Are you sure you gave it to me? I'm not sure you did."

"Never mind. I'll get another one."

Throughout the rest of the game, while Owen cheered and heckled and added his voice to the communal warcry of "Charge!" Stella knitted and dreamed of faraway places, fame and glory for dear Francis, and herself, the treasured companion, making it all come true through Owen's money. The sweater she knitted was to be a birthday present for Francis. It was the least she could do.

The following Sunday was Bat Day.

Owen had said, "I'd like to take Ronnie to the game. It's time he got his first baseball bat. Would you mind missing this one game?"

"Oh, I think I'll survive. Maybe I'll have some of the girls in for tea." Stella's mind leaped to her invitation list. It was a short one.

"Cackle session, huh? Just be sure the hens have flown the coop before I get home." Owen chuckled and Stella smiled.

"Don't worry, dear," she said. "It'll all be over before the end of the ninth."

Early Sunday afternoon, Stella waved goodbye to Owen as he drove off to pick up their five-year-old grandson. As soon as he was out of sight down the winding drive, she hurried upstairs to dress for the tea party. A brand new blue-silk hostess gown hung ready in her closet. In her bathroom, snatches of old songs tinkled through her head while she smeared her face with a wrinkle-removing masque.

"April in Paris, Arrivederci Roma," she hummed. "I'd like to get you on a slow boat to China. . . ."

Under the masque her skin felt tight and clean and young. She wriggled into her sturdy girdle. Francis X. Lafferty had often remarked on the ugliness of girls who starved themselves into scarecrows. He liked a comfortable, womanly woman, he said. Still and all, Stella felt it was the better part of valor to keep her ample curves under control. The loose-fitting gown would help to minimize their magnificence.

To Stella, without her glasses, the wrinkle masque seemed to have performed as advertised. She made up carefully with just the right touch of blusher to her cheeks. Her eyelids matched the blue of her gown. When she cast her eyes down modestly, her false eyelashes tickled her cheekbones. A final cloud of hairspray, a few strategic dabs of cologne, and Stella felt regal and ready.

She swept down the carpeted stairs, pausing in mid-descent to peer at her domain. The heavy drapes were drawn against the harsh afternoon sun. The tea tray twinkled in the half-light on a low table set before the loveseat. Roses massed in a silver bowl sent their fragrance throughout the house swirling on the cool, centrally conditioned air. All that was needed was music.

Stella floated into the room, tingling with anticipation, and placed a stack of Mantovani records on the spindle of the stereo. Everything was perfect. Too bad Owen didn't appreciate her delicacy and good taste. He seldom came into this room and when he did he fidgeted about so clumsily that Stella feared for the safety of her collection of porcelain figurines. He left smelly cigar butts in her dainty china ashtrays. Just as well, she thought, that he preferred to spend his time in the basement rec room where he could smoke his filthy cigars and munch on limburger and onion sandwiches and watch television with his feet up on the furniture.

On the crest of the surging Mantovani strings, the doorbell rang. Stella peeped between the drawn drapes and saw dear Francis' ancient Volkswagen parked in the drive. Such an undignified car for such a truly noble person. Stella could visualize Francis behind the wheel of a Lincoln Continental, at the very least. She glided to the door, her stomach in and her chin high.

"Good afternoon, dear lady. This single rose is not more glorious in its bloom than she to whom I bring it."

"Oh, Mr. Lafferty. Francis. Dear me!" It crossed Stella's mind that the single rose bore a striking resemblance to those carefully nurtured and tended by her neighbor up the road. But she chased the traitorous notion away. After all, it was the thought that counted. "Won't you come in?"

Stella took the proffered rose and promptly received a thorn in her thumb. She cried out in pain.

"What is it, dear lady? Does this envious rose dare to prick the thumb of beauty? Away with it!" Francis X. Lafferty snatched the stem from Stella and tossed it into the umbrella stand. "Let me see the wound. Ah, there. We'll have it well in no time."

A drop of bright blood appeared on Stella's thumb, and a gleaming white handkerchief materialized in Francis X. Lafferty's hand. His long fingers gently encircled her pudgy paw as he swaddled the injured thumb. Stella could have fainted with delight. She would gladly have bled gallons just to keep his hands holding hers.

"How thoughtless of me," he murmured. "I meant to bring you happiness and have caused you only pain."

"Oh, dear me. It doesn't hurt a bit. Well, hardly at all. And now your handkerchief is stained."

If Stella had been infatuated before, she was besotted as she examined Francis X. Lafferty's blood-spotted handkerchief—so clean, and of such fine linen. But laundered so often the threads had parted here and there. Her confined bosom heaved with the indignity of threadbare handkerchiefs and rackety old cars. Dear Francis should have nothing but the best. And she, Stella, would give it to him, could give it to him, if only Owen . . .

Stella giggled. Francis was pressing his warm lips to her hand.

"Oh, my goodness," she squealed. "Kiss it and make it well."

"If only I could, dear lady. If only I were free to kiss away all your cares. What joy it would give me to see the flowers of contentment bloom in your eyes. If I dared hope . . ."

"Ah, um," said Stella. "Shall we have some tea?"

Stella was rinsing teacups when Owen and Ronnie burst into the kitchen, dispelling her daydream of exotic ocean voyages with Francis X. Lafferty in the deck chair beside her. Dear Francis had done well by the petit fours, she noticed.

"We won, Grandma! We won!" shouted Ronnie, swinging his brand new bat.

"Nine to six!" exclaimed Owen. "What a game! You should have been there, Stella! Hey, what are you all dolled up for? That's some bathrobe you got on!"

"It's not a bathrobe. It's a hostess gown. I had a tea party. Remember?"

"Oh, yeah. Well, go put your running shoes on, old girl, and let's play *ball*!"

"Me! Play ball! You must be out of your mind, Owen Crump."

"Play ball, Grandma! Let's play ball," cried Ronnie, thumping his bat on the floor.

"Aw, come on, Stella. I bought a baseball and Ronnie's got his new bat. Let's just hit a few out in the back yard."

"Please, Grandma. It's a real Louisville bat. Look at it!"

"Well, all right," said Stella. "But just for a few minutes. I've never played baseball."

Reluctantly, Stella ascended the stairs and dragged her old gardening clothes out of the closet. She could hear Owen out in the yard, giving Ronnie instructions on how to hold the bat, when to swing. How different her life could be, she thought, as she tied the laces of her tennis shoes. Oh, things were comfortable enough here. She really couldn't complain about that. But she'd never been anywhere or done anything really exciting. And Owen was so dull and boring, content to spend the rest of his life pottering about, going to ball games, having nights out with his cronies from the box factory. Stella knew that in Owen's hands their lives were safe and secure. But, oh, *so* predictable and dull.

"Stella! Hurry up! We're waiting for you."

"I'm coming," she murmured. "Baseball! At my age! Well, I'll give them exactly ten minutes."

* * *

"Me up first!" shouted Ronnie, swinging the bat in a wide wobbly arc. "Here's old Tony Perez comin' to the plate!"

"Hold on a minute, sport," said Owen. "Let's have ladies first. Show your grandma how to hold the bat."

"Aw, okay. Here, Grandma. Put your one hand here and your other hand here, and stand like this, and hit the ball. That right, Grandpa?"

"It'll do for starts," said Owen. "Now I'll pitch and, Ronnie, you be catcher."

"Okay. Here's old Johnny Bench behind the plate." Ronnie turned his red cap backwards and squatted down behind the flat stone Owen had placed to mark the position of home plate.

Stella felt awkward and ridiculous with her plump hands wrapped around the unwieldy bat, her feet apart and her rump pointing northeast.

"Now, Stella," said Owen, "I'll pitch 'em slow and easy. Don't worry if you don't hit anything. But just in case you do, that's first base over there. A home run is anything that goes beyond the driveway on that side and the rhododendron hedge over there. If you do happen to hit the ball, maybe you should let Ronnie run for you. Ready? Batter up!"

"I'll do my own running, Owen Crump," muttered Stella. The contrast between her undignified position of the moment and the sweet flattery that had poured into her ear an hour ago caused Stella's cheeks to burn with indignation. Francis X. Lafferty had sipped his tea and told her, "You are one of the rare ones, dear lady. But I fear your true worth is known only to a few. Your husband is a lucky man. How I would like to . . . but, no, let that remain unsaid." And *now* look at her, standing out here like a dummy with a baseball bat in her hands, about to make a fool of herself.

Owen went through an elaborate windup and Stella watched his gyrations through narrowed eyes. The ball left his hand and she swung as she had seen so many batters swing, slicing the air hard and clean. The loud crack was a shock to her. The impact shivered her arm clear to the shoulder and set her glasses jiggling. Too surprised to run, she stood and watched the ball fly straight and true, watched amazement take possession of Owen's face in the split second before the ball, with all the force of Stella's yearning behind it, hit him squarely between the eyes. Stella heard a soft, sickening thud.

"Oof," said Owen, and fell over backwards.

"Oh, my goodness," said Stella. "Are you all right?"

"Get up, Grandpa," said Ronnie. "I didn't get my turn yet."

But Owen Crump did not get up. He lay in the grass behind his improvised pitcher's mound, his eyes wide to the cloudless summer sky. Stella's eyes were wide too, with suddenly unlimited possibilities.

"I think you'd better go indoors, Ronnie," said Stella Crump.

Stella felt she looked well in black. It lent her an air of sorrowful mystery and had a slimming effect as well. A merciful release, she thought, the stilted words intended for herself and not for Owen. She hid her jubilation well with sighs and stifled moans and exclamations of "What will I do now?" Stella knew perfectly well what she would do now.

Owen Crump had left his affairs in apple-pie order. His will was brief and to the point. So much for his only daughter, a generous allotment for Ronnie and his infant sister, a sizable donation to the Little League, and the rest to his dearly beloved Stella.

The Garden Club rallied 'round the new widow and Stella bravely accepted their gifts of flowers and small cakes. Her daughter, a thoroughly up-to-the-minute girl, telephoned every day to warn of the dangers of allowing herself to feel guilty. "It was an accident, Ma, no matter what anyone says." Ronnie was taken to a child psychiatrist to exorcise any guilt feelings he might have. But neither Stella nor Ronnie was troubled overmuch with mental anguish. Ronnie because he was a healthy young animal and didn't connect himself with the fateful consequence of Grandma's batting average. And Stella was too busy exploring the prospects of her new status to feel anything but excited and optimistic. On the day of the funeral, Stella stuffed the remaining season tickets down the garbage disposal and listened with satisfaction to their slurping, grinding destruction.

And Francis X. Lafferty became a constant visitor.

"Dear lady," he said, "your sorrow is mine to share, your tears fall into the fertile garden of my heart and water the seeds of concern. Let me help you bear this terrible grief."

Stella let him help. She let him drive her around town in Owen's Cadillac, assisting her with those errands that even a newly bereaved widow must perform. She let him escort her to dinner at expensive restaurants featuring secluded tables and rich pastries. He encouraged her to do her share by picking up the tab.

Tongues wagged as tongues would. The Garden Club was quite enjoyably shocked, and for several meetings did not need to engage a speaker. Stella and Francis provided all the topic that was necessary.

Stella's daughter, that thoroughly up-to-the-minute girl, said, "Look, Ma. Personally, I think he's a fraud. But if he's what you need, enjoy yourself. Hang in there and don't let the old biddies get you down. Only if I were you, I'd think twice about getting married again. Got to run now. Ronnie has to see his shrink, and I have a macrame class in half an hour."

Stella did think twice about getting married. In the weeks following Bat Day, she thought of little else. Marriage to Francis and a honeymoon trip around the world, with Francis bringing his message of love and harmony to ever larger and more enthusiastic audiences. Stella could see it all as if it were already happening. Francis, tall and imposing, receiving the adulation of the crowd, while she sat backstage waiting for him to come to her. He would dedicate books to her, and she would be his inspiration. They would travel from London to Paris to Rome. She thought it might be wise to skip over the Middle East, and was none too sure about Francis' reception in India. They seemed to be on the export side of the guru business there. Tokyo, of course. And then a long stay in Honolulu. She pondered the advisability of hiring a press agent.

Francis said, "Dear, dearest Stella. I hesitate to seem importunate. Unseemly haste in these matters can lead to sad regret. Still, it is my fondest wish . . ."

Stella said, "Yes."

". . . my heart's deepest desire, to dare to hope that you will one day in the not too distant future . . ."

Stella said, "Yes."

". . . consent to become my wife. That is, as soon as a suitable period of mourning has passed, and your heart is able once again to receive the outpourings of another."

Stella said, "Yes."

"What did you say, beloved?"

"I said, 'Yes.' How about three weeks from today?"

Stella and Francis got married on the day that the home team batted its way into the World Series. To Stella, if she had taken notice, it might have seemed a fitting irony. But she was too busy with wedding plans and travel brochures. Even a small discreet wedding took a certain degree of planning. Arrangements had to be made for joint bank accounts and joint credit cards, Francis must have a new wardrobe, starting with four dozen silk handkerchiefs. The Lincoln Continental, Stella thought, could wait until they returned from their travels. The old Cadillac would do until they left. Through it all, Francis smiled indulgently and made occasional heartfelt speeches on the subject of contentment.

Despite all of Stella's efforts, she found it was not possible to schedule a lecture tour at short notice. The Royal Albert Hall stubbornly refused to accommodate Francis until the middle of November. So the trip was postponed and Stella and Francis settled in for a short interval of homely marital bliss before their world travels could begin.

Francis consoled a downcast Stella. "Anywhere on earth with you, dear Stella, is paradise to me. Don't you

The Season Ticket Holder

think we ought to buy a boat? I've always had a yen to play Huck Finn on the river."

"You pick one out, dearest. I've got to keep after these travel agents and the speaker's bureau or we'll never get this trip off the ground."

So intent was Stella on planning each last detail of this fabulous trip around the world, she scarcely noticed that Francis spent more and more time puttering about on his new toy, a 25-foot cabin cruiser. Or that when he was at home, he'd taken to hanging about the rec room in the basement with his feet on the furniture watching television and munching swiss cheese and salami sandwiches.

One day, after a particularly fruitless telephone exchange with a booking agent in Brussels, Stella slammed the receiver down and almost wept with sheer frustration. She was tempted to abandon the lecture part of the trip. But that was the point of the whole thing, after all. The tour was her wedding gift to her husband, and she couldn't just give up this wonderful opportunity for dear Francis to deliver his message to the world and become as well known as Billy Graham, or the Maharishi, at the very least. Still, it would be such a help if he would take just the slightest interest in the practical side of becoming an inspirational figure on an international scale.

Stella pouted and rubbed her tired eyes, thereby multiplying the tiny creases, folds, and pouches that adorned her face. She was too annoyed to care. She heard the powerful hum of the Cadillac's engine in the drive and tried, unsuccessfully, to arrange her face into a semblance of contentment. Dear Francis always seemed to take it as a personal insult if she appeared even slightly discontent.

The front door opened and Francis bounded into the house with an even greater display of youthful enthusiasm than usual.

"I've got them, Stella dearest!" he shouted. "The tickets! I've got them! Oh, you don't know how long I've waited for them. And now, thanks to you, I've finally got them. Now I am truly content."

"Tickets? What tickets? I haven't even gotten our itinerary straightened out yet. How could you get the tickets?"

"No, Stella dearest. You don't understand. I guess I've never really told you how much I've always wanted to have season tickets to the football games. And now I've got them. And we won't have to miss a single game. Isn't that wonderful? I think I'll go get myself a beer."

Francis cavorted out into the kitchen. Stella heard the refrigerator door slam, and the old familiar hissing pop of the easy-open beer can. Football! He'd never mentioned football. If anything, football was worse than baseball. All those hulking great bodies charging up and down a muddy field. Sitting in the stands, cold and damp, with her fingers too chilled to knit. And all that noise. Oh, no! How could he do this to her? And what about their trip?

Stella marched determinedly into the kitchen. Francis was sitting at the kitchen table poring over a schedule and sipping from a can.

"What about our trip? And the least you could do is pour that disgusting beer into a glass!"

"Stella, dearest," soothed Francis. "Have I done something to disturb you? You seem suddenly so discontent. You know I can't bear to have you emitting waves of displeasure. It upsets my own balance of contentment, and just when I'm feeling so eternally grateful to you. Please don't spoil it for both of us."

"But what about our trip?" she asked again. "I've just about got things lined up and we could leave next month if all goes well."

"Yes, but don't you think we could postpone it just a little bit longer? After all, we've already been delayed and it would be much more pleasant to travel in the springtime. Don't you think?"

"Oh, I see," said Stella, clamping her jaw shut on all the vicious malcontented words struggling to leap off her tongue. Oh, I could kill him, she raged inwardly. Bean him with his precious football, bop him with a goalpost, punt him over the moon. But none of these measures seemed even remotely feasible.

The Season Ticket Holder

Stella turned and marched out of the kitchen. Resolutely, she climbed the stairs, muttering to herself.

"Just you wait, Francis X. Lafferty. *Dear* Francis. Just you wait. It's going to be my turn next. I'm going to be the next season ticket holder around here."

She smiled as she remembered her recent prowess with a baseball bat. It could have been beginner's luck, but then again maybe she was just a natural athlete. *She* would get the next set of season tickets, and she would watch the players carefully.

"And then, dearest Francis," she murmured, "we'll just see what a novice can do with a hockey puck."

The Last Downhill

CLARK HOWARD

Harlow carried his skis to the base of the lower chair lift and sat down on a bench to put them on.

"Well, Mr. Harlow," said Jerry, the lift operator, "you're almost the last one at the lodge this season. Nearly everyone else has left."

"I'm not *almost* the last," Harlow corrected. "I *am* the last."

"Not quite," said Jerry. "A new guest checked in last night."

Harlow locked on his right ski. "New guest? Who?"

"Don't know. Haven't even seen him. But Mr. Boles called from the desk and said to keep the lift running after you went up; said the new guest would be going up, too."

Harlow stood up and tensed his toes and arch, adjusting the fit. "Did Boles say what the new guest's name was?"

"No, sir. But that looks like him coming now." Jerry bobbed his chin toward the 300-yard trail that led from the lodge to the lift.

Harlow squinted toward the moving figure. The man's gait looked vaguely familiar—or was he just imagining it? "Kind of unusual for someone to check in on the last day of the season, isn't it?"

Jerry shrugged. "Skiers are like golfers, Mr. Harlow; sometimes they don't know when to quit. No offense."

Harlow stared at the advancing figure for another few seconds, then said, "Get the lift moving. I'm ready."

He dropped onto the first chair that swung by and settled into it for the ten-minute trip up to the first ridge. On the way up, he twisted to look back down at the lone figure moving toward the lift base. He couldn't get it out of his mind that the walk was familiar. Could it possibly be one of them?

Alan?

Pudge?

Leo?

The four of them had grown up on skis. When they were eight and ten, they had easily mastered the junior runs around Moose Head, where they all lived. At twelve and fourteen they were experts on the intermediate slopes. By the time they were sixteen, they were better than most adults and the great high runs from the unseen summits were as familiar to them as their own bedrooms. Everyone in town talked about how they constantly tried to out-do one another, and how they were so equal in skill it was hard to tell them apart on the upper snowfields. Even Pudge, who was twenty pounds overweight, held his own in dexterity and maneuverability with his leaner, trimmer companions.

Pudge was Harlow's cousin; Alan and Leo were not related to them, but the four had grown up closer than brothers, practically inseparable. Over the years they had done everything together: played Pop Warner football and American Legion baseball, built a treehouse, gone to see *Shane* nine times, rode a freight train down the mountain to Salinas and hitchhiked back, worked the fruit groves during the summer, the ski runs on weekends during the school year. And in everything they were as near equal as possible. Four young colts in a dead-heat every time they left the gate.

Then, in their senior year of high school, Harlow pulled ahead of them by just an edge. On the slopes. Alan, Pudge, and Leo noticed it first, then the rest of the town. On the downhill runs, Harlow became just a shade better.

At the first ridge, Harlow dropped out of the chair and pushed over to the edge to look down. Back at the base he could see the other man just getting into the chair for the ride up. Even if it was one of them, he thought, what would it matter? He had a ten-minute lead and was better than any of them.

He'd been better since they were all seventeen years old. Better all through the decade of their twenties. And their thirties. And now, at forty-one, he was still better. None of them could catch him on the downhill. Especially on the high ones where he could pick up speed and momentum.

He pushed over to the self-operated control box for the middle lift that went up to the second ridge, another fifteen minutes higher. Activating it, he slipped into the first chair across the pad and started his second ascent. Looking back, he could see that the man coming up on the lower lift had put on a bright red ski cap.

Alan, he thought. Alan had always worn bright red ski caps. Usually ones that Marcy had knitted for him. Marcy was the head cheerleader their last year in high school. Her family had moved to the mountains from Kansas, so she didn't know how to ski. Everybody said she looked like Debbie Reynolds. She and Alan were steadies. Harlow, Pudge, and Leo were forever trying to get Alan to tell them whether he'd made it with Marcy or not, but Alan would never say. Pudge and Leo did not think he had; Harlow disagreed with them. Harlow was sure Marcy was not a virgin. But he had to wait until two years after they graduated to prove it.

Harlow had stopped in at the drugstore where Marcy worked, the day after Alan left for the Army.

"So old Alan is a soldier-boy now," he said, drinking a fountain Coke. "Hup-two-three-four."

"Don't joke about it," Marcy said, wiping off the marble countertop. "I just hope he doesn't get hurt."

"He'll be all right," Harlow assured her. "It's just a police action, not a real war. More like guard duty. Old Alan will come marching home in a couple of years and you two can get married and start making babies." As Marcy bent over the counter, Harlow got a glimpse down her dress. "You know, Marce, Alan and I are best friends. He asked me to look after you while he was gone."

Marcy gave him a dubious look. "Sure he did."

"No, listen, really, I'm serious. He said he wanted to make sure you didn't just sit around bored all the time. He asked me to take you to a movie now and then. But I've got a better idea than that."

"I'll bet you have."

"Be serious, Marce. You know how Alan was always going to teach you how to ski, but you two never seemed to get around to it? Well, what if I was to teach you while he was away? Wouldn't that be a great surprise for him when he came home?"

Marcy beamed. "Why, that's a wonderful idea!"

"Yeah. You two could really have fun on the slopes together. What do you say?"

She said yes, and that had been the start of it with them.

Harlow took her out every weekend. He patiently worked her on the beginners' run; patiently worked her on the longer intermediate slopes; patiently worked her on the gradual bowls and the easy snowfields; and patiently worked her into bed with him one Saturday night nearly a year after Alan had left.

"God, I'm so ashamed," she said when it was over.

"I don't see why. You've obviously done it before."

"Only with Alan. And we're going to be married."

Harlow took her in his arms. "Come on now. This is 1955. The world is growing up. What you and I do can't hurt anyone. Alan will never know."

And he probably never would have. Except that Marcy became pregnant. And Harlow arranged for her to go to San Francisco to an abortionist. Abortions were still being done on kitchen tables in 1955. That was where Marcy died: on a kitchen table.

When Alan got back from the army and learned all the details, he swore he'd kill Harlow. But by that time, Harlow had left town.

At the upper ridge, Harlow dropped out of the chair and turned at once to look back down to the lower ridge. The other man on the lift had reached the lower ridge five minutes before Harlow reached the upper, and Harlow was anxious to see if he was coming any higher. He was not; he was standing next to the control box, one hand on it, looking up at Harlow. I'm fifteen minutes ahead of him now instead of ten, Harlow thought. That had always been very important to Harlow: staying a comfortable distance ahead of other people.

He watched as the figure below kept staring up at him. Then, in a movement that made Harlow involuntarily shiver, the man waved to him. Actually waved. Raised one hand and gave it a little twist of the wrist.

Just like Pudge used to do. Harlow's mouth went dry as he saw the man activate the middle lift and hop onto a chair to come up.

Pudge? Could it actually be Pudge? Could he have dried out, come back from the depths of alcoholism, got himself in shape again, and gone back to the skis?

Harlow grunted softly. Not that it mattered. Pudge could not catch him anyway. Could not even keep up with him. Never had been able to.

Harlow's father and Pudge's father had been brothers. They and their wives had been killed in a jet crash on the way to Bermuda. A third brother, Harlow and Pudge's Uncle Thomas, had been made their guardian until they came of age. Thomas was a bachelor, in the lumber business back in Michigan. He took their insurance money and made both boys his partners. Pudge went off to college to learn accounting, but Harlow, who had never liked school, went right to work in the lumber mill. He stayed at Uncle Thomas's right side: in the forest, cutting and sawing; on the lakes, sending the wood downstream; at the mill, grading, processing; and by the time Pudge got his degree and returned, Harlow knew as much about the business as Uncle Thomas did.

"You ought to let me take over for you, Uncle," Harlow told the older man. "Let me do the work. You'll still get your third. What's the matter, don't you think I can do it?"

"You could do it, all right," his uncle said. "But I'd be afraid of the shortcuts you like to take. I've seen you order trees cut that needed another year of growth; seen you grade wood high when it should've been graded low; seen you sell outside our contracts for a kickback. Your ethics need to mature a little, my boy. You need to develop a sense of values beyond immediate profit. I expect it'll be a while before I can let you take over."

Uncle Thomas was an ex-lumberjack and a hard-drinking man. Pudge, Harlow learned, had also developed a taste for hard liquor while at college. Uncle Thomas and Pudge started drinking together. Before long it became a common sight to see the older man and his nephew at a corner table in the big saloon near the mill. Sometimes they could even be seen stumbling out together, arm-in-arm.

One bitterly cold January night, as Uncle Thomas and Pudge were walking along the dock on their way home, a six-foot log rolled off the top of the next day's load and knocked them both into the icy lake. Some other customers from the saloon heard their cries and managed to pull Pudge out; but Uncle Thomas got caught under an ice floe and drowned. No one was ever able to figure out how just one log got loose from the chained stack.

After Harlow and Pudge inherited the business, Harlow took over running it while Pudge mostly just kept on drinking. Pudge blamed himself for Uncle Thomas's death, and Harlow did nothing to dissuade him from the notion. The more Pudge stayed drunk, the better Harlow liked it. Eventually Harlow went to court and had Pudge committed to a sanatorium for alcoholics, and Pudge's half of the business put under his guardianship. Harlow heard some years later that Pudge had been convinced by a psychiatrist that he was blameless in Uncle Thomas's death, and Pudge had even subsequently hinted to some friends that he suspected Harlow of letting loose the log that hit them. That kind of talk did not bother Harlow, however. By then he had disposed of the lumber business, absorbed Pudge's share, and moved on to new pastures.

Harlow activated the upper lift and took a chair all the way to the summit of the mountain. It was a ten-minute ride and when he reached the top he looked back and saw the other man just getting off at the second ridge. He was still a good ten minutes ahead of him. As soon as the man—whoever he was—boarded the upper lift and got far enough above the ridge to prevent his jumping out of the chair, Harlow would push off and start down the run. As fast as he was on the downhill, and as familiar as he had become with the slopes during the past three weeks, he would be back on the bottom, at the lodge, packed and in his car, by the time this man—who would have to take it very slowly—got halfway down.

Harlow pushed over to the guardrail and waited. And watched. The man in the red cap stood right where Harlow had stood a few minutes earlier, except that he was looking up instead of down. He made no move to activate the upper lift, which had stopped as soon as Harlow had dropped off at the summit. He didn't seem to be in any hurry, Harlow thought. He was just looking up at Harlow, and looking around at the sky and the terrain, from where he was up to where Harlow was. Okay, sport, take your time, Harlow thought. I can wait it out as long as you can.

Harlow looked at the sky, too. It was slate-blue, solid and clear, with a dazzling high-altitude sun. The temperature, he guessed, was in the mid-twenties, the air thin and exhilarating. It had snowed during the early morning and from the summit it looked as if there was a whole mountain of untracked powder. It was a beautiful sight, one that Harlow would have enjoyed immensely had it not been for the other man down on the ridge.

Looking back down, Harlow's eyes widened as he saw the figure bend and scoop up enough fresh snow for a snowball. The man rolled it over and over, packing it tighter between his mittened hands; then he tossed it up, caught it once, and threw it at a nearby ponderosa. It hit the tree dead-center and splattered.

Harlow watched transfixed. It's Leo, he thought. It had to be Leo. A thousand times as a boy he had seen Leo do that exact same thing: make a snowball, toss it up and catch it first, then hit a tree dead-center.

When Harlow sold the lumber business, he moved to Minneapolis and became a building contractor. It seemed like the natural thing to do. Several retail lumber dealers who had bought his inferior grades of wood were in Minneapolis, so he knew who to do business with. He had plenty of capital; all he really needed was a front man. He put in a long distance call to his old boyhood pal, Leo.

"Harlow, where the hell are you?" Leo asked, surprised. "Quite a few people are looking for you: Marcy's two brothers, Alan, Pudge and his lawyers—"

"Never mind who's looking for me, Leo. What are you doing in the way of work these days?"

"Working uptown at Walgreen's. I'm the assistant manager," Leo said proudly.

"A drugstore clerk!" Harlow scoffed.

"It's not a bad job," Leo said defensively. "Got some nice fringe benefits."

"Yeah, free razor blades. Listen, Leo, how would you like to make some serious money? I'm about to go into a new business where I really don't know anybody. I need a right-hand man, somebody I can trust. Are you interested?"

"Is it legal?"

"Of course it's legal," Harlow said, trying to sound indignant.

Leo was interested. Harlow swore him to secrecy, then told him where he was. He sent Leo enough money for him and his family to leave town quietly. After Leo joined Harlow in Minneapolis, they established Prestige Homes and started purchasing land. Soon they began to erect a tract of townhouses in the $75,000 range.

"You're the organized one, Leo, so I'm putting you in charge of running the general office," Harlow told him. "I'm going to be out in the field supervising the construction, ordering materials, and that sort of thing. I'll also be doing the selling and promoting, so I won't have any time for paperwork. You handle the money for us; I'll pass invoices on to you and you can see that they get paid."

Leo was gratified at his responsible position. He was also impressed with the expertise Harlow showed in establishing the business, acquiring the land and building permits, subcontracting the surveying and all the necessary craftsmen, and personally ordering the lumber and all the other materials needed. It pleased him to see how much everyone liked Harlow, and how well he treated all the people associated with Prestige Homes. Leo began to think that the people back home who spoke badly of Harlow were very much mistaken about him.

"I was as leery of this move as you were at first," he told his wife after they had been in Minneapolis a month, "but now I think it's going to work out just fine. Can you believe Harlow's paying me *three* times what I was getting at the drugstore? I really don't mind buying my razor blades at all!"

Business boomed. People bought the townhouses as fast as the bank would approve their loans. Within four months the first ones were completed, the city safety inspector approved them for occupancy, and families began to move in.

At every opportunity, Harlow praised Leo for his work. "Bringing you into this business was the smartest move I ever made," he said with a pat on the back. "The way you've run this office has been more help than you can imagine. I've been able to devote my time to the building and selling without a single worry about the office procedure and the paperwork. Speaking of paperwork, incidentally, we topped off six more units yesterday. Sign these certificates of completion for me, will you?"

Leo was so accustomed by then to signing reams of paper every week that he did it without a second thought. The certificates of completion were statements attesting that all top-grade materials had been used in the construction of the townhouses: top-grade lumber, cement mix, wiring, and plumbing. The certificates were filed with the city safety office when a final safety inspection was requested. The final inspection was a cursory one: carpets laid properly, heating apparatus vented properly, electrical outlets capped—that sort of thing. The important inspections were supposed to have been done during construction, when the inspector could *see* the cement mix, the wiring, the pipes—and the lumber. But the inspector who conducted those inspections was driving a new car, a gift from Harlow.

Sometimes inferior materials in a home go undetected for years. Second-grade lumber, for instance, might take a decade to deteriorate, and then present no more serious a problem than some minor refurbishing. But in the case of the Prestige Homes townhouses, the builder—and one buyer—were not so lucky. Thirty-seven days after the Lemmer family moved into Unit Number 268, the landing between the first and second floors collapsed and killed Mr. Lemmer.

It was the biggest building scandal to hit Minneapolis in years. Construction was ordered suspended at once. State investigators arrived to inspect some still unfinished units. Samples of the low-grade lumber being used were impounded. The city inspector who had approved for occupancy the Lemmer dwelling was suspended. Harlow and Leo were both indicted by a grand jury.

At the subsequent trial it was shown by Harlow's attorney that at no time had he ever put his signature on any document connected with Prestige—not an order, an invoice, a check, a sub-contract, a sales contract, or (most important) a certificate of completion. It had all been Leo, right down the line. Leo had signed the order for low-grade lumber; Leo had paid for it; and Leo had signed the certificate attesting that *high*-grade lumber had been used in the Lemmer townhome. Clearly, Leo was the culprit.

Harlow was acquitted. Leo got eight years.

So now Leo's back, Harlow thought, looking down from the summit of the ski run. The man in the red cap was still on the middle ridge, looking up at him. Harlow grunted softly. It was obvious to him what Leo planned to do. Wait on the middle ridge until Harlow started his downhill run, then push off the ridge and intercept him somewhere halfway down the mountain. Clever. But not clever enough.

Or was it? Harlow looked behind him, past the back side of the mountain. On the horizon, clearly visible, was a line of black that looked like dirty fumes from an exhaust.

A storm.

Damn, Harlow thought. One of those early spring snowstorms that came out of nowhere. Very cold, very quiet, little or no wind. He could not tell how fast it was moving—but surely it would be over the run to the lodge within an hour.

He looked back down at Leo. Or was it Pudge? No, it was Leo. The waiting game was definitely on Leo's side: he could simply stay on the ridge until the storm forced Harlow to make a downhill run.

Harlow wet his dry, cold lips. Pushing over, he looked down the back side of the mountain. He saw a long, easy run down a gently sloping bowl that dropped about a thousand feet to a tree line. Beyond that, although he could not see it, was probably another run, perhaps two or three, the rest of the way down. At the bottom would be the highway, going around the base of the mountain to the lodge. Harlow smiled. Suppose he were to ski down the back side before Pudge—Leo, that is—even knew he was off the summit? Once he made it to the highway, it would be easy to pick up a ride around to the lodge. Leo would think he was still up on the summit. And by the time he became suspicious enough to ride the upper lift to the top to see for himself, Harlow could be back at the lodge and on the road.

Harlow again looked across the sky where the storm was brewing. Definitely moving this way, he told himself. Got to decide one way or another.

He pushed back to the summit rail and looked down at the ridge again. The red cap was still clearly visible, not moving.

Okay, Harlow made up his mind, the back side it is then. He stood at the rail for several moments, long enough to be seen. Then he pushed away, buttoned the collar of his ski jacket, and put his mittens back on. After staying out of sight for five minutes, he moved back to the rail and let himself be seen again. By then he was sure that Leo was used to his disappearing for several minutes at a time.

So long, chump, he thought as he pushed away for the last time. He slid quickly to the back lip of the summit, paused just seconds to put his goggles in place and close his face flap, and pushed skillfully over the edge.

The entire back side of the mountain was an uninterrupted sheet of untracked powder, the top few inches still loose from its early-morning fall. As Harlow made his run, high, billowing plumes of snow curled up in his wake. It was a magnificent run, one of the best of his life. It had been a long time since he had felt such elation.

At the bottom of the run, near the first tree line, he turned into a smooth, professional halt and looked around. He was on a flat meadow, or maybe a frozen pond, about a fourth of the way down. There was no other run in sight. Beyond the stand of trees, he thought: that's where it's likely to be. He pushed forward across the level ground, toward the trees. Before he got to them, his shadow suddenly vanished from in front of him. Looking up, he saw that the first small dark clouds of the storm had arrived; one of them had blotted out the sun.

Pushing onward, he reached the trees, zigzigged through them—finding that they were very shallow—and cleared them on the other side. And there was the next run, a shorter one, leading down to the next lower ridge. Just as he started to push off, a glimpse of color caught his attention. He looked up at one of the ridges above the trees—and saw a figure in a red cap cutting down a narrow, twisting run like a professional. What the hell—? That couldn't be Leo, he thought. *Or* Pudge. Neither of them had ever developed lower leg movements that good. He frowned deeply. Alan? Had it been Alan all along? Of course, the red ski cap—

Without further thought, Harlow went over the side. It was an easy run, high but not steep, not long enough to make him winded. Halfway down he ran into snow: large, wet flakes, drifting straight down. When he reached the next ridge, he was immediately aware that it was becoming noticeably colder. He glided into a brace of sapling pines and moved under their umbrella boughs to rest.

But he did not rest long. Above him, still moving swiftly toward him, was Leo. Or rather, Alan.

Harlow pushed off the ridge onto the next run. It was longer than the second one, but still not as long as the first. As he plunged downward, he became aware that the sun was completely blocked out now, with only the gray daylight left; and the falling snow was thickening around him like a white curtain. Halfway down the run, the snow became so heavy that for most of a minute he was actually skiing blind. He had never done that before; it gave him an eerie feeling.

He was in a half-crouch, leaning to his right, when he

hit the tree. It caught him between the shoulder and elbow, and spun him all the way around, knocking him flat. There was a sharp *craaaack!* sound and for a terrible, frightening moment he was afraid one of his skis had broken. Ignoring his throbbing arm, he pushed himself erect and threw his goggles up to examine the skis. They were both all right. He swallowed dryly: thank God.

He looked around. He was on a level ridge trail that wound through a thick stand of ponderosas, very tall ponderosas, close to fifty feet he estimated. Blocked by the high branches, the snow was not falling as heavily where he stood. It was as if he were in a huge, silent tent, absolutely white except for the poker-straight trees that held up its roof. His eyes were watering. Pulling off one mitten, he wiped them with his fingers. As he put the mitten back on, he saw the red ski cap again.

It was coming toward him through the trees, a slowly moving spot of color in a sea of pure white. He sucked in his breath. Alan? Pudge? Leo? Who the hell was it? But, he thought, it made no difference who it was. No difference at all. He had to escape from whomever it was. He had to run. . . .

He looked down at the ground. The falling snow, even as light as it was in the trees, had already covered up his tracks and his ski poles, which were still on the ground. If he moved now, he would make fresh tracks and could be followed. But if he stayed where he was, if he *hid* . . .

Next to where Harlow stood, there was a twelve-foot drift banked up against a tall ponderosa. He unlocked his skis and knelt beside the drift. He tried to dig with both hands but his right arm was too sore to move it, so he used his left hand only, scooping out a cave in the drift. When he had dug it large enough to squeeze into, he turned and sat back in it, knees drawn up in front of him. He glanced at his skis; they were almost covered with fresh snow. And the newly falling flakes were beginning to cover him also, camouflaging him in his cave.

Squinting, Harlow searched for the red ski cap. He

saw it: off to the left at about ten o'clock, some fifteen yards away. It was impossible, because of the falling snow, to see any more of the figure; just the bright red cap. With maddening slowness, it moved across in front of him. Ten o'clock, twelve o'clock, two o'clock. Then it disappeared into the whiteness. Harlow chuckled to himself. Fool.

His right arm was throbbing and he carefully touched it. Through the ski jacket he could feel a massive swelling. So that was what the cracking sound had been: his arm.

He blinked his eyelids, which were becoming heavy with snow. He wanted to get up and get back on his skis, but somehow he could not manage it. With his left hand he reached out of the cave and stuck his mittened fingers into the fresh layer of snow. There was about three inches of it, which meant it was falling at the rate of nine or ten inches an hour. That discovery, and the sensation that he was growing very warm, made him realize suddenly that he had to get out; he had to have help.

"Alan!" he yelled.

No answer.

"Pudge!"

No answer.

"Leo!"

No answer.

He called their names over and over for half an hour. Then the white world became silent again.

In the coffee shop at the lodge, Collins, the mountain ranger, tossed his red ski cap on the counter and warmed his hands around a mug of steaming chocolate.

"Anything from the highway crew?" Boles asked him.

"Nothing," Collins replied. "He didn't make it down, I'm afraid." He sighed heavily. "Damn! I came so *close* to catching him. You know, I thought it was my imagination when I first saw the guy. In all the years I've been coming down from the lookout cabin on those back slopes, that's the first time I ever saw another skier. Was he the only one up there today?"

The Last Downhill

"No, that fellow at the front table went up, too. Only to the second ridge, though. He had intended going all the way to the summit but he hadn't been on skis for a while. After giving it some thought, he came on down the two lower runs."

"Smart," said Collins. He glanced at the man, at the ordinary red ski cap similar to his own lying next to the man's plate. "Who is he anyway?"

The lodge manager shrugged. "Just a salesman. Name's Phil Casey. Car threw a rod. It's laid up in Hickey's Garage; he sent to Sacramento for a part. Said he thought as long as he was stranded, he might as well get in a little skiing. Only got to do the one downhill run, though, before the storm hit. Tough luck."

"Better luck than the other fellow had," Collins commented.

He wondered if the other skier had frozen to death yet, and sipped at his steaming chocolate.

The Other Runner

JOHN LUTZ

I jog. Like people all over this mechanized world who have discovered the benefits of jogging, of what really is old-fashioned running.

I'm tired now, in my third mile this evening. I feel that I can't make it the mile and a half back to my cabin, but a part of me deep down knows that I will.

What I'm running on is an old bridle path. It once was cinder, but the mountain thunderstorms and melting snows have worn it to the hard gray surface on which I now struggle. The path is approximately two and one-half miles long, meandering in a roughly circular route around Mirror Lake. For an instant I can glimpse through the trees and see the cedar shake roof of my small cabin, and as always the sight strengthens my determination to reach that point of triumph.

The Other Runner

Around and above me the woods are green and shadowed, and occasionally I hear birds twitter in alarm at my approach, or a squirrel or rabbit bolt unseen for cover. I negotiate a slight rise, one of the most grueling stretches of my morning runs, and my thighs suddenly ache under the uphill strain, my breath rasping in louder, quicker rhythm.

Then the high path levels out, sweeps in a sloping crescent to the south. A steep drop on my left, steep rising bare mountain face on my right. At my feet Mirror Lake suddenly glitters blue-green, a jewel nestled deep in a rough green setting.

I draw breath and resolution as I turn onto the final leg of my run, a series of small rises, then a long gentle grade to my cabin. That final downgrade is the best of the run, the very sweetest. Lovely gravity.

Half an hour later I've showered, and I sit now on the wooden porch of my cabin, my feet propped up on the porch rail, a cold can of low-calorie beer on the wicker table beside me. Totally relaxed, I wait for darkness.

I've been jogging for six weeks, since my divorce became final. When Marsha left me I took stock of myself, decided I needed to lose ten to fifteen pounds, strengthen my heart and lungs for the coming lonely battle with encroaching age. I was 43 in March.

Of course age and weight weren't my only reasons for taking up jogging. Tension. Jogging is one of the greatest tension relievers there is, and I was under more tension during the divorce, the unexpected bitterness, than I would ever have guessed I could bear.

And perhaps I couldn't have borne it without the escape and spiritual experience of running, and the isolation of this tiny cabin near Mirror Lake. I've been here two weeks now, and each day I'm gladder I came. Oh, the tension remains, but now I easily hold it at bay.

Seclusion heals. And there is only one other occupied house on the lake, a large flat-roofed modern structure that juts from the side of the east hill like the imbedded prow of a ship. The Mulhaneys are staying there, Dan and Iris. Dan looks to be a few years older than my 43, a beefy, graying man with a sad-pug, brutal face. Iris I've seen once, as she stood staring into the lake, a lithe, long-waisted woman with long brown hair and graceful neck. One of those women who somehow by their silent presence will be able to exercise an attraction for men even into old age, woman not just alive but aflame—coldly aflame.

I've not yet spoken to either of the Mulhaneys; it was from the talkative shopkeeper at the one-pump gas station-grocery store near Daleville that I learned their identities. Though Dan Mulhaney I see almost every day. He's a morning jogger. Always a few minutes either side of nine o'clock he pads wearily past my kitchen window as I'm drinking my coffee. We wave to each other. He's never stopped; he can't break stride.

But one morning he does stop.

Mulhaney simply ceases exerting effort and his bulky white-clad form decelerates to a walk with machine-like inevitability. I stand up from the table and take half a dozen steps out onto the porch.

"Morning," Mulhaney says. "Thought I oughta introduce myself." He holds out a perspiring hand. "Dan Mulhaney."

"Earl Crydon." I shake the hand.

"Wife and I are staying in the house up on the hill. Here to get away from things."

"That's why I'm here myself."

"Vacation?"

"No, I'm a free-lance writer, so my office can pretty well travel with me."

Mulhaney rubs large hairy hands on his shapeless T-shirt, stands silently, expectantly.

"Been jogging long?" I ask.

"About three months. I'm up to six miles. How about you?"

"I can do a bit over five, which is quite an improvement over my first outing. I run in the evenings, after things have cooled."

Mulhaney suddenly seems ill at ease. I offer him coffee.

The Other Runner

"Better not, but thanks." He begins jogging easily in place to keep up his circulation. "I better get moving before I get stiff." He fades backward, waves, graceful for a big man, then turns and strikes a practiced, moderate pace. He jogs in the opposite direction from myself—clockwise. There is about him an air of mild confusion.

Next morning, as I sit sipping coffee in my crude pine-paneled kitchen, I hear Mulhaney's approach at exactly two minutes to nine. When he comes into view I raise my hand to wave, but he doesn't look in my direction. His pace is faster than usual, and on his perspiring flushed face is an expression of perplexity, of muted fright. Almost as if he is running *from* something.

"Morning!" I call through the window.

His head jerks in my direction and he smiles mechanically, gives a tentative wave. The rhythmic beat of his footsteps recedes.

That evening, as I jog through long shadows past the precariously balanced Mulhaney house, I can hear shouting coming from inside, a man and a woman, abrupt, heated words that are only desperate, indecipherable sounds when they reach my ears. I jog on.

The next several mornings I watch Mulhaney jog past my cabin window and each time his beefy face wears that same quizzical, fearful expression. Then, on Friday morning, I hear the broken, slowing rhythm of his footsteps, and even before he comes into view I know that he's stopping to talk. I finish my coffee and rise to walk onto the porch to greet him.

Mulhaney invites me to join him and his wife that evening for cocktails and some outdoor-grilled steaks—after I've returned from jogging, of course. I accept, some side of me faintly resenting this intrusion on my self-imposed isolation, and tell him I'll run earlier this evening so I can be there at dinner time. We decide on eight o'clock.

I get to the Mulhaney house at five minutes to eight, feeling fresh and relaxed after my early run and cool shower. Dan Mulhaney is waiting for me by a redwood gate at the top of a long winding flight of mossy stone steps that leads to the side of the jutting, angled house. We shake hands as he works a pitted metal latch and opens the gate.

"My wife Iris," he says, pride of possession in his voice.

Iris is standing near a white steel table on a brick veranda bordered by thick twisted ivy. She's wearing white shorts and a violet-colored blouse that brings out the violet of her eyes. She smiles. "A drink, Mr. Crydon? Scotch, martini, beer?"

"Beer. And it's Earl, Mrs. Mulhaney."

"Then it's Iris." As she walks toward an open door she says, "I understand you're a compulsive exerciser like my husband."

"I like to run."

I walk with Mulhaney to a no-frills barbecue pit and examine three still-raw steaks.

"Extra-lean," he assures me, as Iris returns with my beer in a glass and with her own martini glass replenished. We drift to the center of the veranda and sit at the white metal table. There is a hole in the center of the table for an umbrella, and round plastic coasters for our glasses.

"Beautiful place," I say, looking around me at glass and squared redwood. A red Porsche convertible squats in the gravel drive.

Iris shrugs. "I hate it."

I raise my glass and look at her, noticing the sheen of her eyes and the faint flush on her cheeks. The results of more than one or two martinis. "But you're staying here," I say.

"Daniel's idea." Her fingertips brush a faded purplish splotch on the side of her neck.

"Both of us had the idea, actually," Mulhaney says quickly. He swivels in his chair to check the wink of flame above the rim of the barbecue pit. "Hey, I better keep an eye on those steaks." He stands and moves away.

"The salad's tossed," Iris says after him. She fixes a violet stare on me. "Daniel sort of twisted my arm to get me to come up here, Earl." A sip of martini. "Marital difficulties. Private matter."

I shift in my hard white chair, slightly embarrassed. "No need to tell me about it, Iris. I'm not qualified to give advice." I wonder how "sort of" was the arm twisting.

"You're not married?"

"Divorced."

Even her smile is violet. There is an unmistakable intensity there.

"I've had enough woman trouble to hold me for a while," I say, and truthfully.

"Well done?" Dan Mulhaney calls to me, probing the largest steak with a long-tined fork.

"Sure," I tell him, "go ahead and burn it."

Iris smiles at me and rises to get the salad.

Again that expression on Mulhaney's face, as if someone—or something—is chasing him.

I sit by my kitchen window, sipping coffee, and glance at my watch. He's early this morning.

The next morning he stops to talk.

"Hot for morning," he says, wiping his glistening face with his T-shirt.

I lean on a cedar porch post. "It is if you're jogging." I can see that Mulhaney is bothered by something more than the heat.

"Any large wild animals around here?" he asks. "I mean, have you ever seen any foxes, bobcats or—anything?"

"Never anything bigger than a rabbit. There used to be bears and cougars in this area, but not for years."

He nods, his broad red face grotesque with a frown in the harsh morning light. "Have you ever been around hunting dogs, Crydon?"

"Not often."

"You can walk where there are a dozen of them lying in the sun, watching you and not watching you. Nothing happens. But if you run they'll sometimes chase you as if you were game."

"Instinct."

Mulhaney seems hesitant to speak further, but he does. "In the evenings, when you're running, do you ever get the feeling that something's—well, behind you?"

"I never have."

"There's an old Gaelic saying to the effect that if you run fast enough long enough, something is bound to give chase."

"Like the hunting dogs. And you think something's chasing you?"

"I don't think it—it's a feeling. Imagination, I guess. But I'm not the imaginative sort." He snorts an embarrassed laugh. "If I were you I'd think Dan Mulhaney was due for a psychiatric checkup."

"Have you ever considered turning around?" I asked him. "Running back toward whatever you think is behind you?"

I'm surprised by the fear in his eyes. "No, no, I couldn't do that."

As he stands talking to me, helpless in all his aging bulk, I feel a wash of deep pity for Mulhaney, of comradeship. I tell him to wait and I go into the cabin. When I return I hand him my revolver. Perhaps this seems extreme, but it is only a small-caliber target pistol. And what if Mulhaney is right? What if something is running behind him, stalking him? This is reasonably wild country.

"Carry this tucked in your belt if you'd like," I say. "If nothing else, it should make you feel more secure."

He holds the small pistol before him in gratitude and surprise. "You don't have to do this."

"Why shouldn't I? I haven't fired that gun in over a year, so I won't miss it."

"I'll pay you for it."

"Give it back to me when you leave here, or when you feel you haven't any more use for it."

Mulhaney grins, tucks the pistol into the waistband of his shorts beneath his baggy T-shirt. He really is grateful. We shake hands and he jogs up the path, his footsteps somehow more confident on the hard earth.

I go inside, pour another cup of coffee, and wonder if I've made a mistake.

But the pistol has nothing to do with Thursday's tragedy.

At ten o'clock in the morning a horn honks outside my cabin, a series of abrupt, frantic blasts. I walk to the door and see Iris sitting behind the wheel of the red Porsche. Her hair is tangled, wild. Her eyes are wild.

"I need your help, Earl! Something's happened to Dan!"

I shut the cabin door and trot to the car. "Where is he?"

"On the path. He went jogging this morning as he always does, but he didn't return. I went looking for him, found him lying on the ground. He—he doesn't seem to be breathing."

I move around and get in on the passenger side of the car. Iris rotates the wheel expertly, turns around in the front yard of my cabin, and the Porsche roars back up the path.

Dan Mulhaney is on the highest part of the path, where the hill drops abruptly toward the lake on one side and to the smooth rock that rises steeply to a wooded crest on the other. He is lying on his stomach, his body curiously hunched, his head twisted as if he's straining to get air. We get out of the Porsche almost before it stops rocking, and I know immediately Daniel Mulhaney is dead.

As I'm feeling automatically and hopelessly for vital signs, my hand touches the cool steel revolver still tucked in Mulhaney's waistband. He is lying on the gun, concealing it.

"Does your cabin have a phone?" I ask Iris.

She nods, staring at her husband. "He's so still, so wax-like. He's dead . . ."

"We can't be sure. Go to your cabin and call a doctor, Iris. I'll stay here."

She nods once, gets into the Porsche, and backs some distance to a wide space at the base of the rise, where she can turn the car around. When she is out of sight I reach beneath Mulhaney's body and remove the gun. It hasn't been fired. I tuck it inside my belt, beneath my shirt. I didn't count on this happening; I don't even have a permit for the gun.

"It looks like a heart attack," the doctor says, 45 minutes later, as Iris and I look on. The doctor sighs and slowly stands. He's a middle-aged but somehow older-appearing man from nearby Daleville, a general practitioner. "You say he jogged regularly?"

"Faithfully," Iris says. She seems to be in mild shock.

The doctor shakes his graying head. "It's a pattern. Overweight, middle-aged, probably high blood pressure. Trying to run like a man of twenty-five and his heart gave out, would be my guess. Thousands of them die like this across the country every year. It's a pattern."

"He was so . . . so healthy," Iris says.

"Maybe he just thought he was," the doctor answers softly. "An ambulance is on the way. We'll take him to Mathers' Funeral Home in Daleville if that's agreeable with you, Mrs. Mulhaney."

Iris nods.

"Why don't you take Mrs. Mulhaney home, give her this with a glass of water." He hands me a small white pill and glances at Iris. "A sedative. Nothing strong."

I get into the car beside Iris and she backs down the road, turns the car, and drives slowly toward her jutting redwood cabin. There is little I can say to her that will help, so I stare straight ahead in silence.

At the cabin she thanks me, assures me that she'll be all right, and with the small white pill clenched in her hand goes inside.

Half an hour later, from my cabin window, I see the ambulance carrying Dan Mulhaney's body carefully negotiating the narrow path. No need for speed, flashing lights, or siren. For the first time since the divorce I take a strong drink, sour mash bourbon on the rocks. I feel a sadness out of proportion to my mere familiarity with Dan Mulhaney.

It's impossible for me to work the rest of the afternoon. Clouds have moved into the area, casting even more gloom, and each hour brings a stronger threat of rain.

At five o'clock, much earlier than usual, I decide that I should run to beat the rain. It takes me only a few minutes to get into my jogging shoes, gray shorts, and faded red T-shirt. The gun I lent Mulhaney is still loaded, and rather than take time to unload it, or leave it in the cabin while I'm gone, I transfer it to the waistband of my shorts. Jogging is what I need to shake off my depression, to obscure the impressions of this morning.

I'm breathing hard by the time I reach the scene of Mulhaney's death. For an instant I feel a shuddering dread, then reassure myself by remembering that Mulhaney was older than my 43 years, as well as overweight. I jog past the death site, instinctively avoiding the exact spot where the body was found. I find myself running between the tire tracks of the Porsche, tracks that must have been left when Iris drove along the path and discovered the body, and when she drove us back to try to help Mulhaney.

And I wonder, why would she come back this way, the long way, instead of continuing past my cabin, the way the car was pointed? That way we could have reached Mulhaney in less than a minute. As my feet pound along the path, I see in the gray dust this morning's footprints from Mulhaney's shoes, exactly like my own footprints only reversed. But his footprints don't describe a straight line; rather they move from one side of the path to the other, with varying spaces between them. He must have staggered in considerable pain before falling.

As I continue to run I keep staring down at the footprints pointing in the opposite direction from the way I'm jogging. Mulhaney staggered an incredible distance, almost all the way up the steepening hill. Why would a man in that much pain continue to run, to push himself? I know what that takes, even without the agonizing spasms of a heart attack.

I stop running.

Still breathing hard, I walk slowly back the way I came.

Now I can see the more subtle veerings of one set of tire tracks, hardly noticeable unless under close scrutiny. The zigzag, irregular patterns of Mulhaney's footprints are paralleled and bounded by the snaking set of tire tracks.

I stop walking where Mulhaney's body was found and backhand the sweat from my forehead.

It's a cold sweat.

She killed him. Dogged him up the hill with the car, at a point where he was already exhausted from over an hour of jogging. On one side of the path the bare face of the mountain rising steep and smooth, and on the other side the long drop to the lake. He had to keep running until he collapsed. If Mulhaney hadn't been dead on the path, Iris probably would have pushed his body over the edge to fall toward the lake. An accident, it would seem. Iris knew her husband was dead when she came to me for help.

Thunder suddenly crashes, echoing about me, but still it doesn't rain. I jog on toward my cabin, through air charged by the imminent storm.

A tingling of alarm through my body, and I hear the car's strangely atavistic roar.

The Porsche rounds the curve near my cabin and speeds toward me. I know it will reach the base of the hill before I can. *I will be in the same position Mulhaney was in!*

Iris works it artfully, varying her speed, always a split second from running me down, keeping me gasping, struggling to gain precious inches of life-sustaining ground.

As I glance back, I see her behind the wheel, her hair flowing beautifully, a fixed dreamy expression on her face. I know why Mulhaney didn't use the gun, know how much, in his possessive, brutish fashion, he must have loved her. I've no such compunctions, only chilling fear.

Unlike Mulhaney, I've had my brief respite while examining the tire tracks and footprints, enough to regain some of my stamina. I put on a burst of speed, draw the gun from my waistband, and twist my body to fire as accurately as possible. The gun kicks in my hand and I see astonishment on Iris' face.

It takes three shots to stop her. The Porsche stalls and nestles against the rocky side of the hill, one rear wheel off the ground. The windshield is starred and Iris is slumped sobbing over the steering wheel. I walk back and see no blood. She isn't hit.

"I was afraid you'd jog early," she says from the cradle of her arms on the steering wheel. "Was watching your cabin, hoping you wouldn't leave." Her head flies back and she stares madly at the sky. "It was supposed to rain!" She begins pounding the steering wheel with her fist. "It was supposed to rain early this afternoon and wash away the tracks!"

I help her out of the car and we walk toward her cabin to phone the county sheriff. Iris sobs, cursing almost with every step. Right now I'm sure she hates the weather forecaster even more than she hated her husband.

I live year-round in the city now. And I still jog. As my feet pound the hard earth I sometimes wonder about Daniel Mulhaney, if he really thought he was being pursued, stalked, or if he had some sort of premonition of his death, sensed some manifestation of his wife's hate.

An uneasiness comes over me at times as I run through lengthening evening shadows, and I remember what the prematurely aged doctor at Mirror Lake said. *It's a pattern* . . . And I remember what Dan Mulhaney said about how if you run fast enough long enough, something is bound to give chase.

And now and then I glance behind me.

Storm

ED McBAIN

I.

The girl with Cotton Hawes had cold feet.

He didn't know what to do about her feet because he'd already tried everything he could think of, and they were still cold. He had to admit that driving in subzero temperatures with a storm some fifteen minutes behind him wasn't exactly conducive to warm pedal extremities. But he had turned the car heater up full, supplied the girl with a blanket, taken off his overcoat and wrapped that around her—and she still had cold feet.

The girl's name was Blanche Colby, a very nice euphonic name which she had adopted the moment she entered show business. That had been a long time ago. Blanche's real name was Bertha Cooley, but a press agent those many years back told her that Bertha Cooley sounded like a mentholated Pullman, and not a dancer. Blanche Colby had class, he told her, and if there was one thing Bertha Cooley wanted, it was class. She had taken the new name and gone into the chorus of a hit musical twenty-two years ago, when she was only fifteen. She was now thirty-seven, but all those years of prancing the boards had left her with a youthful body, lithe and long-legged. She was still, with a slight assist from Clairol, a soft honey-blonde. Her green eyes were intelligent and alert. Her feet, unfortunately, *ahhhh*, her feet.

"How are they now?" he asked her.

"Freezing," she said.

"We're almost here," Hawes told her. "You'll like this place. One of the guys on the squad—Hal Willis—comes up here almost every weekend he's off. He says the skiing is great."

"I know a dancer who broke her leg in Switzerland," Blanche said.

"Skiing?"

"Sure, skiing."

"You've never skied before?"

"Never."

"Well . . ." Hawes shrugged. "Well, I don't think you'll break any legs."

"That's reassuring," Blanche said. She glanced through the window on her side of the car. "I think that storm is catching up to us."

"Just a few flurries."

"I wonder how serious it'll be. I have a rehearsal Monday night."

"Four to six inches, they said. That's not very much."

"Will the roads be open?"

"Sure. Don't worry."

"I know a dancer who got snowed in for six days in Vermont," Blanche said. "It wouldn't have been so bad, but she was with a Method actor."

"Well, I'm a cop," Hawes said.

"Yeah," Blanche answered noncommittally.

They were silent for several moments. The light snow

flurries drifted across the road, turning it into a dreamlike, white, flowing stream. The headlights illuminated the shifting macadam. Sitting behind the wheel, Hawes had the peculiar feeling that the road was melting. He was glad to see the sign of Rawson Mountain Inn. He stopped the car, picking out the sign from the tangle of other signs announcing accommodations in the area. He set the car in motion again, turning left over an old wooden bridge, the timbers creaking as the convertible passed over them. A new sign, blatant red and white, shouted the features of the area—a sixteen-hundred-foot mountain, two chair lifts, a T-Bar, a rope tow, and, definitely not needed with a storm on the way, a snow-making machine.

The inn lay nestled in the foothills at the base of the mountain. The trees around the inn were bare, standing in gaunt silhouette against the snow-threatening sky. Snow-nuzzled lights beckoned warmly. He helped Blanche out of the car, put on his overcoat, and walked with her over old packed snow to the entrance. They stamped their feet in the doorway and entered the huge room. A fire was going at one end of the room. Someone was playing the piano. A handful of tired weekday skiers were sprawled around the fireplace, wearing very fashionable after-ski boots and sweaters, drinking from bottles onto which they'd hand-lettered their names. Blanche went directly to the fire, found a place on one of the couches, and stretched her long legs to the blaze. Hawes found the desk, tapped a bell on it, and waited. No one appeared. He tapped the bell again. A skier passing the desk said, "He's in the office. Over there on your left."

Hawes nodded, found the door marked OFFICE, and knocked on it. A voice inside called, "Yes, come in," and Hawes twisted the knob and entered.

The office was larger than he'd expected, a good fifteen feet separating the entrance door from the desk at the opposite end of the room. A man in his late twenties sat behind the desk. He had dark hair and dark brows pulled low over deep brown eyes. He was wearing a white shirt open at the throat, a bold reindeer-imprinted sweater over it. He was also wearing a plaster cast on his right leg. The leg was stretched out stiffly in front of him, the foot resting on a low ottoman. A pair of crutches leaned against the desk, within easy reach of his hands. Hawes was suddenly glad he'd left Blanche by the fire.

"You're not a new skier, I hope," the man said.

"No, I'm not."

"Good. Some of them get scared by the cast and crutches."

"Was it a skiing accident?" Hawes asked.

The man nodded. "Spiral break of the tibia and fibula. Someone forgot to fill in a sitzmark. I was going pretty fast, and when I hit the hole . . ." He shrugged. "I won't be able to walk without the crutches for at least another month."

"That's too bad," Hawes said. He paused, and then figured he might as well get down to business. "I have a reservation," he said. "Adjoining rooms with bath."

'Yes, sir. What was the name on that?"

"Cotton Hawes and Blanche Colby."

The man opened a drawer in his desk and consulted a typewritten sheet. "Yes, sir," he said. "Two rooms in the annex."

"The annex?" Hawes said. "Where's that?"

"Oh, just a hundred yards or so from the main building, sir."

"Oh. Well, I guess that'll be . . ."

"And that's *one* bath, you understand."

"What do you mean?"

"They're adjoining rooms, but the bathroom is in 104. 105 doesn't have a bath."

"Oh. Well, I'd like two rooms that *do* have baths," Hawes said, smiling.

"I'm sorry, sir. 104 and 105 are the only available rooms in the house."

"The fellow I spoke to on the phone . . ."

"Yes, sir, that's me. Elmer Wollender."

"How do you do?" Hawes said. "You told me both rooms had baths."

"No, sir. You said you wanted adjoining rooms with

bath, and I said I could give you adjoining rooms with bath. And that's what I've given you. Bath. Singular."

"Are you a lawyer, Mr. Wollender?" Hawes asked, no longer smiling.

"No, sir. Out of season, I'm a locksmith."

"What are you in season?"

"Why, a hotel-keeper, sir," Wollender said.

"Don't test the theory," Hawes answered. "Let me have my deposit back, Mr. Wollender. We'll find another place to stay."

"Well, sir, to begin with, we can't make any cash refunds, but we'll be happy to keep your deposit here against another time when you may wish . . ."

"Look, Mr. Wollender," Hawes said menacingly, "I don't know what kind of a . . ."

"And of course, sir, there *are* lots of places to stay here in town, but none of them, sir, *none* of them have any private baths at all. Now if you don't mind walking down the hall . . ."

"All I know is . . ."

". . . and sharing the john with a hundred other skiers, why then . . ."

"You told me on the phone . . ."

"I'm sure you can find other accommodations. The *lady*, however, might enjoy a little privacy." Wollender waited while Hawes considered.

"If I give her 104 . . ." Hawes started and then paused. "Is that the room with the bath?"

"Yes, sir, 104."

"If I give her that room, where's the bath for 105?"

"Down at the end of the hall, sir. And we *are* right at the base of the mountain, sir, and the skiing *has* been excellent, and we're expecting at least twelve inches of fresh powder."

"The radio said four to six."

"That's in the city, sir. We normally get a lot more snow."

"Like what I got on the phone?" Hawes asked. "Where do I sign?"

2.

Cotton Hawes was a detective, and as a member of the 87TH Squad he had flopped down in a great many desirable and undesirable rooms throughout the city and its suburbs. Once, while posing as a dock walloper, he had taken a furnished room overlooking the River Harb, and had been surprised during the night by what sounded like a band of midgets marching at the foot of his bed. The midgets turned out to be giants, or at least giants of the species *Rattus muridae*—or as they say in English, rats. He had turned on the light and picked up a broom, but those brazen rat bastards had reared back on their hind legs like boxers and bared their teeth, and he was certain the pack of them would leap for his throat. He had checked out immediately.

There were no rats in rooms 104 and 105 of the annex to Rawson Mountain Inn. Nor was there very much of anything else, either. Whoever had designed the accommodations was undoubtedly steeped in Spartan philosophy. The walls were white and bare, save for a single skiing poster over each bed. There was a single bed in each room, and a wooden dresser painted white. A portable cardboard clothes closet nestled in the corner of each room. The room Hawes hoped to occupy, the one without the bath, was excruciatingly hot, the vents sending in great waves of heated air. The room with the bath, Blanche's room, was unbearably cold. The single window was rimmed with frost, the floor was cold, the bed was cold, the heating ducts and vents were either clogged or blocked, but certainly inoperative.

"And *I'm* the one with the cold feet," Blanche said.

"I'd let you have the heated room," Hawes said gallantly, "but this is the one with the bath."

"Well, we'll manage," Blanche said. "Shall we go down for the bags?"

"I'll get them," Hawes answered. "Stay in my room for now, will you? There's no sense freezing in here."

"I may get to like your room," Blanche said archly,

and then turned and walked past him through the connecting door.

He went down the long flight of steps to the front porch, and then beyond to where the car was parked. The rooms were over the ski shop, which was closed for the night now, silent and dark. He took the two valises out of the trunk, and then pulled his skis from the rack on top of the car. He was not a particularly distrustful man, but a pair of Head skis had been stolen from him the season before, and he'd been a cop long enough to know that lightning sometimes *did* strike twice in the same place. In his right hand, and under his right arm, he carried the two bags. In his left hand, and under his left arm, he carried his skis and his boots. He struggled through the deepening snow and onto the front porch. He was about to put down the bags in order to open the door when he heard the heavy thud of ski boots on the steps inside. Someone was coming down those steps in a hell of a hurry.

The door opened suddenly, and a tall thin man wearing black ski pants and a black-hooded parka came onto the porch, almost colliding with Hawes. His face was narrow, handsome in a fine-honed way, the sharply hooked nose giving it the edged striking appearance of an ax. Even in the pale light filtering from the hallway, Hawes saw that the man was deeply tanned, and automatically assumed he was an instructor. The guess was corroborated by the Rawson Mountain insignia on the man's right sleeve, an interlocking R and M in bright red letters. Incongruously, the man was carrying a pair of white figure skates in his left hand.

"Oh, I'm sorry," he said. His face broke into a grin. He had spoken with an accent, German or Swedish, Hawes couldn't tell which.

"That's all right," Hawes said.

"May I help you?"

"No, I think I can manage. If you'd just hold the door open for me . . ."

"It will be my pleasure," the man said, and he almost clicked his heels together.

"Has the skiing been good?" Hawes asked as he struggled through the narrow doorway.

"Fairly good," the man answered. "It will be better tomorrow."

"Well, thanks," Hawes said.

"My pleasure."

"See you on the mountain," Hawes said cheerfully and continued up the steps. There was something slightly ridiculous about the entire situation, the adjoining rooms with only one bath, the pristine cells the rooms had turned out to be, the heat in one, the cold in the other, the fact that they were over the ski shop, the fact that it had begun snowing very heavily, even the hurried ski instructor with his polite Teutonic manners and his guttural voice and his figure skates, there was something faintly reminiscent of farce about the whole setup. He began chuckling as he climbed the steps. When he came into his room, Blanche was stretched out on his bed. He put down the bags.

"What's so funny?" she asked.

"I've decided this is a comic-opera hotel," Hawes said. "I'll bet the mountain out there is only a backdrop. We'll go out there tomorrow morning and discover it's painted on canvas."

"This room is nice and warm," Blanche said.

"Yes, it is," Hawes answered. He slid his skis under the bed, and she watched him silently.

"Are you expecting burglars?"

"You never can tell." He took off his jacket and pulled his holstered service revolver from his back hip pocket.

"You going to wear that on the slopes tomorrow?" Blanche asked.

"No. You can't get a gun into those zippered pockets."

"I think I'll stay in *this* room tonight," Blanche asked.

"Whatever you like," Hawes said. "I'll take the icebox next door."

"Well, actually," she said, "that wasn't exactly what I had in mind."

"Huh?"

"Don't detectives kiss people?"

"Huh?"

"We've been out twice together in the city, and we've just driven three hours alone together in a car, and you've never once tried to kiss me."

"Well, I . . ."

"I wish you would," Blanche said thoughtfully. "Unless, of course, there's a department regulation against it."

"None that I can think of," Hawes said.

Blanche, her hands behind her head, her legs stretched luxuriously, suddenly took a deep breath and said, "I think I'm going to like this place."

3.

There were sounds in the night.

Huddled together in the single bed, the first sound of which they were aware was the noise of the oil burner. At regularly spaced intervals, the thermostat would click, and there would be a thirty-second pause, and then a 707 jet aircraft would take off from the basement of the old wooden building. Hawes had never heard a noisier oil burner in his life. The aluminum ducts and vents provided a symphony all their own, too, expanding, contracting, banging, clanking, sighing, exhaling, whooshing. Down the hall, the toilet would be flushed every now and again, the noise sounding with cataract sharpness on the still mountain air.

There was another noise. A rasping sound, the narrow shrill squeak of metal upon metal. He got out of bed and went to the window. A light was burning in the ski shop below, casting a yellow rectangle onto the snow. Sighing, he went back to bed and tried to sleep.

Down the corridor, there was the constant thud of ski boots as guests returned to their rooms, the slamming of doors, the occasional high giggle of a girl skier intoxicated by the mountain air.

Voices.

". . . will mean a slower track for the slalom . . ."

"Sure, but everyone'll have the same handicap . . ."
Fading.
More voices.
". . . don't even think they'll open the upper trails."
"They have to, don't they?"
"Not Dead Man's Fall. They won't even be able to get up there with all this snow. Seventeen inches already, and no end in sight."

The 707 taking off again from the basement. The vents beginning their orchestral suite, the ducts supplying counterpoint. And more voices, raised in anger.

". . . because he thinks he's God almighty!"
"I tell you you're imagining things."
"I'm warning you! Stay away from him!"
A young girl's laughter.
"I'm warning you. If I see him . . ."
Fading.

At two o'clock in the morning, the Cats started up the mountain. They sounded like Rommel's mechanized cavalry. Hawes was certain they would knock down the outside walls and come lumbering into the room. Blanche began giggling.

"This is the noisiest hotel I've ever slept in," she said.
"How are your feet?"
"Nice and warm. You're a very warm man."
"You're a very warm girl."
"Do you mind my sleeping in long johns?"
"I thought they were leotards."
"Leotard is singular," Blanche said.
"Singular or plural, those are the sexiest long johns I've ever seen."
"It's only the girl in them," Blanche said modestly. "Why don't you kiss me again?"
"I will. In a minute."
"What are you listening for?"
"I thought I heard an unscheduled flight a moment ago."
"What?"
"Didn't you hear it? A funny buzzing sound?"
"There are so many noises . . ."

"Shhhh."

They were silent for several moments. They could hear the Cats grinding their way up the mountain. Someone down the hall flushed the toilet. More boots in the corridor outside.

"Hey!" Blanche said.

"What?"

"You asleep?"

"No," Hawes answered.

"That buzzing sound you heard?"

"Yes?"

"It was my blood," she told him, and she kissed him on the mouth.

4.

It was still snowing on Saturday morning. The promised storm had turned into a full-fledged blizzard. They dressed in the warm comfort of the room, Blanche putting on thermal underwear, and then two sweaters and stretch pants, the extra clothing padding out her slender figure. Hawes, standing six feet two inches tall in his double-stockinged feet, black pants and black sweater, presented a one-hundred-and-ninety-pound V-shaped silhouette to the window and the gray day outside.

"Do you think I'll get back in time for Monday night's rehearsal?" Blanche asked.

"I don't know. I'm supposed to be back at the squad by six tomorrow night. I wonder if the roads are open."

They learned during breakfast that a state emergency had been declared in the city and in most of the towns lining the upstate route. Blanche seemed blithely indifferent to the concept of being snowbound. "If there's that much snow," she said, "they'll cancel rehearsal, anyway."

"They won't cancel the police department," Hawes said.

"The hell with it," Blanche said happily. "We're here now, and there's marvelous snow, and if the skiing is good it'll be a wonderful weekend."

"Even if the skiing is *lousy*," Hawes said, "it'll be a wonderful weekend."

They rented boots and skis for her in the ski rental shop, and then took to the mountain. Both chair lifts were in operation, but as one of the midnight voices had prophesied, the upper trails were not yet opened. A strong wind had arisen, and it blew the snow in driving white sheets across the slopes. Hawes took Blanche to the rope tow first, had her practice climbing for a while, teaching her to edge and to herringbone, and then illustrated the use of the tow—left hand clamped around the rope, right hand and arm behind the back and gripping the rope. The beginner's slope was a gentle one, but Blanche seemed immediately capable of more difficult skiing. She was a trained dancer, and she automatically thought of the skis as part of a difficult stage costume, encumbering movement, but simply something to overcome. With remarkable co-ordination, she learned how to snowplow on the beginner's slope. By midmorning, she had graduated to the T-Bar, and was beginning to learn the rudiments of the stem christie. Hawes patiently stayed with her all morning, restricting his own skiing to the elementary slopes. He was becoming more and more grateful for the snow-clogged roads. With the roads impassable, the number of weekend skiers was limited; he and Blanche were enjoying weekday skiing on a Saturday, and the fresh snow made everything a delight.

After lunch, she suggested that he leave her alone to practice for a while. Hawes, who was itching to get at the chair lift and the real trails, nonetheless protested that he was perfectly content to ski with her on the baby slopes. But Blanche insisted, and he finally left her on the slope serviced by the T-Bar, and went to the longest of the chair lifts, Lift A.

He grinned unconsciously as he approached the lift. Eight or ten skiers were waiting to use the chairs, as compared to the long lines one usually encountered on weekends. As he approached the loading area, he caught a blur of black movement from the corner of his eye, turned and saw his German or Swedish ski instructor from the night before *wedeln* down the mountain, and then turning, parallel in a snow-spraying stop near the lift. He did not seem to recognize Hawes, but Hawes was not at all surprised. Every skier on the line was wearing a hooded parka, the hoods covering their heads and tied securely beneath their chins. In addition, all the skiers were wearing goggles, most with tinted yellow lenses in defense against the grayness of the day, some with darker lenses in spite of the grayness. The result, in any case, was almost total anonymity. Male and female, they all looked very much alike. They could have been a band of Martians waiting to be taken to a leader. Instead, they were waiting for chairs. They did not have to wait very long.

The chairs on their cable kept rounding the bend, came past the grinding machinery. Hawes moved into position, watched the girl ahead of him sit abruptly as the chair came up under her behind. He noticed that the chair gave a decided lurch as it cleared the platform, and he braced himself for the expected force, glanced back over his shoulder as another chair rounded the turn. Ski poles clutched in his left hand, his right hand behind him to grip the edge of the chair as it approached, he waited. The chair was faster and had a stronger lurch than he'd anticipated. For a moment, he thought it would knock him down. He gripped the edge of the seat with his mittened right hand, felt himself sliding off the seat, and automatically grabbed for the upright supporting rod with his left hand, dropping his poles.

"Dropped your poles!" one of the loaders shouted behind him.

"We'll send them up!" the other loader called.

He turned slightly in the chair and looked back. He could see one of the loaders scrambling to pick up his poles. There were two empty chairs behind him, and then a skier got into the third chair, and the loader handed him the poles Hawes had dropped. Behind that chair, two other skiers shared a chair. The wind and the snow made it difficult to see. Hawes turned his head abruptly, but the wind was even stronger coming down the mountain.

The chair ahead of him was perhaps thirty feet away, but he could barely make out the shadowy figure of the person sitting in it. All he saw was a dim silhouette obscured by blinding snow and keening wind. He could feel snow seeping under the edges of his hood. He took off his mittens and tightened the string. Quickly, before the biting cold numbed his fingers, he put the mittens on again.

The lift was a new one, and it pulled the chairs silently up the mountain. On his right, Hawes could see the skiers descending, a damn fool snowplowing out of control down a steep embankment pocked with moguls, an excellent skier navigating turns in parallel precision. The wind keened around and under his hood, the only sound on the mountain. The ride was a pleasant one, except for the wind and the cold. In some spots, the chair was suspended some thirty feet above the snow below. In other places, the chair came as close as six feet to the ground. He was beginning to anticipate the descent. He saw the unloading station ahead, saw the sign advising him to keep the tips of his skies up, and prepared to disembark. The skier ahead of him met with difficulty as he tried to get off his chair. The snow had been falling too heavily to clear, and there was no natural downgrade at the top of the lift; the chair followed its occupant, rather than rising overhead at the unloading point. The girl ahead of Hawes was almost knocked off her feet by her own chair. She managed to free herself as the chair gave a sharp lurch around the bend to begin its trip down the mountain again. Hawes concentrated on getting off the chair. Surprisingly, he did so with a minimum of effort and without poles, and then waited while the two empty chairs passed by. The third following chair approached the station. A man clambered off the chair, handed Hawes his poles with a "These yours?" and skied to the crest of the slope. Hawes stood just outside the station booth, hanging his poles over his wrists. He was certain that the fourth chair behind his had contained *two* skiers at the bottom of the lift, and yet it seemed to be approaching now with only a single person in it. Hawes squinted through the snow, puzzled. Something seemed odd about the person in the fourth chair, something was jutting into the air at a curious angle—a ski? a leg? a . . . ?

The chair approached rapidly.

The skier made no move to disembark.

Hawes opened his eyes wide behind his yellow-tinted goggles as the chair swept past the station.

Through the driving snow, he had seen a skier slumped limply. And sticking out of the skier's chest at a malicious angle over the heart, buffeted by the wind and snow so that it trembled as if it were alive, thrust deep through the parka and the clothing beneath it like an oversized, slender aluminum sword, was a ski pole.

5.

The chair gave its sharp lurch as it rounded the bend.

The skier slid from the seat as the chair made its abrupt turn. Skis touched snow, the body fell forward, there was a terrible snapping sound over the keening of the wind, and Hawes knew instantly that a leg had been broken as bone yielded to the unresisting laminated wood and the viselike binding. The skier fell face downward, the ski pole bending as the body struck the snow, one leg twisted at an impossible angle, the boot still held firmly in its binding.

For a moment, there was only confusion compounded.

The wind and the snow filled the air, the body lay motionless, face down in the snow as the chair whipped around the turn and started its descent. An empty chair swept past, another, a third, and then a chair came into view with a man poised to disembark, and Hawes shouted to the booth attendant, "Stop the lift!"

"What?"

"Stop the goddamn lift!"

"What? What?"

Hawes moved toward the body lying in the snow just as the man on the chair decided to get off. They collided in a tangle of poles and skis, the relentless chair pushing them along like a bulldozer, sending them sprawling onto the body in the snow, before it snapped around for its downward passage. The booth attendant finally got the message. He ran into the small wooden shack and threw the control switch. The lift stopped. There was a deeper silence on the mountain.

"You okay?" he called.

"I'm fine," Hawes said. He got to his feet and quickly unsnapped his bindings. The man who'd knocked him down was apologizing profusely, but Hawes wasn't listening. There was a bright red stain spreading into the snow where the impaled skier had fallen. He turned the body over and saw the ashen face and sightless eyes, saw the blood-soaked parka where the pole had been pushed through the soft and curving breast into the heart.

The dead skier was a young girl, no more than nineteen years old.

On the right sleeve of her black parka was the insignia of a Rawson Mountain ski instructor, the interlocking R and M in red as bright as the blood which seeped into the thirsty snow.

"What is it?" the booth attendant shouted. "Shall I get the ski patrol? Is it an accident?"

"It's no accident," Hawes said, but his voice was so low that no one heard him.

6.

As befitted this farcical hotel in this comic-opera town, the police were a band of Keystone cops led by an inept sheriff who worked on the premise that a thing worth doing was a thing worth doing badly. Hawes stood by helplessly as he watched these cracker-barrel cops violate each and every rule of investigation, watched as they mishandled evidence, watched as they made it hopelessly impossible to gain any information at all from whatever slender clues were available.

The sheriff was a gangling oaf named Theodore Watt who, instead of putting Lift A out of commission instantly while his men tried to locate the victim's chair, instead rode that very lift to the top of the mountain, followed by at least three dozen skiers, hotel officials, reporters, and local cretins who undoubtedly smeared any latent prints lingering on *any* of the chairs, and made the task of reconstructing the crime almost impossible. One girl, wearing bright lavender stretch pants and a white parka, climbed off the chair near the booth and was promptly informed there was blood all over the seat of her pants. The girl craned her neck to examine her shapely behind, touched the smear of blood, decided it was sticky and obscene, and almost fainted dead away. The chair, meantime, was happily whisking its way down the mountain again to the loading station where, presumably, another skier would again sit into a puddle of the dead girl's blood.

The dead girl's name, as it turned out, was Helga Nilson. She was nineteen years old and had learned to ski before she'd learned to walk, as the old Swedish saying goes. She had come to America when she was fifteen, had taught in the ski school at Stowe, Vermont, for two years before moving down to Mt. Snow in that same fair state, and then abandoning Vermont and moving to Rawson Mountain, further south. She had joined the Rawson ski school at the beginning of the season, and seemed to be well-liked by all the instructors and especially by many beginning skiers who, after one lesson with her, repeatedly asked for "Helga, the little Swedish girl."

The little Swedish girl had had a ski pole driven into her heart with such force that it had almost exited through her back. The pole, bent out of shape when Helga fell from the chair, was the first piece of real evidence the Keystone cops mishandled. Hawes saw one of the deputies kneel down beside the dead girl, grasp the pole with both hands, and attempt to pull it out of her body.

"Hey, what are you doing?" he shouted, and he shoved the man away from the body.

The man glanced up at him with a baleful upstate eye. "And just who in hell're *you*?" he asked.

"My name's Cotton Hawes," Hawes said. "I'm a detective. From the city." He unzipped the left hip pocket of his ski pants, pulled out his wallet, and flashed the tin. The deputy seemed singularly unimpressed.

"You're a little bit aways from your jurisdiction, ain't you?" he said.

"Who taught you how to handle evidence?" Hawes asked heatedly.

Sheriff Watt sauntered over to where the pair were arguing. He grinned amiably and said, "What seems to be the trouble here, hmmm?" He sang out the "hmmm," his voice rising pleasantly and cheerfully. A nineteen-year-old girl lay dead at his feet, but Sheriff Watt thought he was an old alumnus at Dartmouth's Winter Carnival.

"Feller here's a city detective," the deputy said.

"That's good," Watt said. "Pleased to have you with us."

"Thanks," Hawes said. "Your man here was just smearing any latent prints there may be on that weapon."

"What weapon?"

"The ski pole," Hawes said. "What weapon do you think I . . . ?"

"Oh, won't be no fingerprints on that, anyway," Watt said.

"How do you know?"

"No damn fool's gonna grab a piece of metal with his bare hands, is he? Not when the temperature's ten below zero, now is he?"

"He might have," Hawes said. "And while we're at it, don't you think it'd be a good idea to stop that lift? You've already had one person smearing up whatever stuff you could have found in the . . ."

"I got to get my men up here before I order the lift stopped," Watt said.

"Then restrict it to the use of your men."

"I've already done that," Watt said briefly. He turned back to his deputy. "Want to let me see that pole, Fred?"

"Sheriff, you let him touch that pole again, and . . ."

"And *what*?"

". . . and you may ruin . . ."

"Mister, you just let me handle this my own which-way, hmmm? We been in this business a long time now, and we know all about skiing accidents."

"This wasn't an accident," Hawes said angrily. "Somebody shoved a ski pole into that girl's chest, and that's not . . ."

"I know it wasn't an accident," Watt said. "That was just a manner of speaking. Let me have the pole, Fred."

"Sheriff . . ."

"Mister, you better just shut up, hmmm? Else I'll have one of my men escort you down the mountain, and you can warm your feet by the fire."

Hawes shut up. Impotently, he watched while the deputy named Fred seized the ski pole in both hands and yanked it from Helga's chest. A spurt of blood followed the retreating pole, welled up into the open wound, overflowed it, was sopped up by the sodden sweater. Fred handed the bent pole to the sheriff. Watt turned it over and over in his big hands.

"Looks like the basket's been taken off this thing," he said.

The basket, Hawes saw, had indeed been removed from the bottom of the aluminum pole. The basket on a ski pole is a circular metal ring perhaps five inches in diameter, crossed by a pair of leather thongs. A smaller ring stamped into the thongs fits over the end of the pointed pole and is usually fastened by a cotter pin or a tight rubber washer. When the basket is in place on the end of a pole, it prevents the pole from sinking into the snow, thereby enabling the skier to use it in executing turns or maintaining balance. The basket had been removed from this particular pole and, in addition, someone had sharpened the normally sharp point so that it was as thin as a rapier. Hawes noticed this at once. It took the sheriff a little while longer to see that he was holding a razor-sharp weapon in his hands, and not a normally pointed pole.

"Somebody been working on the end of this thing," he said, the dawn gradually breaking.

A doctor had come up the lift and was kneeling beside the dead girl. To no one's particular surprise, he pronounced her dead. One of the sheriff's bumbling associates began marking the position of the body, tracing its outline on the snow with a blue powder he poured liberally from a can.

Hawes couldn't imagine what possible use this imitation of investigatory technique would serve. They were marking the position of the body, true, but this didn't happen to be the scene of the crime. The girl had been murdered on a chair somewhere between the base of the mountain and the top of the lift. So far, no one had made any attempt to locate and examine the chair. Instead, they were sprinkling blue powder onto the snow, and passing their big paws all over the murder weapon.

"May I make a suggestion?" he asked.

"Sure," Watt said.

"That girl got on the lift with someone else. I know because I dropped my poles down there, and when I turned for a look, there were two people in that chair. But when she reached the station here, she was alone."

"Yeah?" Watt said.

"Yeah. I suggest you talk to the loader down below. The girl was a ski instructor, and they may have recognized her. Maybe they know who got on the chair with her."

"Provided anyone did."

"Someone did," Hawes said.

"How do you know?"

"Because . . ." Hawes took a deep breath. "I just told you. I *saw* two people in that chair."

"How far behind you?"

"Four chairs behind."

"And you could see four chairs behind you in this storm, hmmm?"

"Yes. Not clearly, but I could see."

"I'll just bet you could," Watt said.

"Look," Hawes insisted, "someone was in that chair with her. And he undoubtedly jumped from the chair right after he killed her. I suggest you start combing the ground under the lift before this snow covers any tracks that might be there."

"Yes, we'll do that," Watt said. "When we get around to it."

"You'd better get around to it soon," Hawes said. "You've got a blizzard here, and a strong wind piling up drifts. If . . ."

"Mister, I hadn't *better* do anything. You're the one who'd just better butt his nose out of what we're trying to do here."

"What is it you're trying to do?" Hawes asked. "Compound a felony? Do you think your murderer's going to sit around and wait for you to catch up to him? He's probably halfway out of the state by now."

"Ain't nobody going noplace, mister," Watt said. "Not with the condition of the roads. So don't you worry about that. I hate to see anybody worrying."

"Tell that to the dead girl," Hawes said, and he watched as the ski patrol loaded her into a basket and began taking her on her last trip down the mountain.

7.

Death is a cliché, a tired old saw.

He had been a cop for a good long time now, starting as a rookie who saw death only from the sidelines, who kept a timetable while the detectives and the photographers and the assistant M.E. and the laboratory boys swarmed around the victim like flies around a prime cut of rotten meat. Death to him, at that time, had been motion-picture death. Standing apart from death, being as it were a uniformed secretary who took the names of witnesses and jotted in a black book the arrivals and departures of those actually concerned with the investigation, he had watched the proceedings dispassionately. The person lying lifeless on the sidewalk, the person lying on blood-soaked sheets, the person hanging from a light fixture, the person eviscerated by the onrushing front grille of an automobile, these were all a trifle unreal to Hawes, representations of death, but not death itself, not that grisly son of a bitch.

Storm

When he became a detective, they really introduced him to death.

The introduction was informal, almost casual. He was working with the 30TH Squad at the time, a very nice respectable squad in a nice respectable precinct where death by violence hardly ever came. The introduction was made in a rooming house. The patrolman who had answered the initial squeal was waiting for the detectives when they arrived. The detective with Hawes asked, "Where's the stiff?" and the patrolman answered, "He's in there," and the other detective turned to Hawes and said, "Come on, let's take a look."

That was the introduction.

They had gone into the bedroom where the man was lying at the foot of the dresser. The man was fifty-three years old. He lay in his undershorts on the floor in the sticky coagulation of his own blood. He was a small man with a pinched chest. His hair was black and thinning, and bald patches showed his flaking scalp. He had probably never been handsome, even when he was a youth. Some men do not improve with age, and time and alcohol had squeezed everything out of this man, and drained him dry until all he possessed was sagging flesh and, of course, life. The flesh was still there. The life had been taken from him. He lay at the foot of the dresser in his undershorts, ludicrously piled into a heap of inert flesh, so relaxed, so impossibly relaxed. Someone had worked him over with a hatchet. The hatchet was still in the room, blood-flecked, entangled with thin black hair. The killer had viciously attacked him around the head and the throat and the chest. He had stopped bleeding by the time they arrived, but the wounds were still there to see, open and raw.

Hawes vomited.

He went into the bathroom and vomited. That was his introduction to death.

He had seen a lot of death since, had come close to being dead himself. The closest, perhaps, was the time he'd been stabbed while investigating a burglary. The woman who'd been burglarized was still pretty hysterical when he got there. He asked his questions and tried to comfort her, and then started downstairs to get a patrolman. The woman, terrified, began screaming when he left. He could hear her screams as he went down the stair well. The superintendent of the building caught him on the second floor landing. He was carrying a bread knife, and he thought that Hawes was the burglar returned, and he stabbed repeatedly at his head, ripping a wound over his left temple before Hawes finally subdued him. They let the super go; the poor guy had actually thought Hawes was the thief. And then they'd shaved Hawes' red hair to get to the wound, which time of course healed as it does all wounds, leaving however a reminder of death, of the closeness of death. The red hair had grown in white. He still carried the streak over his temple. Sometimes, particularly when it rained, death sent little signals of pain to accompany the new hair.

He had seen a lot of death, especially since he'd joined the 87TH, and a lot of dying. He no longer vomited. The vomiting had happened to a very young Cotton Hawes, a very young and innocent cop who suddenly awoke to the knowledge that he was in a dirty business where the facts of life were the facts of violence, where he dealt daily with the sordid and grotesque. He no longer vomited. But he still got angry.

He had felt anger on the mountain when the young girl fell out of the chair and struck the snow, the ski pole bending as she dropped into that ludicrously ridiculous posture of the dead, that totally relaxed and utterly frightening posture. He had felt anger by juxtaposition, the reconstruction of a vibrant and life-bursting athlete against the very real image of the same girl, no longer a girl, only a worthless heap of flesh and bones, only a body now, a corpse, "Where's the stiff?"

He had felt anger when Theodore Watt and his witless assistants muddied the residue of sudden death, allowing the killer a precious edge, presenting him with the opportunity for escape—escape from the law and from the outrage of humanity. He felt anger now as he walked back to the building which housed the ski shop and the rooms overhead.

The anger seemed out of place on the silent mountain. The snow still fell, still and gentle. The wind had died, and now the flakes drifted aimlessly from overhead, large and wet and white, and there was a stillness and a peace to Rawson Mountain and the countryside beyond, a lazy white quiet which denied the presence of death.

He kicked the packed snow from his boots and went up the steps.

He was starting down the corridor toward his room when he noticed the door was slightly ajar. He hesitated. Perhaps Blanche had come back to the room, perhaps . . .

But there was silence in the corridor, a silence as large as noise. He stopped and untied the laces of his boots. Gently, he slipped them from his feet. Walking as softly as he could—he was a big man and the floor boards in the old building creaked beneath his weight—he approached the room. He did not like the idea of being in his stockinged feet. He had had to kick men too often, and he knew the value of shoes. He hesitated just outside the door. There was no sound in the room. The door was open no more than three inches. He put his hand against the wood. Somewhere in the basement, the oil burner clicked and then *whooooomed* into action. He shoved open the door.

Elmer Wollender, his crutches under his arms, whirled to face him. His head had been bent in an attitude of . . . prayer, was it? No. Not prayer. He had been listening, that was it, listening *to* something, or *for* something.

"Oh, hello, Mr. Hawes," he said. He was wearing a red ski parka over his white shirt. He leaned on his crutches and grinned a boyish, disarming grin.

"Hello, Mr. Wollender," Hawes said. "Would you mind telling me, Mr. Wollender, just what the hell you're doing in my room?"

Wollender seemed surprised. His eyebrows arched. He tilted his head to one side, almost in admiration, almost as if he too would have behaved in much the same way had he come back to *his* room and found a stranger in it. But the admiration was also tinged with surprise. This was obviously a mistake. Head cocked to one side, eyebrows arched, the boyish smile on his mouth, Wollender leaned on his crutches and prepared to explain. Hawes waited.

"You said the heat wasn't working, didn't you?" Wollender said. "I was just checking it."

"The heat's working fine in this room," Hawes said. "It's the room next door."

"Oh." Wollender nodded. "Oh, is that it?"

"That's it, yes."

"No wonder. I stuck my hand up there to check the vent, and it seemed fine to me."

"Yes, it would be fine," Hawes said, "since there was never anything wrong with it. I told you at the desk this morning that the heat wasn't working in 104. This is 105. Are you new here, Mr. Wollender?"

"I guess I misunderstood you."

"Yes, I guess so. Misunderstanding isn't a wise practice, Mr. Wollender, especially with your local cops crawling all over the mountain."

"What are you talking about?"

"I'm talking about the girl. When those imitation cops begin asking questions, I suggest . . ."

"What girl?"

Hawes looked at Wollender for a long time. The question on Wollender's face and in his eyes looked genuine enough, but could there possibly be someone on the mountain who still had not heard of the murder? Was it possible that Wollender, who ran the inn, the center of all activity and gossip, did not know Helga Nilson was dead?

"The girl," Hawes said. "Helga Nilson."

"What about her?"

Hawes knew enough about baseball to realize you didn't throw your fast ball until you'd tried a few curves. "Do you know her?" he asked.

"Of course I know her. I know all the ski instructors. She rooms right here, down the hall."

"Who else rooms here?"

"Why?"

"I want to know."

"Just her and Maria," Wollender said. "Maria Fiers. She's an instructor, too. And, oh yes, the new man, Larry Davidson."

"Is he an instructor?" Hawes asked. "About this tall?"

"Yes."

"Hooked nose? German accent."

"No, no. You're thinking of Helmut Kurtz. And that's an Austrian accent." Wollender paused. "Why? Why do you want to . . . ?"

"Anything between him and Helga?"

"Why, no. Not that I know of. They teach together, but . . ."

"What about Davidson?"

"Larry Davidson?"

"Yes."

"Do you mean, is he dating Helga, or . . ."

"Yes, that's right."

"Larry's married," Wollender said, "I would hardly think . . ."

"What about you?"

"I don't understand."

"You and Helga. Anything?"

"Helga's a good friend of mine," Wollender said.

"Was," Hawes corrected.

"Huh?"

"She's dead. She was killed on the mountain this afternoon."

There was the fast ball, and it took Wollender smack between the eyes. "Dea—" he started, and then his jaw fell slack, and his eyes went blank. He staggered back a pace, colliding with the white dresser. The crutches dropped from his hands. He struggled to maintain his balance, the leg with the cast stiff and unwieldy; he seemed about to fall. Hawes grabbed at his elbow and pulled him erect. He stooped down for Wollender's crutches and handed them to him. Wollender was still dazed. He groped for the crutches, fumbled, dropped them again. Hawes picked them up a second time, and forced them under Wollender's arms. Wollender leaned back against the dresser. He kept staring at the wall opposite, where a poster advertising the pleasures of Kitzbühel was hanging.

"She . . . she took too many chances," he said. "She always went too fast. I told her . . ."

"This wasn't a skiing accident," Hawes said. "She was murdered."

"No." Wollender shook his head. "No."

"Yes."

"No. Everyone liked Helga. No one would . . ." He kept shaking his head. His eyes stayed riveted to the Kitzbühel poster.

"There are going to be cops here, Mr. Wollender," Hawes said. "You seem like a nice kid. When they start asking questions, you'd better have a more plausible story than the one you invented about being in my room. They're not going to fool around. They're looking for a killer."

"Why . . . why do you *think* I came here?" Wollender asked.

"I don't know. Maybe you were looking for some pocket money. Skiers often leave their wallets and their valu—"

"I'm not a thief, Mr. Hawes," Wollender said with dignity. "I only came here to give you some heat."

"That makes it even," Hawes answered. "The cops'll be coming here to give *you* some."

8.

He found the two loaders in the lodge cafeteria. The lifts had been closed at four-thirty, the area management having reached the conclusion that most skiing accidents took place in the waning hours of the afternoon, when poor visibility and physical exhaustion combined to create gentle havoc. They were both burly, grizzled men wearing Mackinaws, their thick hands curled around coffee mugs. They had been loading skiers onto chairs ever since the area was opened, and they worked well together as a team. Even their dialogue seemed concocted in one mind, though it issued from two mouths.

"My name's Jake," the first loader said. "This here is Obey, short for Obadiah."

"Only I ain't so short," Obadiah said.

"He's short on brains," Jake said and grinned. Obadiah returned the grin. "You're a cop, huh?"

"Yes," Hawes said. He had shown them his buzzer the moment he approached them. He had also told an outright lie, saying he was helping with the investigation of the case, having been sent up from the city because there was the possibility a known and wanted criminal had perpetrated the crime, confusing his own doubletalk as he wove a fantastic monologue which Jake and Obadiah seemed to accept.

"And you want to know who we loaded on them chairs, right? Same as Teddy wanted to know."

"Teddy?"

"Teddy Watt. The sheriff."

"Oh. Yes," Hawes said. "That's right."

"Whyn't you just ask *him*?" Obadiah said.

"Well, I have," Hawes lied. "But sometimes a fresh angle will come up if witnesses can be questioned directly, do you see?"

"Well, we ain't exactly witnesses," Jake said. "We didn't see her get killed, you know."

"Yes, but you did load her on the chair, didn't you?"

"That's right. We did, all right."

"And someone was in the chair with her, is that right?"

"That's right," Jake said.

"Who?" Hawes asked.

"Seems like everybody wants to know *who*," Jake said.

"Ain't it the damnedest thing?" Obadiah said.

"Do you remember?" Hawes asked.

"We remember it was snowing, that's for sure."

"Couldn't hardly see the chairs, it was snowing that hard."

"Pretty tough to reckernize one skier from another with all that wind and snow, wouldn't you say, Obey?"

"Next to impossible," Obadiah answered.

"But you did recognize Helga," Hawes suggested.

"Oh, sure. But she said hello to us, you see. She said, 'Hello, Jake. Hello, Obey.' And also, she took the chair closest to the loading platform, the inside chair. The guy took the other chair."

"Guy?" Hawes asked. "It was a man then? The person who took the chair next to her was a man?"

"Well, can't say for sure," Jake said. "Was a time when men's ski clothes was different from the ladies', but that don't hold true no more."

"Not by a long shot," Obadiah said.

"Nowadays, you find yourself following some pretty girl in purple pants, she turns out to be a man. It ain't so easy to tell them apart no more."

"Then you don't know whether the person who sat next to her was a man or a woman, is that right?" Hawes asked.

"That's right."

"Coulda been either."

"Did this person say anything?"

"Not a word."

"What was he wearing?"

"Well, we ain't established it was a *he*," Jake reminded him.

"Yes, I know. I meant the . . . the person who took the chair. It'll be easier if we give him a gender."

"Give him a *what*?"

"A gen— If we assume for the moment that the person was a man."

"Oh." Jake thought this over. "Okay, if you say so. Seems like pretty sloppy deduction to me, though."

"Well, I'm not actually making a deduction. I'm simply trying to facilitate . . ."

"Sure, I understand," Jake said. "But it's sure pretty sloppy."

Hawes sighed. "Well . . . what *was* he wearing?"

"Black," Jake said.

"Black ski pants, black parka," Obadiah said.

"Any hat?" Hawes asked.

"Nope. Hood on the parka was pulled clear up over the head. Sunglasses over the eyes."

"Gloves or mittens?" Hawes asked.

"Gloves. Black gloves."

"Did you notice whether or not there was an insignia on the man's parka?"

"What kind of insignia?"

"An R-M interlocked," Hawes said.

"Like the instructors wear?" Jake asked.

"Exactly."

"They wear it on their *right* sleeves," Obadiah said. "We told you this person took the outside chair. We couldn'ta seen the right sleeve, even if there *was* anything on it."

Hawes suddenly had a wild idea. He hesitated before he asked, and then thought *What the hell, try it.*

"This person," he said, "was he . . . was he carrying crutches?"

"Carrying *what*?" Jake asked incredulously.

"Crutches. Was his leg in a cast?"

"Now how in hell . . . of *course* not," Jake said. "He was wearing skis, and he was carrying ski poles. Crutches and a cast! My God! It's hard enough getting on that damn lift as it is. Can you just picture . . ."

"Never mind," Hawes said. "Forget it. Did this person say anything to Helga?"

"Not a word."

"Did she say anything to him?"

"Nothing we could hear. The wind was blowing pretty fierce."

"But you heard her when she said hello to you."

"That's right."

"Then if she'd said anything to this person, you might have heard that, too."

"That's right. We didn't hear nothing."

"You said he was carrying poles. Did you notice anything unusual about the poles?"

"Seemed like ordinary poles to me," Jake said.

"Did both poles have baskets?"

Jake shrugged. "I didn't notice. Did you notice, Obey?"

"Both seemed to have baskets," Obadiah said. "Who'd notice a thing like that?"

"Well, you might have," Hawes said. "If there'd been anything unusual, you might have noticed."

"I didn't notice nothing unusual," Obadiah said. "Except I thought to myself this feller must be pretty cold."

"Why?"

"Well, the hood pulled up over his head, and the scarf wrapped almost clear around his face."

"What scarf? You didn't mention that before."

"Sure. He was wearing a red scarf. Covered his mouth and his nose, reached right up to the sunglasses."

"Hmmm," Hawes said, and the table went still.

"You're the fellow dropped his poles on the way up, ain't you?" Jake asked.

"Yes."

"Thought I remembered you."

"If you remember *me*, how come you can't remember the person who took that chair alongside Helga's?"

"You saying I *should*, mister?"

"I'm only asking."

"Well, like maybe if I seen a guy wearing black pants and a black hood, and sunglasses, and a scarf wrapped clear around his face, why maybe then I would recognize him. But, the way I figure it, he ain't likely to be wearing the same clothes right now, is he?"

"I don't suppose so," Hawes said, sighing.

"Yeah, neither do I," Jake answered. "And I ain't even a cop."

9.

Dusk was settling upon the mountain.

It spread into the sky and stained the snow a purple-red. The storm was beginning to taper off, the clouds vanishing before the final triumphant breakthrough of the setting sun. There was an unimaginable hush to the mountain, and the town, and the valley beyond, a hush broken only by the sound of gently jingling skid-chains on hard-packed snow.

He had found Blanche and taken her to the fireplace in the inn, settling her there with a brace of double Scotches and a half-dozen copies of a skiing magazine. Now, with the mountain and the town still, the lifts inoperative, the distant mountain and the town still, the lifts inoperative, the distant snow brushed with dying color, he started climbing the mountain. He worked through the deep snow directly under the lift, the chairs hanging motionless over his head. He was wearing ski pants and after-ski boots designed for lounging beside a fire. He had forsaken his light parka for two sweaters. Before he'd left the room, he had unholstered the .38 and slipped it into the elastic-reinforced waistband of his trousers. He could feel it digging into his abdomen now as he climbed.

The climb was not an easy one.

The snow under the lift had not been packed, and he struggled against it as he climbed, encountering drifts which were impassable, working his way in a zigzagging manner across the lift line, sometimes being forced to leave the high snow for the cat-packed trail to the right of the lift. The light was waning. He did not know how much longer it would last. He had taken a flashlight from the glove compartment of his car, but he began to wonder whether its glow would illuminate very much once the sun had set. He began to wonder, too, exactly what he hoped to find. He was almost certain that any tracks the killer had left would already have been covered by the drifting snow. Again, he cursed Theodore Watt and his inefficient slobs. Someone should have made this climb immediately after they discovered the dead girl, while there was still a possibility of finding a trail.

He continued climbing. After a day of skiing, he was physically and mentally exhausted, his muscles protesting, his eyes burning. He thumbed on the flashlight as darkness climbed the mountain, and pushed his way through knee-deep snow. He stumbled and got to his feet again. The snow had tapered almost completely, but the wind had returned with early evening, a high keening wind that rushed through the tress on either side of the lift line, pushing the clouds from the sky. There was a thin sliver of moon and a scattering of stars. The clouds raced past them like silent dark horsemen, and everywhere on the mountain was the piercing shriek of the wind, a thin scream that penetrated to the marrow.

He fell again.

Loose snow caught under the neck of his sweater, slid down his back. He shivered and tried to brush it away, got to his feet, and doggedly began climbing again. His after-ski boots had not been designed for deep snow. The tops ended just above his ankles, offering no protection whatever. He realized abruptly that the boots were already packed with snow, that his feet were literally encased in snow. He was beginning to regret this whole foolhardy mission, when he saw it.

He had come perhaps a third of the way up the lift line, the mountain in absolute darkness now, still except for the maiden scream of the wind. The flashlight played a small circle of light on the snow ahead of him as he stumbled upward, the climb more difficult now, the clouds rushing by overhead, skirting the thin moon. The light touched something which glinted momentarily, passed on as he continued climbing, stopped. He swung the flashlight back. Whatever had glinted was no longer there. Swearing, he swung the flashlight in a slow steady arc. The glint again. He swung the light back.

The basket was half-covered by the snow. Only one edge of its metallic ring showed in the beam of his light. It had probably been covered completely earlier in the day, but the strong fresh wind had exposed it to view again, and he stooped quickly to pick it up, almost as if he were afraid it would vanish. He was still bending, studying the basket in the light of the flash, when the man jumped onto his back.

The attack came suddenly and swiftly. He had heard nothing but the wind. He had been so occupied with his find, so intent on studying the basket which, he was certain, had come from the end of the ski-pole weapon, that when he felt the sudden weight on his back he did not connect it immediately with an attack. He was simply surprised, and his first thought was that one of the pines had dropped a heavy load of snow from its laden branches, and then he realized this was no heavy load of snow, but by that time he was flat on his belly.

He rolled over instantly. He held the ski pole basket in his left hand, refusing to let go of it. In his right hand, he held the flashlight, and he swung that instantly at the man's head, felt it hitting the man's forearm instead. Something solid struck Hawes' shoulder; a wrench? a hammer? and he realized at once that the man was armed, and suddenly the situation became serious. He threw away the flashlight and groped for the .38 in his waistband.

The clouds cleared the moon. The figure kneeling over him, straddling him, was wearing a black parka, the hood pulled up over his head. A red scarf was wrapped over his chin and his mouth and his nose. He was holding a hammer in his right hand, and he raised the hammer over his head just as the moon disappeared again. Hawes' fingers closed on the butt of the .38. The hammer descended.

It descended in darkness, striking Hawes on his cheek, ripping the flesh, glancing downward and catching his shoulder. Hawes swore violently, drew the .38 in a ridiculously clumsy draw, brought it into firing position, and felt again the driving blow of the other man's weapon, the hammer lashing out of the darkness, slamming with brute force against his wrist, almost cracking the bone. His fingers opened involuntarily. The gun dropped into the snow. He bellowed in pain and tried to kick out at his attacker, but the man moved away quickly, gained his feet, and braced himself in the deep snow for the final assault. The moon appeared again. A thin silvery light put the man in silhouette against the sky, the black hooded head, the face masked by the scarf. The hammer went up over his head.

Hawes kicked out at his groin.

The blow did nothing to stop the man's attack. It glanced off his thigh, missing target as the hammer came down, but throwing him off balance slightly so that the hammer struck without real force. Hawes threw a fist at him, and the man grunted and again the hammer came out of the new darkness. The man fought desperately and silently, frightening Hawes with the fury of his animal strength. They rolled over in the snow, and Hawes grasped at the hood, tried to pull it from the man's head, found it was securely tied in place, and reached for the scarf. The scarf began to unravel. The man lashed out with the hammer, felt the scarf coming free, pulled back to avoid exposing his face, and suddenly staggered as Hawes' fist struck home. He fell into the snow, and all at once, he panicked. Instead of attacking again, he pulled the scarf around his face and began to half run, half stumble through the deep snow. Hawes leaped at him, missing, his hands grabbing air. The man scrambled over the snow, heading for the pines lining the lift. By the time Hawes was on his feet again, the man had gone into the trees. Hawes went after him. It was dark under the trees. The world went black and silent under the pines.

He hesitated for a moment. He could see nothing, could hear nothing. He fully expected the hammer to come lashing out of the darkness.

Instead, there came the voice.

"Hold it right there."

The voice started him, but he reacted intuitively, whirling, his fist pulling back reflexively, and then firing into the darkness. He felt it connecting with solid flesh, heard someone swearing in the dark, and then—surprisingly, shockingly—Hawes heard the sound of a pistol shot. It rang on the mountain air, reverberated under the pines. Hawes opened his eyes wide. A pistol? But the man had only a hammer. Why hadn't . . . ?

"Next time, I go for your heart," the voice said.

Hawes stared into the darkness. He could no longer locate the voice. He did not know where to jump, and the man was holding a pistol.

"You finished?" the man asked.

The beam of a flashlight suddenly stabbed through the darkness. Hawes blinked his eyes against it, tried to shield his face.

"Well, well," the man said. "You never can tell, can you? Stick out your hands."

"What?" Hawes said.

"Stick out your goddamn hands."

Hesitantly, he held out his hands. He was the most surprised human being in the world when he felt the handcuffs being snapped onto his wrists.

10.

The office from which Theodore Watt, sheriff of the town of Rawson, operated was on the main street alongside an Italian restaurant whose neon sign advertised LASAGNA * SPAGHETTI * RAVIOLI. Now that the snow had stopped, the plows had come through and banked snow on either side of the road so that the door of the office was partially hidden by a natural fortress of white. Inside the office, Theodore Watt was partially hidden by the fortress of his desk, the top of which was covered with Wanted circulars, FBI flyers, carbon copies of police reports, a pair of manacles, a cardboard container of coffee, a half-dozen chewed pencil stubs, and a framed picture of his wife and three children. Theodore Watt was not in a very friendly mood. He sat behind his desk-fortress, a frown on his face. Cotton Hawes stood before the desk, still wearing the handcuffs which had been clamped onto his wrists on the mountain. The deputy who'd made the collar, the self-same Fred who had earlier pulled the ski pole from Helga Nilson's chest, stood alongside Hawes, wearing the sheriff's frown, and also wearing a mouse under his left eye, where Hawes had hit him.

"I could lock you up, you know," Watt said, frowning. "You hit one of my deputies."

"You ought to lock *him* up," Hawes said angrily. "If he hadn't come along, I might have had our man."

"You might have, huh?"

"Yes."

"You had no right being on that damn mountain," Watt said. "What were you doing up there?"

"Looking."

"For what?"

"Anything. He gave you the basket I found. Apparently it was important enough for the killer to have wanted it, too. He fought hard enough for it. Look at my cheek."

"Well now, that's a shame," Watt said drily.

"There may be fingerprints on that basket," Hawes said. "I suggest . . ."

"I doubt it. Weren't none on the ski pole, and none on the chair, neither. We talked to the two loaders, and they told us the one riding up with Helga Nilson was wearing gloves. I doubt if there's any fingerprints on that basket at all."

"Well . . ." Hawes said, and he shrugged.

"What it amounts to, hmmmm," Watt said, "is that you figured we wasn't handling this case to your satisfaction, ain't that it? So you figured you'd give us local hicks a little big-time help, hmmmm? Ain't that about it?"

"I thought I could possibly assist in some . . ."

"Then you shoulda come to me," Watt said, "and *asked* if you could help. This way, you only fouled up what we was trying to do."

"I don't understand."

"I've got six men on that mountain," Watt said, "waiting for whoever killed that girl to come back and cover his mistakes. This basket here was one of the mistakes. But did our killer find it? No. Our helpful big-city detective found it. You're a lot of help, mister, you sure are. With all that ruckus on the mountain, that damn killer won't go anywhere near it for a month!"

"I almost had him," Hawes said. "I was going after him when your man stopped me."

"Stopped you, hell! *You're* the one who was stopping *him* from doing his job. Maybe I *ought* to lock you up. There's a thing known as impeding the progress of an investigation. But, of course, you know all about that, don't you? Being a big-city detective. Hmmm?"

"I'm sorry if I . . ."

"And of course we're just a bunch of local hicks who don't know nothing at all about police work. Why, we wouldn't even know enough to have an autopsy performed on that little girl, now would we? Or to have tests made of the blood on that chair, now would we? We wouldn't have no crime lab in the next biggest town to Rawson, would we?"

"The way you were handling the investigation . . ." Hawes started.

". . . was none of your damn business," Watt concluded. "Maybe we like to make our own mistakes, Hawes! But naturally, you city cops never make mistakes. That's why there ain't no crime at all where you come from."

"Look," Hawes said, "you were mishandling evidence. I don't give a damn what you . . ."

"As it turns out, it don't matter because there wasn't no fingerprints on that pole, anyway. And we had to get our men up the mountain, so we had to use the lift. There was a hell of a lot of confusion there today, mister. But I don't suppose big-city cops ever get confused, hmmmm?" Watt looked at him sourly. "Take the cuffs off him, Fred," he said.

Fred looked surprised, but he unlocked the handcuffs. "He hit me right in the eye," he said to Watt.

"Well, you still got the other eye," Watt said drily. "Go to bed, Hawes. We had enough of you for one night."

"What did the autopsy report say?" Hawes asked.

Watt looked at him in something close to astonishment. "You still sticking your nose in this?"

"I'd still like to help, yes."

"Maybe we don't need your help."

"Maybe you can use it. No one here knows . . ."

"There we go with the damn big-city attitu—"

"I was going to say," Hawes said, overriding Watt's voice, "that no one in the area knows I'm a cop. That could be helpful to you."

Watt was silent. "Maybe," he said at last.

"*May* I hear the autopsy report?"

Watt was silent again. Then he nodded. He picked up a sheet of paper from his desk and said, "Death caused by fatal stab wound of the heart, penetration of the auricles and pulmonary artery. That's where all the blood came from, Hawes. Wounds of the ventricles don't usually bleed that much. Coroner figures the girl died in maybe two or three minutes, there was that much loss of blood."

"Anything else?"

"Broke her ankle when she fell out of that chair. Oblique fracture of the lateral malleolus. Examiner also found traces of human skin under the girl's fingernails. Seems like she clawed out at whoever stabbed her, and took a goodly part of him away with her."

"What did the skin tell you?"

"Not a hell of a lot. Our killer is white and adult."

"That's all?"

"That's all. At least, that's all from the skin, except the possibility of using it later for comparison tests—if we ever get anybody to compare it with. We found traces of blood on her fingers and nails, too, not her own."

"How do you know?"

"Blood on the chair, the girl's blood, was in the AB grouping. Blood we found on her hands was in the O grouping, most likely the killer's."

"Then she scratched him enough to cause bleeding."

"She took a big chunk of skin from him, Hawes."

"From the face?"

"Now how in hell would I know?"

"I thought maybe . . ."

"Couldn't tell from the skin sample whether it came from the neck or the face or wherever. She coulda scratched him anyplace."

"Anything else?"

"We found a trail of the girl's blood in the snow under the lift. Plenty of it, believe me, she bled like a stuck pig. The trail started about four minutes from the top. Took her two or three minutes to die. So, assuming the killer jumped from the chair right soon's he stabbed her, then the girl . . ."

". . . was still alive when he jumped."

"That's right."

"Find any tracks in the snow?"

"Nothing. Too many drifts. We don't know whether he jumped with his skis on or not. Have to have been a pretty good skier to attempt that, we figure."

"Well, anyway, he's got a scratch," Hawes said. "That's *something* to look for."

"You gonna start looking tonight?" Watt asked sarcastically.

11.

Blanche Colby was waiting for him when he got back to the room. She was sitting up in his bed propped against the pillows, wearing a shapeless flannel nightgown which covered her from her throat to her ankles. She was holding an apple in her hand, and she bit into it angrily as he entered the room, and then went back to reading the open book in her lap.

"Hi," he said.

She did not answer him, nor did she even look up at him. She continued destroying the apple, continued her pretense of reading.

"Good book?"

"*Excellent* book," she answered.

"Miss me?"

"Drop dead," Blanche said.

"I'm sorry. I . . ."

"Don't be. I enjoyed myself immensely in your absence."

"I got arrested, you see."

"You got *what*?"

"Arrested. Pinched. Pulled in. Collared. Apprehen—"

"I understood you the first time. Who arrested you?"

"The cops," Hawes said, and he shrugged.

"Serves you right." She put down the book. "Wasn't it you who told me a girl was killed on this mountain today? Murdered? And you run off and leave me when a killer . . ."

"I told you where I was going. I told you . . ."

"You said you'd be back in an hour!"

"Yes, but I didn't know I was going to be arrested."

"What happened to your cheek?"

"I got hit with a hammer."

"Good," Blanche said, and she nodded emphatically.

"Aren't you going to kiss my wound?" Hawes asked.

"*You* can kiss my . . ."

"Ah-ah," he cautioned.

"I sat by that damn fireplace until eleven o'clock. Then I came up here and . . . what time is it, anyway?"

"After midnight."

Blanche nodded again. "I would have packed up and gone home, believe me, if the roads were open."

"Yes, but they're closed."

"Yes, damn it!"

"Aren't you glad I'm back?"

Blanche shrugged. "I couldn't care less. I was just about to go to sleep."

"In here?"

"In the other room, naturally."

"Honey, honey . . ."

"Yes, honey-honey?" she mimicked. "*What*, honey-honey baby?"

Hawes grinned. "That's a very lovely nightgown. My grandmother used to wear a nightgown like that."

"I thought you'd like it," Blanche said sourly. "I put it on especially for you."

"I always liked the touch of flannel," he said.

"Get your big hands . . ." she started, and moved away from him swiftly. Folding her arms across the front of her gown, she sat in the center of the bed and stared at the opposite wall. Hawes studied her for a moment, took off his sweaters, and then began unbuttoning his shirt.

"If you're going to undress," Blanche said evenly, "you could at least have the modesty to go into the . . ."

"Shhh!" Hawes said sharply. His hands had stopped on the buttons of his shirt. He cocked his head to one side now and listened. Blanche, watching him, frowned.

"What . . . ?"

"Shhh!" he said again, and again he listened attentively. The room was silent. Into the silence came the sound.

"Do you hear it?" he asked.

"Do I hear what?"

"Listen."

They listened together. The sound was unmistakable, faint and faraway, but unmistakable.

"It's the same buzzing I heard last night," Hawes said. "I'll be right back."

"Where are you going?"

"Downstairs. To the ski shop," he answered, and swiftly left the room. As he went down the corridor toward the steps, a door at the opposite end of the hall opened. A young girl wearing a quilted robe over her pajamas, her hair done in curlers, came into the hallway carrying a towel and a toothbrush. She smiled at Hawes and then walked past him. He heard the bathroom door locking behind her as he went down the steps.

The lights were on in the ski shop. The buzzing sound came from somewhere in the shop, intermittent, hanging on the silent night air, ceasing abruptly, beginning again. He walked silently over the snow, stopping just outside the door to the shop. He put his ear to the wood and listened, but the only sound he heard was the buzzing. He debated kicking in the door. Instead, he knocked gently.

"Yes?" a voice from inside called.

"Could you open up, please?" Hawes said.

He waited. He could hear the heavy sound of ski boots approaching the locked door. The door opened a crack. A sun-tanned face appeared in the opening. He recognized the face at once—Helmut Kurtz, the ski instructor who had helped him the night before, the man he'd seen today on the mountain just before he'd got on the chair lift.

"Oh, hello there," Hawes said.

"Yes? What is it?" Kurtz asked.

"Mind if I come in?"

"I'm sorry, no one is allowed in the shop. The shop is closed."

"Yes, but *you're* in it, aren't you?"

"I'm an instructor," Kurtz said. "We are permitted . . ."

"I just saw a light," Hawes said, "and I felt like talking to someone."

"Well . . ."

"What are you doing, anyway?" Hawes asked casually, and casually he wedged one shoulder against the door and gently eased it open, casually pushing it into the room, casually squeezing his way into the opening, casually shouldering his way past Kurtz, and then squinting past the naked hanging light bulb to the work bench at the far end of the room, trying to locate the source of the buzzing sound which filled the shop.

"You are really not allowed . . ." Kurtz started, but Hawes was already halfway across the room, moving toward the other small area of light where a green-shaded bulb hung over the work bench. The buzzing sound was louder, the sound of an old machine, the sound of . . .

He located it almost at once. A grinding wheel was set up on one end of the bench. The wheel was still spinning. He looked at it, nodded and then flicked the switch to turn it off. Turning to Kurtz, he smiled and said, "Were you sharpening something?"

"Yes, those skates," Kurtz said. He pointed to a pair of white figure skates on the bench.

"Yours?" Hawes asked.

Kurtz smiled. "No. Those are women's skates."

"Whose?"

"Well, I don't think that is any of your business, do you?" Kurtz asked politely.

"I suppose not," Hawes answered gently, still smiling. "Were you in here sharpening something last night, too, Mr. Kurtz?"

"I beg your pardon?"

"I said, were you . . ."

"No, I was not." Kurtz walked up to the bench and studied Hawes slowly and deliberately. "Who *are* you?" he asked.

"My name's Cotton Hawes."

"How do you do? Mr. Hawes, I'm sorry to have to be so abrupt, but you are really not allowed . . ."

"Yes, I know. Only instructors are allowed in here, isn't that right, Mr. Kurtz?"

"After closing, yes. We sometimes come in to make minor repairs on our skis or . . ."

"Or sharpen up some things, huh, Mr. Kurtz?"

"Yes. Like the skates."

"Yes," Hawes repeated. "Like the skates. But you weren't in here last night, were you, Mr. Kurtz?"

"No, I was not."

"Because, you see, I heard what could have been the sound of a file or a rasp or something, and then the sound of this grinding wheel. So you're sure you weren't in here sharpening something? Like skates? Or . . ." Hawes shrugged. "A ski pole?"

"A ski pole? Why would anyone . . . ?" Kurtz fell suddenly silent. He studied Hawes again. "What are you?" he asked. "A policeman?"

"Why? Don't you like policemen?"

"I had nothing to do with Helga's death," Kurtz said immediately.

"No one said you did."

"You implied it."

"I implied nothing, Mr. Kurtz."

"You asked if I were sharpening a ski pole last night. The implication is . . ."

"But you weren't."

"No, I was *not*!" Kurtz said angrily.

"What *were* you sharpening last night?"

"Nothing. I was nowhere near this shop last night."

"Ahh, but you were, Mr. Kurtz. I met you outside, remember? You were coming down the steps. Very fast. Don't you remember?"

"That was earlier in the evening."

"But I didn't say anything about time, Mr. Kurtz. I didn't ask you *when* you were in this shop."

"I was *not* in this shop! Not at any time!"

"But you just said 'That was earlier in the evening.' Earlier than what, Mr. Kurtz?"

Kurtz was silent for a moment. Then he said, "Earlier than . . . than whoever was here."

"You saw someone here?"

"I . . . I saw a light burning."

"When? What time?"

"I don't remember. I went to the bar after I met you . . . and I had a few drinks, and then I went for a walk. That was when I saw the light."

"Where do you room, Mr. Kurtz?"

"In the main building."

"Did you see Helga at any time last night?"

"No."

"Not at any time?"

"No."

"Then what were you doing upstairs?"

"I came to get Maria's skates. Those." He pointed to the figure skates on the bench.

"Maria who?"

"Maria Fiers."

"Is she a small girl with dark hair?"

"Yes. Do you know her?"

"I think I just saw her in the hallway," Hawes said. "So you came to get her skates, and then you went for a drink, and then you went for a walk. What time was that?"

"It must have been after midnight."

"And a light was burning in the ski shop?"

"Yes."

"But you didn't see who was in here?"

"No, I did not."

"How well did you know Helga?"

"Very well. We taught together."

"How well is very well?"

"We were good friends."

"How good, Mr. Kurtz?"

"I *told* you!"

"Were you sleeping with her?"

"How dare you . . ."

"Okay, okay." Hawes pointed to the skates. "These are Maria's, you said?"

"Yes. She's an instructor here, too. But she skates well, almost as well as she skis."

"Are you good friends with her, too, Mr. Kurtz?"

"I am good friends with *everyone*!" Kurtz said angrily. "I am normally a friendly person." He paused. "*Are* you a policeman?"

"Yes. I am."

"I don't like policemen," Kurtz said, his voice low. "I didn't like them in Vienna, where they wore swastikas on their arms, and I don't like them here, either. I had nothing to do with Helga's death."

"Do you have a key to this shop, Mr. Kurtz?"

"Yes. We *all* do. We make our own minor repairs. During the day, there are too many people here. At night, we can . . ."

"What do you mean by *all*? The instructors?"

"Yes."

"I see. Then any of the instructors could have . . ."

The scream was a sentient thing which invaded the room suddenly and startlingly. It came from somewhere upstairs, ripping down through the ancient floor boards and the ancient ceiling timbers. It struck the room with its blunt force, and both men looked up toward the ceiling, speechless, waiting. The scream came again. Hawes got to his feet and ran for the door. *"Blanche,"* he whispered, and slammed the door behind him.

She was standing in the corridor outside the hall bathroom, not really standing, but leaning limply against the wall, her supporting dancer's legs robbed of stance, robbed of control. She wore the long flannel nightgown with a robe over it, and she leaned against the wall with her eyes shut tight, her blond hair disarrayed, the scream unvoiced now, but frozen in the set of her face and the trembling openness of her mouth. Hawes came stamping up the steps and turned abruptly right, and stopped stock still when he saw her, an interruption of movement for only a fraction of a second, the turn, the stop, and then a forward motion again which carried him to her in four headlong strides.

"What is it?" he said.

She could not answer. She clung to the wall with the flat palms of her hands, her eyes still squeezed shut tightly, the scream frozen in her throat and blocking articulation. She shook her head.

"Blanche, what is it?"

She shook her head again, and then pulled one hand from the wall, as if afraid that by doing so she would lose her grip and tumble to the floor. The hand rose limply. It did not point, it only indicated, and that in the vaguest manner, as if it too were dazed.

"The bathroom?" he asked.

She nodded. He turned from her. The bathroom door was partly open. He opened it the rest of the way, rushing into the room, and then stopping instantly, as if he had run into a stone wall.

Maria Fiers was inside her clothing and outside of it. The killer had caught her either dressing or undressing, had caught her in what she supposed was privacy, so that one leg was in the trousers of her pajamas and the other lay twisted beneath her body, naked. Her pajama top had ridden up over one delicately curved breast, perhaps as she fell, perhaps as she struggled. Even her hair seemed in a state of uncertain transition, some of it held firmly in place by curlers, the rest hanging in haphazard abandon, the loose curlers scattered on the bathroom floor. The hook latch on the inside of the door had been ripped from the jamb when the door was forced. The water in the sink was still running. The girl lay still and dead in her invaded privacy, partially clothed, partially disrobed, surprise and terror wedded in the death mask of her face. A towel was twisted about her throat. It had been twisted there with tremendous force, biting into the skin with such power that it remained twisted there now, the flesh torn and overlapping it in places, the coarse cloth almost embedded into her neck and throat. Her tongue protruded from her mouth. She was bleeding from her nose where her face had struck the bathroom tile in falling.

He backed out of the room.

He found a pay telephone in the main building, and from there he called Theodore Watt.

12.

Blanche sat on the edge of the bed in room 105, shivering inside her gown, her robe, and a blanket which had been thrown over her shoulders. Theodore Watt leaned disjointedly against the dresser, puffed on his cigar, and said, "Now you want to tell me exactly what happened, Miss Colby?"

Blanche sat shivering and hunched, her face pale. She searched for her voice, seemed unable to find it, shook her head, nodded, cleared her throat, and seemed surprised that she could speak. "I . . . I was alone. Cotton had gone down to see what . . . what the noise was."

"What noise, Hawes?" Watt asked.

"A grinding wheel," he answered. "Downstairs in the ski shop. I heard it last night, too."

"Did you find who was running the wheel?"

"Tonight, it was a guy named Helmut Kurtz. He's an instructor here, too. Claims he was nowhere near the shop last night. But he did see a light burning after midnight."

"Where's he now?"

"I don't know. Sheriff, he was with me when the girl was killed. He couldn't possibly have . . ."

Watt ignored him and walked to the door. He opened

it, and leaned into the corridor. "Fred," he said, "find me Helmut Kurtz, an instructor here."

"I got that other guy from down the hall," Fred answered.

"I'll be right with him. Tell him to wait."

"What other guy?" Hawes asked.

"Instructor in 102. Larry Davidson." Watt shook his head. "Place is crawling with goddamn instructors, excuse me, miss. Wonder there's any room for guests." He shook his head again. "You said you were alone, Miss Colby."

"Yes. And I . . . I thought I heard something down the hall . . . like . . . I didn't know what. A loud sudden noise."

"Probably the bathroom door being kicked in," Watt said. "Go on."

"And then I . . . I heard a girl's voice saying, 'Get out of here! Do you hear me? Get out of here!' And . . . and then it was quiet, and I heard someone running down the hall and down the steps, so I . . . I thought I ought to . . . to look."

"Yes, go on."

"I went down the . . . the hallway and looked down the steps, but I didn't see anyone. And then, when I . . . when I was starting back for the room, I . . . I heard the water running in the bathroom. The . . . the door was open, so I . . . Oh Jesus, do I *have* to?"

"You found the girl, is that right?"

"Yes," Blanche said, her voice very low.

"And then you screamed."

"Yes."

"And then Hawes came upstairs, is that right?"

"Yes," Hawes said. "And I called you from the main building."

"Um-huh," Watt said. He went to the door and opened it. "Want to come in here, Mr. Davidson?" he asked.

Larry Davidson came into the room hesitantly. He was a tall man, and he stooped as he came through the doorway, giving an impression of even greater height, as if he had to stoop to avoid the top of the door frame. He was wearing dark trousers and a plaid woolen sports shirt. His hair was clipped close to his scalp. His blue eyes were alert, if not wary.

"Guess you know what this is all about, huh, Mr. Davidson?" Watt asked.

"Yes, I think so," Davidson answered.

"You don't mind answering a few questions, do you?"

"No. I'll . . . I'll answer anything you . . ."

"Fine. Were you in your room all night, Mr. Davidson?"

"Not all night, no. I was up at the main building part of the time."

"Doing what?"

"Well, I . . ."

"Yes, Mr. Davidson, what were you doing?"

"I . . . I was fencing. Look, I didn't have anything to do with this."

"You were *what*, Mr. Davidson?"

"Fencing. We've got some foils and masks up there, and I . . . I was fooling around. Look, I *know* Helga was stabbed, but . . ."

"What time did you get back here, Mr. Davidson?"

"About . . . about ten-thirty, eleven."

"And you've been in your room since then?"

"Yes."

"What did you do when you got back here?"

"I wrote a letter to my wife, and then I went to sleep."

"What time did you go to sleep?"

"About midnight."

"Did you hear any loud noise in the hall?"

"No."

"Did you hear any voices?"

"No."

"Did you hear Miss Colby when she screamed?"

"No."

"Why not?"

"I guess I was asleep."

"You sleep in your clothes, Mr. Davidson?"

"What? Oh. Oh, no. Your fellow . . . your deputy said I could put on some clothes."

"What *were* you sleeping in?"

"My pajamas. Listen, I barely knew those girls. I only joined the school here two weeks ago. I mean, I knew them to talk to, but that's all. And the fencing is just a coincidence. I mean, we always fool around with the foils. I mean, ever since I came here, somebody's been up there fooling around with . . ."

"How many times did you scream, Miss Colby?" Watt asked.

"I don't remember," Blanche said.

"She screamed twice," Hawes said.

"Where were you when you heard the screams, Hawes?"

"Downstairs. In the ski shop."

"But you were in your room, right down the hall, Mr. Davidson, and you didn't hear anything, hmmm? Maybe you were too busy . . ."

And suddenly Davidson began crying. His face twisted into a grimace, and the tears began flowing, and he said, "I didn't have anything to do with this, I swear. Please, I didn't have anything to do with it. Please, I'm married, my wife's in the city expecting a baby, I *need* this job, I didn't even *look* at those girls, I swear to God, what do you want me to do? Please, please."

The room was silent except for his sobbing.

"I swear to God," he said softly. "I swear to God. I'm a heavy sleeper. I'm very tired at night. I swear. Please. I didn't do it. I only knew them to say hello. I didn't hear anything. Please. Believe me. Please. I *have* to keep this job. It's the only thing I know, skiing. I can't get involved in this. Please."

He lowered his head, trying to hide the tears that streamed down his face, his shoulders heaving, the deep sobs starting deep inside him and reverberating through his entire body.

"Please," he said.

For the first time since the whole thing had started, Watt turned to Hawes and asked his advice.

"What do you think?" he said.

"I'm a heavy sleeper, too," Hawes said. "You could blow up the building, and I wouldn't hear it."

13.

On Sunday morning, the church bells rang out over the valley.

They started in the town of Rawson, and they rang sharp and clear on the mountain air, drifting over the snow and down the valley. He went to the window and pulled up the shade, and listened to the sound of the bells, and remembered his own youth and the Reverend Jeremiah Hawes who had been his father, and the sound of Sunday church bells, and the rolling, sonorous voice of his father delivering the sermon. There had always been logic in his father's sermons. Hawes had not come away from his childhood background with any abiding religious fervor—but he had come away with a great respect for logic. "To be believed," his father had told him, "it must be reasonable. And to be reasonable, it must be logical. You could do worse than remembering that, Cotton."

There did not seem to be much logic in the killing of Helga Nilson and Maria Fiers, unless there was logic in wanton brutality. He tried to piece together the facts as he looked out over the peaceful valley and listened to the steady tolling of the bells. Behind him, Blanche was curled in sleep, gently breathing, her arms wrapped around the pillow. He did not want to wake her yet, not after what she'd been through last night. So far as he was concerned, the weekend was over; he could not ski with pleasure anymore, not this weekend. He wanted nothing more than to get away from Rawson Mountain, no, that wasn't quite true. He wanted to find the killer. That was what he wanted more than anything else. Not because he was being paid for the job, not because he wanted to prove to Theodore Watt that maybe big-city detectives *did* have a little something on the ball—but only because the double murders filled him with a sense of outrage.

He could still remember the animal strength of the man who'd attacked him on the mountain, and the thought of that power directed against two helpless young girls angered Hawes beyond all reason.

Why? he asked himself.

Where is the logic?

There was none. No logic in the choice of the victims, and no logic in the choice of the scene. Why would anyone have chosen to kill Helga in broad daylight, on a chair suspended anywhere from six to thirty feet above the ground, using a ski pole as a weapon? A ski pole sharpened to a deadly point, Hawes reminded himself, don't forget that. This thing didn't just happen, this was no spur-of-the-moment impulse, this was planned and premeditated, a pure and simple Murder One. Somebody had been in that ski shop the night before the first murder, using a file and then a grinding wheel, sharpening that damn pole, making certain its end could penetrate a heavy ski parka, *and* a ski sweater, *and* a heart.

Then there must have been logic to the choice of locale, Hawes thought. Whoever killed Helga had at least planned far enough ahead to have prepared a weapon the night before. And admitting the existence of a plan, then logic could be presupposed, and it could further be assumed that killing her on the chair lift was a *part* of the plan—perhaps a very necessary part of it.

Yes, that's logic, he thought—*except that it's illogical.*

Behind him, Blanche stirred. He turned to look at her briefly, remembering the horror on her face last night, contrasting it now with her features relaxed in sleep. She had told the story to Watt three times, had told him again and again how she'd found the dead girl.

Maria Fiers, twenty-one years old, brunette, a native of Montpelier, Vermont. She had begun skiing when she was six years old, had won the women's slalom four times running, had been an instructor since she was seventeen. She skated, too, and had been on her high school swimming team, an all-around athlete, a nice girl with a gentle manner and a pleasant smile—dead.

Why?

She lived in the room next door to Helga's, had known Helga for close to a year. She had been nowhere near the chair lift on the day Helga was killed. In fact, she had been teaching a beginner's class near the T-Bar, a good distance from the chair lift. She could not have seen Helga's murder, nor Helga's murderer.

But someone had killed her nonetheless.

And if there were a plan, and if there were supposed logic to the plan, and if killing Helga on a chair halfway up the mountain was part of that logic, then the death of Maria Fiers was also a part of it.

But how?

The hell with it, Hawes thought. I can't think straight anymore. I want to crack this so badly that I can't think straight, and that makes me worse than useless. So the thing to do is to get out of here, wake Blanche and tell her to dress and pack, and then pay my bill and get out, back to the city, back to the 87TH where death comes more frequently perhaps, and just as brutally—but not as a surprise. I'll leave this to Theodore Watt, the sheriff who wants to make his own mistakes. I'll leave it to him and his nimble-fingered deputies, and maybe they'll bust it wide open, or maybe they won't, but it's too much for me, I can't think straight anymore.

He went to the bed and woke Blanche, and then he walked over to the main building, anxious to pay his bill and get on his way. Someone was at the piano, practicing scales. Hawes walked past the piano and the fireplace and around the corner to Wollender's office. He knocked on the door, and waited. There was a slight hesitation on the other side of the door, and then Wollender said, "Yes, come in," and Hawes turned the knob.

Everything looked exactly the way it had looked when Hawes checked in on Friday night, an eternity ago. Wollender was sitting behind his desk, a man in his late twenties with dark hair and dark brows pulled low over deep brown eyes. He was wearing a white shirt open at the throat, a bold reindeer-imprinted sweater over it. The plaster cast was still on his right leg, the leg stretched out stiffly in front of him, the foot resting on a low ottoman. Everything looked exactly the same.

"I want to pay my bill," Hawes said. "We're checking out."

He stood just inside the door, some fifteen feet from the desk. Wollender's crutches leaned against the wall near the door. There was a smile on Wollender's face as he said, "Certainly," and then opened the bottom drawer of the desk and took out his register and carefully made out a bill. Hawes walked to the desk, added the bill, and then wrote a check. As he waved it in the air to dry the ink, he said, "What *were* you doing in my room yesterday, Mr. Wollender?"

"Checking the heat," Wollender said.

Hawes nodded. "Here's your check. Will you mark this bill 'Paid,' please?"

"Be happy to," Wollender said. He stamped the bill and handed it back to Hawes. For a moment, Hawes had the oddest feeling that something was wrong. The knowledge pushed itself into his mind in the form of an absurd caption: WHAT'S WRONG WITH THIS PICTURE? He looked at Wollender, at his hair, and his eyes, and his white shirt, and his reindeer sweater, and his extended leg, and the cast on it, and the ottoman. Something was different. This was not the room, not the picture as it had been on Friday night. WHAT'S WRONG WITH THIS PICTURE? he thought, and he did not know.

He took the bill. "Thanks," he said. "Have you heard any news about the roads?"

"They're open all the way to the Thruway. You shouldn't have any trouble."

"Thanks," Hawes said. He hesitated, staring at Wollender. "My room's right over the ski shop, you know," he said.

"Yes, I know that."

"Do you have a key to the shop, Mr. Wollender?"

Wollender shook his head. "No. The shop is privately owned. It doesn't belong to the hotel. I believe the proprietor allows the ski instructors to . . ."

"But then, you're a locksmith, aren't you?"

"What?"

"Isn't that what you told me when I checked in? You said you were a locksmith out of season, didn't you?"

"Oh. Oh, yes. Yes, I did." Wollender shifted uneasily in the chair, trying to make his leg comfortable. Hawes looked at the leg again, and then he thought, Damn it, what's wrong?

"Maybe you went to my room to listen, Mr. Wollender. Is that possible?"

"Listen to what?"

"To the sounds coming from the ski shop below," Hawes said.

"Are the sounds that interesting?"

"In the middle of the night, they are. You can hear all sorts of things in the middle of the night. I'm just beginning to remember all the things I heard."

"Oh? What did you hear?"

"I heard the oil burner clicking, and the toilet flushing, and the Cats going up the mountain, and someone arguing down the hall, and somebody filing and grinding in the ski shop." He was speaking to Wollender, but not really speaking to him. He was, instead, remembering those midnight voices raised in anger, and remembering that it was only later he had heard the noises in the shop, and gone to the window, and seen the light burning below. And then a curious thing happened. Instead of calling him "Mr. Wollender," he suddenly called him "Elmer."

"Elmer," he said, "something's just occurred to me."

Elmer. And with the word, something new came into the room. With the word, he was suddenly transported back to the interrogation room at the 87TH, where common thieves and criminals were called by their first names, Charlie, and Harry, and Martin, and Joe, and where this familiarity somehow put them on the defensive, somehow rattled them and made them know their questioners weren't playing games.

"Elmer," he said, leaning over the desk, "it's just occurred to me that since Maria couldn't have *seen* anything on the mountain, maybe she was killed because she *heard* something. And maybe what she heard was the same arguing I heard. Only *her* room is right next door to Helga's. And maybe she knew *who* was arguing." He hesitated. "That's pretty logical, don't you think, Elmer?"

"I suppose so," Wollender said pleasantly. "But if you know who killed Maria, why don't you go to . . ."

"I don't know, Elmer. Do *you* know?"

"I'm sorry. I don't."

"Yeah, neither do I, Elmer. All I have is a feeling."

"And what's the feeling?" Wollender asked.

"That you came to my room to listen, Elmer. To find out how much *I* had heard the night before Helga was murdered. And maybe you decided I heard too damn much, and maybe that's why I was attacked on the mountain yesterday."

"Please, Mr. Hawes," Wollender said, and a faint superior smile touched his mouth, and his hand opened limply to indicate the leg in the cast.

"Sure, sure," Hawes said. "How could I have been attacked by a man with his leg in a cast, a man who can't get around without crutches? Sure, Elmer. Don't think that hasn't been bugg—" He stopped dead. "Your crutches," he said.

"What?"

"Your crutches! Where the hell are they?"

For just an instant, the color went out of Wollender's face. Then, quite calmly, he said, "Right over there. Behind you."

Hawes turned and looked at the crutches, leaning against the wall near the door.

"Fifteen feet from your desk," he said. "I thought you couldn't walk without them."

"I . . . I used the furniture to . . . to get to the desk. I . . ."

"You're lying, Elmer," Hawes said, and he reached across the desk and pulled Wollender out of the chair.

"My leg!" Wollender shouted.

"Your leg, my ass! How long have you been walking

on it, Elmer? Was that why you killed her on the mountain? So that . . ."

"I didn't kill anybody!"

". . . so that you'd have a perfect alibi? A man with his leg in a cast couldn't possibly ride a lift or jump from it, could he? Unless he'd been in and out of that cast for God knows how long!"

"My leg is broken! I can't walk!"

"Can you *kill*, Elmer?"

"I didn't kill her!"

"Did Maria hear you arguing, Elmer?"

"No. No . . ."

"Then why'd you go after her?"

"I didn't!" He tried to pull away from Hawes. "You're crazy. You're hurting my leg! Let go of . . ."

"*I'm* crazy? You son of a bitch, *I'm* crazy? You stuck a ski pole in one girl and twisted a towel around . . ."

"I didn't, I didn't!"

"We found the basket from your pole!" Hawes shouted.

"What basket? I don't know what . . ."

"Your fingerprints are all over it!" he lied.

"You're crazy," Wollender said. "How could I get on the lift? I can't walk. I broke the leg in two places. One of the bones came right through the skin. I couldn't get on a lift if I wanted . . ."

"The skin," Hawes said.

"What?"

"The skin!" There was a wild look in his eyes now. He pulled Wollender closer to him and yelled, "Where'd she scratch you?"

"What?"

He seized the front of Wollender's shirt with both hands, and then ripped it open. "Where's the cut, Elmer? On your chest? On your neck?"

Wollender struggled to get away from him, but Hawes had his head captured in both huge hands now. He twisted Wollender's face viciously, forced his head forward, pulled back the shirt collar.

"Let go of me!" Wollender screamed.

"What's this, Elmer?" His fingers grasped the adhesive bandage on the back of Wollender's neck. Angrily, he tore it loose. A healing cut, two inches long and smeared with iodine, ran diagonally from a spot just below Wollender's hairline.

"I did that myself," Wollender said. "I bumped into . . ."

"Helga did it," Hawes said. "When you stabbed her! The sheriff's got the skin, Elmer. It was under her fingernails."

"No," Wollender said. He shook his head.

The room was suddenly very still. Both men were exhausted. Hawes kept clinging to the front of Wollender's shirt, breathing hard, waiting. Wollender kept shaking his head.

"You want to tell me?"

Wollender shook his head.

"How long have you been walking?"

Wollender shook his head again.

"Why'd you keep your leg in the cast?"

Again, Wollender shook his head.

"You killed two young girls!" Hawes bellowed. He was surprised to find himself trembling. His hand tightened on the shirt front, the knuckles showing white through his skin. Perhaps Wollender felt the sudden tension, perhaps Wollender knew that in the next instant Hawes would throttle him.

"All right," he said. His voice was very low. "All right."

"Why'd you keep wearing the cast?"

"So . . . so . . . so she wouldn't know. So she would think I . . . I was . . . was unable to walk. And that way, I could . . . could watch her. Without her knowing."

"Watch who?"

"Helga. She . . . She was my girl, you see. I . . . I loved her, you see."

"Yeah, you loved her enough to kill her," Hawes said.

"That's *not* why I . . ." He shook his head. "It was because of Kurtz. She kept denying it, but I knew about them. And I warned her. You have to believe that I warned her. And I . . . I kept the cast on my leg to . . . to fool her."

"When did it come off?" Hawes asked.

"Last week. The . . . the doctor took it off right in this room. He did a bivalve, with an electric saw, cut it right down the side. And . . . and when he was gone, I . . . . I figured I could put the two halves together again, and . . . and . . . hold it in place with . . . with tape. That way, I could watch her. Without her knowing I could get around."

"And what did you see?"

"You *know* what I saw!"

"Tell me."

"Friday night, she . . . I . . . I saw Kurtz leaving the annex. I knew he'd been with her."

"He was there to pick up Maria's skates," Hawes said. "To sharpen them."

"No!" Wollender shouted, and for a moment there was force in his voice, a vocal explosion, fury and power, and Hawes remembered again the brute strength of Wollender's attack on the mountain. Wollender's voice died again. "No," he said softly, "you're mistaken. He was with Helga. I know. Do you think I'd have killed her if . . ." His voice caught. His eyes suddenly misted. He turned his head, not looking at Hawes, staring across the room, the tears solidifying his eyes. "When I went up to her room, I warned her," he said, his voice low. "I told her I had seen him, seen him with my own eyes, and she . . . she said I was imagining things. And she laughed." His face went suddenly tight. "She laughed, you see. She . . . she shouldn't have laughed." His eyes filled with tears, had a curiously opaque look. "She shouldn't have laughed," he said again. "It wasn't funny. I loved her. It wasn't funny."

"No," Hawes said wearily. "It wasn't funny at all."

14.

The storm was over.

The storm which had started suddenly and filled the air with fury was gone. The wind had died after scattering the clouds from the sky. They drove in the warm comfort of the convertible, the sky a clear blue ahead of them, the snow banked on either side of the road.

The storm was over.

There were only the remains of its fury now, the hard-packed snow beneath the automobile, and the snow lining the roads, and the snow hanging in the branches of the trees. But now it was over and done, and now there was only the damage to count, and the repairs to be made.

He sat silently behind the wheel of the car, a big redheaded man who drove effortlessly. His anger was gone, too, like the anger of the storm. There was only a vast sadness inside him.

"Cotton?" Blanche said.

"Mmmm?" He did not take his eyes from the road. He watched the winding white ribbon and listened to the crunch of snow beneath his heavy-duty tires, and over that the sound of her voice.

"Cotton," she said, "I'm very glad to be with you."

"I am, too."

"In spite of everything," she said, "I'm very, very glad."

He did a curious thing then. He suddenly took his right hand from the wheel and put it on her thigh, and squeezed her gently. He thought he did it because Blanche was a very attractive girl with whom he had just shared a moment of communication.

But perhaps he touched her because death had suddenly shouldered its way into that automobile, and he had remembered again the two young girls who had been Wollender's victims.

Perhaps he touched her thigh, soft and warm, only as a reaffirmation of life.

Dead on the Pin

JOHN D. MacDONALD

My name is Joe Desmon, and I'm manager of the Wonderland Bowling Alley on the turnpike three miles out of town. I've held the job ever since I got back from Vietnam. The hours are long, but I'm not kicking. I've got a little stashed away and I'm getting the experience, and someday I'm going to have my own layout and hire some stupid guy to keep the crazy hours I keep.

The town needs more alleys, and so the leagues are stacked. The way it is now, they've got me working twenty-six hours a day during the season. All the time I'm yapping at the waitresses or calming down some clown full of beer or ducking the big looping passes made by the members of the Industrial Girls' League. That in addition to paying all the bills, keeping track of the cash, running the snacks and beer business, seeing that the equipment stays in shape, renting shoes, and giving lessons.

So it seemed like almost too much to expect when one day about three months ago this little guy showed up and asked if I could hire him to do jobs around the place. Said his name was Johnson. He was edging close to fifty, with the top of his head up to about my chin. He was the sort of little man you would push out of your way, but not if you looked close. There were hard, blunt bones in his face and a pair of pale-blue expressionless eyes and a tight slit for a mouth. He had a thick look through the shoulders, and his arms hung almost down to his knees, with big square wrists.

He was well dressed, and I figured he'd be out of my salary range. I asked him how much he had to make and he said, "Whatever you can give me, kid."

"How about seventy-five a week, and I'm not kid. I'm Mr. Desmon."

"That'll be fine, Mr. Desmon. Just dandy."

"For that dough you brush down the alleys whenever they're clear, mop the floors, empty the ashtrays, check the equipment, and scrub the restrooms. And anything else I can think up."

He said mildly, "I'd like a chance to bowl a little, too."

I took a quick look at his right thumb. It had that swollen, bent-back look of a man who has done a lot of it. But I didn't see any calluses. His hands looked pink and soft.

I wasn't behind and it was a slack hour. I said, "How about a quick one?"

I had my own ball and shoes behind the counter. He picked a pair of shoes out of the rental rack and spent at least five long minutes finding a ball to suit him.

With my double and spare in the first three frames and his two splits and a miss, I felt pretty arrogant. When I got my strike in the fourth, it made my fill on the third frame a fat 69 to his 27. I started to get bored, but in his fourth frame, his ball ducked into the pocket for one of the prettiest cleanest strikes I have ever seen. His ball had been curving in too fast before that, giving him those thin Brooklyn hits.

And so while I got spare, strike, spare, he got three more of those boomers, where all the pins jumped into the pit in unison.

He looked at me and said, "Mr. Desmon, do you fire people you can't beat?"

"What do you think I am? No. And I'm not beat yet."

"Just asking, ki—Mr. Desmon."

So he kept chucking them in there, and in the end he had put eight strikes in a row together, and he wiped me out, 235 to 202.

So I said, "Okay. And I think you could keep right on wiping me out. You're not fired."

He grinned for the first time. It came and went so quickly I almost missed it. He wanted to know if he could practice a little when his work was done. I told him to be my guest.

I kept an eye on him. He did his work and got along well enough with the rest of my people. He got along by staying out of the way. After the first month I began to throw some lessons his way, giving him a cut. He had perfect style, laying the ball down so smoothly it wouldn't have dented the top of a custard pie. He could pick up the flaws and point them out and demonstrate how to cure them. He eased the pressure on me, but I never did really get to know the man.

When he bowled, it was either alone or with me, just before we closed the joint in the small hours. I began to keep a pocket score on him.

As he was leaving one night I said, "Hey, Johnson. Wait a minute."

He turned around. "What?"

"In the last ten games you've rolled, you've averaged two-twenty-one."

"So?"

"So I'd like to wangle you a spot on one of the pro leagues. You're as steady as a rock. How about it? I know an outfit that could use a new anchor man."

He walked slowly back toward me. For one funny moment he was the boss and I was a stooge working for him. He said, "Drop the idea, Desmon. I don't like it."

"But why? I should think it would please you."

"Just say that I don't like to bowl with people. Maybe I blow up under pressure. Put it any way you want, but don't go talking up my game. Understand?"

I almost said, Yes, sir.

He walked off into the night. I shrugged and went back to the books.

All of that should have been a tip-off. I should have gotten wise, maybe, the night Billy Carr came in. Billy has the sort of reputation that makes me wish I had the nerve to tell him not to come back. He's young and tall and sleek, somehow like a big cat. He had two of his boys with him. He's considered locally to be a pretty heavy stud. Anyway, the three of them came in, got shoes, shucked off their coats, and changed shoes down at the semicircular bench, ready to do some bowling.

Johnson was walking down the alley pushing the wide brush, wearing the lamb's wool mitts over his shoes.

I was too far away to stop it. Billy Carr grabbed a ball off the rack and rolled it down at Johnson. Johnson heard it coming. He looked around and sidestepped it, but it hit the brush and knocked it out of his hands.

He turned and walked slowly back up the middle of the alley toward where Billy stood laughing.

Between laughs, Billy said, "Did I scare you, pop?"

"You scared me plenty," Johnson said mildly. He grabbed the front of Billy's shirt and tossed him into the rack. Billy tumbled over it and landed on his shoulders. One of the hired boys reached for a sap as he moved in on Johnson. Johnson caught his wrist, ripped the sap out of his hand, and belted him flush across the mouth with it. The hired boy sat down and began to spit out teeth.

The other hired boy was reaching. "I wouldn't!" Johnson said in a low voice. And the boy didn't.

Their sole remaining gesture of defiance was to throw the shoes at me as they went out.

I said to Johnson, "That wasn't smart. They might give you a bad time outside."

He gave me a look of surprise. "Those three? Grow up, ki—Mr. Desmon."

They didn't bother Johnson, and they didn't come back.

Last week I woke up and there was a man sitting on a chair beside my bed. I shut my eyes hard, and when I opened them again he was still there.

"Good morning, Joe," he said.

"How did you get in here? What do you want? Is this a gag?"

He handed me a picture. A double picture. Full face and profile. With numbers. "Know this man?"

"Johnson. He works for me."

"Not exactly Johnson. Dan Brankel is a better name. Wanted in five western states for armed robbery and murder. Rumored to be a onetime associate and business partner of Al Nussbaum. Did some work with the King gang. That was a long time ago. He skipped the country with a fat bankroll. He's been where we couldn't touch him. By we, I mean the FBI. A while back we got a tip that he had moved. Since then we've been waiting for him to show up. We've been checking bowling alleys. That was his passion in the old days. So with your help, Joe . . ."

I was a wreck all day. I tried to charge people for more games than they'd rolled. I cussed out the waitresses, and one of my best ones quit on me. I even broke down and drank some of my own beer during business hours.

While the leagues were on, I was worse. No matter how tightly I held on to the edge of the desk, my hands still shook.

But I couldn't hold the clock back. The diehards finally pulled out, the last of them, at quarter to two. I said to Johnson, "Game tonight?" I barely managed to keep the quiver out of my voice.

He nodded and went to get his ball and shoes. Somehow he'd managed to buy them out of his pay. When he came back, I said, "Back in a minute. Got to check the doors."

Just the two of us were left in the place. I went to the

side door, slammed it hard, then opened it silently and put the little wedge in it to hold it open.

The light controls were near my desk. I killed everything except the small light over the desk and the lights on the one alley we would use. My heart was swinging from my tonsils.

Johnson popped his thumb out of the hole on the ball, lined his sights, and swung a sweet ball down the alley. It made a low drone as it rolled. Then it hooked into the pocket, and the pins went down with a single smash.

The rack crashed down and I took my first ball. Even though I had used a lot of chalk, my hands were still greasy with sweat. The ball slipped, hung on the edge all the way down, and plinked off the ten pin.

Johnson said mildly, "Getting the hard one first?"

I laughed too loud and too long and stopped too abruptly. I got eight more on my second ball and Johnson marked the miss.

A nightmare game. I didn't dare turn around. I was afraid I'd see one of the men slipping silently in, and my face would give me away. Johnson was bowling like a machine. I piled up misses and splits, and I even threw one gutter ball. Each ball he rolled was just right. Once in the sixth frame one pin wavered and threatened to stay up, but finally it went down.

We had never talked much while bowling. I had to bite my tongue to keep from babbling to him. It might have made him suspicious.

It didn't hit me between the eyes until he marked up his eighth straight strike. And suddenly I realized, that if he kept on, I might see the first perfect game I have ever seen. It was a little bit easier then to forget the figures silently closing in.

He put in the ninth strike and the tenth. I had a miss on the ninth, for a score to that point of one-twenty-one. Worst game of the past three years.

After the tenth strike he said softly, "You know, this might be it. I never had one of those fat three-hundred games before. I've always wanted one."

"Don't jinx yourself talking about it," I said.

Dead on the Pin

He put the eleventh ball in the pocket for a clean strike. "One more," he said. The ball was trundling back up the rails when I saw the little flurry of movement down near the pin setter. That was my signal.

I said, as nonchalantly as I could, "Wait a second. Got to get cigarettes."

As I turned and walked up the stairs he took his ball off the rack, walked slowly back, and chalked his fingers, pulling the towel through them.

I ran the last few steps to the desk, wiped my hand across the light panel, turning on every light in the place.

They had crept up in the darkness. They were in a half circle around him. He looked very small and old and tired standing down there.

"Okay, Dan," one of them said. "End of the line. All out. Put the ball down slowly and lie on the floor, your arms spread."

A dozen weapons were pointed at him.

In a weary voice he said, "You win. Let me heave this last ball down the alley."

Before he could get an answer, he moved over and turned to face the pins. From the angle where I stood, higher than the others, I saw his left hand flick from his belt up to his mouth. He swallowed something.

He stood for a long second, then started his stride. Halfway to the foul line his smooth stride wavered. The ball thumped hard, bounced, and he went down on his face across the foul line.

He was a dead man when he hit the floor. Even I knew that. I dimly heard the hoarse shout of anger and disappointment.

But I had my eyes on the ball. It rolled with pathetic slowness. It wavered in toward the head pin, hit the head pin on the left side. The pins toppled slowly, all but the six pin. It stood without a waver. A pin rolled slowly across the alley, nudged the rebel, and tumbled it off into the pit.

As though I was walking in my sleep, I went back down the stairs, took the black crayon, marked in the last strike, and drew the 300, making the zeros fat and bold.

I knew he was a crook. I knew he was cruel and lawless. They told me about the way he shot the Nevada bank clerk in the stomach. But I also know that he was a homesick guy who came back to the only thing he liked to do and scrubbed out lavatories for the privilege of doing it.

Maybe there's something wrong with me.

Because I don't think I'm ever going to like the game as much as I used to.

The Affair of the "Avalanche Bicycle and Tyre Co., Limited"

ARTHUR MORRISON

I.

Cycle companies were in the market everywhere. Immense fortunes were being made in a few days and sometimes little fortunes were being lost to build them up. Mining shares were dull for a season, and any company with the word "cycle" or "tyre" in its title was certain to attract capital, no matter what its prospects were like in the eyes of the expert. All the old private cycle companies suddenly were offered to the public, and their proprietors, already rich men, built themselves houses on the Riviera, bought yachts, ran racehorses, and left business for ever. Sometimes the shareholders got their money's worth, sometimes more, sometimes less—sometimes they got nothing but total loss; but still the game went on. One could never open a newspaper without finding, displayed at large, the prospectus of yet another cycle company with capital expressed in six figures at least, often in seven. Solemn old dailies, into whose editorial heads no new thing ever found its way till years after it had been forgotten elsewhere, suddenly exhibited the scandalous phenomenon of "broken columns" in their advertising sections, and the universal prospectuses stretched outrageously across half or even all the page—a thing to cause apoplexy in the bodily system of any self-respecting manager of the old school.

In the midst of this excitement it chanced that the firm of Dorrington & Hicks were engaged upon an investigation for the famous and long-established "Indestructible Bicycle and Tricycle Manufacturing Company," of London and Coventry. The matter was not one of sufficient intricacy or difficulty to engage Dorrington's personal attention, and it was given to an assistant. There was some doubt as to the validity of a certain patent having reference to a particular method of tightening the spokes and truing the wheels of a bicycle, and Dorrington's assistant had to make inquiries (without attracting attention to the matter) as to whether or not there existed any evidence, either documentary or in the memory of veterans, of the use of this method, or anything like it, before the year 1885. The assistant completed his inquiries and made his report to Dorrington. Now I think I have said that, from every evidence I have seen, the chief matter of Dorrington's solicitude was his own interest, and just at this time he had heard, as had others, much of the money being made in cycle companies. Also, like others, he had conceived a great desire to get the confidential advice of somebody "in the know"—advice which might lead him into the "good thing" desired by all the greedy who flutter about at the outside edge of the stock and share market. For this reason Dorrington determined to make this small matter of the wheel patent an affair of personal report. He was a man of infinite resource, plausibility and good-companionship, and there was money going in the cycle trade. Why then should he lose an opportunity of making himself pleasant in the inner groves of that trade, and catch whatever might come his way—information, syndicate shares, directorships, anything? So that Dorrington made himself master of his assistant's information, and proceeded to the head office of the "Indestructible" company on Holborn Viaduct, resolved to become the entertaining acquaintance of the managing director.

On his way his attention was attracted by a very elaborately fitted cycle shop, which his recollection told him was new. "The Avalanche Bicycle and Tyre Company" was the legend gilt above the great plate-glass window, and in the window itself stood many brilliantly enamelled and plated bicycles, each labelled on the frame with the flaming red and gold transfer of the firm; and in the midst of all was another bicycle covered with dried mud, of which, however, sufficient had been carefully cleared away to expose a similar glaring transfer to those that decorated the rest—with a placard announcing that on this particular machine somebody had ridden some incredible distance on bad roads in very little more than no time at all. A crowd stood about the window and gaped respectfully at the placard, the bicycles, the transfers, and the mud, though they paid little attention to certain piles of folded white papers, endorsed in bold letters with the name of the company, with the suffix "limited" and the word "prospectus" in bloated black letters below. These, however, Dorrington observed at once, for he had himself that morning, in common with several thousand other people, received one by post. Also half a page of his morning paper had been filled with a copy of that same prospectus, and the afternoon had brought another copy in the evening paper. In the list of directors there was a titled name or two, together with a few unknown names—doubtless the "practical men." And below this list there were such positive promises of tremendous dividends, backed up and proved beyond dispute by such ingenious piles of businesslike figures, every line of figures referring to some other line for testimonials to its perfect genuineness and accuracy, that any reasonable man, it would seem, must instantly sell the hat off his head and the boots off his feet to buy one share at least, and so make his fortune for ever. True, the business was but lately established, but that was just it. It had rushed ahead with such amazing rapidity (as was natural with an avalanche) that it had got altogether out of hand, and orders couldn't be executed at all; wherefore the proprietors were reluctantly compelled to let the public have some of the luck. This was Thursday. The share list was to be opened on Monday morning and closed inexorably at four o'clock on Tuesday afternoon, with a merciful extension to Wednesday morning for the candidates for wealth who were so unfortunate as to live in the country. So that it behoved everybody to waste no time lest he be numbered among the unlucky whose subscription-money should be returned in full, failing allotment. The prospectus did not absolutely say it in so many words, but no rational person could fail to feel that the directors were fervently hoping that nobody would get injured in the rush.

Dorrington passed on and reached the well-known establishment of the "Indestructible Bicycle Company." This was already a limited company of a private sort, and had been so for ten years or more. And before that the concern had had eight or nine years of prosperous experience. The founder of the firm, Mr. Paul Mallows, was now the managing director, and a great pillar of the cycling industry. Dorrington gave a clerk his card, and asked to see Mr. Mallows.

Mr. Mallows was out, it seemed, but Mr. Stedman, the secretary, was in, and him Dorrington saw. Mr. Stedman was a pleasant, youngish man, who had been a famous amateur bicyclist in his time, and was still an enthusiast. In ten minutes business was settled and dismissed, and Dorrington's tact had brought the secretary into a pleasant discursive chat, with much exchange of anecdote. Dorrington expressed much interest in the subject of bicycling, and, seeing that Stedman had been a racing man, particularly as to bicycling races.

"There'll be a rare good race on Saturday, I expect," Stedman said. "Or rather," he went on, "I expect the fifty miles record will go. I fancy our man Gillett is pretty safe to win, but he'll have to move, and I quite expect to see a good set of new records on our advertisements next week. The next best man is Lant—the next fellow, you know—who rides for the 'Avalanche' people."

"Let's see, they're going to the public as a limited company, aren't they?" Dorrington asked casually.

Stedman nodded, with a little grimace.

"You don't think it's a good thing, perhaps," Dorrington said, noticing the grimace. "Is that so?"

"Well," Stedman answered, "of course I can't say. I don't know much about the firm—nobody does, as far as I can tell—but they seem to have got a business together in almost no time; that is, if the business is as genuine as it looks at first sight. But they want a rare lot of capital, and then the prospectus—well, I've seen more satisfactory ones, you know. I don't say it isn't all right, of course, but still I shan't go out of my way to recommend any friends of mine to plunge on it."

"You won't?"

"No, I won't. Though no doubt they'll get their capital, or most of it. Almost any cycle or tyre company can get subscribed just now. And this 'Avalanche' affair is both, and it is well advertised, you know. Lant has been winning on their mounts just lately, and they've been booming it for all they're worth. By jove, if they could only screw him up to win the fifty miles on Saturday, and beat our man Gillett, that *would* give them a push! Just at the correct moment too. Gillett's never been beaten yet at the distance, you know. But Lant can't do it—though, as I have said, he'll make some fast riding—it'll be a race, I tell you."

"I should like to see it."

"Why not come? See about it, will you? And perhaps you'd like to run down to the track after dinner this evening and see our man training—awfully interesting, I can tell you, with all the pacing machinery and that. Will you come?"

Dorrington expressed himself delighted, and suggested that Stedman should dine with him before going to the track. Stedman, for his part, charmed with his new acquaintance—as everybody was at a first meeting with Dorrington—assented gladly.

At that moment the door of Stedman's room was pushed open and a well-dressed, middle-aged man, with a shaven, flabby face, appeared. "I beg pardon," he said, "I thought you were alone. I've just ripped my finger against the handle of my brougham door as I came in— the screw sticks out. Have you a piece of sticking plaster?" He extended a bleeding finger as he spoke. Stedman looked doubtfully at his desk.

"Here is some court plaster," Dorrington exclaimed, producing his pocket-book. "I always carry it—it's handier than ordinary sticking plaster. How much do you want?"

"Thanks—an inch or so."

"This is Mr. Dorrington, of Messrs. Dorrington & Hicks, Mr. Mallows," Stedman said. "Our managing director, Mr. Paul Mallows, Mr. Dorrington."

Dorrington was delighted to make Mr. Mallows' acquaintance, and he busied himself with a careful strapping of the damaged finger. Mr. Mallows had the large frame of a man of strong build who had had much hard bodily work, but there hung about it the heavier, softer flesh that told of a later period of ease and sloth. "Ah, Mr. Mallows," Stedman said, "the bicycle's the safest thing, after all! Dangerous things these broughams!"

"Ah, you younger men," Mr. Mallows replied, with a slow and rounded enunciation, "you younger men can afford to be active. We elders—"

"Can afford a brougham," Dorrington added, before the managing director began the next word. "Just so— and the bicycle does it all; wonderful thing the bicycle!"

Dorrington had not misjudged his man, and the oblique reference to his wealth flattered Mr. Mallows. Dorrington went once more through his report as to the spoke patent, and then Mr. Mallows bade him good-bye.

"Good day, Mr. Dorrington, good day," he said. "I

am extremely obliged by your careful personal attention to this matter of the patent. We may leave it with Mr. Stedman now, I think. Good day. I hope soon to have the pleasure of meeting you again." And with clumsy stateliness Mr. Mallows vanished.

2.

"So you don't think the 'Avalanche' good business as an investment?" Dorrington said once more as he and Stedman, after an excellent dinner, were cabbing it to the track.

"No, no," Stedman answered, "don't touch it! There's better things than that coming along presently. Perhaps I shall be able to put you in for something, you know, a bit later; but don't be in a hurry. As to the 'Avalanche,' even if everything else were satisfactory, there's too much 'booming' being done just now to please me. All sorts of rumours, you know, of their having something 'up their sleeve,' and so on; mysterious hints in the papers, and all that, as to something revolutionary being in hand with the 'Avalanche' people. Perhaps there is. But why they don't fetch it out in view of the public subscription for shares is more than I can understand, unless they don't want too much of a rush. And as to that, well they don't look like modestly shrinking from anything of that sort up to the present."

They were at the track soon after seven o'clock, but Gillett was not yet riding. Dorrington remarked that Gillett appeared to begin late.

"Well," Stedman explained, "he's one of those fellows that afternoon training doesn't seem to suit, unless it is a bit of walking exercise. He just does a few miles in the morning and a spurt or two, and then he comes on just before sunset for a fast ten or fifteen miles—that is, when he is getting fit for such a race as Saturday's. Tonight will be his last spin of that length before Saturday, because tomorrow will be the day before the race. Tomorrow he'll only go a spurt or two, and rest most of the day."

They strolled about inside the track, the two highly "banked" ends whereof seemed to a near-sighted person in the centre to be solid erect walls, along the face of which the training riders skimmed, fly-fashion. Only three or four persons beside themselves were in the enclosure when they first came, but in ten minutes' time Mr. Paul Mallows came across the track.

"Why," said Stedman to Dorrington, "here's the Governor! It isn't often he comes down here. But I expect he's anxious to see how Gillett's going, in view of Saturday."

"Good evening, Mr. Mallows," said Dorrington. "I hope the finger's all right? Want any more plaster?"

"Good evening, good evening," responded Mr. Mallows heavily. "Thank you, the finger's not troubling me a bit." He held it up, still decorated by the black plaster. "Your plaster remains, you see—I was a little careful not to fray it too much in washing, that was all." And Mr. Mallows sat down on a light iron garden chair (of which several stood here and there in the enclosure) and began to watch the riding.

The track was clear, and dusk was approaching when at last the great Gillett made his appearance on the track. He answered a friendly question or two put to him by Mallows and Stedman, and then, giving his coat to his trainer, swung off along the track on his bicycle, led in front by a tandem and closely attended by a triplet. In fifty yards his pace quickened, and he settled down into a swift even pace, regular as clockwork. Sometimes the tandem and sometimes the triplet went to the front, but Gillett neither checked nor heeded as, nursed by his pacers, who were directed by the trainer from the centre, he swept along mile after mile, each mile in but a few seconds over the two minutes.

"Look at the action!" exclaimed Stedman with enthusiasm. "Just watch him. Not an ounce of power wasted there! Did you ever see more regular ankle work? And did anybody ever sit a machine quite so well as that? Show me a movement anywhere above the hips!"

"Avalanche Bicycle and Tyre Co., Ltd."

"Ah," said Mr. Mallows, "Gillett has a wonderful style—a wonderful style, really!"

The men in the enclosure wandered about here and there on the grass, watching Gillett's riding as one watched the performance of a great piece of art—which, indeed, was what Gillett's riding was. There were, besides Mallows, Stedman, Dorrington and the trainer, two officials of the Cyclists' Union, an amateur racing man named Sparks, the track superintendent and another man. The sky grew darker, and gloom fell about the track. The machines became invisible, and little could be seen of the riders across the ground but the row of rhythmically working legs and the white cap that Gillett wore. The trainer had just told Stedman that there would be three fast laps and then his man would come off the track.

"Well, Mr. Stedman," said Mr. Mallows, "I think we shall be all right for Saturday."

"Rather!" answered Stedman confidently. "Gillett's going great guns, and steady as a watch!"

The pace now suddenly increased. The tandem shot once more to the front, the triplet hung on the rider's flank, and the group of swishing wheels flew round the track at a "one-fifty" gait. The spectators turned about, following the riders round the track with their eyes. And then, swinging into the straight from the top end, the tandem checked suddenly and gave a little jump. Gillett crashed into it from behind, and the triplet, failing to clear, wavered and swung, and crashed over and along the track too. All three machines and six men were involved in one complicated smash.

Everybody rushed across the grass, the trainer first. Then the cause of the disaster was seen. Lying on its side on the track, with men and bicycles piled over and against it, was one of the green painted light iron garden chairs that had been standing in the enclosure. The triplet men were struggling to their feet, and though much cut and shaken, seemed the least hurt of the lot. One of the men of the tandem was insensible, and Gillett, who from his position had got all the worst of it, lay senseless too, badly cut and bruised, and his left arm was broken.

The trainer was cursing and tearing his hair. "If I knew who'd done this," Stedman cried, "I'd *pulp* him with that chair!"

"Oh, that betting, that betting!" wailed Mr. Mallows, hopping about distractedly; "see what it leads people into doing! It can't have been an accident, can it?"

"Accident? Skittles! A man doesn't put a chair on a track in the dark and leave it there by accident. Is anybody getting away there from the outside of the track?"

"No, there's nobody. He wouldn't wait till this; he'd clear off a minute ago and more. Here, Fielders! Shut the outer gate, and we'll see who's about."

But there seemed to be no suspicious character. Indeed, except for the ground-man, his boy, Gillett's trainer, and a racing man, who had just finished dressing in the pavilion, there seemed to be nobody about beyond those whom everybody had seen standing in the enclosure. But there had been ample time for anybody, standing unnoticed at the outer rails, to get across the track in the dark, just after the riders had passed, place the obstruction, and escape before the completion of the lap.

The damaged men were helped or carried into the pavilion, and the damaged machines were dragged after them. "I will give fifty pounds gladly—more, a hundred," said Mr. Mallows, excitedly, "to anybody who will find out who put the chair on the track. It might have ended in murder. Some wretched bookmaker, I suppose, who has taken to many bets on Gillett. As I've said a thousand times, betting is the curse of all sport nowadays."

"The governor excites himself a great deal about betting and bookmakers,' Stedman said to Dorrington, as they walked towards the pavilion, "but, between you and me, I believe some of the 'Avalanche' people are in this. The betting bee is always in Mallows' bonnet, but as a matter of fact there's very little betting at all on cycle races, and what there is is little more than a matter of half-crowns or at most half-sovereigns on the day of the race. No bookmaker ever makes a heavy book first. Still there *may* be something in it this time, of course. But look at the 'Avalanche' people. With Gillett away their man can certainly win on Saturday, and if only the weather keeps fair he can almost as certainly beat the record; just at present the fifty miles is fairly easy, and it's bound to go soon. Indeed, our intention was that Gillett should pull it down on Saturday. He was a safe winner, bar accidents, and it was good odds on his altering the record, if the weather were any good at all. With Gillett out of it Lant is just about as certain a winner as our man would be if all were well. And there would be a boom for the 'Avalanche' company, on the very eve of the share subscription! Lant, you must know, was very second-rate till this season, but he has improved wonderfully in the last month or two, since he has been with the 'Avalanche' people. Let him win, and they can point to the machine as responsible for it all. 'Here,' they will say in effect, 'is a man who could rarely get in front, even in second-class company, till he rode an "Avalanche." Now he eats the world's record for fifty miles on it, and makes rings round the topmost professionals!' Why, it will be worth thousands of capital to them. Of course the subscription of capital won't hurt us, but the loss of the record may, and to have Gillett knocked out like this in the middle of the season is serious."

"Yes, I suppose with you it is more than a matter of this one race."

"Of course. And so it will be with the 'Avalanche' company. Don't you see, with Gillett probably useless for the rest of the season, Lant will have it all his own way at anything over ten miles. That'll help to boom up the shares and there'll be big profit made on trading in them. Oh, I tell you this thing seems pretty suspicious to me."

"Look here," said Dorrington, "can you borrow a light for me, and let me run over with it to the spot where the smash took place? The people have cleared into the pavilion and I could go alone."

"Certainly. Will you have a try for the governor's hundred?"

"Well, perhaps. But anyway there's no harm in doing you a good turn if I can, while I'm here. Some day perhaps you'll do me one."

"Right you are—I'll ask Fielders, the ground-man."

A lantern was brought, and Dorrington betook himself to the spot where the iron chair still lay, while Stedman joined the rest of the crowd in the pavilion.

Dorrington minutely examined the grass within two yards of the place where the chair lay, and then, crossing the track and getting over the rails, did the same with the damp gravel that paved the outer ring. The track itself was of cement, and unimpressionable by footmarks, but nevertheless he scrutinized that with equal care, as well as the rails. Then he turned his attention to the chair. It was, as I have said, a light chair made of flat iron strip, bent to shape and riveted. It had seen good service, and its present coat of green paint was evidently far from being its original one. Also it was rusty in places, and parts had been repaired and strengthened with crosspieces secured by bolts and square nuts, some rusty and loose. It was from the back at the top, that Dorrington secured some object—it might have been a hair—which he carefully transferred to his pocketbook. This done, with one more glance round, he betook himself to the pavilion.

A surgeon had arrived, and he reported well of the chief patient. It was a simple fracture, and a healthy subject. When Dorrington entered, preparations were beginning for setting the limb. There was a sofa in the pavilion, and the surgeon saw no reason for removing the patient till all was made secure.

"Found anything?" asked Stedman in a low tone of Dorrington.

Dorrington shook his head. "Not much," he answered at a whisper, "I'll think it over later."

Dorrington asked one of the Cyclists' Union officials for the loan of a pencil and, having made a note with it, immediately, in another part of the room, asked Sparks, the amateur, to lend him another.

Stedman had told Mr. Mallows of Dorrington's late

employment with the lantern, and the managing director now said quietly, "You remember what I said about rewarding anybody who discovered the perpetrator of this outrage, Mr. Dorrington? Well, I was excited at the time, but I quite hold to it. It is a shameful thing. You have been looking about the grounds, I hear. I hope you have come across something that will enable you to find something out. Nothing will please me more than to have to pay you, I'm sure."

"Well," Dorrington confessed, "I'm afraid I haven't seen anything very big in the way of a clue, Mr. Mallows; but I'll think a bit. The worst of it is, you never know who these betting men are, do you, once they get away? There are so many, and it may be anybody. Not only that, but they may bribe anybody."

"Yes, of course—there's no end to their wickedness, I'm afraid. Stedman suggests that trade rivalry may have had something to do with it. But that seems an uncharitable view, don't you think? Of course we stand very high, and there are jealousies and all that, but this is a thing I'm sure no firm would think of stooping to, for a moment. No, it's betting that is at the bottom of this, I fear. And I hope, Mr. Dorrington, that you will make some attempt to find the guilty parties."

Presently Stedman spoke to Dorrington again. "Here's something that may help you," he said. "To begin with, it must have been done by someone from the outside of the track."

"Why?"

"Well, at least every probability's that way. Everybody inside was directly interested in Gillett's success, excepting the Union officials and Sparks, who's a gentleman and quite above suspicion, as much so, indeed, as the Union officials. Of course there was the ground-man, but he's all right, I'm sure."

"And the trainer?"

"Oh, that's altogether improbable—altogether. I was going to say—"

"And there's that other man who was standing about; I haven't heard who he was."

"Right you are. I don't know him either. Where is he now?"

But the man had gone.

"Look here, I'll make some quiet inquiries about that man," Stedman pursued. "I forgot all about him in the excitement of the moment. I was going to say that although whoever did it could easily have got away by the gate before the smash came, he might not have liked to go that way in case of observation in passing the pavilion. In that case he could have got away (and indeed he could have got into the grounds to begin with) by way of one of those garden walls that bound the ground just by where the smash occurred. If that were so he must either live in one of the houses, or must know somebody that does. Perhaps you might put a man to smell about along the road—it's only a short one; Chisnall Road's the name."

"Yes, yes," Dorrington responded patiently. "There might be something in that."

By this time Gillett's arm was in a starched bandage and secured by splints, and a cab was ready to take him home. Mr. Mallows took Stedman away with him, expressing a desire to talk business, and Dorrington went home by himself. He did not turn down Chisnall Road. But he walked jauntily along toward the nearest cab-stand, and once or twice he chuckled, for he saw his way to a delightfully lucrative financial operation in cycle companies, without risk of capital.

The cab gained, he called at the lodgings of two of his men assistants and gave them instant instructions. Then he packed a small bag at his rooms in Conduit Street, and at midnight was in the late fast train for Birmingham.

3.

The prospectus of the "Avalanche Bicycle and Tyre Company" stated that the works were at Exeter and Birmingham. Exeter is a delightful town, but it can scarcely be regarded as the centre of the cycle trade; neither is it in especially easy and short communication with Bir-

"Avalanche Bicycle and Tyre Co., Ltd." 215

mingham. It was the sort of thing that any critic anxious to pick holes in the prospectus might wonder at, and so one of Dorrington's assistants had gone by the night mail to inspect the works. It was from this man that Dorrington, in Birmingham, about noon on the day after Gillett's disaster, received this telegram—

> Works here old disused cloth-mills just out of town. Closed and empty but with big new signboard and notice that works now running are at Birmingham. Agent says only deposit paid—tenancy agreement not signed.—Farrish.

The telegram increased Dorrington's satisfaction, for he had just taken a look at the Birmingham works. They were not empty, though nearly so, nor were they large; and a man there had told him that the chief premises, where most of the work was done, were at Exeter. And the hollower the business the better prize he saw in store for himself. He had already, early in the morning, indulged in a telegram on his own account, though he had not signed it. This was how it ran—

> Mallows, 58, Upper Sandown Place, London, W.
> Fear all not safe here. Run down by 10.10 train without fail.

Thus it happened that at a little later than half past eight Dorrington's other assistant, watching the door of No. 58, Upper Sandown Place, saw a telegram delivered, and immediately afterwards Mr. Paul Mallows in much haste dashed away in a cab which was called from the end of the street. The assistant followed in another. Mr. Mallows dismissed his cab at a theatrical wig-maker's in Bow Street and entered. When he emerged in little more than forty minutes' time, none but a practised watcher, who had guessed the reason for the visit, would have recognized him. He had not assumed the clumsy disguise of a false beard. He was "made up" deftly. His colour was heightened, and his face seemed thinner.

There was no heavy accession of false hair, but a slight crepe-hair whisker at each side made a better and less pronounced disguise. He seemed a younger, healthier man. The watcher saw him safely off to Birmingham by the ten minutes past ten train, and then gave Dorrington note by telegraph of the guise in which Mr. Mallows was travelling.

Now this train was timed to arrive at Birmingham at one, which was the reason Dorrington had named it in the anonymous telegram. The entrance to the "Avalanche" works was by a large gate, which was closed, but which was provided with a small door to pass a man. Within was a yard, and at a little before one o'clock Dorrington pushed open the small door, peeped, and entered. Nobody was about in the yard, but what little noise could be heard came from a particular part of the building on the right. A pile of solid "export" crates stood to the left, and these Dorrington had noted at his previous call that morning as making a suitable hiding-place for temporary use. Now he slipped behind them and awaited the stroke of one. Prompt at the hour a door on the opposite side of the yard swung open, and two men and a boy emerged and climbed one after another through the little door in the big gate. Then presently another man, not a workman, but apparently a sort of overseer, came from the opposite door, which he carelessly let fall-to behind him, and he also disappeared through the little door, which he then locked. Dorrington was now alone in the sole active works of the "Avalanche Bicycle and Tyre Company, Limited."

He tried the door opposite and found it was free to open. Within he saw in a dark corner a candle which had been left burning, and opposite him a large iron enameling oven, like an immense safe, and round about, on benches, were strewn heaps of the glaring red and gold transfer which Dorrington had observed the day before on the machines exhibited in the Holborn Viaduct window. Some of the frames had the label newly applied, and others were still plain. It would seem that the chief business of the "Avalanche Bicycle and Tyre Company,

Limited" was the attaching of labels to previously nondescript machines. But there was little time to examine further, and indeed Dorrington presently heard the noise of a key in the outer gate. So he stood and waited by the enamelling oven to welcome Mr. Mallows.

As the door was pushed open Dorrington advanced and bowed politely. Mallows started guiltily, but, remembering his disguise, steadied himself, and asked gruffly, "Well, sir, and who are you?"

"I," answered Dorrington with perfect composure, "I am Mr. Paul Mallows—you may have heard of me in connection with the 'Indestructible Bicycle Company.'"

Mallows was altogether taken aback. But then it struck him that perhaps the detective, anxious to win the reward he had offered in the matter of the Gillett outrage, was here making inquiries in the assumed character of the man who stood, impenetrably disguised, before him. So after a pause he asked again, a little less gruffly, "And what may be your business?"

"Well," said Dorrington, "I did think of taking shares in this company. I suppose there would be no objection to the managing director of another company taking shares in this?"

"No," answered Mallows, wondering what all this was to lead to.

"Of course not; I'm sure *you* don't think so, eh?" Dorrington, as he spoke, looked in the other's face with a sly leer, and Mallows began to feel altogether uncomfortable. "But there's one thing," Dorrington pursued, taking out his pocket-book, though still maintaining his leer in Mallows' face—"one other thing. And by the way, *will* you have another piece of court plaster now I've got it out? Don't say no. It's a pleasure to oblige you, really." And Dorrington, his leer growing positively fiendish, tapped the side of his nose with the case of court plaster.

Mallows paled under the paint, gasped, and felt for support. Dorrington laughed pleasantly. "Come, come," he said, "don't be frightened. I admire your cleverness, Mr. Mallows, and I shall arrange everything pleasantly, as you will see. And as to the court plaster, if you'd rather not have it you needn't. You have another piece on now, I see. Why didn't you get them to paint it over at Clarkson's? They really did the face very well, though! And there again you were quite right. Such a man as yourself was likely to be recognized in such a place as Birmingham, and that would have been unfortunate for both of us—*both* of us, I assure you. . . . Man alive, don't look as though I was going to cut your throat! I'm not, I assure you. You're a smart man of business, and I happen to have spotted a little operation of yours, that's all. I shall arrange easy terms for you. . . . Pull yourself together and talk business before the men come back. Here, sit on this bench."

Mallows, staring amazedly in Dorrington's face, suffered himself to be led to a bench, and sat on it.

"Now," said Dorrington, "the first thing is a little matter of a hundred pounds. That was the reward you promised if I should discover who broke Gillett's arm last night. Well, I *have*. Do you happen to have any notes with you? If not, make it a cheque."

"But—but—how—I mean who!—who—"

"Tut, tut! Don't waste time, Mr. Mallows. *Who?* Why, yourself, of course. I knew all about it before I left you last night, though it wasn't quite convenient to claim the reward then, for reasons you'll understand presently. Come, that little hundred."

"But what—what proof have you? I'm not to be bounced like this, you know." Mr. Mallows was gathering his faculties again.

"Proof? Why, man alive, be reasonable! Suppose I have none—none at all? What difference does that make? Am I to walk out and tell your fellow directors where I have met you—here—or am I to have that hundred? More, am I to publish abroad that Mr. Paul Mallows is the moving spirit in the rotten 'Avalanche Bicycle Company'?"

"Well," Mallows answered reluctantly, "if you put it like that—"

"But I only put it like that to make you see things

reasonably. As a matter of fact your connection with this new company is enough to bring your little performance with the iron chair near proof. But I got at it from the other side. See here—you're much too clumsy with your fingers, Mr. Mallows. First you go and tear the tip of your middle finger opening your brougham door, and have to get court plaster from me. Then you let that court plaster get frayed at the edge, and you still keep it on. After that you execute your very successful chair operation. When the eyes of the others are following the bicycles you take the chair in the hand with the plaster on it, catching hold of it at the place where a rough, loose, square nut protrudes, and you pitch it on to the track so clumsily and nervously that the nut carries away the frayed thread of the court plaster with it. Here it is, you see, still in my pocket-book, where I put it last night by the light of the lantern; just a sticky black silk thread, that's all. I've only brought it to show you I'm playing a fair game with you. Of course I might easily have got a witness before I took the thread off the nut, if I had thought you were likely to fight the matter. But I knew you were not. You can't fight, you know, with this bogus company business known to me. So that I am only showing you this thread as an act of grace, to prove that I have stumped you with perfect fairness. And now the hundred. Here's a fountain pen, if you want one."

"Well," said Mallows glumly, "I suppose I must, then." He took the pen and wrote the cheque. Dorrington blotted it on the pad of his pocket-book and folded it away.

"So much for that!" he said. "That's just a little preliminary, you understand. We've done these little things just as a guarantee of good faith—not necessarily for publication, though you must remember that as yet there's nothing to prevent it. I've done you a turn by finding out who upset those bicycles, as you so ardently wished me to do last night, and you've loyally fulfilled your part of the contract by paying the promised reward—though I must say that you haven't paid with all the delight and pleasure you spoke of at the time. But I'll forgive you that, and now that the little *hors-d'oeuvre* is disposed of, we'll proceed to serious business."

Mallows looked uncomfortably glum.

"But you mustn't look so ashamed of yourself, you know," Dorrington said, purposely misinterpreting his glumness. "It's all business. You were disposed for a little side flutter, so to speak—a little speculation outside your regular business. Well, you mustn't be ashamed of that."

"No," Mallows observed, assuming something of his ordinarily ponderous manner; "no, of course not. It's a little speculative deal. Everybody does it, and there's a deal of money going."

"Precisely. And since everybody does it, and there is so much money going, you are only making your share."

"Of course." Mr. Mallows was almost pompous by now.

"Of course." Dorrington coughed slightly. "Well now, do you know, I am exactly the same sort of man as yourself—if you don't mind the comparison. *I* am disposed for a little side flutter, so to speak—a little speculation outside my regular business. I also am not ashamed of it. And since everybody does it, and there is so much money going—why, *I* am thinking of making *my* share. So we are evidently a pair, and naturally intended for each other!"

Mr. Paul Mallows here looked a little doubtful.

"See here, now," Dorrington proceeded. "I have lately taken it into my head to operate a little on the cycle share market. That was why I came round myself about that little spoke affair, instead of sending an assistant. I wanted to know somebody who understood the cycle trade, from whom I might get tips. You see I'm perfectly frank with you. Well, I have succeeded uncommonly well. And I want you to understand that I have gone every step of the way by fair work. I took nothing for granted, and I played the game fairly. When you asked me (as you had anxious reason to ask) if I had found anything, I told you there was nothing very big—and see what a little thing the thread was! Before I came away from the pavilion I made sure that you were really the only man there with black court plaster on his fingers. I had noticed the hands of every man but two, and I made an excuse of borrowing something to see those. I saw your thin pretence of suspecting the betting men, and I played up to it. I have had a telegraphic report on your Exeter works this morning—a deserted cloth mills with nothing on it of yours but a sign-board, and only a deposit of rent paid. *There* they referred to the works here. *Here* they referred to the works there. It was very clear, really! Also I have had a telegraphic report of your make-up adventure this morning. Clarkson does it marvellously, doesn't he? And, by the way, that telegram bringing you down to Birmingham was not from your confederate here, as perhaps you fancied. It was from me. Thanks for coming so promptly. I managed to get a quiet look round here just before you arrived, and on the whole conclusion I come to as to the 'Avalanche Bicycle and Tyre Company, Limited,' is this: A clever man, whom it give me great pleasure to know," with a bow to Mallows, "conceives the notion of offering the public the very rottenest cycle company ever planned, and all without appearing in it himself. He finds what little capital is required; his two or three confederates help to make up a board of directors, with one or two titled guinea pigs, who know nothing of the company and care nothing, and the rest's easy. A professional racing man is employed to win races and make records, on machines which have been specially made by another firm (perhaps it was the 'Indestructible,' who knows?) to a private order, and afterwards decorated with the name and style of the bogus company on a transfer. For ordinary sale, bicycles of the 'trade' description are bought—so much a hundred from the factors, and put your own name on 'em. They come cheap, and they sell at a good price—the profit pays all expenses and perhaps a bit over; and by the time they all break down the company will be successfully floated, the money—the capital—will be divided, the moving spirit and his confederates will have disappeared, and the guinea-pigs will be left to stand the racket—if there is a racket. And the moving spirit will remain unsuspected, a man of account in the trade all the time! Admirable! All the work to be done at the 'works' is the sticking on of labels and a bit of enamelling. Excellent, all round! Isn't that about the size of your operations?"

"Well, yes," Mallows answered, a little reluctantly, but with something of modest pride in his manner, "that was the notion, since you speak so plainly."

"And it shall be the notion. All—everything—shall be as you have planned it, with one exception, which is this. The moving spirit shall divide his plunder with me."

"*You?* But—but—why, I gave you a hundred just now!"

"Dear, dear! Why will you harp so much on that vulgar little hundred? That's settled and done with. That's our little personal bargain in the matter of the lamentable accident with the chair. We are now talking of bigger business—not hundreds, but thousands, and not one of them, but a lot. Come now, a mind like yours should be wide enough to admit of a broad and large view of things. If I refrain from exposing this charming scheme of yours I shall be promoting a piece of scandalous robbery. Very well then, I want my promotion money, in the regular way. Can I shut my eyes and allow a piece of iniquity like this to go on unchecked, without getting anything by way of damages for myself? Perish the thought! When all expenses are paid, and the confederates are sent off with as little as they will take, you and I will divide fairly, Mr. Mallows, respectable brothers in rascality. Mind, I might say we'd divide to begin with, and leave you to pay expenses, but I am always fair to a partner in anything of this sort. I shall just want a little guarantee, you know—it's safest in such matters as these; say a bill at six months for ten thousand pounds—which is very low. When a satisfactory division is made you shall have the bill back. Come—I have a bill-stamp ready, being so much convinced of your reasonableness as to buy it this morning, though it cost five pounds."

"But that's nonsense—you're trying to impose. I'll

give you anything reasonable—half is out of the question. What, after all the trouble and worry and risk that I've had?"

"Which would suffice for no more than to put you in gaol if I held up my finger!"

"But hang it, be reasonable! You're a mighty clever man, and you've got me on the hip, as I admit. Say ten per cent."

"You're wasting time, and presently the men will be back. Your choice is between making half, or making none, and going to gaol into the bargain. Choose!"

"But just consider—"

"Choose!"

Mallows looked despairingly about him. "But really," he said, "I want the money more than you think. I—"

"For the last time—choose!"

Mallow's despairing gaze stopped at the enamelling oven. "Well, well," he said, "if I must, I must, I suppose. But I warn you, you may regret it."

"Oh dear no, I'm not so pessimistic. Come, you wrote a cheque—now I'll write the bill. 'Six months after date, pay to me or my order the sum of ten thousand pounds for value received'—excellent value too, *I* think. There you are!"

When the bill was written and signed, Mallows scribbled his acceptance with more readiness than might have been expected. Then he rose, and said with something of brisk cheerfulness in his tone, "Well, that's done, and the least said the soonest mended. You've won it, and I won't grumble any more. I think I've done this thing pretty neatly, eh? Come and see the 'works.'"

Every other part of the place was empty of machinery. There were a good many finished frames and wheels, bought separately, and now in course of being fitted together for sale; and there were many more complete bicycles of cheap but showy make to which nothing needed to be done but to fix the red and gold "transfer" of the "Avalanche" company. Then Mallows opened the tall iron door of the enamelling oven.

"See this," he said; "this is the enamelling oven. Get

in and look round. The frames and other different parts hang on the racks after the enamel is laid on, and all those gas jets are lighted to harden it by heat. Do you see that deeper part there by the back?—go closer."

Dorrington felt a push at his back and the door was swung to with a bang, and the latch dropped. He was in the dark, trapped in a great iron chamber. "I warned you," shouted Mallows from without; "I warned you you might regret it!" And instantly Dorrington's nostrils were filled with the smell of escaping gas. He realized his peril on the instant. Mallows had given him the bill with the idea of silencing him by murder and recovering it. He had pushed him into the oven and had turned on the gas. It was dark, but to light a match would mean death instantly, and without the match it must be death by suffocation and poison of gas in a very few minutes. To appeal to Mallows was useless—Dorrington knew too much. It would seem that at last a horribly fitting retribution had overtaken Dorrington in death by a mode parallel to that which he and his creatures had prepared for others. Dorrington's victims had drowned in water—and now Dorrington himself was to drown in gas. The oven was of sheet iron, fastened by a latch in the centre. Dorrington flung himself desperately against the door, and it gave outwardly at the extreme bottom. He snatched a loose angle-iron with which his hand came in contact, dashed against the door once more, and thrust the iron through where it strained open. Then, with another tremendous plunge, he drove the door a little more outward and raised the angle-iron in the crack; then once more, and raised it again. He was near to losing his senses, when, with one more plunge, the catch of the latch, not designed for such treatment, suddenly gave way, the door flew open, and Dorrington, blue in the face, staring, stumbling and gasping, came staggering out into the fresher air, followed by a gush of gas.

Mallows had retreated to the rooms behind, and thither Dorrington followed him, gaining vigour and fury at every step. At sight of him the wretched Mallows sank in a corner, sighing and shivering with terror. Dorrington reached him and clutched him by the collar. There should be no more honour between these two thieves now. He would drag Mallows forth and proclaim him aloud; and he would keep that £10,000 bill. He hauled the struggling wretch across the room, tearing off the crêpe whiskers as he came, while Mallows supplicated and whined, fearing that it might be the other's design to imprison *him* in the enamelling oven. But at the door of the room against that containing the oven their progress came to an end, for the escaped gas had reached the lighted candle, and with one loud report the partition wall fell in, half burying Mallows where he lay, and knocking Dorrington over.

Windows fell out of the building, and men broke through the front gate, climbed into the ruined rooms and stopped the still escaping gas. When the two men and the boy returned, with the conspirator who had been in charge of the works, they found a crowd from the hardware and cycle factories thereabout, surveying with great interest the spectacle of the extrication of Mr. Paul Mallows, managing director of the "Indestructible Bicycle Company," from the broken bricks, mortar, bicycles and transfers of the "Avalanche Bicycle and Tyre Company, Limited," and the preparations for carrying him to a surgeon's where his broken leg might be set. As for Dorrington, a crushed hat and a torn coat were all his hurts, beyond a few scratches. And in a couple of hours it was all over Birmingham, and spreading to other places, that the business of the "Avalanche Bicycle and Tyre Company" consisted of sticking brilliant labels on factors' bicycles, bought in batches; for the whole thing was thrown open to the general gaze by the explosion. So that when, next day, Lant won the fifty miles race in London, he was greeted with ironical shouts of "Gum on yer transfer!" "Hi! mind your label!" "Where did you steal that bicycle?" "Sold yer shares?" and so forth.

Somehow the "Avalanche Bicycle and Tyre Company, Limited," never went to allotment. It was said that a few people in remote and benighted spots, where news never came till it was in the history books, had applied for shares, but the bankers returned their money, doubtless to their extreme disappointment. It was found politic, also, that Mr. Paul Mallows should retire from the directorate of the "Indestructible Bicycle Company"—a concern which is still, I believe, flourishing exceedingly.

As for Dorrington, he had his hundred pounds reward. But the bill of £10,000 he never presented. Why, I do not altogether know, unless he found that Mr. Mallows' financial position, as he had hinted, was not altogether so good as was supposed. At any rate, it was found among the notes and telegrams in this case in the Dorrington deed-box.

Tomorrow's Murder

STUART PALMER

"There is only one reason in the world why my husband would buy a revolver!"

A thin, stony-eyed blonde, wrapped in chinchilla and righteous wrath, made her abrupt exit from the office of Inspector Oscar Piper on this line, punctuating it with a slam of the door which dislodged a framed photograph of the Headquarters' Pistol Team (1922).

The silence surged softly backward into the reception room, and then an angular schoolteacher, complete with cotton umbrella and worn leather handbag, rose to her feet and stepped catlike over the fragments of broken glass.

The Inspector was scribbling a report. "Oh, so it's you!" was the greeting.

"Oscar, what did that woman want?" Miss Hildegarde Withers' curiosity was getting the best of her.

He looked up wearily. "Just another hysterical dame who has the idea that her husband plans to bump her off. But I told her that the Homicide Squad has enough to do without worrying over tomorrow's murders. I said she'd better leave town . . ."

"Tomorrow's murders!" echoed the schoolteacher thoughtfully. "Coming events cast their shadows . . . please go on, Oscar."

He sighed, and then as usual gave in. "That's about all there is to it. That woman was the former Mavis Dewitt-Brown-Hopkinson. Current husband is Wilfred Parks, polo star. He was what they call a polo bum, selling horses to maintain himself, when she discovered him. Anyway, it seems that he received a small but heavy express package a week ago. Told her it was some new spurs."

"And pray how did she know he lied?"

"I asked that," Piper said. "She told me that a man doesn't usually keep his spurs under his pillow at night, nor wear them in his hip pocket at a dance."

"Any mention of motive for this forthcoming homicide?"

"Not money, anyway," Piper declared. "It seems that Parks doesn't draw more than half of the generous allowance she gives him. I asked if her husband had any reason for being jealous, and she said not to be silly, of course he had. But he wasn't usually jealous, and even then most of the time he was worried about the wrong person. Even of the family doctor, she said.

"So you see, there's nothing in it. Just a jittery dame with her conscience troubling her. But if she did get bumped off, after asking me for protection, I'd be in a tight spot . . ."

"Oscar, I'm not so sure that anything will happen to that woman," she decided. "But I smell a smoke screen."

He gnawed thoughtfully at a long, green cigar. "You mean that the dame is getting set for a self-defense plea after she kills him?"

Miss Withers shrugged. "Possibly. But perhaps it is

the family doctor who should be leaving town!" She picked up her handbag, grasped her umbrella firmly. "I'm off, Oscar. Off on the trail of tomorrow's murder!"

All was peace and quiet in the Inspector's office until next day when he returned from lunch to find an urgent message asking him to call a Long Island number. In a moment he was listening to a familiar Bostonian accent. He cut in, protested feebly.

"What? Leave my desk and come out to hell-and-gone? It's impossible. Besides, that case is dead. I called the Parks home this morning and the maid says that Mrs. Parks sailed for Bermuda last night."

"Really, Oscar?" Miss Withers' voice was cool and crisp. "And of course you checked to see whether there was a ship sailing for Bermuda last night?" There was a slight pause, and then: "Well, I did. And there wasn't!"

So it was that the Inspector went out to Long Island's depths and was met by Miss Withers at the Norwood station. "Oscar," was her greeting, "you're going to see Wilfred Parks, the famous nine-goal polo star, perform this afternoon at the Shorelands Club."

"And why am I?"

"Because this is a new kind of mystery, Oscar. Usually you have a victim and must search for the killer. Here—" and she led the way toward a waiting taxicab— "here we have a killer and must search for the victim."

As Miss Withers and the Inspector found camp chairs near the end of the line she expressed a hope that it wasn't all over. Her remark caught the attention of a small, wiry person in a worn trench coat, who sat in the chair at her left with his worn riding boots propped on another in front of him. "It's only the end of the second chukker, ma'am," he informed her.

For some years Miss Withers had cultivated the knack of falling into conversation with strangers. She studied for a moment this dry little man, whose small bald spot gave him the monkish effect of a tonsure. "Could you tell me," she began, "just who is the great Mr. Parks? We only came because we wanted to see him in action."

"Parks is number three in the blue jersey," the stranger informed her. "See—the big man drinking from the silver thermos."

Wilfred Parks had a strong but petulant face, undisciplined and uncontrolled, Miss Withers thought. She watched him take a gulp from the thermos, then make a wry face and spit on the grass. He tossed the silver bottle to a blanket, and then strode to where a boyish groom held the reins of a dancing, spotted horse. Parks swung his big loose body up into the saddle and speedily joined the double line of players at the edge of the field. The umpire wheeled his horse and bowled a ball of glistening white willowroot between them.

Then things began to happen with a rapidity which quite bewildered Miss Withers and even the Inspector, who had been half drowsing in the warm sun, snapped to attention. Two mallets swung—a man in red caught the ball and smacked it a few yards down the field. He spurred forward and tried to hit it again, but a man in blue unkindly crashed alongside, putting him out of the play and at the same time sending the ball backward with a wild whirl of his stick.

For a moment the red-jerseyed player hung over the neck of his horse, clutching wildly at the sky. "There he goes," muttered the man who sat beside Miss Withers. He groped for a black kit-bag beside him, and then relaxed as the player miraculously regained his saddle, wheeled his horse, and took off after the ball again.

"Are you the doctor here?" Miss Withers queried.

"I'm Dr. Harris," he admitted. "As a reward for hanging around with my splints they let me go in as a substitute when anything happens to one of the star players, like Parks." The doctor shot her a glance. "You're not friends of his?"

"Of Mrs. Parks," Miss Withers hazarded.

"Parks isn't playing his best game today. That man ought to have a complete physical exam," Dr. Harris remarked, half to himself.

Miss Withers nudged the bored Inspector, and said, "Oh, Dr. Harris—then you're the family doctor?"

By this time Dr. Harris had given up resenting her questions.

"I have attended Mavis from measles to wisdom teeth to an appendectomy last March," he said dryly. "As for her latest husband, I've seen him though a green-stick fracture of the ulna and two collar-bone smashes."

Just when the Inspector was growing restless a gasp went up from the crowd. Down the field a strange transformation had come over Parks. One wild sweep of his stick had pulled the ball out of the air over his head and sent it forward into a tangle of red and blue players. Under the rider the spotted horse also seemed inspired to super-equine endeavor, for like a maddened centaur the man and beast plunged into the fray and emerged on the farther side, with the ball rolling easily beside them. Parks raised his mallet, pointed his left shoulder . . .

A frantic man in red swung at the ball, but Parks's clubhead came quickest, snapping the ball almost half the length of the field in a long high arc. Eight horses raced after it, eight men dug spur and lashed whip. But there was no stopping this new Parks. Ridden off the ball by the desperate Reds, blocked and bumped and hemmed in, he still somehow managed to reach that scarred white globule and snap it between the goal posts in a seemingly impossible tail shot.

The players speedily lined up for another throw-in, and again there was a wild scurry of confusion as every man swung at it and every man missed. It was a pony's hoof which finally knocked the ball into the clear, and then the crowd stirred as they saw a big "3" on the blue jersey that flashed after it.

Parks rose high in his irons, reins slack on the withers of the spotted horse and his left shoulder twisted down at the ball. The heavy face under his white-cork helmet was contorted with supreme effort and then, just as the pony's flashing fore legs came up to the ball, the rider snapped the stick back, down, and forward in a terrific forehand drive.

There was the sharp musical snap of a truly hit ball,

and the willowroot rose and floated bright and fair down the field.

The eyes of the crowd turned after it, and the other seven men raced after it. So that, as it happened, Miss Hildegarde Withers and one other person were the only ones watching the man in the blue jersey as he slumped in the saddle, rolled sideways, and then plunged headlong to the turf.

The spotted horse, stumbling a little, trotted to the sideboards and fell to nibbling grass. Wilfred Parks lay motionless. Miss Withers knew suddenly that he would never rise again. "Oscar, this is what we came to see," said the schoolteacher grimly.

"The doctor says it's concussion," Inspector Oscar Piper announced importantly as he approached the spot near the sideboards where Miss Withers has been waiting. But she nodded absently and went on patting the nose of the spotted pony, who stared apathetically past her at the white-lipped, boyish groom who held his rein.

"This is Tad Alfers—Mr. Piper," she introduced them. "Tad is—or was—Mr. Parks's groom."

The boy seemed hurt at that. "I'm just working as a groom until something better comes along," he hastened to explain. "I was studying to be a veterinary surgeon, but I had to give it up temporarily."

Miss Withers was looking down at the bright blanket where were spread out all the dead man's polo mallets. "By the way," she said softly, "just where is Mr. Parks's silver thermos? Or did that have an accident, too?"

The young groom didn't know. But people were always switching stuff around here. His voice trailed away again as he saw that both Miss Withers and the Inspector were staring at the gold combination cigaret case and lighter in his hand.

Alfers smiled. "He—Mr. Parks, I mean—gave me this for Christmas. He'd give you the shirt off his back."

The Inspector was growing impatient. "One question more," Miss Withers put in. "Where could we reach you in case something comes up?"

Tad Alfers hesitated. "Well—I generally sleep on a cot here at the stables . . ."

"You're not married, then?"

He blushed. "Well—I'm thinking about it."

Miss Withers beamed at him. Red about the neck and ears, Alfers led the spotted pony toward the stables, jerking nervously as the horse stumbled and almost fell when they crossed the low sideboards.

They walked slowly past the line of empty chairs toward the main gate where they found a taxi and joined the procession of cars which rolled slowly along the asphalt drive toward town.

It was, in the main, a tranquil journey, except for the moment when a shrill siren sounded behind them. A rather sporty open roadster cut past, on the wrong side of the road, and there was the red sign PHYSICIAN above the rear license plate.

"Harris! Wonder where he's off to in such a hurry?" said the Inspector.

Miss Withers refused to speculate. But she leaned forward and tapped sharply on the glass. "Instead of the railroad station, you may drive us to the County Sheriff's office," she commanded.

The Inspector frowned. "Now Hildegarde, you know I can't go butting in on a thing like this, without a leg to stand on except your hunches. . . ."

"You should be more observant, Oscar," she told him. "The Sheriff will listen to us. Because I happened to notice that Dr. Harris had a silver thermos bottle beside him on the seat!"

When the Inspector, with some help from Miss Withers, had laid most of their cards on the table, Sheriff Oakes nodded. Then he reached for his telephone, dialed a number and said: "Is Doctor there? Yeah . . . hello, Paul. Can you come over to my office right away? Uh huh. Right away."

Dr. Harris, somewhat annoyed, arrived and was ushered in. "These folks," said the Sheriff quietly, "just come in with quite a story worked out. They're sorta accusing you of the theft of a silver thermos bottle."

The doctor's smile hardened. He sat down, lighted a cigaret. "Why, yes," he said. "Naturally."

"Naturally?" cut in the Inspector. "Then you, too—"

Dr. Harris nodded. "It's a long story—but you see, Parks had an idea that once, in the East-West tournament last month, somebody tried to drug that water bottle . . . with the idea of slowing up his game. So today—well, I thought the bottle ought to be analyzed."

The others all leaned forward, hanging on his words. "And what was in the thermos?" demanded Miss Withers.

"Hydrogen dioxide," Dr. Harris informed her. "H_2O."

"You mean—just plain water?" Piper cut in incredulously.

Harris nodded. "Nothing there to hurt him unless he drowned in it."

It was at this point that the Sheriff suddenly stood up, the smile on his fat face a very set one now. "You folks satisfied now?"

"We had no business to go barging in," Piper told her as they left the office. "We've got to go back where we belong, and stop stepping on the Sheriff's toes . . ."

"You're going, not I," Miss Withers snapped. "Murder is every citizen's business. Good afternoon!" And so she turned and left him.

The Inspector had barely reached his home on Manhattan when the telephone shrieked its summons, and the familiar voice of Hildegarde Withers greeted him.

"You may be interested to know that just after we left the office of Sheriff Oakes, he ordered an autopsy performed on the body of Wilfred Parks."

"Yeah? Just taking precautions, that's all. . . ."

"No, Oscar. Do you know who's performing that autopsy at this very moment? It's Dr. Harris!"

There was silence at the Inspector's end of the line. Then—"O.K., Hildegarde. I'll go over to the Parks apartment and see what I can find out. You stick around the Sheriff's office and let me know how the autopsy comes out."

Questioned by Inspector Oscar Piper was Eve Simpson, parlormaid in the Parks home, who stated that as God was her judge she had packed Mrs. Parks's clothes for a trip to Bermuda, including Mothersills for *mal de mer*. No, she didn't think that Mrs. Parks had ever given her husband any reason to be jealous. Of course the doctor did come rather often, but Mrs. Parks had been very delicate since her operation.

Somewhat conflicting was the testimony of Mrs. Mabel Rogers, cook-housekeeper in the Parks home, who swore on her sacred oath that if anything had happened to the poor young master it was the work of that green-eyed lath of a woman, Mavis. Pressed for more damning details, Mrs. Rogers said that once, a few months before, Mrs. Parks had gone to a party aboard Mr. Tom Van Orpet's yacht, and hadn't come home until 8 A.M.

Charles Togo, butler to Mr. Tom Van Orpet, when reached by telephone at the Van Orpet penthouse on Sutton Place, gave vague information as to the fact that Mr. Van Orpet was cruising somewhere on Long Island Sound in the *Penguin III*.

"There it is," said the Inspector when Miss Withers called him back much later that same evening. "Just servants' gossip, but if it does you any good—" He cut short her thanks. "Has the doctor turned in his verdict of accidental death yet?"

Miss Withers hesitated. Then "Yes, and no. Yes, he turned it in, and no, it wasn't accidental death!"

The Inspector whistled. "What?"

"Dr. Harris discovered that Wilfred Parks was poisoned."

"What kind of poison?"

"Oil of something—mirbane I think it was. There are limits to what even I can hear through the closed door of the Sheriff's inner office, Oscar."

He could understand that. "Nice going, Hildegarde. Well, that clears the doctor, anyway."

"Oscar, you're really improving!" Miss Withers told him. "If you'll come down here again I'll let you help me interview the one witness that we've neglected."

"Huh? Oh, you mean the good-looking groom with the fancy cigaret case?"

Miss Withers didn't mean Alfers at all. "I was referring to the spotted horse," she told the Inspector. "In my opinion that horse is more likely to—"

Here the Inspector exploded. "Phooey," he told her, which she correctly interpreted to mean that he was not interested in interviewing horses, that he was sick and tired of the Parks murder, and that he was going to bed and would not further answer his telephone.

So Hildegarde Withers started out alone. Whatever may have been her intentions in regard to interviewing the spotted horse, it was to Dr. Harris that she went first. The crisp little medico had not, as she had half feared, started for Bermuda or other distant points. He was at home, a spacious and rambling abode in one of the better streets of the little city. He admitted her genially, wearing a purple-silk dressing gown.

"You didn't disturb me a bit," he said. "I was just boning up on poisons a bit before making out my official report." And he led the way to his study.

He took down a fat volume. "Here it is in Peterson, Haines and Webster," he said. " 'Nitrobenzine, known as essence or oil of mirbane, a pale-yellow, oily liquid, used commercially in the manufacture of explosives, in making aniline dyes, soaps, perfumes, and patent medicines. Symptoms . . . first a stimulation of body and mind, followed in a few minutes by numbness, dizziness and disturbance of vision. Later Cheyne-Stokes respiration going directly into coma and death. The face becomes grayish blue, the nails and lips purple. Death within an hour, particularly swift when the poison is absorbed through the skin or nasal passages rather than swallowed . . .' "

Miss Withers gulped. "That's enough," she begged off. "There is no doubt that Parks died of this?"

Dr. Harris shook his head.

"Could it have been from something he ate or drank?"

Dr. Harris shrugged. "Might have been in his lunch."

"I wonder," said Miss Withers casually, "if the spotted horse had lunch with its master today?"

The doctor frowned, almost dropped the book, and then said hopefully, "Now if that's all the questions, ma'am, I'd like to get on with my report."

Miss Withers rose to go. "Just one more question, Doctor. Do you always carry a gun in the pocket of your dressing gown?"

He did not even bat an eye. Slowly he pulled a small automatic from his pocket and pointed it at her, butt first. "I just wanted to examine this more carefully," he told her. "You see, I found this gun in the pocket of Parks's riding breeches!"

It was brand new, fully loaded and had never been fired. So Mavis Parks has been telling the truth, after all. Or else . . .

By the time a taxicab had deposited her at the gate of Shorelands, Miss Withers was heartily wishing that she had borrowed the little automatic from Dr. Harris.

"Tomorrow would do just as well," she told herself. Then she shook her head and started valiantly toward the stables. Suddenly she noticed that there was a light in the stables.

It was a faint light, which seemed to pulsate, to swing and glow and die away . . . and come again. It was a furtive light, sneaky . . .

"Flashlight," hazarded the schoolteacher.

She went on, tiptoeing softly over cobblestones. Once, as she was poised in the shadows alongside the stables, a long, sad visage appeared out of nowhere and went *whoosh* almost in her face, then swiftly withdrew inside its stall again. Miss Withers gulped, and backed hastily away. Backed, as it happened, into something very hard that pressed against her spine.

"Reach!" said a determined voice. And she reached. A flashlight blinded her, and then her captor said: "Oh, so it's only you!" Mr. Tad Alfers had, it developed, held her up with the end of his flashlight in lieu of a pistol.

"What are you doing here at this hour?" she accused him. It was part of Miss Withers' philosophy to attack first.

Alfers said why wouldn't he be up, with a sick horse on his hands? And he showed her the stall where lay the spotted horse that Parks had ridden that afternoon. The beast lay on its side, eyes glazed, breathing thickly.

"Another mystery, eh?" the schoolteacher said. "I thought I was near the solution of all our mysteries a few moments ago when I saw your flashlight over there." And she pointed.

Tad Alfers stiffened. "But you didn't," he said. "I mean—I wasn't. That's the tack rooms over there—where we keep saddles and bridles and so forth."

He turned and ran, Miss Withers following him as best she could. They came to the tack room, and Alfers switched on the light. There were rows of saddles, neatly hanging on pegs. There were bridles and halters, sheets and blankets neatly monogrammed, bandages and polo mallets and bottles. But there was no marauder here. There was no sign of any marauder—except for one empty peg in the row of saddles.

Alfers turned to face Miss Withers. "I guess you're barking up the wrong tree," he told her. "I guess maybe you better get back to minding your business, ma'am, and I'll get back to tending my sick horse."

He left her very swiftly. So swiftly, indeed, that it was not for several moments that Miss Withers realized the fact that in his haste he had disappeared in the opposite direction to the stable in which the spotted horse had been. Back to the town she went, still wondering.

"One ticket to Penn Station," she said wearily to the clerk. And then there was a brusque voice behind her.

"No you don't, Hildegarde," said the Inspector, grinning. "I don't wonder you're surprised to see me. But I thought you ought to know. We've found Mavis Parks."

"Where was she, on Van Orpet's yacht?" demanded Miss Withers.

The Inspector winced. "You knew? Well, maybe you didn't know that she tried to commit suicide tonight by jumping overboard, and that she is being rushed to shore by the Coast Guard!"

Piper's smile of triumph was somewhat cut short by the abrupt departure of his audience. "Come on, Oscar!" was her only explanation as he caught up with her in the station exit.

"Come on where?" he quite naturally demanded. But Miss Withers was already giving directions to a taxi driver.

"Fourteen two Pinewood—the residence of Dr. Harris!" she commanded. "And step on it."

The driver stepped. "Now, Hildegarde," complained the Inspector as they approached the doctor's house, "I don't see—"

"You don't see the meaning of the thermos bottle and the cigaret case and the stumbling horse and the jittery wife? Neither did I, Oscar, neither did I. Until just now."

Miss Withers led the way up the walk, but instead of ringing the front bell she impelled the Inspector on through the garden, on to the window from which the doctor had spied upon her only a short time before. Piper stood beside her and peered in through the window.

The room was dark except for a shaded lamp at the desk, where appeared to be a very sharp knife. Dr. Harris moved to one side, and the two Peeping Toms saw that what he was slicing was nothing less than the leather cantle of a saddle . . . slicing off thin strips.

Somebody else was watching the doctor, watching from an inner doorway of the room. They could only mark a shadowy outline, a waiting, formless figure . . .

"We seem for once to have arrived at the crucial moments," Miss Withers whispered. "Oscar, have you got a gun?"

He nodded. Inside the room Dr. Harris pushed aside the wrecked saddle, dropped slices of the leather into a glass retort. He referred again to a thick tome, started to rise—

Just at that moment the shadowy figure in the room's inner doorway rushed forward, seizing the doctor from behind. The retort with its strange contents crashed to the floor, and both men fell against the desk, knocking the shade from the light.

It was Tad Alfers, a white-faced avenging Tad Alfers, who wrestled so fiercely and so silently with the doctor. Harris twisted, struck out blindly, but he was no match for the younger man.

The Inspector was trying to raise the window. "Never mind that," cried Miss Withers. "Use your gun, Oscar. Shoot!"

"No need for that," he grunted. "Young Alfers is doing all right. Let him nab our man for us . . ."

Then the amazed Inspector felt Miss Withers seize his gun hand, squeeze it . . .

A shot smashed wildly through the glass, the slug burying itself harmlessly in the ceiling. But Alfers let go his grasp of the doctor's throat, turned toward the window for a moment in blank amazement.

The moment was long enough for Dr. Harris, who picked up Peterson, Haines and Webster and with that massive tome struck Alfers on the back of the neck. Tad Alfers took two steps forward, and then his arms slackened and he went down on his face.

"Meet the murderer of Wilfred Parks," said Miss Withers sweetly.

"Oil of mirbane, well soaked into the saddle," was the verdict of Dr. Harris. He showed Miss Withers a retort filled with scraps of leather and a cloudy liquid which had a ring of bright carmine, already turning green. "Morpurgo's test," he confided.

The Inspector was finishing a neat seat of knots upon the person of Tad Alfers. "You see, Oscar," Miss Withers said, "the polo pony showed some of the symptoms of the poisoning, too—including the temporary blindness which made it fall over the sideboards. So it must have been the saddle . . ."

The Inspector gave his prisoner a last shove and stood up. "I get that," he confessed. "I thought all along it must have been the water bottle, but I was wrong."

"You were right, Oscar," Miss Withers corrected. "Alfers did try poison in the water bottle, but his employer detected it. He even complained that someone was trying to dope him, and bought a gun for protection. So Alfers had to try a more subtle way. He admitted studying to be a veterinary, and must have known quite a bit about poisons . . ." She looked down at the prisoner. "Isn't that true, Mr. Alfers?"

The boy stared up at them, his dull, smoky eyes filled with hate. But he did not speak.

"Where does Mrs. Parks come into all this?" Piper demanded. "Bursting into my office, and then leaving town, and finally trying to kill herself . . ."

"*Cherchez la femme*, Oscar," the schoolteacher told him. "You heard Mr. Alfers here tell me that he was thinking of getting married. That—and the gold cigaret case—should have told us. A man gives a gold cigaret case to an employe who has only worked for him a few months? Fiddlesticks, Oscar. But a woman might—a silly woman with more money than sense, and a liking for handsome young men," Miss Withers sniffed. "Mavis Parks has been married and divorced four or five times."

Dr. Harris interrupted. "But Mavis had no idea of divorcing Willy Parks—and the glamour of his polo rating—"

"Of course not," Miss Withers agreed. "Which was why the ambitious Mr. Alfers here thought that it would be wise to remove Parks. And then why shouldn't he marry her—and her millions? Am I right, Mr. Alfers?"

The man on the floor started talking then, and kept on until he was safe in the Bayside County Jail, a prisoner of the pleased but bewildered Sheriff Oakes. "You folks seem to have turned everything upside down, and committed a couple of misdemeanors and maybe a felony in shooting off that there gun, but I guess I got to let you get away with it," he decided.

"It was a Mr. Emerson," Miss Withers told him, "who said 'In skating over thin ice our safety is our speed'!"

Trojan Horse

ELLERY QUEEN

"Whom," demanded Miss Paula Paris across the groaning board, "do you like, Mr. Queen?"

Mr. Queen instantly mumbled: "You," out of a mouthful of Vermont turkey, chestnut stuffing, and cranberry sauce.

"I didn't mean that, silly," Miss Paris, nevertheless pleased. "However, now that you've brought the subject up—will you say such pretty things when we're married?"

Mr. Ellery Queen paled and, choking, set down his weapons. When he had first encountered the lovely Miss Paris, Hollywood's reigning goddess of gossip, Miss Paris had been suffering from homophobia, or morbid fear of man; she had been so terrified of crowds that she had not for years set foot outside her virginal white frame house in the Hollywood hills. Mr. Queen, stirred by a nameless emotion, determined to cure the lady of her psychological affliction. The therapy, he conceived, must be both shocking and compensatory; and so he made love to her.

And lo! although Miss Paris recovered, to his horror Mr. Queen found that the cure may sometimes present a worse problem than the affliction. For the patient promptly fell in love with her healer; and the healer did not himself escape certain excruciating emotional consequences.

His precious liberty faced with this alluring menace, Mr. Queen now choked over the luscious Christmas dinner which Miss Paris had cunningly cooked with her own slim hands and served *en tête-à-tête* in her cosy maple and chintz dining-room.

"Oh, relax," pouted Miss Paris. "I was joking. What makes you think I'd marry a creature who studies cut throats and chases thieves for the enjoyment of it?"

"Horrible fate for a woman," Mr. Queen hastened to agree. "Besides, I'm not good enough for you."

"Darned tootin' you're not! But you haven't answered my question. Do you think Carolina will lick USC next Sunday?"

"Oh, the Rose Bowl game," said Mr. Queen, discovering his appetite miraculously. "More turkey, please! . . . Well, if Ostermoor lives up to his reputation, the Spartans should breeze in."

"Really?" murmured Miss Paris. "Aren't you forgetting that Roddy Crockett is the whole Trojan backfield?"

"Southern California Trojans, Carolina Spartans," said Mr. Queen thoughtfully, munching. "Spartans versus Trojans . . . Sort of modern gridiron Siege of Troy."

"Ellery Queen, that's plagiarism or—or something! You read it in my column."

"Is there a Helen for the lads to battle over?" grinned Mr. Queen.

"You're *so* romantic, Queenikins. The only female involved is a very pretty, rich, and sensible co-ed named Joan Wing, and she *isn't* the kidnaped love of any of the Spartans."

"Curses," said Mr. Queen, reaching for the brandied plum pudding. "For a moment I thought I had something."

"But there's a Priam of a sort, because Roddy Crockett is engaged to Joan Wing, and Joanie's father, Pop Wing, is just about the noblest Trojan of them all."

"Maybe you know what you're talking about, beautiful," said Mr. Queen, "but *I* don't."

"You're positively the worst-informed man in California! Pop Wing is USC's most enthusiastic alumnus, isn't he?"

"Is he?"

"You mean you've never heard of Pop Wing?" asked Paula incredulously.

"Not guilty," said Mr. Queen. "More plum pudding, please."

"The Perennial Alumnus? The Boy Who Never Grew Up?"

"Thank you," said Mr. Queen. "I beg your pardon?"

"The Ghost of Exposition Park and the LA Coliseum, who holds a life seat for all USC football games? The unofficial trainer, rubber, water-boy, pep-talker, Alibi Ike, booster, and pigskin patron-in-chief to the Trojan eleven? Percy Squires 'Pop' Wing, Southern California '04, the man who sleeps, eats, and breathes only for Trojan victories and who married and, failing a son, created a daughter for the sole purpose of snaring USC's best fullback in years?"

"Peace, peace; I yield," moaned Mr. Queen, "before the crushing brutality of the characterization. I now know Percy Squires Wing as I hope never to know anyone again."

"Sorry!" said Paula, rising briskly. "Because directly after you've filled your bottomless tummy with plum pudding we're going Christmas calling on the great man."

"No!" said Mr. Queen with a shudder.

"You want to see the Rose Bowl game, don't you?"

"Who doesn't? But I haven't been able to snap a brace of tickets for love or money."

"Poor Queenie," purred Miss Paris, putting her arm about him.

"You're *so* helpless. Come on watch me wheedle Pop Wing out of two seats for the game!"

The lord of the château whose towers rose from a magnificently preposterous parklike estate in Inglewood proved to be a flat-bellied youngster of middle age, almost as broad as he was tall, with a small bald head set upon small ruddy cheeks, so that at first glance Mr. Queen thought he was viewing a Catawba grape lying on a boulder.

They came upon the millionaire seated on his hams in the center of a vast lawn, arguing fiercely with a young man who by his size—which was herculean—and his shape—which was cuneiform—and his coloring—which was coppery—could only be of the order *footballis*, and therefore Mr. Wing's future son-in-law and the New Year's Day hope of the Trojans.

They were manipulating wickets, mallets, and croquet balls in illustration of a complex polemic which apparently concerned the surest method of frustrating the sinister quarterback of the Carolina eleven, Ostermoor.

A young lady with red hair and a saucy nose sat cross-legged on the grass near by, her soft blue eyes fixed on the brown face of the young man with that naked worshipfulness young ladies permit themselves to exhibit in public only when their young men have formally yielded. This, concluded Mr. Queen without difficulty, must be the daughter of the great man and Mr. Roddy Crockett's fiancée, Joan Wing.

Mr. Wing hissed a warning to Roddy at the sight of Mr. Queen's unfamiliar visage, and for a moment Mr. Queen felt uncomfortably like a spy caught sneaking into the enemy's camp. But Miss Paris hastily vouched for his devotion to the cause of Troy, and for some time there were Christmas greetings and introductions, in the course of which Mr. Queen made the acquaintance of two persons whom he recognized instantly as the hybrid genus *house-guest perennialis*. One was a bearded gentleman with high cheek-bones and a Muscovite manner (pre-Soviet) entitled the Grand Duke Ostrov; the other was a thin, dark, whiplike female with inscrutable black eyes who went by the astonishing name of Madame Mephisto.

These two barely nodded to Miss Paris and Mr. Queen; they were listening to each word which dropped from the lips of Mr. Percy Squires Wing, their host, with the adoration of novitiates at the feet of their patron saint.

The noble Trojan's ruddiness of complexion, Mr. Queen pondered, came either from habitual exposure to the outdoors or from high blood-pressure; a conclusion which he discovered very soon was accurate on both counts, since Pop Wing revealed himself without urging as an Izaak Walton, a golfer, a Nimrod, a mountain-climber, a polo-player, and a racing yachtsman; and he was as squirmy and excitable as a small boy.

The small-boy analogy struck Mr. Queen with greater force when the Perennial Alumnus dragged Mr. Queen off to inspect what he alarmingly called "my trophy room." Mr. Queen's fears were vindicated; for in a huge vaulted chamber presided over by a desiccated, gloomy, and monosyllabic old gentleman introduced fantastically as "Gabby" Huntswood, he found himself inspecting as heterogeneous and remarkable an assemblage of junk as ever existed outside a small boy's dream of Paradise.

Postage-stamp albums, American college banners, mounted wild-animal heads, a formidable collection of match-boxes, cigar bands, stuffed fish, World War trench helmets of all nations . . . all were there; and Pop Wing beamed as he exhibited these priceless treasures, scurrying from one collection to another and fondling them with such ingenuous pleasure that Mr. Queen sighed for his own lost youth.

"Aren't these objects too—er—valuable to be left lying around this way, Mr. Wing?" he inquired politely.

"Hell, no. Gabby's more jealous of their safety than I am!" shouted the great man. "Hey, Gabby?"

"Yes, sir," said Gabby; and he frowned suspiciously at Mr. Queen.

"Why, Gabby made me install a burglar-alarm system. Can't see it, but this room's as safe as a vault."

"Safer," said Gabby, glowering at Mr. Queen.

"Think I'm crazy, Queen?"

"No, no," said Mr. Queen, who meant to say "Yes, yes."

"Lots of people do," chuckled Pop Wing. "Let 'em. Between 1904 and 1924 I just about vegetated. But something drove me on. Know what?"

Mr. Queen's famous powers of deduction were unequal to the task.

"The knowledge that I was making enough money to retire a young man and kick the world in the pants. And I did! Retired at forty-two and started doing all the things I'd never had time or money to do when I was a shaver. Collecting things. Keeps me young! Come here, Queen, and look at my *prize* collection." And he pulled Mr. Queen over to a gigantic glass case and pointed gleefully, an elder Penrod gloating over a marbles haul.

From his host's proud tone Mr. Queen expected to gaze upon nothing less than a collection of the royal crowns of Europe. Instead, he saw a vast number of scuffed, streaked, and muddy footballs, each carefully laid upon an ebony rest, and on each a legend lettered in gold leaf. One that caught his eye read: ROSE BOWL, 1930. USC 47–PITT 14. The others bore similar inscriptions.

"Wouldn't part with 'em for a million dollars," confided the great man. "Why, the balls in this case represent every Trojan victory for the past fifteen years!"

"Incredible!" exclaimed Mr. Queen.

"Yes, sir, right after every game they win the team presents old Pop Wing with the pigskin. What a collection!" And the millionaire gazed worshipfully at the unlovely oblate spheroids.

"They must think the world of you at USC."

"Well, I've sort of been of service to my Alma Mater," said Pop Wing modestly, "especially in football. Wing Athletic Scholarship, you know; Wing Dorm for Varsity athletes; and so on. I've scouted prep schools for years, personally; turned up some mighty fine Varsity material. Coach is a good friend of mine. I guess—" and he drew a happy breath—"I can have just about what I damn well ask for at the old school!"

"Including football tickets?" said Mr. Queen quickly, seizing his opportunity. "Must be marvelous to have that kind of drag. I've been trying for days to get tickets for the game."

The great man surveyed him. "What was your college?"

"Harvard," said Mr. Queen apologetically. "But I yield to no man in my ardent admiration of the Trojans. Darn it, I did want to watch Roddy Crockett mop up those Spartan upstarts."

"You did, huh?" said Pop Wing. "Say, how about you and Miss Paris being my guests at the Rose Bowl Sunday?"

"Couldn't think of it—" began Mr. Queen mendaciously, already savoring the joy of having beaten Miss Paris, so to speak, to the turnstiles.

"Won't hear another word." Mr. Wing embraced Mr. Queen. "Say, long as you'll be with us, I'll let you in on a little secret."

"Secret?" wondered Mr. Queen.

"Rod and Joan," whispered the millionaire, "are going to be married right after the Trojans win next Sunday!"

"Congratulations. He seems like a fine boy."

"None better. Hasn't got a cent, you understand—worked his way through—but he's graduating in January and . . . shucks! he's the greatest fullback the old school ever turned out. We'll find something for him to do. Yes, sir, Roddy's last game . . ." The great man sighed. Then he brightened. "Anyway, I've got a hundred thousand dollar surprise for my Joanie that ought to make her go right out and raise another triple-threat man for the Trojans!"

"A—how much of a surprise?" asked Mr. Queen feebly.

But the great man looked mysterious. "Let's go back and finish cooking that boy Ostermoor's goose!"

New Year's Day was warm and sunny; and Mr. Queen felt strange as he prepared to pick up Paula Paris and escort her to the Wing estate, from which their party was to proceed to the Pasadena stadium. In his quaint Eastern fashion, he was accustomed to don a mountain of sweater, scarf, and overcoat when he went to a football game; and here he was *en route* in a sports jacket!

"California, thy name is Iconoclast," muttered Mr. Queen, and he drove through already agitated Hollywood streets to Miss Paris's house.

"Heavens," said Paula, "you can't barge in on Pop Wing that way."

"What way?"

"Minus the Trojan colors. We've got to keep on the old darlin's good side, at least until we're safely in the stadium. Here!" And with a few deft twists of two lady's handkerchiefs Paula manufactured a breast-pocket kerchief for him in cardinal and gold.

"I see you've done yourself up pretty brown," said Mr. Queen, not unadmiringly; for Paula's figure was the secret envy of many better-advertised Hollywood ladies, and it was clad devastatingly in a cardinal-and-gold creation that was a cross between a suit and a dirndl, to Mr. Queen's inexperienced eye, and it was topped off with a perky, feathery hat perched nervously on her blue-black hair, concealing one bright eye.

"Wait till you see Joan," said Miss Paris, rewarding him with a kiss. "She's been calling me all week about *her* clothes problem. It's not every day a girl's called on to buy an outfit that goes equally well with a football game and a wedding." And as Mr. Queen drove off towards Inglewood she added thoughtfully: "I wonder what that awful creature will wear. Probably a turban and seven veils."

"What creature?"

"Madame Mephisto. Only her real name is Suzie Lucadamo, and she quit a dumpy little magic and mind-reading vaudeville act to set herself up in Seattle as a seeress—you know, we positively guarantee to pierce the veil of the Unknown? Pop met her in Seattle in November during the USC–Washington game. She wangled a Christmas-week invitation out of him for the purpose, I suppose, of looking over the rich Hollywood sucker-field without cost to herself."

"You seem to know a lot about her."

Paula smiled. "Joan Wing told me some—Joanie doesn't like the old gal nohow—and I dug out the rest . . . well, you know, darling, I know everything about *everybody*."

"Then tell me," said Mr. Queen. "Who exactly is the Grand Duke Ostrov?"

"Why?"

"Because," replied Mr. Queen grimly, "I don't like His Highness, and I do like—heaven help me!—Pop Wing and his juvenile amusements."

"Joan tells me Pop likes you, too, the fool! I guess in his adolescent way he's impressed by a real, live detective. Show him your G-man badge, darling." Mr. Queen glared, but Miss Paris's gaze was dreamy. "Pop may find it handy having you around today, at that."

"What d'ye mean?" asked Mr. Queen sharply.

"Didn't he tell you he had a surprise for Joan? He's told everyone in Los Angeles, although no one knows what it is but your humble correspondent."

"And Roddy, I'll bet. He did say something about a 'hundred thousand dollar surprise.' What's the point?"

"The point is," murmured Miss Paris, "that it's a set of perfectly matched star sapphires."

Mr. Queen was silent. Then he said: "You think Ostrov—"

"The Grand Duke," said Miss Paris, "is even phonier than Madame Suzie Lucadamo Mephisto. *His* name is Louie Batterson, and he hails from the Bronx. Everybody knows it but Pop Wing." Paula sighed. "But you know Hollywood—live and let live; you may need a sucker yourself someday. Batterson's a high-class deadbeat. He's pulled some awfully aromatic stunts in his time. I'm hoping he lays off our nostrils this sunny day."

"This," mumbled Mr. Queen, "is going to be one heck of a football game, I can see that."

Bedlam was a cloister compared with the domain of the Wings. The interior of the house was noisy with decorators, caterers, cooks, and waiters; and with a start Mr. Queen recalled that this was to be the wedding day of Joan Wing and Roddy Crockett.

They found their party assembled in one of the formal gardens—which, Mr. Queen swore to Miss Paris, outshone Fontainebleau—and apparently Miss Wing had solved her dressmaking problem, for while Mr. Queen could find no words to describe what she was wearing, Mr. Roddy Crockett could, and the word was "sockeroo."

Paula went into more technical raptures, and Miss Wing clung to her gridiron hero, who looked a little pale; and then the pride of Troy went loping off to the wars, leaping into his roadster and waving farewell with their cries of good cheer in his manly, young, and slightly mashed ears.

Pop Wing ran down the driveway after the roadster, bellowing: "Don't forget that Ostermoor defense, Roddy!"

And Roddy vanished in a trail of dusty glory; the noblest Trojan of them all came back shaking his head and muttering: "It ought to be a pipe!"; flunkies appeared bearing mounds of canapés and cocktails; the Grand Duke, regally Cossack in a long Russian coat gathered at the waist, amused the company with feats of legerdemain—his long soft hands were very fluent—and Madame Mephisto, minus the seven veils, but, as predicted, wearing the turban, went into a trance and murmured that she could see a "glorious Trojan vic-to-ree"—all the while Joan Wing sat smiling dreamily into her cocktail and Pop Wing pranced up and down vowing that he had never been cooler or more confident in his life.

And then they were in one of Wing's huge seven-passenger limousines—Pop, Joan, the Grand Duke, Madame, Gabby, Miss Paris, and Mr. Queen—bound for Pasadena and the fateful game.

And Pop said suddenly: "Joanie, I've got a surprise for you."

And Joan dutifully looked surprised, her breath coming a little faster; and Pop drew out of the right-hand pocket of his jacket a long leather case, and opened it, and said with a chuckle: "Wasn't going to show it to you till tonight, but Roddy told me before he left that you look so beautiful I ought to give you a preview as a reward. From me to you, Joanie. Like 'em?"

Joan gasped: "*Like* them!" and there were exclamations of "Oh!" and "Ah!," and they saw lying upon black velvet eleven superb sapphires, their stars winking royally—a football team of perfectly matched gems.

"Oh, *Pop*!" moaned Joan, and she flung her arms about him and wept on his shoulder, while he looked pleased and blustery, and puffed and closed the case and returned it to the pocket from which he had taken it.

"Formal opening tonight. Then you can decide whether you want to make a necklace out of 'em or a bracelet or what." And Pop stroked Joan's hair while she sniffled against him; and Mr. Queen, watching the Grand Duke of Ostrov, *né* Batterson, and Madame Mephisto, *née* Lucadamo, thought they were very clever to have concealed so quickly those involuntary expressions of avarice.

Surrounded by his guests, Pop strode directly to the Trojans' dressing-room, waving aside officials and police and student athletic underlings as if he owned the Rose Bowl and all the multitudinous souls besieging it.

The young man at the door said: "Hi, Pop," respectfully, and admitted them under the envious stares of the less fortunate mortals outside.

"Isn't he grand?" whispered Paula, her eyes like stars; but before Mr. Queen could reply there were cries of: "Hey! Femmes!" and "Here's Pop!" and the Coach came over, wickedly straight-arming Mr. Roddy Crockett, who was lacing his doeskin pants, aside, and said with a wink: "All right, Pop. Give it to 'em."

And Pop, very pale now, shucked his coat and flung it on a rubbing table; and the boys crowded round, very quiet suddenly; and Mr. Queen found himself pinned between a mountainous tackle and a behemoth of a guard who growled down at him: "Hey, you, stop squirming. Don't you see Pop's gonna make a speech?"

And Pop said, in a very low voice: "Listen, gang. The last time I made a dressing-room spiel was in '33. It was on a January first, too, and it was the day USC played Pitt in the Rose Bowl. That day we licked 'em thirty-three to nothing."

Somebody shouted: "Yay!" but Pop held up his hand.

"I made three January first speeches before that. One was in '32, before we knocked Tulane over by a score of twenty-one to twelve. One was in 1930, the day we beat the Panthers forty-seven to fourteen. And the first in '23, when we took Penn State by fourteen to three. And that was the first time in the history of the Rose Bowl that we represented the Pacific Coast Conference in the inter-sectional classic. There's just one thing I want you men to bear in mind when you dash out there in a few minutes in front of half of California."

The room was very still.

"I want you to remember that the Trojans have played in four Rose Bowl games. And I want you to remember that the Trojans have *won* four Rose Bowl games," said Pop.

And he stood high above them, looking down into their intent young faces; and then he jumped to the floor, breathing heavily.

Hell broke loose. Boys pounded him on the back; Roddy Crockett seized Joan and pulled her behind a locker; Mr. Queen found himself pinned to the door, hat over his eyes, by the elbow of the Trojan center, like a butterfly to a wall; and the Coach stood grinning at Pop, who grinned back, but tremulously.

"All right, men," said the Coach. "Pop?" Pop Wing grinned and shook them all off, and Roddy helped him into his coat, and after a while Mr. Queen, considerably the worse for the wear, found himself seated in Pop's box directly above the fifty-yard line.

And then, as the two teams dashed into the Bowl across the brilliant turf, to the roar of massed thousands, Pop Wing uttered a faint cry.

"What's the matter?" asked Joan quickly, seizing his arm. "Aren't you feeling well, Pop?"

"The sapphires," said Pop Wing in a hoarse voice, his hand in his pocket. "They're gone."

Kick-off! Twenty-two figures raced to converge in a tumbling mass, and the stands thundered, the USC section fluttering madly with flags . . . and then there was a groan that rent the blue skies, and deadly, despairing silence.

For the Trojans' safety man caught the ball, started forward, slipped, the ball popped out of his hands, the Carolina right end fell on it—and there was the jumping, gleeful Spartan team on the Trojans' 9-yard line, Carolina's ball, first down, and four plays for a touchdown.

And Gabby, who had not heard Pop Wing's exclamation, was on his feet shrieking: "But they can't *do* that! Oh, heavens— Come *on*, USC! Hold that line!"

Pop glanced at Mr. Huntswood with bloodshot surprise, as if a three-thousand-year-old mummy had suddenly come to life; and then he muttered: "Gone. Somebody's—picked my pocket."

"What!" whispered Gabby; and he fell back, staring at his employer with horror.

"But thees ees fantastic," the Grand Duke exclaimed.

Mr. Queen said quietly: "Are you positive, Mr. Wing?"

Pop's eyes were on the field, automatically analyzing the play; but they were filled with pain. "Yes, I'm sure. Some pickpocket in the crowd . . ."

"No," said Mr. Queen.

"Ellery, what do you mean?" cried Paula.

"From the moment we left Mr. Wing's car until we entered the Trojan dressing-room we surrounded him completely. From the moment we left the Trojan dressing-room until we sat down in this box, we surrounded him completely. No, our pickpocket is one of this group, I'm afraid."

Madame Mephisto shrilled: "How dare you! Aren't you forgetting that it was Mr. Crockett who helped Mr. Wing on with his coat in that dressing-room?"

"You—" began Pop in a growl, starting to rise.

Joan put her hand on his arm and squeezed, smiling at him. "Never mind her, Pop."

Carolina gained two yards on a plunge through center. Pop shaded his eyes with his hands, staring at the opposite lines.

"Meester Queen," said the Grand Duke coldly, "that ees an insult. I demand we all be—how you say?—searched."

Pop waved his hand wearily. "Forget it. I came to watch a football game." But he no longer looked like a small boy.

"His Highness's suggestion," murmured Mr. Queen, "is an excellent one. The ladies may search one another; the men may do the same. Suppose we all leave here together—in a body—and retire to the rest rooms?"

"Hold 'em," muttered Pop, as if he had not heard. Carolina gained 2 yards more on an off-tackle play. Five yards to go in two downs. They could see Roddy Crockett slapping one of his linesmen on the back.

The lines met, and buckled. No gain.

"D'ye see Roddy go through that hole?" muttered Pop.

Joan rose and, rather imperiously, motioned Madame and Paula to precede her. Pop did not stir. Mr. Queen motioned to the men. The Grand Duke and Gabby rose. They all went quickly away.

And still Pop did not move. Until Ostermoor rifled a flat pass into the end zone, and a Carolina end came up out of the ground and snagged the ball. And then it was Carolina 6, USC 0, the big clock indicating that barely a minute of the first quarter's playing time had elapsed.

"Block that kick!"

Roddy plunged through the Spartan line and blocked it. The Carolina boys trotted back to their own territory, grinning.

"Hmph," said Pop to the empty seats in his box; and then he sat still and simply waited, an old man.

The first quarter rolled along. The Trojans could not get out of their territory. Passes fell incomplete. The Spartan line held like iron.

"Well, we're back," said Paula Paris. The great man looked up slowly. "We didn't find them."

A moment later Mr. Queen returned, herding his two companions. Mr. Queen said nothing at all; he merely shook his head, and the Grand Duke Ostrov looked grandly contemptuous, and Madame Mephisto tossed her turbaned head angrily. Joan was very pale; her eyes crept down the field to Roddy, and Paula saw that they were filled with tears.

Mr. Queen said abruptly: "Will you excuse me, please?" and left again with swift strides.

The first quarter ended with the score still 6 to 0 against USC and the Trojans unable to extricate themselves from the menace of their goal post . . . pinned back with inhuman regularity by the sharp-shooting Mr. Ostermoor. There is no defense against a deadly accurate kick.

When Mr. Queen returned, he wiped his slightly moist brow and said pleasantly: "By the way, Your Highness, it all comes back to me now. In a former incarnation—I believe in that life your name was Batterson, and you were the flower of an ancient Bronx family—weren't you mixed up in a jewel robbery?"

"Jewel robbery!" gasped Joan, and for some reason she looked relieved. Pop's eyes fixed coldly on the Grand Duke's suddenly oscillating beard.

"Yes," continued Mr. Queen, "I seem to recall that the fence tried to involve you, Your Highness, saying you were the go-between, but the jury wouldn't believe a fence's word, and so you went free. You were quite charming on the stand, I recall—had the courtroom in stitches."

"It's a damn lie," said the Grand Duke thickly, without the trace of an accent. His teeth gleamed wolfishly at Mr. Queen from their thicket.

"You thieving four-flusher—" began Pop Wing, half-rising from his seat.

"Not yet, Mr. Wing," said Mr. Queen.

"I have never been so insulted—" began Madame Mephisto.

"And you," said Mr. Queen with a little bow, "would be wise to hold your tongue, Madame Lucadamo."

Paula nudged him in a fierce mute inquiry, but he shook his head. He looked perplexed.

No one said anything until, near the end of the second quarter, Roddy Crockett broke loose for a 44-yard gain, and on the next play the ball came to rest on Carolina's 26-yard line.

Then Pop Wing was on his feet, cheering lustily, and even Gabby Huntswood was yelling in his cracked, unoiled voice: "Come on, Trojans!"

"Attaboy, Gabby," said Pop with the ghost of a grin. "First time I've ever seen you excited about a football game."

Three plays netted the Trojans 11 yards more: first down on Carolina's 15-yard line! The half was nearly over. Pop was hoarse, the theft apparently forgotten. He groaned as USC lost ground, Ostermoor breaking up two plays. Then, with the ball on Carolina's 22-yard line, with time for only one more play before the whistle ending the half, the Trojan quarterback called for a kick formation and Roddy booted the ball straight and true between the uprights of the Spartans' goal.

The whistle blew. Carolina 6, USC 3.

Pop sank back, mopping his face. "Have to do better. That damn Ostermoor! What's the matter with Roddy?"

During the rest period Mr. Queen, who had scarcely watched the struggle, murmured: "By the way, Madame, I've heard a good deal about your unique gift of

Trojan Horse

divination. We can't seem to find the sapphires by natural means; how about the supernatural?"

Madame Mephisto glared at him. "This is no time for jokes!"

"A true gift needs no special conditions," smiled Mr. Queen.

"The atmosphere—scarcely propitious—"

"Come, come, Madame! You wouldn't overlook an opportunity to restore your host's hundred thousand dollar loss?"

Pop began to inspect Madame with sudden keen curiosity.

Madame closed her eyes, her long fingers at her temples. "I see," she murmured, "I see a long jewel-case . . . yes, it is closed, closed . . . but it is dark, very dark . . . it is in a, yes, a dark place . . ." She sighed and dropped her hands, her dark lids rising. "I'm sorry. I can see no more."

"It's in a dark place, all right," said Mr. Queen dryly. "It's in my pocket." And to their astonishment he took from his pocket the great man's jewel-case.

Mr. Queen snapped it open. "Only," he remarked sadly, "it's empty. I found it in a corner of the Trojans' dressing-room."

Joan shrank back, squeezing a tiny football charm so hard it collapsed. The millionaire gazed stonily at the parading bands blaring around the field.

"You see," said Mr. Queen, "the thief hid the sapphires somewhere and dropped the case in the dressing-room. And we were all there. The question is: Where did the thief cache them?"

"Pardon me," said the Grand Duke. "Eet seems to me the theft must have occurred in Meester Wing's car, after he returned the jewel-case to his pocket. So perhaps the jewels are hidden in the car."

"I have already," said Mr. Queen, "searched the car."

"Then in the Trojan dressing-room!" cried Paula.

"No, I've also searched there—floor to ceiling, lockers, cabinets, clothes, everything. The sapphires aren't there."

"The thief wouldn't have been so foolish as to drop them in an aisle on the way to this box," said Paula thoughtfully. "Perhaps he had an accomplice—"

"To have an accomplice," said Mr. Queen wearily, "you must know you are going to commit a crime. To know that you must know there will be a crime to commit. Nobody but Mr. Wing knew that he intended to take the sapphires with him today—is that correct, Mr. Wing?"

"Yes," said Pop. "Except Rod— Yes. No one."

"Wait!" cried Joan passionately. "I know what you're all thinking. You think Roddy had—had something to do with this. I can see it—yes, even you, Pop! But don't you see how silly it is? Why should Rod steal something that will belong to him anyway? I *won't* have you thinking Roddy's a thief!"

"I did not," said Pop feebly.

"Then we're agreed the crime was unpremeditated and that no accomplice could have been provided for," said Mr. Queen. "Incidentally, the sapphires are not in this box. I've looked."

"But it's ridiculous!" cried Joan. "Oh, I don't care about losing the jewels, beautiful as they are; Pop can afford the loss; it's just that it's such a mean, dirty thing to do. Its very cleverness makes it dirty."

"Criminals," drawled Mr. Queen, "are not notoriously fastidious, so long as they achieve their criminal ends. The point is that the thief has hidden those gems somewhere—the place is the very essence of his crime, for upon its simplicity and later accessibility depends the success of his theft. So it's obvious that the thief's hidden the sapphires where no one would spot them easily, where they're unlikely to be found even by accident, yet where he can safely retrieve them at his leisure."

"But heavens," said Paula, exasperated, "they're not in the car, they're not in the dressing-room, they're not on any of us, they're not in this box, there's no accomplice . . . it's impossible!"

"No," muttered Mr. Queen. "Not impossible. It was done. But how? How?"

The Trojans came out fighting. They carried the pigskin slowly but surely down the field toward the Spartans' goal line. But on the 21-yard stripe the attack stalled. The diabolical Mr. Ostermoor, all over the field, intercepted a forward pass on third down with 8 yards to go, ran the ball back 51 yards, and USC was frustrated again.

The fourth quarter began with no change in the score; a feeling that was palpable settled over the crowd, a feeling that they were viewing the first Trojan defeat in Rose Bowl history. Injuries and exhaustion had taken their toll of the Trojan team; they seemed dispirited, beaten.

"When's he going to open up?" muttered Pop. "That trick!" And his voice rose to a roar. "Roddy! Come on!"

The Trojans drove suddenly with the desperation of a last strength. Carolina gave ground, but stubbornly. Both teams tried a kicking duel, but Ostermoor and Roddy were so evenly matched that neither side gained much through the interchange.

Then the Trojans began to take chances. A long pass—successful. Another!

"Roddy's going to town!"

Pop Wing, sapphires forgotten, bellowed hoarsely; Gabby shrieked encouragement; Joan danced up and down; the Grand Duke and Madame looked politely interested; even Paula felt the mass excitement stir her blood.

But Mr. Queen sat frowning in his seat, thinking and thinking as if cerebration were a new function to him.

The Trojans clawed closer and closer to the Carolina goal line, the Spartans fighting back furiously but giving ground, unable to regain possession of the ball.

First down on Carolina's 19-yard line, with seconds to go!

"Roddy, the kick! The kick!" shouted Pop.

The Spartans held on the first plunge. They gave a yard on the second. On the third—the inexorable hand of the big clock jerked towards the hour mark—the Spartans' left tackle smashed through USC's line and smeared the play for a 6-yard loss. Fourth down, seconds to go, and the ball on Carolina's 24-yard line!

"If they don't go over next play," screamed Pop, "the game's lost. It'll be Carolina's ball and they'll freeze it . . . *Roddy!*" he thundered. *"The kick play!"*

And, as if Roddy could hear that despairing voice, the ball snapped back, the Trojan quarterback snatched it, held it ready for Roddy's toe, his right hand between the ball and the turf . . . Roddy darted up as if to kick, but as he reached the ball he scooped it from his quarterback's hands and raced for the Carolina goal line.

"It worked!" bellowed Pop. "They expected a place kick to tie—and it worked! *Make it, Roddy!*"

USC spread out, blocking like demons. The Carolina team was caught completely by surprise. Roddy wove and slithered through the bewildered Spartan line and crossed the goal just as the final whistle blew.

"We win! We win!" cackled Gabby, doing a war dance.

"Yowie!" howled Pop, kissing Joan, kissing Paula, almost kissing Madame.

Mr. Queen looked up. The frown had vanished from his brow. He seemed serene, happy.

"Who won?" asked Mr. Queen genially.

But no one answered. Struggling in a mass of worshipers, Roddy was running up the field to the 50-yard line; he dashed up to the box and thrust something into Pop Wing's hands, surrounded by almost the entire Trojan squad.

"Here it is, Pop," panted Roddy. "The old pigskin. Another one for your collection, and a honey! Joan!"

"Oh, Roddy."

"My boy," began Pop, overcome by emotion; but then he stopped and hugged the dirty ball to his breast.

Roddy grinned and, kissing Joan, yelled: "Remind me that I've got a date to marry you tonight!" and ran off towards the Trojan dressing-room followed by a howling mob.

Trojan Horse

"Ahem!" coughed Mr. Queen. "Mr. Wing, I think we're ready to settle your little difficulty."

"Huh?" said Pop, gazing with love at the filthy ball. "Oh." His shoulders sagged. "I suppose," he said wearily, "we'll have to notify the police—"

"I should think," said Mr. Queen, "that that isn't necessary, at least just yet. May I relate a parable? It seems that the ancient city of Troy was being besieged by the Greeks, and holding out very nicely, too; so nicely that the Greeks, who were very smart people, saw that only guile would get them into the city. And so somebody among the Greeks conceived a brilliant plan, based upon a very special sort of guile; and the essence of this guile was that the Trojans should be made to do the very thing the Greeks has been unable to do themselves. You will recall that in this the Greeks were successful, since the Trojans, overcome by curiosity and the fact that the Greeks had sailed away, hauled the wooden horse with their own hands into the city and, lo! that night, when all Troy slept, the Greeks hidden within the horse crept out, and you know the rest. Very clever, the Greeks. May I have that football, Mr. Wing?"

Pop said dazedly: "Huh?"

Mr. Queen, smiling, took it from him, deflated it by opening the valve, unlaced the leather thongs, shook the limp pigskin over Pop's cupped hands . . . and out plopped the eleven sapphires.

"You see," murmured Mr. Queen, as they stared speechless at the gems in Pop Wing's shaking hands, "the thief stole the jewel-case from Pop's coat pocket while Pop was haranguing his beloved team in the Trojan dressing-room before the game. The coat was lying on a rubbing table and there was such a mob that no one noticed the thief sneak over to the table, take the case out of Pop's coat, drop it in a corner after removing the sapphires, and edge his way to the table where the football to be used in the Rose Bowl game was lying, still uninflated. He loosened the laces surreptitiously, pushed the sapphires into the space between the pigskin wall and the rubber bladder, tied the laces, and left the ball apparently as he had found it.

"Think of it! All the time we were watching the game, the eleven sapphires were in this football. For one hour this spheroid has been kicked, passed, carried, fought over, sat on, smothered, grabbed, scuffed, muddied—with a king's ransom in it!"

"But how did you know they were hidden in the ball," gasped Paula, "and who's the thief, you wonderful man?"

Mr. Queen lit a cigaret modestly. "With all the obvious hiding places eliminated, you see, I said to myself: 'One of us is a thief, and the hiding place must be accessible to the thief after this game.' And I remembered a parable and a fact. The parable I've told you, and the fact was that after every winning Trojan game the ball is presented to Mr. Percy Squires Wing."

"But you can't think—" began Pop, bewildered.

"Obviously you didn't steal your own gems," smiled Mr. Queen. "So, you see, the thief had to be someone who could take equal advantage with you of the fact that the winning ball is presented to you. Someone who saw that there are two ways of stealing gems: to go to the gems, or to make the gems come to you.

"And so I knew that the thief was the man who, against all precedent and his taciturn nature, has been volubly imploring the Trojan team to win this football game; the man who knew that if the Trojans won the game the ball would immediately be presented to Pop Wing, and who gambled upon the Trojans; the man who saw that, with the ball given immediately to Pop Wing, he and he exclusively, custodian of Pop's wonderful and multifarious treasures, could retrieve the sapphires safely unobserved—grab the old coot, Your Highness!—Mr. Gabby Huntswood."

The Return of Cardula

JACK RITCHIE

"Albert's last words were 'No snow.' "

I frowned thoughtfully. People do seem to babble the oddest things when they depart this world. Especially murder victims. "What were the weather conditions at the time of Albert's death?" I asked.

"The temperature was in the low seventies. You couldn't *buy* snow on a night like that."

Which reminded me. "Now be utterly honest with me, sir. In the vernacular of the underworld, snow often refers to drugs of one kind or another. Were you and Albert by any chance involved in drugs?"

His expression indicated that he was clearly above that sort of thing. "We wouldn't touch anything that heavy. We were just ordinary thieves."

* * *

I had arrived at my office at nine P.M.

I closed the window against the night air, hung up my cape, and proceeded to unlock the door to my waiting room.

I found a client already seated there. I always leave the door between my waiting room and the hall unlocked. He seemed startled to see me. "Were you inside there all the time?"

I smiled economically. "Have you been out here long?"

"About twenty minutes."

He was a small man of middle years with blinking eyes and a nervous manner. He studied me dubiously, as people have a tendency to do when they first meet me. "Are you Cardula?"

"Yes." I showed him into my office and offered him a chair.

He sat down. "I finally couldn't stand it any longer. I decided that I ought to see a private detective and find out what could be done. I was going to go the first thing tomorrow morning, but when I looked up names in the phone book I saw that your display ad said Night Hours, so I decided to come here right away and get it over with." He hesitated. "Is a private eye something like a priest or a lawyer? I mean if you tell him something does he keep it to himself?"

"Sir, I assure you that anything you have to tell me will travel no further."

That satisfied him. "My name is Walter Pierce. I'd like you to solve a murder."

"Sir," I said, "I do not wish to discourage business, but the regular police possess the numbers, the expertise, and the communications needed to handle matters as grave as murder. Contrary to popular belief, private detectives rarely, if ever, deal with murder."

"But the police still haven't found the murderer and I don't think they ever will."

"When did this murder occur?"

"About two months ago."

"And the victim?"

"Albert Marshall. Albert and me were partners. We were together for more than thirty years. In jail and out. Mostly in. We'd get caught together, serve time together, and get paroled together."

Naturally I wanted to hear more about that. "Jail?"

He nodded. "The fact of the matter is that Albert and me were thieves. Mostly burglary, but also whatever else came along. That's why we were at the ball park. Not to see the game—we never even read the sports pages of the newspapers—but to go through the locker rooms while the players were out on the field. You know, scoop up anything we could lay our hands on—watches, wallets, rings, anything that looked valuable."

"Wouldn't you expect to find somebody in the rooms watching the players' possessions?"

"Sometimes there'd be somebody there and sometimes not. Whenever we found anybody, we'd just pretend we were lost and walk out again."

He rubbed his jaw. "Well, this time we did things a little different because of the layout. There was this long low corridor, like a tunnel, under the stands leading to the locker rooms and it made a turn. If we both went in there and something happened that we didn't expect we could get trapped. So we decided that one of us would stay at the entrance, like a lookout, and the other would go inside and do the job. If anybody showed up while Albert was at work, I'd stall him long enough so Albert could finish up inside and get out of there."

Pierce sighed. "So I stood there and watched Albert disappear down the corridor. And two minutes later I saw Albert again—only this time he had one hand tight against his chest and he was staggering. He came back up to me, his eyes wide, and said, 'No snow.' Then he dropped dead at my feet.

"At first I thought it was a heart attack, but then I saw the hole in his chest. There wasn't much blood—just around the edges of the wound and on Albert's hand. What I figure happened is that somebody was there in the locker room, only Albert didn't know it. When he saw Albert going through the lockers collecting, this unknown person grabbed a gun and fired."

"Did you hear the shot?"

"No. Where I was standing the noise from the fans must have drowned it out. So there I was with Albert's body, but I couldn't go to the police because I hadn't reported to my parole officer for over a year and that could get me into a lot of trouble. So I just had to leave Albert lying there and let somebody else find his body."

Pierce shook his head sadly. "Albert was even smaller than I am and weighed ten pounds less. You could have said boo and Albert would have dropped everything and run like a rabbit. There wasn't no cause to shoot him."

Now I vaguely remembered reading a newspaper item about the body of a man being found in a corridor under the stands at the County Stadium. The police had speculated that he might have been the victim of a robbery attempt that went awry.

I reflected. "If Albert was shot by someone in the locker room, why didn't that person come forward and admit as much? I don't remember reading anything to that effect in the newspapers."

Pierce smiled thinly. "Nobody ever came forward. Whoever shot Albert wasn't too proud of what he'd done. Maybe because it was really murder. I was hoping the police would find him, but since that doesn't look likely anymore I decided to come to you and see if anything can be done about it."

"Whose locker room had Albert been rifling? The home team's or the visitors'?"

"The home team. If everything went right we were going to go through the visitors' next."

When Pierce left, I pondered. Who had killed Albert? A locker-room attendant? Or perhaps even a player who had lagged behind for some reason? A visit to the stadium might be in order.

I found the evening's newspaper in the waiting room and turned to the sports pages. Ah, good, there was a game tonight.

The Return of Cardula

It was approximately four miles to the County Stadium—as the crow flies, so to speak—and when I arrived I descended to a dark spot behind the last seats in the upper grandstand.

I studied the playing field far below. Even with my ultra-keen eyesight I could barely distinguish the numbers on the backs of the players. Clearly I had to get a better view.

I strode down the ramp to the lower grandstand and then down the aisle to the box seats near the diamond. I found two empty seats and took one of them, which gave me an excellent close view of the players. I purchased a score card and settled down to observe. A beer vendor passed and I was sorely tempted—however, I am on a strict high-protein diet.

I am by no means a baseball aficionado—however, I am not totally ignorant of the game. I have, through occasional video viewing, natural curiosity, and longevity, acquired at least a working knowledge of the game and even recognition of certain of the more important individuals in the sport.

From the scoreboard in left field, I learned that I had entered the stadium in the last half of the sixth inning. The home team led the Yankees, 4 to 2, and was at bat. There were two outs, Gary on first base, and Seiler at bat.

I noticed that I was drawing some attention from those seated about me. Perhaps I should have worn one of my sports jackets rather than the red-lined cape.

Seiler walked on four pitched balls, putting men on first and second. Monson stepped into the batter's box and swung at the first pitch. He sent a fly ball to Winfield, the Yankee left fielder, and that ended the inning.

I now became aware of a middle-aged couple standing in the aisle glowering at me. They remained thus for a few minutes more and then departed. However, they soon returned, this time accompanied by an usher.

He regarded me sternly. "Are you sure you got the right seat, mister? These people think you're in one of theirs and they got the ticket stubs to prove it."

The pair nodded confirmation and held up their stubs. "We had car trouble and just got here," the man said.

I managed to look perplexed. "Isn't this Section Eight?"

Obviously it was not and the usher said, "Nope."

I rose immediately. "My apologies, madam and sir. I seem to have made an error."

I left them and wandered up and down the aisles until I found another vacant seat in Section Five.

The Yankees went down one-two-three in the top half of the seventh.

I now found the same usher who had accosted me before at my side. This time he was accompanied by a policeman.

The usher spoke. "I been watching you, mister. This ain't Section Eight either."

I blinked surprise. "It isn't?"

"No. Let's see your ticket stub. If you paid to get in here, you got a ticket stub."

I searched several of my pockets and then chuckled. "I seem to have lost my stub. It was here just a moment ago." Then I appealed to his reason. "Oh, well, what difference does it really make *which* seat I take? As long as it was empty."

The policeman took the opposite view. "Mister, no stub, no seat." He took me by the arm and began escorting me to the exit.

I could, of course, have tossed him, the usher, and several dozen of the interested spectators to the winds, but I detest being the center of attention. It brings a blush to my cheeks, which can be quite a strain.

The policeman guided me all the way down the exit ramp and out of the stadium before he released his hold.

"For shame, mister. You look like you got money and still you sneak into the stadium."

When he disappeared, I walked to the ticket windows only to discover that they were all closed. Nevertheless, I reentered the stadium, this time finding a place under the roof of the upper grandstand.

The score was still 4 to 2 and remained that way as

the inning ended. The Yankees trotted in for their turn at the plate and our team took the field. I watched our pitcher, a young left hander, wind up and throw the first ball of the eighth inning. A perfect strike.

Then I blinked and nearly lost my grip on the rafter.

I stared at the pitcher as he threw a slider for strike two.

So *that* was it.

In the top half of the ninth, Piniella hit a home run for the Yankees with nobody on, but it wasn't enough and they lost the game 4 to 3.

After the game I remained in the area waiting for the players to show, change to mufti, and exit.

When they did, some of them went to private automobiles in the parking lot and others to the team bus.

I followed the bus closely as it made its way out of the lot and onto the freeway. It took the team back downtown and debarked them at the Atkinson Hotel.

I managed to be in the same elevator which took Monson, the pitcher, up to the twelfth floor. When he unlocked the door of his room, I shouldered in before he could close it again. He backed up, startled. "Who are you?"

I proffered my card and he glanced at it without touching. I smiled. "I am here to see that justice is done."

He swallowed. "Justice? What justice?"

"Oh, come now. You know perfectly well that I am referring to the murder of one Albert Marshall on an evening two months ago at the County Stadium."

His face paled.

I was rather proud of my deductions and now I proceeded to expound. "Let me refresh your memory, sir. On that night two months ago, you were pitching. However, you were not at your best. You were shelled from the mound and sent to the showers. Being sent to the showers can be interpreted literally or figuratively, depending upon the manager of a team. And your manager was literal. You descended into the bowels of the stadium to the locker room. You removed your uniform.

"I deduce that you had just finished your shower and were still in the shower room toweling yourself when Albert Marshall entered the adjoining locker room, his mission being to pilfer anything portable. If you had been still showering, Marshall would have heard the water running and fled immediately.

"As you reentered the locker room you saw Marshall at work. You sneaked to your locker, removed a pistol from therein, made your presence known, and shot him."

Monson sank slowly into a chair.

I smiled grimly. "Marshall was sorely wounded, but still had the strength to flee. And then suddenly the full realization of what you had done struck you. Even if the man was a thief caught in the act, why does a six-foot-three-inch two-hundred-pound man in the prime of life find it necessary to use a weapon against a middle-aged five-foot thief? It might possibly even be considered murder. You could get into real trouble if you admitted the shooting. So you decided to say nothing at all."

Monson sighed heavily and shook his head. "No. It wasn't like that. It was an accident. The gun didn't even belong to me. It's Seiler's. He has the locker next to mine and he collects guns. He just bought that one for his collection. I didn't know it was loaded and I never held a pistol before in my life. I was just going to point the gun, but I guess it had a hair trigger or maybe I was just too nervous and it went off.

"I was really stunned when it happened. I just stood there, not knowing what to do or think when he staggered out. I was still in shock when the team came in after the game. And then I learned that he was dead and the police thought he was the victim of a holdup attempt."

Monson looked me full in the eye. "I was going to go to the police and tell them what happened, but then all kinds of other thoughts came to my mind. Like this is my first year in the majors and we're pennant contenders. And all my life I dreamed about pitching in a World Series. So I finally decided I'd say nothing until the end of the season or the World Series, whichever came last.

And *then* I'd go to the police and be ready to go to jail, if that was in the cards. But now that you know what happened, I guess I'd better go to the police right now."

I thought over his words. "You say the team is a pennant contender?"

He nodded. "With any luck at all, we'll make it."

I pondered a bit more, pacing back and forth a few times while he watched. Then I came to a decision. "Well, perhaps it won't do any actual harm if you waited until the end of the season or the World Series."

He brightened. "You really think so?"

"You have my permission."

The next evening, I was waiting in my office when Pierce appeared.

He listened while I related the previous night's events and then became reflective. "You really think he'll go to the police after the World Series?"

"Yes, I believe so. He seemed quite sincere to me. I think we can trust him," I said.

"How old is he?"

"I'd guess about twenty-one or -two."

Pierce mulled a bit more. "Well, if it had been murder, like I thought, that would be one thing. But if it was an accident, I can't see what good it will do for the kid to report to the police. I mean it can't do Albert any good. He's dead. And Monson is still a young man. He could ruin his whole life and career. Maybe he should just keep his mouth shut forever and let sleeping dogs lie."

I smiled. "My sentiments exactly. I will speak to him again."

Pierce now asked the question for which I had been waiting. "How did you manage to pinpoint Monson? After all, there are a lot of other players who could have done it."

I chuckled. "When Monson undressed for the showers, I suspect that he tossed, flung, or otherwise draped his uniform shirt over the edge of his open locker door. The name Monson in lower case *and* upside down, means nothing. However, in upper case—as it appeared on his uniform—and upside down, it becomes NOSNOW.

"As you said, Albert knew absolutely nothing about baseball or he might have recognized Monson. But all he saw was someone standing next to a uniformed shirt which carried the letters NOSNOW. As far as Albert was concerned, that could very well have been the player's name. When he conveyed that information to you, he chose to pronounce it 'No snow,' which is as reasonable as any."

After Pierce left, I locked the office and went off to the County Stadium. This time I wore my sports jacket and bought a ticket.

We beat the Yankees again, 6 to 1.

This Won't Kill You
REX STOUT

At the end of the sixth inning the score was Boston 11, New York 1. I would not have believed that the day would ever come when, seated in a lower box between home and first, at the seventh and deciding game of a World Series between New York and Boston, I would find myself glomming a girl. I am by no means above glomming a girl if she is worthy, but not at a ball game, where my mind is otherwise occupied. That awful day, though, I did.

The situation was complex and will have to be explained. It was a mess even before the game started. Pierre Mondor, owner of a famous restaurant in Paris, was visiting New York and was our house guest at Nero Wolfe's old brownstone on West 35TH Street. He got the notion, somehow, that Wolfe had to take him to a baseball game, and Wolfe as his host couldn't refuse. Tickets were no problem, since Emil Chisholm, oil millionaire and part owner of the New York team, considered himself deeply in Wolfe's debt on account of a case we had handled for him a few years back.

So that October afternoon, a Wednesday, I got the pair of them—the noted private detective and the noted chef—up to the ball park. It was twenty past one, only ten minutes to game time, and the stands were jammed. I motioned to Mondor, and he slid in and sat. Wolfe stood and glared down at the wooden slats and metal arms. Then he glared at me.

"Are you out of your senses?" he demanded.

"I warned you," I said coldly. "It was designed for men, not mammoths."

He tightened his lips, moved his bulk, lowered it, and tried to squeeze between the arms. No. He grasped the rail in front with both hands, wriggled loose, and perched on the edge of the seat.

Mondor called to me across the great expanse of Wolfe's back: "I depend with confidence on you, Arshee! You must make clear as it develops! What are the little white things?"

I love baseball, I love the New York team, I had 50 bucks up on that game, but I would have got up and gone but for one thing: It was working hours and Wolfe pays my salary, and there were too many people, some of them alive and loose, who felt strongly that he had already lived too long. He is seldom out in the open, easy to get at, and when he is I like to be nearby. So I gritted my teeth and stuck.

The ground crew finished smoothing off and hauled their drags away; the umpires did a huddle, the home team trotted out on the field to their stations; the throng gave with a lusty, excited roar; we all stood up for *The Star-Spangled Banner*, and then sat down again. After southpaw Ed Romeike, 22-4 for the season, had burned a few over for the range, Lew Baker, the catcher, fired it to Tiny Garth at second. The Boston lead-off man came to the white line, the plate umpire said go, and Romeike looked around at the field, toed the rubber, went into his tricky windup, and shot a fast one over the outside corner for strike one. The crowd let out a short, sharp yell.

My personal nightmare was bad enough. Mondor was our guest, and trying to tell a foreigner what a base on balls is during a World Series game, with two men on, two down, and Oaky Asmussen at bat, is hard on the nerves. As for Wolfe, it wasn't so much the sight of him there in his concentrated misery; it was the certainty that by tomorrow he would have figured out a way to blame it on me, and that would start a feud.

Bad enough, but more was to come, and not for me alone. One fly had plopped into the soup even before the game started, when the line-up was announced and Tiny Garth was named for second base, with no explanation. A buzz of amazement had filled the stands. Why not Nick Ferrone? Ferrone, a lanky, big-eared kid just up from the bush five months back, had fielded and batted himself so far to the front that it was taken for granted he would be voted rookie of the year. He had been spectacular in the first six games of the Series, batting .427. Where was he today? Why Garth?

Then the game. That was no personal nightmare of mine; it was all too public. In the first inning Con Prentiss, New York's shortstop, bobbled an easy grounder, and two minutes later Lew Baker, the catcher, trying to nab a runner at second, threw the ball six feet over Garth's head into the outfield. With luck the visitors scored only one run. In the second inning Nat Neill, center fielder, misjudged a fly he could have walked under, tried to run in three directions at once, and had to chase it to the fence; and soon after that, Prentiss grabbed a hard-hit ball on the hop and hurled it into the dirt three paces to the left of third base. By the time they got three out, Boston had two more runs.

As the New York team came in for their turn at bat in the second, bitter sarcasms from the stands greeted them. Then our section was distracted by an incident. A man in a hurry came plunging down the aisle, bumping my elbow as he passed, and pulled up alongside a front box occupied by six men, among them the Mayor of New York and oilman Emil Chisholm, who had provided our tickets. The man spoke into the ear of Chisholm, who looked anything but happy. Chisholm said something to his boxmates, arose, and beat it up the aisle double-quick, followed by cutting remarks from nearby fans who had recognized him.

As my eyes went back to the arena, Con Prentiss, New York shortstop, swung at a floater and missed by a mile.

There is no point in my retailing the agony. As I said, at the end of the sixth the score was 11 to 1. Romeike was hurling all right, but his support would have been pitiful on a sand lot. Joe Eston, the third baseman, and Nat Neill had each made two errors, and Con Prentiss and Lew Baker three apiece. As they came to the dugout in the sixth one wit yelled, "Say it ain't true, Joe!" at Eston, and the crowd, recognizing that classic moan to Shoeless Joe Jackson, let out a howl. They were getting really rough. As for me, I had had plenty of the tragedy out on the diamond and was looking around for something less painful, when I caught sight of the girl, in a box off to my right.

I glommed her, not offensively. There were two of them. One was a redhead who would start to get plump in a couple of years; almost worthy, but not quite. The other one, the glommee, had light-brown hair and dark-brown eyes, and was fully qualified. I had the feeling that she was not a complete stranger, that I had seen her somewhere before, but couldn't place her.

The pleasure it gave me to look at her was not pure, because it was adulterated with resentment. She looked happy. Her eyes sparkled. Apparently she liked the way things were going. There is no law barring enemy fans from a ball park, but I resented it. Nevertheless, I continued the glommation. She was the only object I had seen there that day, on or off the field, that didn't make me want to shut my eyes.

Something came between her and me. A man stopped at my elbow, and asked my ear, "Are you Archie Goodwin?"

I told him yes.

"Is that Nero Wolfe?"

I nodded.

"Mr. Chisholm wants him in the clubhouse, quick."

I reflected for two seconds, decided that this was straight from heaven, and slid forward to tell Wolfe: "Mr. Chisholm invites us to the clubhouse. We'll avoid the crush. There's a chair there. He wants to see you."

He didn't growl, "What about?" He didn't even growl. He muttered something to Mondor, pulled himself erect, and side-stepped past me to the aisle. Mondor came after him. The courier led the way and I brought up the rear. As we went up the concrete steps single file a shout came from somewhere on the left:

"Go get 'em, Nero! Sic 'em!"

Such is fame. . . .

"This is urgent!" Emil Chisholm squeaked. "It's urgent!"

There was no chair in the clubroom of the size Wolfe likes and needs, but there was a big leather couch, and he was on it, breathing hard and scowling. Mondor was seated over against the wall, out of it. Chisholm, a hefty, broad-shouldered guy, with a wide, thick mouth and a long, straight nose, was too upset to stand or sit, so he was boiling around. I was standing near an open window. Through it came a sudden swelling roar from the crowd out in the stands.

"Shut that window!" Chisholm barked.

I did so.

"I'm going home," Wolfe stated in his most conclusive tone. "But not until they have left. Perhaps, if you will tell me briefly—"

"We've lost the Series!" Chisholm shouted.

Wolfe closed his eyes, and opened them again. "If you'll keep your voice down," he suggested. "I've had enough noise today. If losing the Series is your problem, I'm afraid I can't help."

"No. Nobody can." Chisholm stood facing him. "I blew up. I'm sorry. I've got to get hold of myself. This is what happened: Out there before the game Art got a suspicion—

"Art?"

"Art Kinney, our manager. Naturally, he was watching the boys like a hawk, and he got a suspicion something was wrong. That first—"

"Why was he watching them like a hawk?"

"That's his job! He's manager!" Chisholm realized he was shouting again, stopped, clamped his jaw, and clenched his fists. After a second he went on: "Also, Nick Ferrone had disappeared. He was here with them in the clubhouse, he had got into uniform; then, after they went out to the dugout, he just wasn't there. Art sent Doc Soffer back here to get him, but he couldn't find him. He was simply gone. Art had to put Garth at second base. Naturally, he was on edge, and he noticed things—the way some of the boys looked and acted—that made him suspicious. Then—"

A door opened and a guy came running in, yelling, "Fitch hit one and Neill let it get by, and Asmussen scored! Fitch went on to third!"

I recognized him, chiefly by his crooked nose, which had got in the way of a line drive back in the twenties, when he was a star infielder. It was Beaky Durkin, now a New York scout, with a new lease on life because he had dug up Nick Ferrone out in Arkansas.

Chisholm yelled at him, "Get out!" He took a threatening step. "Get out!" . . . "Hey, Doc! Come in here!"

Durkin, backing out, collided with a man in the doorway. This was Doc Soffer, New York's veteran medico, bald, wearing black-rimmed glasses; he had a long torso and short legs. Entering, he looked as if his ten best-paying patients had just died on him.

"I can't sweat it, Doc," Chisholm told him. "I'm going nuts! This is Nero Wolfe. You tell him."

"Who are you?" Wolfe demanded.

Soffer stopped before him. "I'm Dr. Horton Soffer," he said, clipping it. "Four of my men have been drugged. They're out there now, trying to play ball, and they can't." He stopped, looking as if he were about to break down and cry, gulped, and went on:

"They didn't seem right, there in the dugout. I noticed it and so did Kinney. That first inning there was no doubt about it, something was wrong. The second inning it was even worse—and the same four men, Baker, Prentiss, Neill, and Eston. I got an idea, and came here to investigate. You see that cooler?"

He pointed to a big, white-enameled refrigerator standing against a wall.

Wolfe nodded. "Well?"

"It contains mostly an assortment of drinks in bottles. I know my men's habits, every little habit they've got and every big one, too. I know that after they get into uniform before a game those four men—the four I named—have the habit of getting a bottle of Beebright out of the cooler."

"What is Beebright?"

"It's a carbonated drink that's supposed to have honey in it instead of sugar. Each of those four men drinks a bottle of it, or part of one, before he goes out to the field, practically without exception. And it was those four that were off—terrible! I never saw anything like it. That's how I got my idea. I told Kinney, and he said to come and see.

"Usually the clubhouse boy cleans up here after the men leave for the field, but this being the deciding game of the World Series, today he didn't. Stuff was scattered around—as you see it, it still is—and there was a Beebright bottle there on that table with a little left in it. It didn't smell wrong, and I didn't want to waste any tasting it. I had sent for Mr. Chisholm, and when he came we decided what to do. He sent for Beaky Durkin, who had a seat in the grandstand, because he knew Ferrone better than anyone else. We thought he might have some idea that would help explain what had happened to Ferrone and those four other boys. I took the Beebright down the street to a drugstore, and made two tests. The first one, Ranwez's, didn't prove anything, but that was probably because it is limited—"

"Negatives may be skipped," Wolfe muttered.

"I'm telling you what I did," Soffer snapped. "Ranwez's test took over half an hour. The second, Ekkert's, took less. I did it twice, to check. It was conclusive. The Beebright contained sodium phenobarbital. I couldn't get the quantity, in a hurry like that, but on a guess it was two grains, possibly a little more, in the full bottle. Anyone can get hold of it. Certainly that would be no problem for a big-time gambler who wanted to clean up on a World Series game."

Chisholm swore, audibly and at length.

Doc Soffer nodded. "And somebody put it in the bottles, knowing those four men would drink it just before the game. All he had to do was remove the caps, drop the tablets in, replace the caps, and shake the bottles a little—not much, because it's very soluble. They must have been placed in the refrigerator not much before noon; otherwise someone else might have drunk them. Besides, if they were fixed very far in advance, the drinks would have gone stale and the men would have noticed it. So it must have been someone—"

Chisholm had marched to the window. He whirled and yelled, "Ferrone did it! He did it and lammed!"

Doc Soffer said, "I don't know about that, but I've got to tell Art—" He almost ran from the room.

Beaky Durkin appeared again. He came through the door and halted, facing Chisholm. He was trembling and his face was white, all but the crooked nose.

"Not Nick," he said hoarsely. "Not that boy. Nick didn't do it!"

"Oh, no?" Chisholm was bitter. "Did I ask you? A fine rookie of the year you brought in from Arkansas! Where is he? Bring him here and let me get my hands on him! Go find him!"

Beaky looked bewildered. "Go where?"

"How do I know? He's your pet, not mine," Chisholm said savagely. "Get him and bring him in and I'll offer him a new contract—that will *be* a contract. Now beat it!"

Durkin lifted helpless hands, but turned and left the room.

Wolfe grunted. "Sit down, please," he told Chisholm. "When I address you I want to look at you, and my neck is not elastic. . . . Thank you, sir. You want to hire me for a job?"

"Yes. I want—"

"Please. Is this correct? Four of your best players, drugged as described by Dr. Soffer, could not perform properly, and as a result a game is lost and a World Series?"

"We're losing it." Chisholm's head swung toward the window and back again. "Art's pulling out the drugged men, but of course it's lost."

"And you assume a gambler or a group of gamblers is responsible. How much could he or they win on a game?"

"On today's game, any amount. Fifty thousand, or double that, easy."

"I see. Then you need the police. At once."

Chisholm shook his head. "I don't want to. Baseball is a wonderful game, the best and cleanest game on earth. This is the dirtiest thing that's happened in baseball in 30 years, and it's got to be handled right and handled fast. You're the best detective in the business, and you're right here. With a swarm of cops trooping in, who knows what'll happen! If we have to have them later, all right, but now you're here. Go to it!"

Wolfe was frowning. "You think this Nick Ferrone did it."

"I don't know!" Chisholm was yelling again. "How do I know what I think? He's a harebrained kid just out of the sticks, and he's disappeared. What does that look like?"

Wolfe nodded. "Very well." He drew a deep sigh. "I can at least make some gestures, and see." He aimed a finger at the door Beaky Durkin and Doc Soffer had used. "Is that an office?"

"It leads to Kinney's office—the manager's."

"Then it has a phone. You will call police headquarters and report the disappearance of Nick Ferrone, and ask them to find him. Such a job, when urgent, is beyond my resources. Tell them nothing more for the present if you want it that way. Where do the players change clothing?"

"Through there." Chisholm indicated another door. "That's the locker room. The shower room is beyond."

Wolfe's eyes came to me: "Archie. You will look around all premises adjoining this room. This room you can leave to me."

"Anything in particular?" I asked.

"No. You have good eyes and a head of sorts. Use them."

"I could wait to phone the police," Chisholm suggested, "until you—"

"No," Wolfe snapped. "In ten minutes you can have every cop in New York looking for Mr. Ferrone, and it will cost you ten cents. Spend it. I charge more for less."

Chisholm went out, through the door at the left. I thought I might as well start in that direction, and followed him across a hall and into another room. It was good-sized, furnished with desk, chairs, and accessories. Beaky Durkin sat in a corner with his ear to a radio tuned low, and Doc Soffer was there with him. Chisholm barked, "Shut that thing off!" and crossed to a desk with a phone.

Under other circumstances I would have enjoyed having a look at the office of Art Kinney, the New York manager, but I was on a mission and there was too big an audience. I about-faced and backtracked to the clubroom. As I crossed to the door in the far wall, Wolfe was standing by the open door of the refrigerator with a bottle of Beebright in his hand, holding it at arm's length, sneering at it, and Mondor was beside him.

I passed through the door and was in a room both long and wide, with two rows of lockers, benches and stools, and a couple of chairs. The locker doors were marked with numbers and names. I tried three; they were locked. Through a doorway at the left was the shower room. I went to the far end, glancing in at each of the shower stalls, was disappointed to see no pillbox that might have contained sodium phenobarbital, and returned to the locker room.

In the middle of the row on the right was the locker marked "Ferrone." Its door was locked. With my portable key collection I could have operated, but I don't take it along to ball games, and nothing on my personal ring was usable. It seemed to me that the inside of that locker was the first place that needed attention, so I returned to the clubroom, made a face at Wolfe as I went by, and entered Kinney's office. Chisholm had finished phoning and was seated at a desk, staring at the floor. Beaky Durkin and Doc Soffer had their ears glued to the radio.

I asked Chisholm, "Have you got a key to Ferrone's locker?"

His head jerked up. "No. I think Kinney has a master key. I don't know where he keeps it."

"Fifteen to two," Durkin informed us, or maybe he was just talking to himself. "New York batting in the ninth, two down. Garth got a home run, bases empty. It's all—"

"Shut up!" Chisholm yelled at him.

Since Kinney would soon be with us, and since Ferrone's locker had first call, I thought I might as well wait there for him. However, with our client sitting there glaring at me it would be well to display some interest and energy, so I moved. I went to the filing cabinets and looked them over. I opened a door, saw a hall leading to stairs going down, and shut the door. I crossed to another door in the opposite wall, and opened that.

Since I hadn't the faintest expectation of finding anything pertinent beyond that door, let alone a corpse, I must have made some sign of surprise, but if so it wasn't noticed. I stood for three seconds, then slipped inside and squatted long enough to get an answer to the main question. I arose, backed out, and addressed Soffer:

"Take a look here, Doc. I think he's dead."

He made a noise, stared, and moved. I marched into the clubroom and crossed to the couch where Wolfe was sitting.

"Found something," I told him. "Nick Ferrone, in uniform, on the floor of a closet, with a baseball bat alongside him and his head smashed in. He's dead, according to me, but Doc Soffer is checking, if you want an expert opinion."

Wolfe grunted. "Call the police."

"Yes, sir. A question: Any minute the ballplayers will be coming in here. The cops won't like it if they mess around. Do we care? It won't be Cramer. This is the Bronx, not Manhattan. Do we—?"

A bellow, Chisholm's, came through: "Wolfe! Come in here!"

Wolfe got up, growling. "We owe the police nothing, but we have a client—I think we have. I'll see. Meanwhile, you stay here. Everyone entering this room remains, under surveillance." He headed for Kinney's office.

Another door opened, the one in the west wall, and Nat Neill, New York's center fielder, entered the clubroom, his jaw set and his eyes blazing. Following him came Lew Baker, the catcher. Behind them, on the stairs, was a clatter of footsteps.

The game was over. New York had lost. . . .

Another thing I don't take along to ball games is a gun, but that day there was a moment when I wished I had. After any ordinary game, even a lost one, I suppose the team might have been merely irritated if, on getting to the clubhouse, they found a stranger backed up against the door to the locker room telling them they could not pass. But that day they were ready to plug one another, so why not a stranger?

The first dozen were ganging me, about to start using hands, when Art Kinney, the manager, appeared. He strode, tight-lipped, through to his office and the gang let up to consider; all but Bill Moyse, the second-string catcher, six-feet-two and over 200 pounds. He had come late, after Kinney. He strode up to me, making fists, and announced that his wife was waiting for him, he was going in to change, and either I would move or he would move me.

One of his teammates called: "Show him her picture, Bill! That'll move him!"

Moyse whirled and leaped. Hands grabbed for him but he kept going. Whether he reached his target or not I can't say, because, first, I was staying put and it was quite a mix-up, and, second, I was seeing something that wasn't present. The mention of Moyse's wife and her picture had done it. What I was seeing was a picture of a girl that had appeared in the *Gazette* a couple of months back, with a caption tagging her as the show-girl bride of William Moyse, the ballplayer; and it was the girl I had been glomming in a nearby box when the summons had come from Chisholm. No question about it. That was interesting.

Meanwhile, Moyse was doing me a service by making a diversion. Three or four men had hold of him, and others were gathered around his target, Con Prentiss, the shortstop. They were all jabbering. Prentiss, who was wiry and tough, was showing his teeth in a grin, not an attractive one. Moyse suddenly whirled again and was heading back for me. It was useless to start slugging that mountain of muscle, and I was set to try locking him, when a loud voice came from the doorway to the manager's office:

"Here! Attention, all of you!"

It was Art Kinney. His face was absolutely white and his neck cords were twitching, as they all turned toward him.

"I'm full up," he said, half hysterical. "This is Nero Wolfe, the detective. He'll tell you something."

Muttering began as Kinney stepped aside and Wolfe took his place in the doorway. The great man's eyes swept over them, and then he spoke:

"You deserve an explanation, gentlemen, but the police are coming and there's not much time. You have just lost a ball game by knavery. Four of you were drugged, in a drink called Beebright, and could not perform properly. You will learn—"

They drowned him out. It was an explosion of astonished rage.

"Gentlemen!" Wolfe thundered. "Will you listen?" He glowered. "You will learn more of that later, but there is something more urgent. The dead body of one of your colleagues, Mr. Nick Ferrone, has been discovered on these premises. He was murdered. It is supposed, naturally, that the two events, the drugging and the murder, are connected. In any case, if you do not know what a murder investigation means to everyone within reach, innocent or not, you are about to learn. For the moment you will not leave this room. When the police arrive they will tell you—"

Heavy feet were clomping in the hall. The door swung open and a uniformed cop stepped in, followed by three others. The one in front, a sergeant, halted and demanded indignantly:

"What's all this? Where is it?"

The team looked at the cops, and hadn't a word to say. . . .

Inspector Hennessy of Bronx Homicide was tall and straight, silver-haired, with a bony face and quick-moving gray eyes. Two years before he had told Nero Wolfe that if he ever again tried poking into a murder in the Bronx he would be escorted to the Harlem River and dunked. But when, at 9 o'clock that evening, Hennessy breezed through the clubroom, passing in front of the leather couch where Wolfe was seated, with a ham sandwich in one hand and a bottle of beer in the other, he didn't even toss him a glance. He was much too busy.

The Police Commissioner was in Manager Kinney's office with Chisholm and others. The Bronx District Attorney and an assistant were in the locker room, along with an assortment of Homicide men, giving various athletes their third or fourth quiz. There were still a couple of dozen city employees in the clubhouse, though the scientists—the photographers and fingerprint hounds—had all finished and gone.

I had standing as the finder of the corpse, but also I was a part of Wolfe. Technically, Wolfe was not poking into a murder; he had been hired by Chisholm, before the corpse had been found, to find out who had doped the ballplayers. However, in gathering facts for relay to Wolfe I had not discriminated. I saw Nick Ferrone's locker opened and the contents examined, with no startling disclosures.

While I was in Kinney's office watching a basket squad load the corpse and carry it out, I heard a lieutenant on the phone giving instructions for a roundup of gamblers throughout the metropolitan area. A little later I picked up a bunch of signed statements from a table, and sat down and read them through, without anyone noticing. By that time the commissioner and the district attorney had arrived, and they had eight or nine quiz posts going in the various rooms, and Hennessy was doing his best to keep it organized.

I collected all I could for Wolfe. The bat that had been used to crack Ferrone's skull was no stock item, but a valued trophy. With it, years back, there had been a belted grand slam home run that had won a pennant, and it had been displayed on a wall rack in the manager's office. The murderer could have simply grabbed it from the rack. It had no usable fingerprints. Of eight bottles of Beebright left in the cooler, the two in front had been doped and the other six had not. No other drinks had been tampered with. Everyone had known of the liking of those four—Baker, Prentiss, Neill, and Eston—for Beebright, and their habit of drinking a bottle of it before a game. No good prints. No sign anywhere of a container of sodium phenobarbital tablets.

There were a thousand other negatives; for instance, the clubhouse boy, Jimmie Burr. The custom was that when he wasn't around, the players would put chits in a little box for what they took; and he hadn't been around. For that game someone had got him a box seat, and he had beat it to the grandstand while most of the players were in the locker room, changing. A sergeant jumped on it: Who had got him out of the way by providing a ticket for a box seat? But it had been Art Kinney himself, the manager.

Around 8 o'clock they turned a big batch loose. Twenty men, including coaches and the bat boy, were allowed to go to the locker room to change, under surveillance, and then let out, with instructions to keep available. They were not in the picture as it then looked.

It was established that Ferrone had arrived at the clubhouse shortly after 12 o'clock and had got into uniform; a dozen of the men had been in the locker room with him. He had been present during a pre-game session with Kinney in the clubroom, and no one remembered seeing him leave afterward. When they trooped out and down the stairs and emerged onto the field, Ferrone's absence was not noticed until they had been in the dugout for some minutes.

As the cops figured it, he couldn't have been slammed with a baseball bat in Kinney's office only a few yards away, while the team was in the clubroom, and therefore all who had unquestionably left for the field with the gang, and had stayed there, were in the clear until further notice. With them went Pierre Mondor, who had wanted to see a ball game and had picked a beaut.

As I said, when Inspector Hennessy breezed through the clubroom at 9 o'clock, coming from the locker room and headed for Kinney's office, he didn't even toss a glance at the leather couch where Wolfe and I were seated. He disappeared. But soon he was back again, speaking from the doorway:

"Come in here, will you, Wolfe?"

"No," Wolfe said. "I'm eating."

"The commissioner wants you."

"Is he eating?" Waiting for no reply, Wolfe turned his head and bellowed, "Mr. Skinner! I'm dining!"

It wasn't very polite, I thought, to be sarcastic about the sandwiches and beer Chisholm had provided. Hennessy started a remark which indicated that he agreed with me, but it was interrupted by the appearance of Commissioner Skinner at his elbow. Hennessy stepped in and aside, and Skinner approached the couch, followed by Chisholm.

Skinner kept it friendly: "I've just learned that four men who were told they could go are still here: Baker, Prentiss, Neill, and Eston. When Inspector Hennessy asked them why, they told him that Mr. Chisholm had asked them to stay. Mr. Chisholm says that he did so at your suggestion. He understood that you wanted to speak with them after our men have all left. Is that correct?"

Wolfe nodded. "I made it quite plain, I thought."

"M-m." The commissioner regarded him. "You see, I know you fairly well. You wouldn't dream of hanging on here half the night to speak with those men merely as a routine step in an investigation. And, besides, at Mr. Chisholm's request you have already been permitted to speak with them, and with several others. You're cooking something. Those are the four men who were drugged, but they left the clubhouse for the field with the rest of the team, so the way we figure it, none of them killed Ferrone. How do you figure it?"

Wolfe swallowed the last of a well-chewed bite. "I don't."

Hennessy growled and set his jaw.

Skinner said, "I don't believe it," with his tone friendlier than his words. "You're cooking something," he insisted. "What's the play with those four men?"

Wolfe shook his head. "No, sir."

Hennessy took a step forward. "Look," he said; "this is the Bronx. You don't turn *this* murder into a parlor game."

Wolfe raised brows at him. "Murder? I am not concerned with murder. Mr. Chisholm hired me to investigate the drugging of his employees. The two events may, of course, be connected, but the murder is your job. And they were not necessarily connected. I understand that a man named Moyse is in there now with the district attorney"—Wolfe aimed a thumb at the door to the locker room—"because it has been learned that he has twice within a month assaulted Mr. Ferrone physically through resentment at Ferrone's interest in his wife, injudiciously displayed. And that Moyse did not leave the clubhouse with the others, but arrived at the dugout three or four minutes later, just before Ferrone's absence was noticed. For your murder, Mr. Hennessy, that should be a help; but it doesn't get me on with my job—disclosure of the culprit who drugged the drinks. Have you charged Mr. Moyse?"

"No." Hennessy was curt. "So you're not interested in the murder?"

"Not as a job, since it's not mine. But if you want a comment from a specialist, you're closing your lines too soon."

"We haven't closed any lines."

"You let twenty men walk out of here. You are keeping Moyse for the reasons given. You are keeping Dr. Soffer, I suppose, because when Ferrone was missing in the dugout Soffer came here to look for him, and he could have found him here alive and killed him. You are keeping Mr. Durkin, I suppose again, because, he, too, could have been here alone with Ferrone. He says he left the clubhouse shortly before the team did and went to his seat in the grandstand, and stayed there. Has he been either contradicted or corroborated?"

"No."

"Then you regard him as vulnerable on opportunity?"

"Yes."

"Are you holding Mr. Chisholm for the same reason?"

Chisholm made a noise. Skinner and Hennessy stared. Skinner said, "We're not holding Mr. Chisholm."

"You should be, for consistency," Wolfe declared. "This afternoon, when I reached my seat in the stands, at twenty minutes past one, the mayor and others were there in a nearby box, but Mr. Chisholm was not. He arrived a few minutes later. He has told me that when he arrived with his party, about 1 o'clock, he had the others escorted to the stands, that he started for the clubhouse for a word with his employees, that he was delayed by the crowd and decided it was too late, and then proceeded to the box. If the others are vulnerable on opportunity, so is he."

They made remarks, all three of them, not appreciative.

Wolfe put the beer bottle to his lips, tilted it, and swallowed. He put the bottle down empty.

"I was merely," he said mildly, "commenting on the murder as a specialist. As for my job, learning who drugged the drinks, I haven't even made a start. How could I in this confounded hubbub? Trampled by an army. I have been permitted to sit here and talk to people, yes, with a succession of your subordinates standing behind me breathing down my neck. Pfui!"

"Very rude, I'm sure," Hennessy said dryly. "The commissioner has asked you, what's the play with those four men?"

Wolfe shook his head. "Not only those four. I included others in my request to Mr. Chisholm: Dr. Soffer, Mr. Kinney, Mr. Durkin, and of course Mr. Chisholm himself. I am not arranging a parlor game. I make a living as a professional detective, and I need their help on this job I've undertaken. I think I know why—engrossed as you are with the most sensational case you've had in years—you're spending all this time chatting with me: You suspect I'm contriving a finesse. Well, I am."

"You are?"

"Yes." Wolfe suddenly was peevish. "Haven't I sat here for five hours submerged in your pandemonium? Haven't you all the facts that I have, and many more besides? Haven't you thousands of men to command—and I but one? One little fact strikes me, as apparently it has not struck you, and in my forlorn desperation I decide to test my interpretation of it. For that test I need help, and I ask Mr. Chisholm to provide it."

"We'll be glad to help," Skinner offered. "Which fact, and how do you interpret it?"

"No, sir." Wolfe was positive. "It is my one slender chance to earn a fee. I intend—"

"But we may not know this fact."

"Certainly you do. I have stated it explicitly during this conversation, but I won't point at it for you. If I did you'd spoil it for me, and, slender as it is, I intend to test it. I am not beset with the urgency of murder, as you are, but I'm in a fix. I don't need a motive strong enough to incite a man to murder, merely one to persuade him to drug some bottled drinks—mildly, far from lethally.

A thousand dollars? Twenty thousand? That would be only a fraction of the possible winnings on a World Series game. As for opportunity, anyone at all could have slipped in here late this morning, before others had arrived, with drugged bottles of that drink and put them in the cooler—and earned a fortune. Those twenty men you let go, Mr. Hennessy—how many of them can you say positively did not drug the drinks?"

The inspector was scowling at him. "I can say that I don't think any of them killed Ferrone."

"Ah, but I'm not after the murderer; that's your job." Wolfe upturned a palm. "You see why I am driven to a forlorn finesse?"

We all turned, as a man came in from the locker room. District Attorney Megalech of the Bronx was as masterful as they come and bald as a doorknob. He strode across and told Skinner and Hennessy he wanted to speak with them, took an elbow of each, and steered them through the door to Kinney's office. Chisholm, uninvited, wheeled and followed them.

Wolfe reached for a sandwich and I arose and stood looking down at him. I asked, "How good is this fact you're saving up?"

"Not very." He chewed and swallowed. "Good enough to try if we get nothing better. Evidently they have nothing at all. You heard them."

"Yeah. You told them they have all the facts you have, but they haven't. The one I gave you about Mrs. Moyse? That's not the one you're interpreting privately?"

"No."

"She might still be around, waiting. I might possibly get something better than the one you're saving. Shall I go try?"

He grunted. I took it for a yes, and moved. Outside the hall door stood a cop. I addressed him: "I'm going down to buy Mr. Wolfe a pickle. Do I need to be passed out or in?"

"You?" He used only the right half of his mouth for talking. "Shoot your way through. Huh?"

"Right. Many thanks." I went. . . .

It was dumb to be so surprised, but I was. I might have known that the news that New York had been doped out of the game and the Series, and that Nick Ferrone, the rookie of the year, had been murdered, would draw a record mob. Downstairs inside the entrance there were sentries, and outside a regiment was stretched into a cordon. I was explaining to a sergeant who I was and telling him I would be returning, when three desperate men, one of whom I recognized, came springing at me. All they wanted was the truth, the whole truth, and nothing but the truth. I had to get really rude. I have been clawed at by newspapermen more than once, but I had never seen them quite as hungry as they were that October night. As they wouldn't shake loose, I dived through the cordon and into the mob.

It looked hopeless. The only parked car in sight on that side of the street were police cars. I pushed through to the fringe of the throng and made my way two blocks south. Having made inquiries of two members of the team hours before, I knew what I was looking for: a light-blue sedan.

I crossed the street and headed for the parking plaza. Two cops in the cordon gave me a look, but it wasn't the plaza they were guarding and I marched on through. In the dim light I could see three cars over at the north end. Closer up, one was a light-blue sedan. I went up to it. Two females on the front seat were gazing at me through the window, and one of them was my glommee. The radio was on. I opened the door and said hello.

"Who are you?" she demanded.

"My name's Archie Goodwin. I'll show credentials if you are Mrs. William Moyse."

"What if I am?"

She was rapidly erasing the pleasant memory I had of her. Not that she had turned homely in a few hours, but her expression was not only unfriendly but sour, and her voice was not agreeable. I got out my wallet and extracted my license card. "If you are who I think you are," I said, "this will identify me."

"Okay, you name's Goodman." She ignored the card. "So what?"

"Not Goodman." I pronounced it for her: "Archie Goodwin. I work for Nero Wolfe, who is up in the clubhouse. I just came from there. Why not turn off the radio?"

"I'd rather turn you off," she said bitterly.

Her companion, the redhead who had been with her in the box, reached for the knob, and the radio died. "Look, Lila," she said earnestly; "you're acting like a sap. Invite him in. He may be human. Maybe Bill sent him."

"What did Walt tell us?" Lila snapped at her. "Nero Wolfe is there working with the cops." She came back at me: "Did my husband send you? Prove it."

I put a foot on the edge of the frame, not aggressively. "That's one reason," I said, "why Mr. Wolfe can't stand women. The way they flop around, intellectually. I didn't say your husband sent me. He didn't. He couldn't even if he wanted to because for the past hour he has been kept in the locker room conversing with a gathering of homicide hounds, and still is. Mr. Wolfe sent me. But in a way it's a personal problem I've got, and no one but you can help me."

"*You've* got a personal problem! *You* have! Take it away."

"I will if you say so, but wait till I tell you. Up to now they have only one reason for picking on your husband. The players left the clubhouse for the field in a bunch—all but one of them, who left later and got to the dugout a few minutes after the others. It was Bill Moyse. They all agreed on that, and Bill admits it. The cops figure that he had seen or heard something that made him suspect Nick Ferrone of doping the drinks—you know about that? That the Beebright was doped?"

"Yes. Walt Goidell told me." She gestured toward the redhead. "Helen's husband. He's on the team."

"And that he stayed behind with Ferrone to put it to him, and Nick got tough, and he got tougher, with a baseball bat. That's how the cops figure it, and that's why they're after Bill. But I have a private reason, confided only to Nero Wolfe, to think that the cops have got it twisted. Mr. Wolfe is inclined to agree with me, but he hasn't told the cops, because he has been hired by Chisholm and wants to earn a fat fee. My private slant is that if Bill did kill Ferrone—please note the 'if'—it wasn't because he caught Ferrone doping the drinks, but the other way around. Ferrone caught Bill doping the drinks, and was going to spill it, and Bill killed him."

She was goggling at me. "You have the nerve—!"

"Hold it. I'm telling you. This afternoon at the game I was in a box. By the sixth inning I had had plenty of the game and looked around for something to take my mind off it, and I saw an extremely attractive girl. I looked at her some more. I had a feeling that I had seen her before, but couldn't place her. The score was 11 to 1, the home team were flat on their faces, and that lovely specimen was exactly what my eyes needed—except for one flaw. She was having a swell time. Her whole face and manner showed it. She liked what was happening out on the field."

She was trying to say something, but I raised my voice a little: "Wait till I tell you. Later, after the game, in the clubhouse, Bill Moyse said his wife was waiting for him, and someone made a crack about showing me her picture. Then it clicked. I remembered seeing a picture of his bride in the *Gazette*, and it was the girl I had seen in the stands. Then, later, I had a chance to ask some of the players some questions, and I learned that she usually drove to games in Bill's light-blue sedan and waited for him after the game. It puzzled me that it made the wife of a New York player happy to see his team getting walloped in the deciding game of a World Series, and Mr. Wolfe agreed. Why were you tickled stiff to see them losing?"

"I wasn't."

"It's perfectly ridiculous," the redhead snorted.

I shook my head. "That won't do. Mr. Wolfe accepts my judgment on girls, and I have told him you were happy. If I go back and report that you flatly deny it, I don't see how he can do anything but tell the cops, and that will be bad. They'll figure that you wanted New

York to lose because you knew Bill did, and why. Then, of course, they'll refigure the murder and get a new answer—that Ferrone found out that Bill had doped the drinks, and Bill killed him. They'll start on Bill all over again and—"

"Stop it!"

"I was only saying, if they—"

The redhead horned in, then. "How dumb can you get?" she demanded. "You say you know girls! Do you know baseball girls? I'm one! I'm Helen Goidell, Walt's wife. I would have liked to slap Lila this afternoon, sitting there gloating, much as I love her. But I'm not a sap like you! She's not married to the team, she's married to Bill! Lew Baker had batted .132 in the first six games of the Series, and he had made four errors and had nine bases stolen on him, and still they wouldn't give Bill a chance. Lila had sat through those six games praying to see Bill walk out—and not once! What did she care about the Series? She wanted to see Bill in it. And look at Baker this afternoon! If he had been doped, all right, but Lila didn't know it then. All she knew was that Bill was probably going to get his chance. What you know about girls, you nitwit!"

She was blazing. I did not blaze back.

"I'm still willing to learn," I said agreeably. "Is she right, Mrs. Moyse?"

"Yes."

"Then I am, too, on the main point? You were pleased to see New York losing?"

"I said she was right."

"Yeah. Then I've still got a problem. If I accept your version, and report to Wolfe accordingly, he'll accept it, too. Whether you think I know girls or not, he does. So that's some responsibility for me. What if you're a lot smoother and trickier than I think you are? Your husband is suspected of murder, and they're still working on him. What if he's guilty and they manage to squeeze out of you what they need to hook him? How will I look if they do? Any suggestions?"

Lila had none. She sat with her head lowered, silent.

This Won't Kill You

"You sound almost human," Helen Goidell said.

"That's deceptive," I told her. "I turn it on and off. If I thought she had something Mr. Wolfe could use I'd stop at nothing, even hair-pulling. But at the moment I really don't think she has. I think she's pure and innocent and wholesome. Her husband is another matter. For her sake, I hope he wriggles out of it somehow, but I'm not taking any bets. The cops seem to like him, and I know cops as well as I do girls." I removed my foot from the car frame. "So long and so forth." I turned to go.

"Wait a minute." It was Lila.

I turned back. Her head was up.

"Is this straight?" she asked.

"Is what straight?"

"You're going to tell Mr. Wolfe you're satisfied about me?"

"Well. Satisfied is quite a word. I'm going to tell him I have bought your explanation of your happiness at the game—or, rather, Mrs. Goidell's."

"You could be a liar."

"Not only could I be, I often am, but not at the moment."

She regarded me. "Maybe you can tell me about Bill," she said. "They don't really think he killed Nick Ferrone, do they?"

"They think maybe he did."

"I know he didn't."

"Good for you. But you weren't there, so you don't have a vote."

She nodded. She was being hard and practical. "Are they going to arrest him? Will they really charge him with murder?"

"I can't say. But Bill is the leading candidate."

"Then I've got to do something. I wish I knew what he's telling them. Do you know?"

"Only that he's denying he knows anything about it. He says he left the clubhouse after the others had gone, because he went back to the locker room to change to other shoes."

She shook her head. "I don't mean that. I mean,

whether he told them—" She stopped. "No. I know he didn't. He wouldn't. He knows something and I know it, too, about a man trying to fix that game. Only, he wouldn't tell, on account of me. I have to go and see someone downtown. Will you come along?"

"To see who?"

"I'll tell you on the way."

Helen Goidell blurted, "For heaven's sake, Lila, do you know what you're saying?"

If Lila replied I missed it, for I was on my way around the car. It was a little headstrong to dash off with a damsel, leaving Wolfe up there with mass-production sandwiches, warm beer, and his one measly little fact he was saving up, but this might be really hot.

By the time I got around to the other door Helen had it open and was getting out. Her feet on the ground, she turned to speak: "I don't want any part of this, Lila. I do not! I wish I'd gone with Walt instead of staying with you!"

She turned and trotted off, toward the street. I climbed in and pulled the door shut.

"She'll tell Walt," Lila said.

I nodded. "Yeah. But does she know where we're going?"

"No."

"Then let's go."

She started the engine, levered to reverse, and backed the car.

Under ordinary circumstances she was probably a pretty good driver, but that night wasn't ordinary for her. Swinging right, there was a little click on my side as we grazed the fender of a stopped car. Rolling up the grade, we slipped between two taxis, clearing by an inch, and both hackmen yelled at her. Stopping for a light at the crest, she turned her head and spoke:

"It's my Uncle Dan. His name is Gale. He came last night and asked me—"

She fed gas and we shot forward, but a car heading uptown and squeezing the light was suddenly there smack in our path. With a lightning reflex her foot hit the brake, the other car zipped by with at least a foot to spare, she fed gas again, and the sedan jerked forward.

I asked her, "Taking the highway?"

"Yes, it's quicker."

"It will be if you make it. Just concentrate on that and let the details wait."

She got to the downtown side of the highway without any actual contact with other vehicles, turned into the left lane and stepped on it. The speedometer said 55 when she spoke again.

"If I go ahead and tell you, I can't change my mind. He wanted me to persuade Bill to fix the game. He said he'd give us $10,000. I didn't even want to tell Bill, but he insisted, so I did. I knew what Bill would say—"

She broke off to do some expert weaving, swerving to the middle lane, then a sprint, then swinging back to the left again in front of a couple of cars that had slowed her down to under 50.

"Look," I told her; "you could gain up to two minutes this way with luck, but getting stopped and getting a ticket would take at least ten. You're driving, okay, but don't try to talk, too."

She didn't argue, but she held the pace. I twisted around to keep an eye on the rear through the window, and stayed that way clear to 57TH Street. We rolled down the ramp and a block south, turned left on 56TH Street, had a green light at Eleventh Avenue, and went through. A little short of Tenth Avenue we turned into the curb and stopped. Lila reached for the hand brake and gave it a yank.

"Let's hear it," I said. "Enough to go on. Is Uncle Dan a gambler?"

"No." Her face turned to me. "I'm afraid of him."

"Then what is he?"

"He runs a drugstore. He owns it. That's where we're going to see him. My father and mother died when I was just a kid, and Uncle Dan has been good to me—as good as he could. If it hadn't been for him I'd have been brought up in an orphans' home. Of course, Bill wanted to tell Art Kinney last night, but he didn't on account of me, and that's why he's not telling the cops."

"Maybe he is telling them, or soon will."

She shook her head. "I know Bill. We decided we wouldn't tell, and that settled it. Uncle Dan made me promise we wouldn't tell before he said what he wanted."

I grunted. "Even so, he was crowding his luck, telling you two about the program before signing you up. If he explained the idea of doping the Beebright—"

"But he didn't! He didn't say how it was to be done. He didn't get that far, because Bill said nothing doing, as I knew he would."

I eyed her. "This was last night?"

"Yes."

"What time?"

"Around 8 o'clock. We had dinner early with Helen and Walt Goidell, and when we got home Uncle Dan was there waiting for us."

"Where's home?"

"Our apartment on Seventy-ninth Street. He spoke to me alone first, and then insisted I had to ask Bill."

"And Bill turned him down flat?"

"Of course he did!"

"Bill didn't see him alone later?"

"Of course not!"

"All right, don't bite. I need to know. Now what?"

"We're going to see him. We're going to tell him that we have to tell the cops, and we're going to try to get him to come along. That's why I wanted you with me, because I'm afraid of him—I mean, I'm afraid he'll talk me out of it. But they've got to know that Bill was asked to fix the game and he wouldn't. If it's hard on Uncle Dan that's too bad, but I can't help it. I'm for Bill, all the way."

I was making myself look at her, for discipline. I was having the normal male impulses at the sight and sound of a good-looking girl in trouble, and they were worse than normal because I was partly responsible. I had given her the impression that the cops were about set to take her Bill on the big one, which was an exaggeration. I hadn't mentioned that one reason they were keeping him was his reaction to the interest Nick Ferrone had shown in her, which of course had no bearing on anyone's attempt to fix a ball game. True, she had been in a mess before I had got to her, but I had shoved her in deeper. What she needed now was understanding and sympathy, and I was all she had. Which was I, a man or a detective?

"Okay," I said, "let's go see Uncle Dan."

The engine was running. She released the hand brake, fed gas, and we rolled. Three minutes got us to Eighth Avenue, where we turned downtown. The car slowed and she pulled in at the curb.

"There it is." She pointed. "Gale's Pharmacy."

It was ten paces down. There were lights in the window, but otherwise it looked drab. I got out and held the door, and she joined me on the sidewalk. She put a hand on my arm.

"You're staying right with me," she stated.

"Absolutely," I assured her. "I'm good with uncles."

As we crossed to the entrance and went inside I was feeling not fully dressed. I have a routine habit of wearing a gun when I'm on a case involving people who may go to extremes, but, as I said, I do not go armed to ball games. However, at first sight of Daniel Gale I did not put him in that category. His drugstore was so narrow that a fat man would have had to squeeze between the soda-fountain stools and the central showcase, and that made it look long, but it wasn't. Five or six customers were on the stools, and the soda jerk was busy.

At the cosmetics counter on the left, a woman was being waited on by a little guy with a pale, tight-skinned face, wearing glasses.

"That's him," Lila whispered to me.

We waited near the door. Uncle Dan, concentrating on the customer, hadn't seen us. Finally the customer made her choice and, as he tore off paper to wrap the purchase, his eyes lifted and he saw Lila. Also, he saw me, beside her. He froze. He held it, rigid, for seconds, then came to, went on with the wrapping job, and was handed a bill by the customer. While he was at the cash register Lila and I crossed to the counter. As he handed the woman her change, Lila spoke:

"Uncle Dan, I've got to tell you—"

She stopped because he was gone. Without speaking, he turned and made for the rear, disappeared behind a partition, and a door closed. I didn't like it, but didn't want to start a commotion by hurdling the counter, so I stepped to the end and circled, went to the door that had closed, and turned the knob. It was locked. There I was, out at first, unless I was prepared to smash the door in.

The soda jerk called, "Hey, Mac, come out of that!"

"It's all right," Lila told him. "I'm his niece—Mr. Gale is my Uncle Dan."

"I never saw you before, lady. . . . You, Mac, come out here where you belong! Whose uncle are you?"

A couple of the fountain customers gave him his laugh. Then the door I was standing by popped open and Uncle Dan was there, beside me.

"Henry!" he called.

"Right here!" the soda jerk called back.

"Take over for a while—I'll be busy. Come here, Lila, will you?"

Lila circled the end of the counter and approached us. There wasn't room enough to be gallant and let her pass, so I followed Gale through the door into the back room ahead of her. It was small, and the stacks of shipping cartons and other objects took most of what space there was. The rows of shelves were crammed with packaged merchandise, except those along the right wall, which held labeled bottles. Gale stopped near the door, and Lila and I went on by.

"We don't want to be disturbed," Gale said, and bolted the door.

"Why not?" I inquired.

He faced me, and from a distance of five arms' lengths, with Lila between us, I had my first good view of the eyes behind the specs. They were cold and deadly.

"Because," he was telling me, "this is a private matter. You see, I recognized you, Mr. Goodwin. Your face is not as well known as your employer's, but it has been in the papers on several occasions, and you were in my mind on account of the news. The radio bulletins have included the detail that Nero Wolfe and his assistant were present and engaged by Mr. Chisholm. So when I saw you with my niece I realized we should talk privately. But you're an impulsive young man, and for fear you may not like what I say, I make conditions. I shall stay here near the door. You will move to that packing case back of you and sit on it, with your hands in sight and making no unnecessary movements. My niece will put the chair here in front of me and sit on it, facing you, between you and me. That way I will feel free to talk.

I thought he was batty. As a setup against one of my impulses, including a gun if I had had one, it made no sense at all. I backed up to the packing case and lowered myself, resting my hands on my knees to humor him. When Lila saw me complying she moved the chair, the only one there, as directed, and sat with her back to her uncle. He, himself, went to a narrow counter, picked up a bottle of colorless liquid, removed the glass stopper, held it to his nose, and sniffed.

"I do not have fainting spells," he said apologetically, "but at the moment I am a little unstrung. Seeing my niece here with you was a real shock for me. I came back here to consider what it might mean, but reached no conclusion. Perhaps you'll explain?"

"Your niece will. Tell him, Lila."

She started to twist around in the chair, but he commanded her: "No, my dear, stay as you were. Face Mr. Goodwin." He took another sniff at the bottle.

She obeyed. "It's Bill," she said. "They're going to arrest him for murder, and they mustn't. They won't, if we tell them how you offered to pay him for fixing the game and he wouldn't do it. He won't tell them, on account of me, so we have to. I know I promised you I wouldn't, but now I've got to. You see how it is, Uncle Dan; I've got to."

"You haven't told the police?"

"No. I thought the best way was to come and get you

to go with me. I was afraid to come alone, because I know how bad it will be for you, but it will be worse for Bill if we don't. Don't you see, Uncle—?"

"Keep your back turned, Lila. I insist on it. That's right; stay that way." He had been talking in an even low tone, but now his voice became thin and strained: "I'll tell you why I want your back to me—so I can't see your face. . . . Remember, Goodwin, don't move! . . . This is a bottle of pure sulphuric acid. I was smelling it just to explain why I had it; of course, it has no smell. I suppose you know what it will do. This bottle is nearly full, and I'm holding it carefully, because one drop on your skin will scar you for life. That's why I want your back to me, Lila. I'm very fond of you, and I don't want to see your face if I have to use this acid. If you move, Lila dear, I'll use it. Or you, Goodwin; especially you. I hope you both understand?"

His hand holding the bottle hovered inches above her head. She looked as if she might keel over, and I urged her, "Sit tight, Lila, and don't scream."

"Yes," Uncle Dan said approvingly. "I should have mentioned that. Screaming would be as bad as moving. I had to tell you about the acid before I discussed matters. I'm not surprised at your fantastic suggestion, Lila, because I know how foolish you can be, but I'm surprised at you, Goodwin. How could you expect me to consent to my complete ruin? Did Lila persuade you that I am an utter fool?"

"I guess she must have," I admitted. "What kind of man are you?"

He proceeded to tell me, and I pretended to listen. I also tried to keep my eyes on his pale, tight-skinned face, but that wasn't easy, because they were fascinated by the bottle he was holding. Meanwhile, my brain was buzzing. Unless he was plain loony the only practical purpose of the bottle must be to gain time—and for what?

". . . and I will," he was saying. "This won't kill you, Lila dear, but it will be horrible, and I don't want to do it unless I have to. Only, you mustn't think I won't. You don't really know me very well, because to you I'm just Uncle Dan. You didn't know that I once had a million dollars and I was an important and dangerous man. There were people who knew me and feared me, but I was unlucky. I have gambled and made fortunes, and lost them. That affects a man's nerves. It changes a man's outlook on life. I borrowed enough money to buy this place, and for years I worked hard and did well—well enough to pay it all back. But that was my ruin. I owed nothing and had a little cash and decided to celebrate by losing $100 to some old friends—just $100, but I didn't lose. I won several thousand. After that I went on, and lost what I had won, and I lost this place.

"So I don't own this place; my friends do. They are very old friends, and they gave me a chance to get this place back. I'm telling you about this, Lila dear, because I want you to understand. I came to you and Bill with that offer because I had to, and you promised me, you swore you would tell no one. I have been an unlucky man, and sometimes a weak one, but I am never going to be weak again— Don't move!"

Lila, who had lifted her head a little, stiffened. I sat gazing at Gale. Obviously, he was stalling for time, but what could he expect to happen? It could be only one thing: he expected somebody to come. He expected help.

As soon as he had seen us he had scooted back here to phone somebody. Help was on the way, the kind of help that would deal with Lila and me efficiently and finally; and big-time gamblers who could provide ten grand to fix a game are just the babies to be ready with that kind of help.

Either he was loony or that was it. But then what? They might come any second; they might be entering the drugstore right now. Any second a knock on the door might come . . .

Gale was talking: "I didn't think you'd tell, Lila, after all I've done for you. You promised me you wouldn't. Now, of course, you've told Goodwin and it can't be helped. If I just tip this bottle a little—"

"Nuts," I said emphatically, but not raising my voice. "You haven't got it staged right." I had my eyes straight on his specs. "Maybe you don't want to see her face, but the way you've got her, with her back to you, it's no good. What if she suddenly ducked, and dived forward? You might get some on her clothes or her feet, but the chair would be in your way. Have you considered that? . . . Better still, what if she suddenly darted sideways in between those cartons? The instant she moved I'd be moving, too, and that would take her out of my path. She'd be taking a chance, but that would be better than sitting there waiting for the next act. Unquestionably, it would be better for her to go sideways—with her head down and her arms out. You see how bum your arrangement is? But if you make her turn and face you—"

She moved. She went sideways, to her left, her head down and her arms out, diving for the cartons.

I lost a tenth of a second because I hadn't dared to pull my feet back ready for the spring, but that was all I lost. I didn't leap, I just went, with all the force my leg muscles could give it. My target was the bottom of the left front leg of the chair, and I went in flat, face down, and had the leg before he could get under way. The impact of the chair knocked him back against the door, and I kept going and grabbed his ankle and jerked.

Of course, the bottle could have landed right on me, but I had to get him off his feet. As I yanked his ankle I kept my face down, and he tumbled. The next thing I knew I was on top of him, pinning him, with a grip on his throat, looking around for the bottle. It had never reached the floor. It had landed on a carton six feet to my right and lay there on its side, the stuff gurgling out. The floor slanted toward the wall, so no flood threatened me.

"Okay, Lila," I said. "I need help."

She was scrambling to her feet. "Did he—did it—?" She giggled.

"No. If you have hysterics I'll tell Bill. Slap yourself; I can't."

"But he—"

"Shut up. Company's coming and we've got to get out

of here. I want some adhesive tape quick." She started looking on shelves and in drawers. "Watch your step," I told her. "That stuff's spreading to the floor. . . . When I said I was good with uncles I didn't mean uncles like him. He's a lulu. He—"

"Here it is."

"Good girl. Tear off a piece six inches long . . . that's it. Now across his mouth good and tight, diagonally. Now one the other way. . . . That ought to do it, thank you, nurse. Now find some nice sterile bandage."

She found that, too, and held his arms while I sat on his knees and tied his ankles. Then I fastened his wrists behind him and anchored the strip of bandage to the handle of a locked drawer. I squatted for a look at the tape on his mouth, gave it a rub, stood up, went to the door, and pushed the bolt.

"Come on," I told her.

I opened the door and she passed through. I followed and pulled the door to. There were customers on the fountain stools, and Henry was selling a man a pack of cigarettes. I paused on my way to the street door to tell him that Mr. Gale would be out soon, then opened the door for Lila. On the sidewalk I told her to wait in the car while I made a phone call.

Up twenty paces was a bar and grill. I went in, found a phone booth, dialed Manhattan Homicide, asked for Sergeant Purley Stebbins, and got him. He wanted to know if I was still up at the ball park.

I told him no. "Where I am," I said, "is top secret. I'm giving you a hot one." I gave him the address of Gale's Pharmacy. 'Get a prowl car there fast, and plenty of reinforcements. Gale, the owner, on information received, was the go-between for the gamblers who fixed the ball game. He's in the back room of his store, gagged and tied."

"Is *this* a gag?"

"No. The reason for the hurry is that I think Gale sent for a rescue squad to deal with certain parties who are no longer there, and it would be nice to get there in time to welcome them. So PD cars should not park in front.

Be sure to tell them not to step in the stuff on the floor that looks like water, because it's sulphuric acid. That's all. Got the address?"

"Yes. Where are you? And—"

"Sorry, I've got a date. This could make you a lieutenant. Step on it."

I went out and back to the car. Lila was on the driver's side, gripping the steering wheel with both hands.

"Move over," I said. "I'll do the driving this time."

She slid across, and I got in and pulled the door to. I sat. Half a minute went by.

"Where are we going?" she asked. Her voice was so weak I barely got it.

"Uptown. Where Bill is." Maybe he was.

"Why don't we start?"

"I phoned for cops. If others come before the cops do I want to get a look at them. In case I forget it later, I want to mention that that was a beautiful dive you made, and the timing couldn't have been better. I'm for you, only spiritually of course, since you're happily married."

"I want to get away from here. I want to see Bill."

"You will. Relax."

We sat, but not for long. It couldn't have been more than four minutes before a pair of cops swung around the corner, headed for the entrance to Gale's Pharmacy, and entered. I pushed the starter button. . . .

It was only half an hour short of midnight when I stopped the car at the curb across the street from the main entrance to the ball park. The mob had dwindled to a few small knots, and of the long line of police cars only three were left. Two cops were having a tête-à-tête in front of the entrance.

Lila was a quick mover. She had got out and circled the car to my side by the time I hit the pavement. I gave her the ignition key and we were crossing the street when suddenly she let out a squawk and started to run. I took another step, and stopped. Bill Moyse was there, emerging from the entrance, with a dick on either side of him and one behind. Lila ended her run in a flying leap and was on him. The startled dicks grabbed for her, and the two uniformed cops started toward them.

I would have liked to deliver Lila to Wolfe, or at least to Hennessy, but there was a fat chance of tearing her loose from her second-string catcher. Also, I did not care to get hung up explaining to a bunch of underlings how I happened to be chauffeuring for Mrs. Moyse, so I detoured around the cluster, made it inside the entrance, and headed for the clubhouse stairs. Hearing heavy footsteps above, starting down, and voices, one of them Hennessy's, I slipped quietly behind a pillar.

Surely Stebbins had informed the Bronx of my phone call about the situation at Gale's Pharmacy, and so surely Hennessy would be inquisitive enough to want to take me along wherever he was going. I didn't risk peeking around the pillar, but, judging from the footsteps, there were four or five men. As soon as they had faded out I went on up the stairs. I was not chipper. I did not have Lila. I had been gone more than two hours. Wolfe might have gone home. They might all be gone.

But they weren't. Wolfe was in the clubroom, on the leather couch, and Chisholm was standing. As I entered, their heads turned to me.

"The police are looking for you," Wolfe said coldly.

"Uh-huh." I played it indifferent. "I just dodged a squad."

"Why did you go to that drugstore?"

I raised the brows. "Oh, you've heard about it?"

"Yes. Mr. Hennessy did, and he was kind enough to tell me." He was dripping sarcasm. "It is a novel experience, learning of your movements through the courtesy of a policeman."

"I was too busy to phone." I glanced at Chisholm. "Maybe I should report privately."

"This is getting to be a farce," Chisholm growled. His tie was crooked, his eyes were bloodshot, and he had a smear of mustard at the side of his mouth.

"No," Wolfe said, to me, not to Chisholm. "Go ahead. But be brief."

I obeyed. With the training and experience I have had

I can report a day of dialogue practically verbatim, but he had said to be brief, so I condensed it, including all essentials. When I finished he was scowling.

"Then you don't know whether Gale was actually involved or not. When he failed with Mr. and Mrs. Moyse he may have quit trying."

"I doubt it."

"You could have resolved the doubt. You were sitting on him. Or you could have brought him here."

I might have made three or four cutting remarks if an outsider hadn't been present. I stayed calm. "Maybe I didn't make it clear," I conceded generously. "It was ten to one he had phoned for help, the kind of help that would leave no doubts to resolve, and it might have come any second. Not that I was scared—I was too busy—but I wanted to see you once more so I could resign. I resign."

"Bosh." Wolfe put his hands on the leather seat for leverage and raised himself to his feet. "Very well. I'll have to try it."

Chisholm put in, "Inspector Hennessy said to notify him immediately if Goodwin showed up."

Wolfe wheeled on him, snarling. "Am I working for you? Yes! Notify Mr. Hennessy? Bah!" He turned and strode through the door that led to Art Kinney's office.

Chisholm and I fell in behind.

They were all in there. The four who were famous athletes didn't look very athletic just at present. Their sap had started draining with the first inning of that awful ball game, and it hadn't stopped for more than ten hours. Lew Baker, catcher, and Con Prentiss, shortstop, were perched on a desk. Joe Eston, third baseman, and Nat Neill, center-fielder, were on chairs.

Art Kinney, the manager, was standing over by a window. Doc Soffer was seated at Kinney's desk, bent over, with his elbows on his knees and his face covered by his hands. Beaky Durkin was propped against a table, saggy and bleary-eyed.

"It had better be good," someone said. I didn't know who, because I was placing a chair for Wolfe where he could see them all without straining his neck. When he was in it, with nothing to spare between the arms, I crossed to a vacant seat over by the radio. Chisholm was there, at my right.

Wolfe's head moved from side to side and back again. "I hope," he said grumpily, "you're not expecting too much."

"I'm through expecting," Kinney muttered.

Wolfe nodded. "I know how you feel, Mr. Kinney. All of you. You are weary and low in spirit. You have been personally and professionally humiliated. You have all been talked at too much. I'm sorry I have to prolong it, but I had to wait until the police were gone. Also, since I have no evidence, I had to let them complete their elaborate and skilled routine in search of some. They got none. Actually, they have nothing but a druggist that Mr. Goodwin got for them."

"They've got Bill Moyse," Con Prentiss rumbled.

"Yes, but on suspicion, not on evidence. Of course I admit, because I must, that I am in the same fix. I, too, have a suspicion but no evidence, only mine is better-grounded. I suspect one of you eight men of drugging the drinks and killing Ferrone. What I—"

They made enough noise to stop him. He held up a palm.

"If you please, gentlemen. I have a question to put. I suspect one of you, but I have no evidence and no way of getting any speedily. That is why I asked Mr. Chisholm to keep you here for consultation with me after the departure of the police. I wanted to ask you: Do you want to help? I would like to tell you the reason for my suspicion and ask you to help me get evidence to support it. I think you can if you will. Well?"

"One of *us*?" Joe Eston demanded.

It was interesting to see them. Naturally, they all had an impulse, all but one, anyway, to look around at faces, but no two of them handled it exactly alike. Chisholm looked straight and full at each in turn. Beaky Durkin sent quick little glances here and there. Doc Soffer, frowning and pursing his lips, turned his head slowly left to right.

"Go ahead!" Kinney blurted. "Have you got something or not?"

"Yes, I have something," Wolfe assured him, "but I don't know how good it is. Without your help it is no good at all."

"We'll help if we can. Let's hear it."

"Well. First the background. Were the two events—the drugging of the drinks and the murder—connected? The reasonable supposition is yes, until and unless it is contradicted. If they were connected, how? Did Ferrone drug the drinks, and did one of his teammates discover it and, enraged, go for him with the bat? It seems unlikely."

Wolfe focused on Beaky Durkin: "Mr. Durkin, you knew Ferrone better than anyone else. You discovered him and got him here. You were his roommate and counselor. You told me that because of his brilliant performance this season his salary for next year would be doubled; that his heart was set on winning today's game and the Series; that winning or losing meant a difference of some two thousand dollars to him personally; that his Series money would pay his debts, with some to spare; and that, knowing him intimately, you are positive that he could not have been bribed to drug the drinks. Is that correct?"

"It sure is." Durkin was hoarse and cleared his throat. "Nick was a swell kid." He looked around as if ready for an argument, but nobody started one.

"Do any of you dispute it?" Wolfe asked.

They didn't.

"Then without evidence it is idiotic to assume that he drugged the drinks. The alternative, suppose that the two events were connected, is the reverse: that someone drugged the drinks and Ferrone knew or suspected it and was going to expose him, and was killed. That is how I see it. Call him X. X could have—"

"Don't beat around the bush," Kinney blurted. "Name him!"

"Presently. X could have put the drugged drinks in the cooler any time during the late morning, as opportunity offered. What led Ferrone to suspect him of skulduggery may not be known, but conjecture offers a wide choice. Ferrone's suspicion may have been only superficial, but to X any suspicion whatever was a mortal menace, knowing, as he did, what was going to happen on the ball field. When Ferrone questioned him he had to act. The two were, of course, in this room together, at the time the rest of you were leaving the clubroom for the field or shortly after. X was, as so many have been, the victim of progressive emergency. At first he needed only money, and to get it he stooped to scoundrelism; but it betrayed him into needing the life of a fellow man."

"Cut the rhetoric," Chisholm snapped. "Name him."

Wolfe nodded. "Naming him is easy. But it is pointless to name him, and expose myself to an action for slander, unless I can enlist your help. As I said, I have no evidence. All I have is a fact about one of you, a fact known to all of you and to the police, which seems to me to point to guilt. But I admit that other interpretations are conceivable. You are better judges of that than I am, and I'm going to present it for your consideration."

He aimed his gaze at Baker and Prentiss, perched on a desk, raised a hand, slowly, and scratched the tip of his nose. His eyes moved to pin Doc Soffer. His head jerked to the left, to focus on Chisholm, and then right, to Beaky Durkin. He spoke:

"I'll illustrate my meaning. Take you, Mr. Durkin. You have accounted for yourself, but you have been neither contradicted nor corroborated. You say you left the clubhouse shortly before the team did and went to your seat in the grandstand."

"That's right." Durkin was still hoarse. "And I didn't kill Nick."

"I didn't say you did. I am merely expounding. You say you remained in your seat, watching the game, until the third inning, when you were sent for by Mr. Chisholm to come to the clubhouse. That, too, is neither contradicted nor corroborated. Certainly you were there when you were sent for, but there is no proof that you had been there continuously since the game started and even before."

"I don't know about proof, but I was. I can probably find the guy that was sitting next to me."

"You didn't leave your seat once during that time?"

"I did not."

Wolfe looked around. "Well, gentlemen. That's the fact I can't explain. Can you?"

They were gawking at him. "Do we have to?" Baker demanded.

"Someone does." Wolfe's voice sharpened: "Consider the situation. Consider the relationship of those two men. The discovery of Ferrone is Durkin's proudest achievement as a baseball scout. He fosters him and treasures him. Today, now yesterday, at the game that was to be the climax of Ferrone's triumphant season, Durkin is in the clubroom and sees Ferrone there in uniform, with the others, young, sound, mighty, valiant. He leaves the clubhouse and goes to a seat in the grandstand. Before long the loud-speaker announces that Garth, not Ferrone, will play second base. Durkin keeps his seat. The players take the field, and the game starts, with no Ferrone. Durkin keeps his seat. They play the first inning badly. Durkin keeps his seat. They play the second inning badly. Durkin keeps—"

"Good lord!" Art Kinney yelled.

"Exactly." Wolfe lifted a hand. "Please, gentlemen, keep your seats. It is clearly fantastic. The announcement that Garth would play second base could have been taken by Durkin merely as a blunder, but when they took the field without Ferrone his consternation would have been insupportable. The one thing he couldn't possibly have done was to stay in his seat. Why did you, Mr. Durkin?"

"I couldn't think—" He tried to clear his throat and almost choked. "What could I do?"

"I don't know. I said I can't explain what you did do, but I can try. Suppose the nonappearance of Ferrone was no surprise to you, because you knew where he was and what had happened to him. Suppose, further, you were in a state of severe systemic shock because you had murdered him. I submit that explanation of your keeping your seat is plausible. Can you offer any other?"

Durkin took two steps. "Look here," he said; "you can't sit there and accuse me of a thing like that. I don't have to stay and take it, and I'm not going to."

He started for the door, but Lew Baker was suddenly there in his path. "Back up, Beaky. I said back up!"

Beaky did so, literally. He backed until his rump hit the edge of the table. He groped for support and braced himself.

Wolfe was grim. "I was supposing, Mr. Durkin, not accusing. But I am now ready to accuse, and I do. I explained, when I was calling you X, how and why you acted." His eyes moved. "Gentlemen, I ask you to look at him. Look at his face, his eyes. Look at his hands, clutching the table in dismay and despair. Yes, I accuse him. I say that that man drugged your drinks, caused you to lose your game, and, threatened with exposure, murdered your teammate."

They were all on their feet, including Art Kinney. They were making threatening sounds.

"Wait!" Wolfe said sharply, and they turned to him. "I must warn you, you approach him at your peril, for I have no proof. It will be gratifying to press a confession out of him, but a confession is not evidence, and we need some. I suggest that you try for it. He did it for money, and surely he was paid something in advance, unless he is a fool. Where is it? Certainly not on his person, since you have all been searched, but it is somewhere, and it would do admirably. Where is it?"

Lew Baker got to Durkin ahead of the others. He told him in a thin, tight voice, so tight it twanged, "I wouldn't want to touch you, Beaky, you dirty rat. Where is it? Where's the jack?"

"Lew, I swear to—"

"Skip it! You fixed us, did you? And Nick—you fixed him. I'd hate to touch you, but if I do—"

The others were there, Kinney and Doc Soffer with them, crowding in on Durkin, who had pulled back onto the table, still gripping the edge. I went to the end of the table and stood. They were all strong and hard, and their nervous systems had had a tough day. Aside from the killing of Nick Ferrone, this was the bird who had made them play ball like half-witted apes in the most important game of their lives, to an audience of fifty million. If they really cut loose there could be another corpse.

"Give me room, fellow," Nat Neill said. "I'm going to plug him."

Durkin didn't flinch. His jaw was quivering and his eyes looked sick, but he didn't flinch.

"This is wrong," Con Prentiss said. "He wants us to hurt him. He'd like to be knocked cold. He's not a coward; he's just a snake. Look at him."

"It's a moral question," Joe Eston said. "That's the way to handle it; it's a moral question."

Art Kinney shouldered between two of them to get his face within ten inches of Durkin's. "Look, Beaky. You've been in baseball 30 years. You know everybody in the majors and we know you. What do you think's going to happen? Where could you light? We've got you here now and we're going to keep you. I'll send for the whole team. How will you like that?"

"I want a lawyer," Durkin said in a sudden burst.

Neill roared. "He wants a lawyer! Get out of the way—I'm going to clip him!"

"No, Beaky, no lawyers," Kinney said. "I'll send for the boys and we'll lock the doors. Where's the money? We know you got it. Where is it?"

Durkin's head went forward, down. Kinney put a fist under his chin and yanked it up and held it. "No, you don't. Look at me. We've got you, but even if we didn't where could you go? Where are you going to sleep and eat? You're done, Beaky. Where's the money?"

"Let me hold his chin," Neill requested. "I'll fix it for him."

"Shut up," Eston told him. "It's a moral question."

Kinney's fist was still propping Durkin's chin. "I think," he said, "the boys ought to have a look at you. They won't be sleeping anyhow, not tonight. Con, get on the phone and find them. You, too, Lew, the one in the clubroom. Get 'em here—get all of 'em you can. And tell them not to spill it. We don't want any cops around until we get—"

"No!" Durkin squawked.

"No what, Beaky?" Kinney removed his fist.

"I didn't mean to kill Nick." He was slobbering. "I swear I didn't, Art. He suspected. He found out I bet a grand against us and he threw it at me. I brought him here to explain. But he wouldn't believe me and was going to tell you, and he got sore and came at me, and I grabbed the bat just to stop him, and when I saw he was dead— You've got to believe me, Art. I didn't want to kill Nick!"

"You got more than a grand for doping the drinks. How much did you get?"

"I'm coming clean, Art. You can check me and I'm coming clean. I got five grand and I've got five more coming. I had to have it, Art, because the bookies had me down and I was sunk. I was listed good if I didn't come through. I had it on me, but with the cops coming I knew we'd be frisked, so I ditched it. You see I'm coming clean, Art. I ditched it there in the radio. I stuffed it in through a slot."

There was a scramble and a race. Prentiss tangled with a chair and went down with it, sprawling. Nat Neill won. He jerked the radio around and started clawing at the back, but the panel was screwed on.

"Here," I said, "I've got a—"

He hauled off and swung with his bare fist, getting his plug out of his system, though not on Durkin. Grabbing an edge of the hole his fist had made, he yanked, and half the panel came off. He looked inside and started to stick his hand in, but I shouldered him, good and hard, and sent him sideways. The others were there, three of them, surrounding me.

"We don't touch it, huh?" I instructed them, and bent down for a look in the radio, and there it was, lodged between a pair of tubes.

"Well?" Wolfe called as I straightened up.

"A good, fat roll," I told him and the world. "The one on the outside is a C."

Beaky Durkin, left to himself on the table, suddenly moved fast. He was on his feet and streaking for the door. Joe Eston, who had claimed it was a moral issue, leaped for him as if he had been a blazing line drive trying to get by, got to him in two bounds, and landed with his right. Durkin went down all the way, slamming the floor with his head, and lay still.

"That will do," Wolfe said, as one who had earned the right to command. "Thank you, gentlemen. I needed help. Archie, get Mr. Hennessy."

I went to Kinney's desk and reached for the phone. At the instant my fingers touched it, it rang. So instead of dialing I lifted it and, feeling cocky, told it, "Nero Wolfe's Bronx office, Archie Goodwin speaking."

"This is Inspector Hennessy. Is Durkin there?"

I said yes.

"Fine. Hold him, and hold him good. We cracked Gale and he spilled everything. Durkin is it. Gale got to him and bought him. You'll get credit for getting Gale—that'll be all right—but I'll appreciate it if you'll hold off and let it be announced officially. We'll be there for Durkin in five minutes. Hold him good."

"We're already holding him good. He's stretched out on the floor. Mr Wolfe hung it on him. Also, we have found a roll of lettuce he cached in the radio."

Hennessy laughed. "You're an awful liar, Goodwin. But you're a privileged character tonight. Have your fun. We'll be there in five minutes."

I hung up and turned to Wolfe: "That was Hennessy. They broke Gale and he unloaded. He gave them Durkin and they're coming for him. Hennessy doesn't believe we've already got him, but of course on that we've got witnesses. The trouble is this: Which of us crossed the plate first, you with your one little fact, or me with my druggist? You can't deny that Hennessy's call came before I started to dial him. How can we settle it?"

We can't. That was months ago, and it's not settled yet.

Murder on the Race Course

JULIAN SYMONS

"With my son up he can do it," Sir Reginald Bartley said emphatically. "There's no better amateur in the country than Harry. I tell you I'm not sorry Baker can't ride him."

There was something challenging in his tone. Trainer Norman Johnson, wooden-faced, bowlegged, said noncommittally, "He can ride, your son, I'm not denying it."

"And Lucky Charm's a fine horse."

"Ay, there's nothing against the horse," Johnson said.

"Then what's the matter with you, man? A few days ago you were keen as mustard, telling me I had a chance of leading in my first Grand National winner. Today you're as enthusiastic as the cat who started lapping a saucer of cream and found it was sour milk."

"I wouldn't want to raise false hopes, Sir Reginald, that's all. Here comes Lucky Charm."

"And here comes Harry."

Private detective Francis Quarles stood with them in the paddock at Aintree and listened to this conversation with interest. Horse racing was one of the few subjects about which he had no specialized knowledge, and he was here only because he had been tracking down the man who later became known as the Liverpool Forger.

Quarles had once cleared up a troublesome series of robberies committed in the chain of department stores owned by Sir Reginald, and when they met again in the Adelphi Hotel the business magnate had invited the private detective to be his guest at Aintree.

In the hotel that morning Quarles had learned that Lucky Charm was a 40-to-1 outsider in this year's Grand National, that his jockey Baker had fallen and thrown out his shoulder on the previous day, and that Lucky Charm would now be ridden by Sir Reginald's son, Harry.

Now he looked at the big-shouldered powerful-looking black horse, with the number 8 on his saddle cloth, being led round by a stable boy. Then he looked at the young man who walked up to them wearing a jacket of distinctive cerise and gold hoops.

"How is it, Harry? All set?" asked Sir Reginald.

"Why not?" Harry Bartley had the kind of dark, arrogant good looks that Quarles distrusted.

"We're all ready to lead him in," Sir Reginald said, with what seemed to Quarles almost fatuous complacency. "We know we've got the horse and the jockey too, Harry my boy."

Johnson said nothing. Harry Bartley pulled a handkerchief out of his breast pocket and blew his nose.

"Got your lucky charm?" the owner persisted.

"Of course." Harry's voice was lightly blurred, as though he had just had a tooth out. From the same pocket he produced a rabbit's foot, kissed it, and put it back carefully.

"There's Mountain Pride," said Sir Reginald a little

wistfully. Mountain Pride, Quarles knew, was the favorite, a bay gelding with a white star on his forehead.

"Time to go." Harry Bartley gave them a casual nod and turned away, walking a little erratically across the paddock to the place where the stable boy stood, holding Lucky Charm. Had he been drinking, Quarles wondered?

"Good luck," his father called. "Better be getting along to the stand." Sir Reginald was a choleric little man, and now his face was purple as he turned to the trainer. "You may not like the boy, but you could have wished him luck."

Johnson's wooden expression did not change. "You know I wish Lucky Charm all the luck there is, Sir Reginald."

"Trouble with Johnson is, he's sulking," Sir Reginald said when they were in the stand. "Insisted Baker should ride the horse when I wanted Harry. I gave way—after all, Baker's a professional jockey. Then, when Baker was injured, he wanted to have some stable boy and I put my foot down."

"What has he got against your son?"

Sir Reginald looked at Quarles out of the corner of one slightly bloodshot eye. "The boy's a bit wild, y'know. Nothing wrong with him, but—a bit wild. There they go."

The horses had paraded in front of the stand and now they were going down to the starting post. Bright March sunlight illuminated the course and even Francis Quarles, who was not particularly susceptible to such things, found something delightful in the scene. The men and women in the stands and the crowd chattering along the rails, the men with their raglans and mackintoshes and the patches of color in women's coats and hats, the ballet-like grace of the horses and the vivid yet melting green of the Aintree background . . .

Quarles pulled himself up on the edge of sentiment. His companion said sharply, "Harry's having trouble."

The horses were at the starting post. Quarles raised

his glasses. After a moment he picked out Lucky Charm. The black horse was refusing to get into line with the rest. Three times Harry Bartley brought him up and he turned away.

Sir Reginald tapped his stick on the ground. "Come on now, Harry. Show him who's master. Never known Lucky Charm to act like this before."

"Is he used to your son?"

The question was not well received. "Harry can ride any horse," Bartley snapped. Then he drew in his breath and his voice joined with thousands of others in the cry, "They're off!"

Now in the stand a mass of binoculars was raised to follow the progress of some thirty horses over some of the most testing fences in the world. Now bookmakers looked anxious, punters let cigars go out, women twisted race cards in gloved hands. Everything depended now on the jumping skill and staying power of horses that had been trained for months in preparation for this day, and on the adeptness of the jockeys in nursing their charges and then urging them forward to moments of supreme endeavor.

The horses came up in a bunch to the first fence, rose to it, cleared it. Thousands of throats exhaled and articulated sighingly the words: "They're over."

They were not all over, Quarles saw. A jockey lay on the ground, a jockey wearing red jacket and white cap. A riderless horse ran on.

On to the second jump and the third, a six-foot ditch with a four-foot-nine fence on the other side of it. Now there was a cry: "O'Grady's down. Double or Quits is down. Bonny Dundee's down."

There were more riderless horses, more jockeys on the ground who stumbled to their feet and ran to the rails when all the horses had passed.

Past Becher's they came and round the Canal Turn and then over Valentine's, the field beginning to string out.

"There's Mountain Pride in front," Sir Reginald cried. "And Johnny Come Lately and Lost Horizon. And Lucky Charm's with them." Almost under his breath he muttered, "But I don't like the way the boy's handling him."

The horses came round toward the stand. Quarles watched the cerise and gold jacket take the fourteenth fence, and it seemed to him that Harry Bartley was not so much riding as desperately clinging to the horse.

They came to the fifteenth fence, the Chair, which is one of the most awkward at Aintree—a six-foot ditch and then a fence five-foot-two in height which rises roughly in a chair's shape.

Mountain Pride soared over, and so did the two horses that followed. Then came the cerise and gold jacket. Lucky Charm rose to the fence and went over beautifully, but as he landed the jockey seemed simply to slip off and lay prone on the turf.

Lucky Charm ran on, the rest of the field thundered by.

Sir Reginald lowered his glasses slowly. "That's that. Not my Grand National, I'm afraid."

Quarles waited for the figure on the turf to get up, but it did not move. Ambulance men beside the jump ran onto the course with a stretcher and bent over the jockey. Still he did not move as they lifted him onto the stretcher.

They watched in stupefaction as the ambulance men carried him away. Then Sir Reginald, his usually ruddy face white as milk, said, "Come on, man, come on."

"What about the race?"

"To hell with the race," Sir Reginald cried. "I want to know what's happened to my son."

The limp body of Harry Bartley was carried round to the course hospital, in the administrative block. Doctor Ferguson, the local doctor, had just begun his examination when the door of the ward was pushed open and a handsome gray-haired man, with a pair of binoculars slung round his neck, came in.

"Ferguson? My name's Ramsay, I'm Harry's doctor. We've met before, up here last year. Is the boy badly hurt?"

"As far as I can see he's received no injury at all.

There's something very wrong though—his pulse is feeble and irregular. Was he subject to any kind of fits, do you know?"

"Harry? Not to my knowledge." Ferguson made way as Doctor Ramsay approached the body and bent over it. He straightened up with a puzzled frown. "Have you smelled round the nose and mouth?"

"No, I haven't. I'd only begun to examine him." Ferguson bent over too and caught the odor of bitter almonds. "My God, he's taken poison!"

"Taken it—or it's been administered to him." Ramsay's face was grave. "The question is what, and how? It's not cyanide, obviously, or he wouldn't be alive now."

"I must telephone—" Doctor Ferguson broke off as Sir Reginald and Francis Quarles, followed by trainer Norman Johnson, came into the room. Ramsay went over to Sir Reginald and placed a hand on his arm.

"Bartley, I won't mince words. You must be prepared for a shock. Harry has been poisoned in some way, and there's very little we can do for him."

"He'll be all right?"

"It's touch and go," Ramsay said evasively. He watched Francis Quarles approach the body. "Who's that?"

Sir Reginald told him.

Quarles bent over the unconscious figure, looked at its pale face and purple lips and nose, sniffed the scent of bitter almonds. He came over to Ramsay, who had now been joined by Ferguson. Sir Reginald introduced the detective.

"Have you gentlemen made up your minds about this case?" Quarles asked. He spoke in a faintly languid manner which made Ramsay, who was brisk and soldierly, bristle slightly.

"Not yet. In your superior wisdom I suppose you have done so."

"Have you considered nitrobenzene?"

"Nitrobenzene," Doctor Ferguson said thoughtfully. "Yes, that would explain the prussic acid symptoms, but I don't see why it should have occurred to you."

"I know little about horse racing, but something about poisoning," Quarles said. "And I had the opportunity of seeing Harry Bartley just before the race. His appearance then seemed to me very strange. His speech was blurred and he walked unsteadily. The thought crossed my mind that he might be drunk, but as you know such an appearance of drunkenness is a common symptom in nitrobenzene poisoning."

There was silence. Ramsay shifted uncomfortably. Sir Reginald said, "What are we waiting for? If there's no ambulance let's get him in to Liverpool in my car."

Ferguson crossed over to Harry Bartley again, felt pulse and heart, and then drew a sheet up over the face.

Ramsay said to Sir Reginald, "He's gone. I wanted to break it gently. There was never any chance."

"But when we came in Ferguson here was telephoning—"

"I was telephoning the police superintendent on the course," Ferguson said. "There'll need to be an investigation. This is a bad business."

Francis Quarles took no part in the flurry of conversation that followed the arrival of the police superintendent and the other officers with him. Instead, he went over to the wooden-faced trainer, Norman Johnson, and took him outside. They paced up and down in hearing of the excited crowds who were cheering the victory of Mountain Pride, and Quarles asked questions.

"Harry Bartley may have died by accident, but I would bet a hundred pounds that he was murdered. Now there's one obvious question I should like to have answered by a racing expert. Is it likely that he was killed to prevent Lucky Charm winning the National?"

Johnson paused for an appreciable time before he said bluntly, "No."

"It's unlikely?"

"You can put it out of your mind. I'm not saying horse racing's pure as snow, Mr. Quarles. Far from it. Horses have been nobbled before now, horses have been doped.

But favorites, not forty-to-one outsiders. And horses, not men."

"You mean—?"

"If anyone wanted to stop Lucky Charm they'd go for the horse, not the man. Kill a horse and get caught, you may go to prison. Kill a man—well, it's murder."

"Sir Reginald seemed very optimistic about his horse's chances in the National. What did you feel?"

The trainer rubbed his chin, making a sound like a saw cutting wood. "With Baker up, he was a good outsider, a nice each-way bet. Hadn't quite the class for it, but you never can tell. He liked Baker, did Lucky Charm."

"And he didn't like Harry Bartley?"

"Hated him. Bartley used the whip more than he needed to. Lucky Charm wasn't a horse you could treat that way. I tried to persuade Sir Reginald to give the ride to another jockey, but it was no good."

"You shared the horse's dislike of Harry Bartley, I gather."

The trainer said nothing. His faded blue eyes stared into the distance, and the Red Indian impassiveness of his features did not change. "Was there a special reason for that?"

Slowly and without passion, Norman Johnson said, "Sir Reginald Bartley is a man I respect and like, none more so. I don't know how he came to have such a son. He couldn't be trusted with a woman, he couldn't be trusted to pay his debts, he was a good rider but he couldn't be trusted to treat a horse decently."

"But there's something personal in your dislike," Quarles insisted.

Johnson brought his blue eyes out of the middle distance and focused them on Quarles. "You'll learn about it soon enough. It might as well be from me. I had a daughter named Mary. She was a good girl until she took up with Harry Bartley. He was always around the stables, every day for weeks, and I was fool enough not to realize what he was after—until Mary went away with him and left me a note. I understood it then well enough. That was six months ago. He walked out on her after a few weeks. She put her head in a gas oven."

"I see."

"When I've worked out my contract with Sir Reginald, I'm asking him to take his horses away."

Quarles said softly, "Some people might call that a motive for murder."

"I don't deny it, Mr. Quarles. It happens that I didn't kill him, that's all." Johnson drove the fist of one hand into the palm of the other, and his voice for the first time vibrated with excitement. "But if you ever find his murderer you'll find he has a personal reason, a reason like mine. For me, I hope you never find him. I say good luck to the man or woman who killed Harry Bartley."

Back in the course hospital Quarles met young Inspector Makepeace, who had been working with him in running down the Liverpool Forger.

Makepeace looked at the private detective with a wry smile. "You seem to manage to be where things happen, Mr. Quarles. I understand you saw young Bartley before the race."

Quarles told him the impression he had formed that Bartley might be drunk, and the outcome of his conversation with Johnson. The Inspector listened with interest.

"I should say Johnson's right, and this was almost certainly the working out of a private enmity. As you say, he's got a motive himself, although I'm keeping an open mind about that. In return I don't mind telling you that we've got a pretty good idea of how the poison was administered. Miss Moore here has been very helpful about that. She was engaged to Harry Bartley."

Miss Jennifer Moore had a round innocent face and dark hair. She had been crying. "But Inspector, I only said—"

"Bear with me a moment," Inspector Makepeace asked. Quarles, whose own sense of modesty was conspicuous by its absence, noted mentally that Makepeace had a good opinion of himself. "I don't know whether you know much about nitrobenzene poisoning, Mr. Quarles?"

"I know that nitrobenzene is comparatively easy to make," Quarles answered. "It is generally taken in the form of a liquid although it is equally poisonous as a vapor. I remember the case of a young man who spilled nitrobenzene on his clothes, became stupefied, finally collapsed in coma and died. But the most interesting thing about it is that there is an interval between taking the poison and its effects appearing, which can vary from a quarter of an hour to three hours, or longer in the case of vapor. Is that what you were going to tell me?"

The Inspector laughed a little uncomfortably. "You're a bit of a walking encyclopedia, aren't you? That's pretty much what I was going to say, yes. You see, if we can trace the course of Bartley's eating and drinking today we should be able to see when he took the poison. Now it so happens that we can do just that. Doctor Ramsay, would you come over here, please?"

The poker-backed doctor came forward.

"I understand Harry Bartley came to see you this morning."

Ramsay nodded. "I'm staying with friends a couple of miles outside Liverpool. Harry rang me up this morning before nine o'clock. He was pretty jittery, wanted something to pep him up. He was out at the place I'm staying before half-past nine and I gave him a couple of pills, and put two more in a box for him in case he needed to take them before the race."

"They were in his clothes in the changing room," Makepeace said to Quarles with a smile. "I can see your eyes fixed thoughtfully on Doctor Ramsay, but Ferguson here assures me that any pills taken at half-past nine must have had effect well before the time of the race. Now, follow the course of events, Quarles. Bartley returned to the hotel by ten o'clock, met Miss Moore in the lobby, and said that he was going up to his room to write some letters. She arranged to pick him up at about twelve, because they were going to a cocktail party. She picked him up then and they went to the party, which was given by a friend of theirs named Lapetaine. There, Miss Moore can testify, Harry Bartley drank just one glass of orange juice."

"What about lunch?" Quarles asked the girl.

She shook her head. "Harry was worried about making the weight. He came and watched Bill and me eat lunch and didn't touch anything, not so much as a piece of toast or a glass of water."

"Bill?"

She colored slightly. "Doctor Ramsay and I have known each other for years. He can bear out what I say. We had lunch on the course, and after it Harry went off to the changing room. Of course he may have drunk something after that."

"Most unlikely," Ferguson said. "Particularly if he was worried about making the weight."

"So you see we're down to the one glass of orange juice." The Inspector smoothed his fair hair with some complacency.

"Apparently," Quarles agreed. "At lunch, did he show any sign of confusion, blurred speech, unsteady walk—anything like that?"

Both Ramsay and Jennifer Moore returned decided negatives.

"Come on now, Mr. Quarles," Makepeace said with a smile. "The fact is you're reluctant to admit that the police are ever quick off the mark, and this time we've surprised you."

"It isn't that, my dear Inspector. Something's worrying me, and I don't quite know what it is. Something that I've seen, or that's happened or that's been said. I shall be interested to know the result of the post-mortem."

"The P.M.?" The Inspector was startled. "Surely you don't doubt that—"

"That he died of nitrobenzene poisoning? No, I don't, but there's still something that tantalizes me about it. Ah, here are his personal possessions."

The detective paused by a table on which a number of articles lay in two separate piles. One of them contained the things Bartley had been wearing during the race, the other came from his clothes in the changing room.

In the first pile were Lucky Charm's saddle, the cerise and gold shirt and cap, and the breeches Bartley had been wearing. Here too, isolated and pathetic, was the rabbit's-foot charm he had kissed; it was neatly ticketed: *Found in pocket.*

The things in the other pile were naturally more numerous—sports jacket, vest, shirt and gray trousers, gold wrist watch, keys on a ring, silver and copper coins, a wallet with notes and other papers, three letters.

Inspector Makepeace picked up one of these letters and handed it to Quarles.

It was a letter written in a sprawling hand by a woman who had used violet ink, and it was full of bitter reproaches, in painfully familiar phrasing. "Cast me off like an old shoe . . . given you everything a woman can give . . . shan't let you get away with it . . . sooner see you dead than married to somebody else."

Why is it, Quarles wondered, that at times of strong emotion, almost all of us express ourselves in clichés? The letter began "Darling Harry" and was signed "Hilary."

"You haven't traced the writer of this letter yet?" The undercurrent of sarcasm in Quarles's voice was so faint that Inspector Makepeace missed it.

"Give us a chance, Mr. Quarles. Between you and me I'm not inclined to attach too much importance to it— shouldn't be surprised to learn that there were half a dozen women in Master Harry's life. I'm more interested in getting a complete list of guests at that cocktail party. Nothing very informative here, I'm afraid."

"On the contrary," Quarles said.

Makepeace stared. "You mean there's something I've missed—"

"You haven't missed anything, but something's missing that should be here. You should be able to deduce it yourself. Now I'm more anxious than ever to know the result of the post-mortem."

* * *

Sir Reginald Bartley paced up and down the drawing room of his suite. His voice had lost none of its vigor, but his appearance was pitiably different from that of the jaunty man who had talked about leading in the Grand National winner twenty-four hours earlier. There was an ushaved patch on his chin, his face was pallid and his hand trembled slightly.

'I want this murderer caught," he said. "I want to see him in the dock. I want to hear the judge pronounce sentence on him. That police Inspector is smart, but I believe you're smarter, Quarles. I want you to investigate this case, and if you catch the man who poisoned my son you can write your own ticket."

Quarles looked at him intently. "Why do you call it a man? There is a general belief that most poisoners are women."

"Man or woman." Sir Reginald made an impatient gesture to indicate that this was merely splitting hairs. "I want them in the dock."

"Then you'll have to be franker with me than you have been so far. You might begin by telling me what you know about Hilary."

"Hilary?" Sir Reginald's surprise seemed genuine. "That's not a name I've ever heard in relation to Harry."

"She wrote an interesting letter to your son." Quarles did not pursue the point. "Norman Johnson said that your son behaved very badly to his daughter."

Sir Reginald blew his nose emphatically. "She was a foolish girl, wouldn't leave him alone. I'm not denying that Harry was sometimes wild. But there was never any real harm to him."

"Johnson's story was that your son lured this girl away from home, lived with her for a short time, then walked out on her. Do you accept that?"

"I've really no idea. Harry was of age. I knew little about that side of his life. I don't see," he added stiffly, "that it's our place to sit in moral judgment on him."

"It's not a question of moral judgment," Quarles said patiently. "I'm trying to get at facts. What do you think of Miss Moore?"

"A very nice girl, very nice indeed," said Sir Reginald emphatically.

"She'd only recently become engaged to your son, I believe?"

"About three weeks ago, yes. She is—was—very much in love with him."

"Doctor Ramsay had known her for years?"

"Yes. Known Harry for many years too, for that matter, ever since he was a boy. Good chap, Ramsay, pulled me through a bad go of pneumonia a couple of years ago, just after my wife died."

Quarles stood up. His eyes, hard and black, stared at Sir Reginald, who bore their gaze uneasily. "I accept the commission. But you will realize, Sir Reginald, that I am no respecter of persons. You are engaging me to discover the truth, regardless of consequences."

Sir Reginald repeated after him, "Regardless of consequences."

In the hotel lobby Quarles heard himself being paged. He stopped the boy and was told that Miss Moore was in the lounge and would like to speak to him. He found her talking in a deserted corner of the room to a dark-skinned, rather too beautifully dressed young man, with a fine large nose.

"This is Jack Lapetaine, who was Harry's great friend," she said. "As a matter of fact, it was through Jack that I met Harry, and it was Jack who gave the cocktail party yesterday."

"Is that so?" Quarles looked at Lapetaine with interest, wondering about his ancestry. Indian perhaps? Turkish? "Are you a racing man, Mr. Lapetaine?"

"I am an art dealer." Lapetaine smiled, showing pointed yellowish teeth. "But I am interested in horse racing, yes. I like the excitement. I like to gamble, I was very fond of Harry. So I came up for the National. I am almost ashamed of it, but I had a good win."

"You backed Mountain Pride?"

"I did. I had just a little flier on Lucky Charm, for

Murder on the Race Course

sentiment's sake as you might say, but I did not think he had quite—how shall I put it?—the class for the race."

"You watched it, of course?"

"No, Mr. Quarles." Lapetaine looked down at his elegant suede shoes. "I was engaged on urgent business."

Jennifer Moore said impatiently, "Look here, Mr. Quarles, there's something I want you to tell me. Has Sir Reginald asked you to investigate this case?" Quarles nodded. "I hope you won't."

"Why not?"

"It can't possibly do any good. Harry's dead, and nothing can bring him back. And it might—well, might embarrass people who haven't any connection with it."

Lapetaine listened with a malicious smile. Quarles said quietly, "I see. Your engagement is very recent, isn't it, Miss Moore?"

"Harry and I met for the first time five weeks ago. It sounds silly, I expect, but we fell in love at first sight. Within a fortnight we were engaged."

"Should I be right in thinking that Doctor Ramsay feels some affection for you, and that you are afraid my investigations may involve him?"

Still with that slightly objectionable smile, Lapetaine said, "I can tell you exactly what Jennifer is afraid of. Ramsay has been sweet on her for years. Now, you know that Harry went out to see Ramsay on the morning of the race to get some pep tablets. What was to stop Ramsay from giving him two more, one of them filled with nitrobenzene, and saying, 'Take one of these at twelve thirty, my boy, and you'll ride as you've never ridden before.' It simply happened that Harry took the poisoned tablet first. The timing would be just about right."

The girl buried her face in her hands. "You shouldn't have—"

"My dear, Mr. Quarles is an intelligent man. I should be surprised if that idea had not already occurred to him."

Quarles looked at him. "You seem to know a good

deal about the operation of nitrobenzene, Mr. Lapetaine."

Unperturbed, the art dealer showed his teeth. "I trained for a medical degree in youth before I—what shall I say?—discovered my vocation."

"There are certain objections to that idea," Quarles began, when a page boy came running up.

"Mr. Quarles, sir. Telephone for you."

On the telephone Quarles heard Inspector Makepeace's voice, raw with irritation. "We've got the result of the P.M. I don't know how you guessed, but you were perfectly right."

"There was no question of guessing," Quarles said indignantly. "My suggestion was the result of deduction from observed facts."

"Anyway, it seems to leave us just where we began."

"Oh, no," Quarles said softly. "I have told you exactly what happened before and during the race. Surely it leaves only one possible explanation."

He went back to the lounge, and addressed Jennifer Moore. "You need not worry any further, Miss Moore, about Doctor Ramsay or anyone else having administered a poisonous pill to Harry Bartley. I have just learned the result of the post-mortem. There was only a trace of nitrobenzene in the stomach."

They looked at him in astonishment, Lapetaine with his mouth slightly open. "I will spell out the meaning of that for you. Harry Bartley was not poisoned by a pill or by the orange juice he drank at your cocktail party, Mr. Lapetaine. He was poisoned by nitrobenzene, yes, but in the form of vapor."

Lapetaine had been surprised by Quarles's revelation but, as the detective admitted to himself with some admiration, the art dealer was a cool card. After the initial shock he nodded.

"Will you excuse me? I must remember to make a note of an appointment." He scribbled something on a sheet of paper torn from a pocket diary and said with a smile, "I am relieved. You will no longer suspect me of poisoning my guest's orange juice, which would hardly have been playing the game, as you might say."

Jennifer Moore seemed bewildered. "I thought it must be the orange juice. If it was vapor, then—well, I simply don't understand. Perhaps it was an accident."

"It was not an accident," Francis Quarles said. "You can see that my investigations may be useful after all, Miss Moore."

"I suppose so," she said a little doubtfully. "Goodbye, Mr. Quarles."

Lapetaine held out his hand to say goodbye, and when Quarles took it he found a piece of paper in his palm. He opened it after they had turned away, and saw that it was the paper torn from Lapetaine's diary.

On it the art dealer had scribbled: *Can you meet me in ten minutes at Kismet Coffee House, down the street?*

Ten minutes later Quarles pushed open the door of the Kismet Coffee House. In one of the cubicles he found the darkly handsome Lapetaine, drinking black coffee.

"Mr. Quarles, you'll think me immensely mysterious, but—"

"Not at all. It was plain enough from your note that you wanted to talk to me when Miss Moore was not present. From that I deduce that you want to talk about a woman connected with Harry Bartley, and that it would upset Miss Moore to hear about her. I admit, however, that I am making no more than an informed guess when I suggest that her name is Hilary."

Lapetaine looked at Quarles with his mouth open, then laughed unconvincingly. "My word, Mr. Quarles, it's not much use trying to keep secrets from you. I didn't know you'd ever heard of Hilary Hall."

"I didn't say that I had. But now that you have told me her full name, you may as well go on with the story. I take it that she was a friend of Harry Bartley's."

"She certainly was. Hilary's a night-club singer, the star at the Lady Love, which is a newish club just off Piccadilly. She's a red-head with a tremendous temper. When she heard that Harry was engaged to be married, she really hit the roof. Harry had played around with a lot of girls in his time, you know."

Quarles nodded. "I do know. But about Miss Hall."

Lapetaine leaned forward. "This I'll bet you *don't* know, Mr. Quarles, and neither does anybody else. Hilary Hall came up here the day before the race, and she came to make trouble. She telephoned Harry that evening and he went to see her, tried to quiet her down, but without much effect. She rang Harry again at the cocktail party I gave the morning before the race, but I spoke to her. I spent the afternoon of the race arguing with her." Lapetaine smiled. "She finally agreed that a thousand pounds might help to soothe her injured feelings. I think you should talk to her."

"I think so too. Why didn't you give this information to the police, Mr. Lapetaine?"

The art dealer looked down at his shoes. "I didn't think Hilary could be involved, but after what you tell me about vapor—I don't know. If I'm going to get into any trouble myself, then with me it's strictly Number One. Hilary's gone back to London. You'll find her at the Lady Love night-club."

Francis Quarles talked on the telephone to the owner of the Lady Love, then took a plane from Liverpool to London. He arrived at the night-club, caught a glimpse of a cabaret-turn ending, and pushed his way backstage among a crowd of blondes and brunettes, wondering as he had often done before why a dozen half-dressed girls should be so much less attractive than one.

He tapped on the door of a room that was labeled *Miss Hall*. A deep, harsh voice said "All right."

Hilary Hall was sitting in front of a looking glass and her reflection frowned out at him. Her beauty was like a physical blow after the commonplace prettiness of the dancing girls outside. Yet on a second look it was not really beauty, Quarles saw, but simply the combination of flaming red hair, a milk-white skin, and certain unusual physical features—the thick brows that almost met

Murder on the Race Course

in the middle, the jutting red underlip, the powerful shoulders.

This was a woman whom you could imagine as a murderess, although such an exercise of the imagination, as Quarles well knew, could easily be misleading.

"I was told you were coming," she said in that rusty, attractive voice. "And I've seen your picture in the papers. What do you want?"

"I would like you to answer some questions."

"I'm on in ten minutes. You've got till then." She had not turned round.

Quarles said, "I can put it simply. You were in love with Harry Bartley. You wrote him a threatening letter after his engagement. You went up to Liverpool to cause trouble."

Her thick brows were drawn together. "So what? He's dead now. I never went near the course, Mr. Detective."

Quarles said softly, "He came to see you the night before the race."

She swung round now and faced him. Her eyes were snapping with temper. She looked magnificent. "Of course he did, after I'd rung him up. He came to pour out all his troubles and say how sorry he was it had to be goodbye. He didn't want to marry that silly little bit he'd got engaged to. She had money, that was all. Can you imagine any man preferring her to me?"

She paused and Quarles, although not particularly susceptible, felt a kind of shiver run down his back.

"He had other troubles too," she said. "A frightful cold that he was afraid might develop into flu and make it difficult for him to ride that damned horse. Said he'd have to do something about it. Altogether, he was pretty low."

"You were very much in love with him?"

Looking down at her scarlet fingernails she said, "He was a man."

With a deprecating cough Quarles said, "But you were prepared to accept a thousand pounds to soothe your feelings."

She struck the dressing table sharply with a clenched

fist. "That filthy Paul Lapetaine's been talking to you. He was after me himself, but he never got to first base. I like men, not dressed-up dolls. Yes, I said I'd take the money. I need it. I knew Harry would never put a ring on my finger. You can think what you like about it."

"What I think," Quarles said abruptly, "is that you're an honest woman."

Her heavy frown changed into a smile. "You're all right."

A head poked through the door and a voice said, "On in two minutes, Miss Hall."

"Look here," she said, "I'm on now, but why don't you stay here? We'll talk afterwards, have a drink. I want to find Harry's murderer as much as you do."

"I should be delighted to have a drink, and honored if you would allow me to take you out to supper," Francis Quarles said. "But we don't have to talk about the case. The case is solved."

Quarles's secretary, Molly Player, was a neatly attractive—but not too attractive—blonde. He had told her something about the people involved in the case, and now as the suspects arrived and she took them all in to Quarles's office overlooking Trafalgar Square, she found some amusement in comparing the detective's remarks with the reality.

Sir Reginald came first, pale and anxious ("self-made man, vulgar and cocky, but really cut to pieces by his son's death," Quarles had said), and he was closely followed by Doctor Ramsay ("every inch a soldier, so military he seems phoney, but in fact he was an army doctor, and a good one").

Then came Jennifer Moore wearing a becoming amount of black, accompanied by elegant Paul Lapetaine. "She looks and talks like a mouse, but that doesn't mean she *is* a mouse," Quarles had said thoughtfully of Miss Moore. Lapetaine he had dismissed briskly. "One of nature's spivs."

Then, on her own, in a glory of furs and radiating bright sex, Hilary Hall. "You can't miss *her*, Molly, any more than you can miss the sun coming out," Quarles said. "An orange sun," he added as an afterthought. "High in the sky, a scorcher."

Last of all, Norman Johnson, the brown-faced bow-legged trainer of Lucky Charm. About him Quarles's comment had been tersest of all. "Poker face."

Molly Player let them all in. Then she sat down and tried to type a report, but found herself making a number of mistakes. She remembered Quarles's last words to her: "One of these six, Molly, is a murderer."

Francis Quarles sat back in the big chair behind his desk, and said pleasantly to the six people, "One of you is a murderer."

His office was large, but it had only four chairs for visitors, so that Paul Lapetaine stretched his elegant legs from a stool, and Doctor Ramsay sat in a window-seat from which he could look down on the square far below with its pigeons, its children, and its lions. Jennifer Moore sat next to Ramsay, as far away as possible from Hilary Hall.

"It may be of interest to you all," Quarles continued didactically, "to know how I discovered the murderer, after Sir Reginald had engaged me to investigate.

"I considered first the question of motive, and I found that five of you had motives for killing Harry Bartley. Johnson, trainer of the horse he rode, hated him because Bartley had treated his daughter badly. Miss Hall had been thrown over by Bartley, and had written him a threatening letter.

"Miss Moore might have discovered that Bartley went to see Miss Hall on the night before the race. She looks like a quiet young lady, but quiet young ladies have been known to poison through jealousy.

"Paul Lapetaine, I should judge, was jealous of Bartley's success with women, and especially with Hilary Hall. Doctor Ramsay was obviously fond of Miss Moore, and had been for years. He must have had bitter feelings when he learned that she was going to marry a man like Harry Bartley."

Ramsay on his window-seat made a motion of protest. Sir Reginald said, "You have no right to talk about my son like that."

Quarles's voice was harsh. "I'm sorry, Sir Reginald. I told you that this inquiry might be disagreeable for you. I don't condone murder, but I must admit that your son strikes me as an unpleasant character.

"Let us move on from motive to opportunity. Bartley was killed by nitrobenzene, and it was thought at first that he had drunk the poison in a glass of orange juice, or perhaps taken it in the form of a pill. There was a thought in Miss Moore's mind, or perhaps Lapetaine put it there, that Doctor Ramsay might have given Bartley a tablet filled with nitrobenzene when Bartley came to see him early on the morning of the race.

"The post-mortem proved conclusively that this idea was mistaken. Dr. Ramsay's pills were perfectly harmless. Bartley had not been killed by nitrobenzene introduced into his stomach. He had been poisoned by it in the form of vapor.

"This was the essential feature of the crime. The last vital clue, however, was provided by Miss Hall. She told me that on the night before the race, when Bartley came to see her, he complained of a bad cold that he feared might develop into influenza."

There was silence in the room. Then Jennifer Moore said timidly, "I suppose I knew that too. I mean, I knew Harry was sniffing a lot and had a bit of a cold, but I still don't understand why it should be important—vital, you said."

"Quite early in the case I said that I remembered an affair in which a young man spilled nitrobenzene on his clothes, became stupefied, collapsed in coma, and died. Something like that happened to Harry Bartley."

"His clothes weren't poisoned." That was Johnson, speaking for the first time.

"No. He was killed by a handkerchief impregnated with nitrobenzene, which he used frequently because he had a cold."

Murder on the Race Course

Hilary Hall objected, in her rusty voice, "I don't believe that that points to anybody in particular."

"There are two other things I should tell you. When I met Harry Bartley in the paddock I noticed that he used a handkerchief to wipe his nose. After the race, when his things were laid out on a table, the handkerchief was no longer there."

"It came out when he fell from the horse," Ramsay suggested.

"No. Because the rabbit's foot which he had tucked into his pocket at the same time was still there. The handkerchief had been taken away—stolen."

Sir Reginald rubbed his chin. "I may be slow, but I simply don't see how that can be possible. Nobody came near Harry's body—" He stopped.

"That isn't true," Quarles said. "But it is true that only one person fulfills all *five* of our murderer's qualifications. He had to be a person who disliked Harry Bartley. He had to possess some knowledge of the properties of nitrobenzene. He had to know that Bartley had a cold, and would frequently wipe his nose with a handkerchief. He had to be a person from whom Bartley would have accepted a handkerchief—having been told that it was impregnated with what our murderer might have said was oil of eucalyptus, good for a cold. Finally he had to be a person who had access to Harry Bartley very soon after he collapsed. He was able to bend over the body—making an examination, shall we say?—and steal the handkerchief.

"The police are outside, Doctor Ramsay. It's no good trying to use that gun in your hip pocket."

Doctor Ramsay was on his feet now, and the gun was in his hand. "I'm not sorry for what I did," he said. "Not in the least. Harry was a dirty little devil with girls, had been since he was a boy. I'd always loved you, Jennifer, although I've never said it. In the wrong age group, I know. When I heard he'd got hold of you I just couldn't stand it. Don't come near me, now. I don't want to hurt anybody else."

"Bill." Jennifer Moore held out a hand to him. "Please don't—"

Ramsay flung up the window. "You don't think I'm going to endure the farce of a trial, do you? It's better this way, for me and for everybody else."

He stepped out onto the ledge, and looked for a moment at the pigeons and the children, the placid lions and Nelson on his pillar.

Then he jumped.

The Hustler

WALTER S. TEVIS

They took Sam out of the office, through the long passageway, and up to the big metal doors. The doors opened, slowly, and they stepped out.

The sunlight was exquisite; warm on Sam's face. The air was clear and still. A few birds were circling in the sky. There was a gravel path, a road, and then, grass. Sam drew a deep breath. He could see as far as the horizon.

A guard drove up in a gray station wagon. He opened the door and Sam got in, whistling softly to himself. They drove off, down the gravel path. Sam did not turn around to look at the prison walls; he kept his eyes on the grass that stretched ahead of them, and on the road through the grass.

When the guard stopped to let him off in Richmond he said, "A word of advice, Willis."

"Advice?" Sam smiled at the guard.

"That's right. You got a habit of getting in trouble, Willis. That's why they didn't parole you, made you serve full time, because of that habit."

"That's what the man told me," Sam said. "So?"

"So stay out of pool rooms. You're smart. You can earn a living."

Sam started climbing out of the station wagon. "Sure," he said. He got out, slammed the door, and the guard drove away.

It was still early and the town was nearly empty. Sam walked around, up and down different streets, for about an hour, looking at houses and stores, smiling at the people he saw, whistling or humming little tunes to himself.

In his right hand he was carrying his little round tubular leather case, carrying it by the brass handle on the side. It was about 30 inches long, the case, and about as big around as a man's forearm.

At ten o'clock he went to the bank and drew out the 600 dollars he had deposited there under the name of George Graves. Only it was 680; it had gathered that much interest.

Then he went to a clothing store and bought a sporty tan coat, a pair of brown slacks, brown suede shoes and a bright green sport shirt. In the store's dressing room he put the new outfit on, leaving the prison-issued suit and shoes on the floor. Then he bought two extra sets of underwear and socks, paid, and left.

About a block up the street there was a clean-looking beauty parlor. He walked in and told the lady who seemed to be in charge, "I'm an actor. I have to play a part in Chicago tonight that requires red hair." He smiled at her. "Can you fix me up?"

The lady was all efficiency. "Certainly," she said. "If you'll just step back to a booth we'll pick out a shade."

A half hour later he was a redhead. In two hours he was on board a plane for Chicago, with a little less than 600 dollars in his pocket and one piece of luggage. He still had the underwear and socks in a paper sack.

In Chicago he took a 14-dollar-a-night room in the best hotel he could find. The room was big, and pleasant. It looked and smelled clean.

He sat down on the side of the bed and opened his little leather case at the top. The two piece billiard cue inside was intact. He took it out and screwed the brass joint together, pleased that it still fit perfectly. Then he checked the butt for tightness. The weight was still firm and solid. The tip was good, its shape had held up; and the cue's balance and stroke seemed easy, familiar; almost as though he still played with it every day.

He checked himself in the mirror. They had done a perfect job on his hair; and its brightness against the green and brown of his new clothes gave him the sporty, racetrack sort of look he had always avoided before. His once ruddy complexion was very pale. Not a pool player in town should be able to recognize him: he could hardly recognize himself.

If all went well he would be out of Chicago for good in a few days; and no one would know for a long time that Big Sam Willis had even played there. Six years on a manslaughter charge could have its advantages.

In the morning he had to walk around town for a while before he found a pool room of the kind he wanted. It was a few blocks off the Loop, small; and from the outside it seemed to be fairly clean and quiet.

Inside, there was a short order and beer counter up front. In back there were four tables; Sam could see them through the door in the partition that separated the lunch room from the pool room proper. There was no one in the place except for the tall, blond boy behind the counter.

Sam asked the boy if he could practice.

"Sure." The boy's voice was friendly. "But it'll cost you a dollar an hour."

"Fair enough." He gave the boy a five dollar bill. "Let me know when this is used up."

The boy raised his eyebrows and took the money.

In the back room Sam selected the best 20-ounce cue he could find in the wall rack, one with an ivory point and a tight butt, chalked the tip, and broke the rack of balls on what seemed to be the best of the four tables.

He tried to break safe, a straight pool break, where you drive the two bottom corner balls to the cushions and back into the stack where they came from, making the cue ball go two rails and return to the top of the table, killing itself on the cushion. The break didn't work, however; the rack of balls spread wide, five of them came out into the table, and the cue ball stopped in the middle. It would have left an opponent wide open for a big run. Sam shuddered.

He pocketed the 15 balls, missing only once—a long shot that had to be cut thin into a far corner—and he felt better, making balls. He had little confidence on the hard ones, he was awkward; but he still knew the game, he knew how to break up little clusters of balls on one shot so that he could pocket them on the next. He knew how to play position with very little English on the cue, by shooting "natural" shots, and letting the speed of the cue ball do the work. He could still figure the spread, plan out his shots in advance from the positions of the balls on the table, and he knew what to shoot at first.

He kept shooting for about three hours. Several times other players came in and played for a while, but none of them paid any attention to him, and none of them stayed long.

The place was empty again and Sam was practicing cutting balls down the rail, working on his cue ball and on his speed, when he looked up and saw the boy who ran the place coming back. He was carrying a plate with a hamburger in one hand and two bottles of beer in the other.

"Hungry?" He set the sandwich down on the arm of a chair. "Or thirsty, maybe?"

Sam looked at his watch. It was 1:30. "Come to think of it," he said, "I am." He went to the chair, picked up the hamburger, and sat down.

"Have a beer," the boy said, affably. Sam took it and drank from the bottle. It tasted delicious.

"What do I owe you?" he said, and took a bite out of the hamburger.

"The burger's 30 cents," the boy said. "The beer's on the house."

"Thanks," Sam said, chewing. "How do I rate?"

"You're a good customer," the boy said. "Easy on the equipment, cash in advance, and I don't even have to rack the balls for you."

"Thanks." Sam was silent for a minute, eating.

The boy was drinking the other beer. Abruptly, he set the bottle down. "You on the hustle?" he said.

"Do I look like a hustler?"

"You practice like one."

Sam sipped his beer quietly for a minute, looking over the top of the bottle, once, at the boy. Then he said, "I might be looking around." He set the empty bottle down on the wooden chair arm. "I'll be back tomorrow; we can talk about it then. There might be something in it for you, if you help me out."

"Sure, mister," the boy said. "You pretty good?"

"I think so," Sam said. Then when the boy got up to leave he added, "Don't try to finger me for anybody. It won't do you any good."

"I won't." The boy went back up front.

Sam practiced, working mainly on his stroke and his position, for three more hours. When he finished his arm was sore and his feet were tired; but he felt better. His stroke was beginning to work for him, he was getting smooth, making balls regularly, playing good position. Once, when he was running balls continuously, racking 14 and 1, he ran 47 without missing.

The next morning, after a long night's rest, he was even better. He ran more than 90 balls one time, missing, finally, on a difficult rail shot.

The boy came back at 1:00 o'clock, bringing a ham sandwich this time and two beers. "Here you go," he said. "Time to make a break."

Sam thanked him, laid his cue stick on the table, and sat down.

"My name's Barney," the boy said.

"George Graves." Same held out his hand, and the boy shook it. "Just," he smiled inwardly at the thought, "call me Red."

"You *are* good," Barney said. "I watched you a couple of times."

"I know." Sam took a drink from the beer bottle. "I'm looking for a straight pool game."

"I figured that, Mister Graves. You won't find one here, though. Up at Bennington's they play straight pool."

Sam had heard of Bennington's. They said it was a hustler's room, a big money place.

"You know who plays pool there, Barney?" he said.

"Sure. Bill Peyton, he plays there. And Shufala Kid, Louisville Fats, Johnny Vargas, Henry Keller, a little guy they call 'The Policeman' . . ."

Henry Keller was the only familiar name; Sam had played him once, in Atlantic City, maybe 14 years ago, but that had been even before the big days of Sam's reputation, before he had got so good that he had to trick hustlers into playing him. That was a long time ago. And then there was the red hair; he ought to be able to get by.

"Which one's got money," he asked, "and plays straight pool?"

"Well," Barney looked doubtful, "I think Louisville Fats carries a big roll. He's one of the old Prohibition boys; they say he keeps an army of hoods working for him. He plays straights. But he's good. And he doesn't like being hustled."

It looked good; but dangerous. Hustlers didn't take it very well to find out a man was using a phony name so he could get a game. Sam remembered the time someone had told Bernie James who he had been playing and Bernie had got pretty rough about it. But this time it was different; he had been out of circulation six years, and he had never played in Chicago before.

"This Fats. Does he bet big?"

"Yes, he bets big. Big as you want." Barney smiled. "But I tell you he's mighty good."

The Hustler

"Rack the balls," Sam said, and smiled back. "I'll show you something."

Barney racked. Sam broke them wide open and started running. He went through the rack, then another, another, and another. Barney was counting the balls, racking them for him each time. When he got to 80 Sam said, "Now I'll bank a few." He banked seven, knocking them off the rails, across, and into the pockets. When he missed the eighth he said, "What do you think?"

"You'll do," Barney said. He laughed. "Fats is good; but you might take him."

"I'll take him," Sam said. "You lead me to him. Tomorrow night you get somebody to work for you. We're going up to Bennington's."

"Fair enough, Mister Graves," Barney said. He was grinning. "We'll have a beer on that."

At Bennington's you took an elevator to the floor you wanted: billiards on the first, pocket pool on the second, snooker and private games on the third. It was an old-fashioned set-up, high ceilings, big, shaded incandescent lights, overstuffed leather chairs.

Sam spent the morning on the second floor, trying to get the feel of the tables. They were different from Barneys, with softer cushions and tighter cloths, and it was a little hard to get used to them; but after about two hours he felt as though he had them pretty well, and he left. No one had paid any attention to him.

After lunch he inspected his hair in the restaurant's bathroom mirror; it was still as red as ever and hadn't yet begun to grow out. He felt good. Just a little nervous, but good.

Barney was waiting for him at the little pool room. They took a cab up to Bennington's.

Louisville Fats must have weighed 300 pounds. His face seemed to be bloated around the eyes like the face of an Eskimo, so that he was always squinting. His arms, hanging from the short sleeves of his white silk shirt, were pink and dough-like. Sam noticed his hands; they were soft looking, white and delicate. He wore three rings, one with a diamond. He had on dark green, wide suspenders.

When Barney introduced him, Fats said, "How are you, George?" but didn't offer his hand. Sam noticed that his eyes, almost buried beneath the face, seemed to shift from side to side, so that he seemed not really to be looking at anything.

"I'm fine," Sam said. Then, after a pause, "I've heard a lot about you."

"I got a reputation?" Fats' voice was flat, disinterested. "Then I must be pretty good maybe?"

"I suppose so," Sam said, trying to watch the eyes.

"You a good pool player, George?" The eyes flickered, scanning Sam's face.

"Fair. I like playing. Straight pool."

"Oh." Fats grinned, abruptly, coldly. "That's my game too, George." He slapped Barney on the back. The boy pulled away, slightly, from him. "You pick good, Barney. He plays my game. You can finger for me, sometime, if you want."

"Sure," Barney said. He looked nervous.

"One thing." Fats was still grinning. "You play for money, George? I mean, you gamble?"

"When the bet's right."

"What you think is a right bet, George?"

"50 dollars."

Fats grinned even more broadly; but his eyes still kept shifting. "Now that's close, George," he said. "You play for a hundred and we play a few."

"Fair enough," Sam said, as calmly as he could.

"Let's go upstairs. It's quieter."

"Fine. I'll take my boy if you don't mind. He can rack the balls."

Fats looked at Barney. "You level with that rack, Barney? I mean, you rack the balls tight for Fats?"

"Sure," Barney said, "I wouldn't try to cross you up."

"You know better than that, Barney. Ok."

They walked up the back stairs to the third floor. There was a small, bare-walled room, well lighted, with chairs lined up against the walls. The chairs were high ones, the type used for watching pool games. There was no one else in the room.

They uncovered the table, and Barney racked the balls. Sam lost the toss and broke, making it safe, but not too safe. He undershot, purposely, and left the cue ball almost a foot away from the end rail.

They played around, shooting safe, for a while. Then Fats pulled a hard one off the edge of the rack, ran 35, and played him safe. Sam jockeyed with him, figuring to lose for a while, only wanting the money to hold out until he had the table down pat, until he had the other man's game figured, until he was ready to raise the bet.

He lost three in a row before he won one. He wasn't playing his best game; but that meant little, since Fats was probably pulling his punches too, trying to take him for as much as possible. After he won his first game he let himself go a little and made a few tricky ones. Once he knifed a ball thin into the side pocket and went two cushions for a break up; but Fats didn't even seem to notice.

Neither of them tried to run more than 40 at a turn. It would have looked like a game between only fair players, except that neither of them missed very often. In a tight spot they didn't try anything fancy, just shot a safe and let the other man figure it out. Sam played safe on some shots that he was sure he could make; he didn't want to show his hand. Not yet. They kept playing and, after a while, Sam started winning more often.

After about three hours he was five games ahead, and shooting better all the time. Then, when he won still another game, Sam said, "You're losing money, Fats. Maybe we should quit." He looked at Barney and winked. Barney gave him a puzzled, worried look.

"Quit? You think we should quit?" Fats took a big silk handkerchief from his side pocket and wiped his face. "How much money you won, George?" he said.

"That last makes 600." He felt, suddenly, a little tense. It was coming. The big push.

"Suppose we play for 600, George." He put the handkerchief back in his pocket. "Then we see who quits."

"Fine." He felt really nervous now, but he knew he would get over it. Nervousness didn't count. At 600 a game he would be in clover and in San Francisco in two days. If he didn't lose.

Barney racked the balls and Sam broke. He took the break slowly, putting to use his practice of three days, and his experience of 27 years. The balls broke perfectly, reracking the original triangle, and the cue ball skidded to a stop right on the end cushion.

"You shoot pretty good," Fats said, looking at the safe table that Sam had left him. But he played safe, barely tipping the cue ball off one of the balls down at the foot of the table and returning back to the end rail.

Sam tried to return the safe by repeating the same thing; but the cue ball caught the object ball too thick and he brought out a shot, a long one, for Fats. Fats stepped up, shot the ball in, played position, and ran out the rest of the rack. Then he ran out another rack and Sam sat down to watch; there was nothing he could do now. Fats ran 78 points and then, seeing a difficult shot, played him safe.

He had been afraid that something like that might happen. He tried to fight his way out of the game, but couldn't seem to get into the clear long enough for a good run. Fats beat him badly—125 to 30—and he had to give back the 600 dollars from his pocket. It hurt.

What hurt even worse was that he knew he had less than 600 left of his own money.

"Now we see who quits." Fats stuffed the money in his hip pocket. "You want to play for another 600?"

"I'm still holding my stick," Sam said. He tried not to think about that "army of hoods" that Barney had told him about.

He stepped up to the table and broke. His hand shook a little; but the break was a perfect one.

In the middle of the game Fats missed an easy shot, leaving Sam a dead set-up. Sam ran 53 and out. He won. It was as easy as that. He was 600 ahead again, and feeling better.

Then something unlucky happened. Downstairs they

The Hustler

must have closed up because six men came up during the next game and sat around the table. Five of them Sam had never seen, but one of them was Henry Keller. Henry was drunk now, evidently, and he didn't seem to be paying much attention to what was going on; but Sam didn't like it. He didn't like Keller, and he didn't like having a man who knew who he was around him. It was too much like that other time. That time in Richmond when Bernie James had come after him with a bottle. That fight had cost him six years. He didn't like it. It was getting time to wind things up here, time to be cutting out. If he could win two more games quick, he would have enough to set him up hustling on the West Coast. And on the West Coast there weren't any Henry Kellers who knew that Big Sam Willis was once the best straight-pool shot in the game.

After Sam had won the game by a close score Fats looked at his fingernails and said, "George, you're a hustler. You shoot better straights than anybody in Chicago shoots. Except me."

This was the time, the time to make it quick and neat, the time to push as hard as he could. He caught his breath, held steady, and said, "You've got it wrong, Fats. I'm better than you are. I'll play you for all of it. The whole 1200."

It was very quiet in the room. Then Fats said, "George, I like that kind of talk." He started chalking his cue. "We play 1200."

Barney racked the balls and Fats broke them. They both played safe, very safe, back and forth, keeping the cue ball on the rail, not leaving a shot for the other man. It was nerve-wracking. Over and over.

Then he missed. Missed the edge of the rack, coming at it from an outside angle. His cue ball bounced off the rail and into the rack of balls, spreading them wide, leaving Fats at least five shots. Sam didn't sit down. He just stood and watched Fats come up and start his run. He ran the balls, broke on the 15TH, and ran another rack. 28 points. And he was just getting started. He had his rack break set up perfectly for the next shot.

Then, as Fats began chalking up, preparing to shoot, Henry Keller stood up from his seat and pointed his finger at Sam.

He was drunk; but he spoke clearly, and loudly. "You're Big Sam Willis," he said. "You're the World's Champion." He sat back in his chair, heavily. "You got red hair, but you're Big Sam." He sat silent, half slumped in the big chair, for a moment, his eyes glassy, and red at the corners. Then he closed his eyes and said, "There's nobody beats Big Sam, Fats. Nobody *never*."

The room was quiet for what seemed to be a very long while. Sam noticed how thick the tobacco smoke had become in the air; motionless, it was like a heavy brown mist, and over the table it was like a cloud. The faces of the men in the chairs were impassive; all of them, except Henry, watching him.

Fats turned to him. For once his eyes were not shifting from side to side. He looked Sam in the face and said, in a voice that was flat and almost a whisper, "You Big Sam Willis, George?"

"That's right, Fats."

"You must be pretty smart, Sam," Fats said, "to play a trick like that. To make a sucker out of me."

"Maybe." His chest and stomach felt very tight. It was like when Bernie James had caught him at the same game, except without the red hair. Bernie hadn't said anything, though; he had just picked up a bottle.

But, then, Bernie James was dead now. Sam wondered, momentarily, if Fats had ever heard about that.

Suddenly Fats split the silence, laughing. The sound of his laughing filled the room, he threw his head back and laughed; and the men in the chairs looked at him, astonished, hearing the laughter. "Big Sam," he said, "you're a hustler. You put on a great act; and fool me good. A great act." He slapped Sam on the back. "I think the joke's on me."

It was hard to believe. But Fats could afford the money, and Sam knew that Fats knew who would be the best if it came to muscle. And there was no certainty whose side the other men were on.

The Hustler

Fats shot, ran a few more balls, and then missed.

When Sam stepped up to shoot he said, "Go ahead, Big Sam, and shoot your best. You don't have to act now. I'm quitting you anyway after this one."

The funny thing was that Sam had been shooting his best for the past five or six games—or thought he had—but when he stepped up to the table this time he was different. Maybe it was Fats or Keller, something made him feel as he hadn't felt for a long time. It was like being the old Big Sam, back before he had quit playing the tournaments and exhibitions, the Big Sam who could run 125 when he was hot and the money was up. His stroke was smooth, steady, accurate, like a balanced, precision instrument moving on well-oiled bearings. He shot easily, calmly, clicking the shots off in his mind and then pocketing them on the table, watching everything on the green, forgetting himself, forgetting even the money, just dropping the balls into the pockets, one after another.

He did it. He ran the game. 125 points, 125 shots without missing. When he finished Fats took 1200 from his still-big roll and counted it out, slowly, to him. He said, "You're the best I've ever seen, Big Sam." Then he covered the table with the oilcloth cover.

After Sam had dropped Barney off he had the cab take him by his hotel and let him off at a little all-night lunch room. He ordered bacon and eggs, over light, and talked with the waitress while she fried them. The place seemed strange, gay almost; his nerves felt electric, and there was a pleasant fuzziness in his head, a dim, insistent ringing sound coming from far off. He tried to think for a moment; tried to think whether he should go to the airport now without even going back to the hotel, now that he had made out so well, had made out better, even, than he had planned to be able to do in a week. But there was the waitress and then the food; and when he put a quarter in the juke box he couldn't hear the ringing in his ears anymore. This was no time for plane trips; it was a time for talk and music, time for the sense of triumph, the sense of being alive and having money again, and then time for sleep. He was in a chromium and plastic booth in the lunch room and he leaned back against the padded plastic backrest and felt an abrupt, deep, gratifying sense of fatigue, loosening his muscles and killing, finally, the tension that had ridden him like a fury for the past three days. There would be plane flights enough tomorrow. Now, he needed rest. It was a long way to San Francisco.

The bed at his hotel was impeccably made; the pale blue spread seemed drum-tight, but soft and round at the edges and corners. He didn't even take off his shoes.

When he awoke, he awoke suddenly. The skin at the back of his neck was itching, sticky with sweat from where the collar of his shirt had been pressed, tight, against it. His mouth was dry and his feet felt swollen, stuffed, in his shoes. The room was as quiet as death. Outside the window a car's tires groaned gently, rounding a corner, then were still.

He pulled the chain on the lamp by the bed and the light came on. Squinting, he stood up, and realized that his legs were aching. The room seemed too big, too bright. He stumbled into the bathroom and threw handfuls of cold water on his face and neck. Then he dried off with a towel and looked in the mirror. Startled, he let go the towel momentarily; the red hair had caught him off guard; and with the eyes now swollen, the lips pale, it was not his face at all. He finished drying quickly, ran his comb through his hair, straightened out his shirt and slacks hurriedly. The startling strangeness of his own face had crystallized the dim, half-conscious feeling that had awakened him, the feeling that something was wrong. The hotel room, himself, Chicago, they were all wrong. He should not be here, not now; he should be on the West Coast, in San Francisco.

He looked at his watch. 4:00 o'clock. He had slept three hours. He did not feel tired, not now, although his bones ached and there was sand under his eyelids. He could sleep, if he had to, on the plane. But the important thing, now, was getting on the plane, clearing out, moving West. He had slept with his cue, in its case, on the bed. He took it and left the room.

The lobby, too, seemed too bright and too empty. But when he had paid his bill and gone out to the street the relative darkness seemed worse. He began to walk down the street hastily, looking for a cab stand. His own footsteps echoed around him as he walked. There seemed to be no cabs anywhere on the street. He began walking faster. The back of his neck was sweating again. It was a very hot night; the air felt heavy against his skin. There were no cabs.

And then, when he heard the slow, dense hum of a heavy car moving down the street in his direction, heard it from several blocks away and turned his head to see it and to see that there was no cablight on it, he knew—abruptly and lucidly, as some men at some certain times know these things—what was happening.

He began to run; but he did not know where to run. He turned a corner while he was still two blocks ahead of the car and when he could feel its lights, palpably, on the back of his neck, and tried to hide in the doorway, flattening himself out against the door. Then, when he saw the lights of the car as it began its turn around the corner he realized that the doorway was too shallow, that the lights would pick him out. Something in him wanted to scream. He pushed himself from his place, stumbled down the street, visualizing in his mind a place, some sort of a place between buildings where he could hide completely and where the car could never follow him. But the buildings were all together, with no space at all between them; and when he saw that this was so he also saw at the same instant that the carlights were flooding him. And then he heard the car stop. There was nothing more to do. He turned around and looked at the car, blinking.

Two men had got out of the back seat; there were two more in front. He could see none of their faces; but was relieved that he could not, could not see the one face that would be bloated like an Eskimo's and with eyes like slits.

The men were holding the door open for him.

"Well," he said. "Hello, boys," and climbed into the back seat. His little leather case was still in his right hand. He gripped it tightly. It was all he had.

Without the Option

P.G. WODEHOUSE

The evidence was all in. The machinery of the law had worked without a hitch. And the beak, having adjusted a pair of pince-nez which looked as though they were going to do a nose dive any moment, coughed like a pained sheep and slipped us the bad news.

"The prisoner, Wooster," he said—and who can paint the shame and agony of Bertram at hearing himself so described?—"will pay a fine of five pounds."

"Oh, rather!" I said. "Absolutely! Like a shot!"

I was dashed glad to get the thing settled at such a reasonable figure. I gazed across what they called the sea of faces till I picked up Jeeves, sitting at the back. Stout fellow, he had come to see the young master through his hour of trial.

"I say, Jeeves," I sang out, "have you got a fiver? I'm a bit short."

"Silence!" bellowed some officious blighter.

"It's all right," I said; "just arranging the financial details. Got the stuff, Jeeves?"

"Yes, sir."

"Good egg!"

"Are you a friend of the prisoner?" asked the beak.

"I am in Mr. Wooster's employment, Your Worship, in the capacity of gentleman's personal gentleman."

'Then pay the fine to the clerk."

"Very good, Your Worship."

The beak gave a coldish nod in my direction, as much as to say that they might now strike the fetters from my wrists; and having hitched up the pince-nez once more, proceeded to hand poor old Sippy one of the nastiest looks ever seen in Bosher Street police court.

"The case of the prisoner Leon Trotsky—which," he said, giving Sippy the eye again, "I am strongly inclined to think an assumed and fictitious name—is more serious. He has been convicted of a wanton and violent assault upon the police. The evidence of the officer has proved that the prisoner struck him in the abdomen, causing severe internal pain, and in other ways interfered with him in the execution of his duties. I am aware that on the night following the annual aquatic contest between the universities of Oxford and Cambridge a certain license is traditionally granted by the authorities, but aggravated acts of ruffianly hooliganism like that of the prisoner Trotsky cannot be overlooked or palliated. He will serve a sentence of thirty days in the Second Division without the option of a fine."

"No, I say—here—hi—dash it all!" protested poor old Sippy.

"Silence!" bellowed the officious blighter.

"Next case," said the beak. And that was that.

The whole affair was most unfortunate. Memory is a trifle blurred; but as far as I can piece together the facts, what happened was more or less this:

Abstemious cove though I am as a general thing, there is one night in the year when, putting all other engagements aside, I am rather apt to let myself go a bit and renew my lost youth, as it were. The night to which I allude is the one following the annual aquatic contest between the universities of Oxford and Cambridge; or, putting it another way, Boat-Race Night. Then, if ever, you will see Bertram under the influence. And on this occasion, I freely admit, I had been doing myself rather juicily, with the result that when I ran into old Sippy opposite the Empire I was in quite fairly bonhomous mood. This being so, it cut me to the quick to perceive that Sippy, generally the brightest of revelers, was far from being his usual sunny self. He had the air of a man with a secret sorrow.

"Bertie," he said as we strolled along toward Piccadilly Circus, "the heart bowed down by weight of woe to weakest hope will cling." Sippy is by way of being an author, though mainly dependent for the necessaries of life on subsidies from an old aunt who lives in the country, and his conversation often takes a literary turn. "But the trouble is that I have no hope to cling to, weak or otherwise. I am up against it, Bertie."

"In what way, laddie?"

"I've got to go tomorrow and spend three weeks with some absolutely dud—I will go further—some positively scaly friends of my Aunt Vera. She has fixed the thing up, and may a nephew's curse blister every bulb in her garden."

"Who are these hounds of hell?" I asked.

"Some people named Pringle. I haven't seen them since I was ten, but I remember them at that time striking me as England's premier warts."

"Tough luck. No wonder you've lost your morale."

"The world," said Sippy, "is very gray. How can I shake off this awful depression?"

It was then that I got one of those bright ideas one does get round about eleven-thirty on Boat-Race Night.

"What you want, old man," I said, "is a policeman's helmet."

"Do I, Bertie?"

"If I were you, I'd just step straight across the street and get that one over there."

"But there's a policeman inside it. You can see him distinctly."

"What does that matter?" I said. I simply couldn't follow his reasoning.

Sippy stood for a moment in thought.

"I believe you're absolutely right," he said at last. "Funny I never thought of it before. You really recommend me to get that helmet?"

"I do, indeed."

"Then I will," said Sippy, brightening up in the most remarkable manner.

So there you have the posish, and you can see why, as I left the dock a free man, remorse gnawed at my vitals. In his twenty-fifth year, with life opening out before him and all that sort of thing, Oliver Randolph Sipperley had become a jailbird, and it was all my fault. It was I who had dragged that fine spirit down into the mire, so to speak, and the question now arose: What could I do to atone?"

Obviously the first move must be to get in touch with Sippy and see if he had any last messages and what not. I pushed about a bit, making inquiries, and presently found myself in a little dark room with whitewashed walls and a wooden bench. Sippy was sitting on the bench with his head in his hands.

"How are you, old lad?" I asked in a hushed, bedside voice.

"I'm a ruined man," said Sippy, looking like a poached egg.

"Oh, come," I said. "It's not so bad as all that. I mean to say, you had the swift intelligence to give a false name. There won't be anything about you in the papers."

"I'm not worrying about the papers. What's bothering me is, how can I go and spend three weeks with the Pringles, starting today, when I've got to sit in a prison cell with a ball and chain on my ankle?"

"But you said you didn't want to go."

"It isn't a question of wanting, fathead. I've got to go. If I don't my aunt will find out where I am. And if she finds out that I am doing thirty days, without the option, in the lowest dungeon beneath the castle moat—well, where shall I get off?"

I saw his point.

"This is not a thing we can settle for ourselves," I said gravely. "We must put our trust in a higher power. Jeeves is the man we must consult."

And having collected a few of the necessary data, I shook his hand, patted him on the back, and tooled off home to Jeeves.

"Jeeves," I said, when I had climbed outside the pick-me-up which he had thoughtfully prepared against my coming, "I've got something to tell you; something important; something that vitally affects one whom you have always regarded with—one whom you have always looked upon—one whom you have—well, to cut a long story short, as I'm not feeling quite myself—Mr. Sipperley."

"Yes, sir?"

"Jeeves, Mr. Souperley is in the sip."

"Sir?"

"I mean, Mr. Sipperley is in the soup."

"Indeed, sir?"

"And all owing to me. It was I who, in a moment of mistaken kindness, wishing only to cheer him up and give him something to occupy his mind, recommended him to pinch that policeman's helmet."

"Is that so, sir?"

"Do you mind not intoning the responses, Jeeves?" I said. "This is a most complicated story for a man with a headache to have to tell, and if you interrupt you'll make me lose the thread. As a favor to me, therefore, don't do it. Just nod every now and then to show that you're following me."

I closed my eyes and marshaled the facts.

"To start with then, Jeeves, you may or may not know that Mr. Sipperley is practically dependent on his Aunt Vera."

"Would that be Miss Sipperley of the Paddock, Beckley-on-the-Moor, in Yorkshire, sir?"

"Yes. Don't tell me you know her!"

"Not personally, sir. But I have a cousin residing in the village who has some slight acquaintance with Miss Sipperley. He has described her to me as an imperious and quick-tempered old lady. . . . But I beg your pardon, sir, I should have nodded."

"Quite right, you should have nodded. Yes, Jeeves, you should have nodded. But it's too late now."

I nodded myself. I hadn't had my eight hours the night before, and what you might call a lethargy was showing a tendency to steal over me from time to time.

"Yes, sir?" said Jeeves.

"Oh—ah—yes," I said, giving myself a bit of a hitch up. "Where had I got to?"

"You were saying that Mr. Sipperley is practically dependent upon Miss Sipperley, sir."

"Was I?"

"You were, sir."

"You're perfectly right; so I was. Well, then, you can readily understand, Jeeves, that he has got to take jolly good care to keep in with her. You get that?"

Jeeves nodded.

"Now mark this closely: The other day she wrote to old Sippy, telling him to come down and sing at her village concert. It was equivalent to a royal command, if you see what I mean, so Sippy couldn't refuse in so many words. But he had sung at her village concert once before and had got the bird in no uncertain manner, so he wasn't playing any return dates. You follow so far, Jeeves?"

Jeeves nodded.

"So what did he do, Jeeves? He did what seemed to him at the moment a rather brainy thing. He told her that, though he would have been delighted to sing at her village concert, by a most unfortunate chance an editor had commissioned him to write a series of articles on the colleges of Cambridge and he was obliged to pop down there at once and would be away for quite three weeks. All clear up to now?"

Jeeves inclined the coconut.

"Whereupon, Jeeves, Miss Sipperley wrote back, saying that she quite realized that work must come before pleasure—pleasure being her loose way of describing the act of singing songs at the Beckley-on-the-Moor concert and getting the laugh from the local toughs; but that, if he was going to Cambridge, he must certainly stay with her friends, the Pringles, at their house just outside the town. And she dropped them a line telling them to expect him on the twenty-eighth, and they dropped another line saying right-ho, and the thing was settled. And now Mr. Sipperley is in the jug, and what will be the ultimate outcome or upshot? Jeeves, it is a problem worthy of your great intellect. I rely on you."

"I will do my best to justify your confidence, sir."

"Carry on, then. And meanwhile pull down the blinds and bring a couple more cushions and heave that small chair this way so that I can put my feet up, and then go away and brood and let me hear from you in—say, a couple of hours, or maybe three. And if anybody calls and wants me, inform them that I am dead."

"Dead, sir?"

"Dead. You won't be so far wrong."

It must have been well toward evening when I woke up with a crick in my neck but otherwise somewhat refreshed. I pressed the bell.

"I looked in twice, sir," said Jeeves, "but on each occasion you were asleep and I did not like to disturb you."

"The right spirit, Jeeves. . . . Well?"

"I have been giving close thought to the little problem which you indicated, sir, and I can see only one solution."

"One is enough. What do you suggest?"

"That you go to Cambridge in Mr. Sipperley's place, sir."

I stared at the man. Certainly I was feeling a good deal better than I had been a few hours before; but I was far from being in a fit condition to have rot like this talked to me.

"Jeeves," I said sternly, "pull yourself together. This is mere babble from the sickbed."

"I fear I can suggest no other plan of action, sir, which will extricate Mr. Sipperley from his dilemma."

"But think! Reflect! Why, even I, in spite of having had a disturbed night and a most painful morning with the minions of the law, can see that the scheme is a loony one. To put the finger on only one leak in the thing, it isn't me these people want to see; it's Mr. Sipperley. They don't know me from Adam."

"So much the better, sir. For what I am suggesting is that you go to Cambridge, affecting actually to be Mr. Sipperley."

This was too much.

"Jeeves," I said, and I'm not half sure there weren't tears in my eyes, "surely you can see for yourself that this is pure banana oil. It is not like you to come into the presence of a sick man and gibber."

"I think the plan I have suggested would be practicable, sir. While you were sleeping, I was able to have a few words with Mr. Sipperley, and he informed me that Professor and Mrs. Pringle have not set eyes upon him since he was a lad of ten."

"No, that's true. He told me that. But even so, they would be sure to ask him questions about my aunt—or rather his aunt. Where would I be then?"

"Mr. Sipperley was kind enough to give me a few facts respecting Miss Sipperley, sir, which I jotted down. With these, added to what my cousin has told me of the lady's habits, I think you would be in a position to answer any ordinary question."

There is something dashed insidious about Jeeves. Time and again since we first came together he has stunned me with some apparently driveling suggestion or scheme or ruse or plan of campaign, and after about five minutes has convinced me that it is not only sound but fruity. It took nearly a quarter of an hour to reason me into this particular one, it being considerably the weirdest to date; but he did it. I was holding out pretty firmly, when he suddenly clinched the thing.

"I would certainly suggest, sir," he said, "that you left London as soon as possible and remained hid for some little time in some retreat where you would not be likely to be found."

"Eh? Why?"

"During the last hour Mrs. Spenser Gregson has been on the telephone three times, sir, endeavoring to get into communication with you."

"Aunt Agatha!" I cried, paling beneath my tan.

"Yes, sir. I gathered from her remarks that she had been reading in the evening paper a report of this morning's proceedings in the police court."

I hopped from the chair like a jack rabbit of the prairie. If Aunt Agatha was out with her hatchet, a move was most certainly indicated.

"Jeeves," I said, "this is a time for deeds, not words. Pack—and that right speedily."

"I have packed, sir."

"Find out when there is a train for Cambridge."

"There is one in forty minutes, sir."

"Call a taxi."

"A taxi is at the door, sir."

"Good!" I said. "Then lead me to it."

The Maison Pringle was quite a bit of a way out of Cambridge, a mile or two down the Trumpington Road; and when I arrived everybody was dressing for dinner. So it wasn't till I had shoved on the evening raiment and got down to the drawing room that I met the gang.

"Hullo-ullo!" I said, taking a deep breath and floating in.

I tried to speak in a clear and ringing voice, but I wasn't feeling my chirpiest. It is always a nervous job for a diffident and unassuming bloke to visit a strange house for the first time; and it doesn't make the thing any better when he goes there pretending to be another fellow. I was conscious of a rather pronounced sinking feeling, which the appearance of the Pringles did nothing to allay.

Sippy had described them as England's premier warts, and it looked to me as if he might be about right. Professor Pringle was a thinnish, baldish, dyspeptic-lookingish cove with an eye like a haddock, while Mrs. Pringle's aspect was that of one who had had bad news round about the year 1900 and never really got over it. And I was just staggering under the impact of these two when I was introduced to a couple of ancient females with shawls all over them.

"No doubt you remember my mother?" said Professor Pringle mournfully, indicating Exhibit A.

"Oh—ah!" I said, achieving a bit of a beam.

"And my aunt," sighed the prof, as if things were getting worse and worse.

"Well, well, well!" I said, shooting another beam in the direction of Exhibit B.

"They were saying only this morning that they remembered you," groaned the prof, abandoning all hope.

There was a pause. The whole strength of the company gazed at me like a family group out of one of Edgar Allan Poe's less cheery yarns, and I felt my *joie de vivre* dying at the roots.

"I remember Oliver," said Exhibit B, looking at me in much the same way as the Bosher Street beak had looked at Sippy before putting on the black cap. "Nasty little boy! He teased my cat."

"Aunt Jane's memory is wonderful, considering that she will be eighty-seven next birthday," whispered Mrs. Pringle with mournful pride.

"What did you say?" asked the Exhibit suspiciously.

"I said your memory was wonderful."

"Ah!" The dear old creature gave me another glare. I could see that no beautiful friendship was to be looked for by Bertram in this quarter. "He chased my Tibby all over the garden, shooting arrows at her from a bow."

At this moment a cat strolled out from under the sofa and made for me with its tail up. Cats always do take to me, which made it all the sadder that I should be saddled with Sippy's criminal record. I stopped to tickle it under the ear, such being my invariable policy, and the Exhibit uttered a piercing cry.

"Stop him! Stop him!"

She leaped forward, moving uncommonly well for one of her years and, having scooped up the cat, stood eyeing me with bitter defiance, as if daring me to start anything. Most unpleasant.

"I like cats," I said feebly.

It didn't go. The sympathy of the audience was not with me. And conversation was at what you might call a low ebb when the door opened and a girl came in.

"My daughter Heloise," said the prof moodily, as if he hated to admit it.

I turned to mitt the female, and stood there with my hand out, gaping. I can't remember when I've had such a nasty shock.

I suppose everybody has had the experience of suddenly meeting somebody who reminded them frightfully of some fearful person. I mean to say, by way of an example, once when I was golfing in Scotland I saw a woman come into the hotel who was the living image of my Aunt Agatha. Probably a very decent sort, if I had only waited to see, but I didn't wait. I legged it that evening, utterly unable to stand the spectacle. And on another occasion I was driven out of a thoroughly festive nightclub because the headwaiter reminded me of my Uncle Percy.

Well, Heloise Pringle, in the most ghastly way, resembled Honoria Glossop.

I think I may have told you before about this Glossop scourge. She was the daughter of Sir Roderick Glossop, the loony doctor, and I had been engaged to her for about three weeks, much against my wishes, when the old boy most fortunately got the idea that I was off my rocker and put the bee on the proceedings. Since then the mere thought of her had been enough to make me start out of my sleep with a loud cry. And this girl was exactly like her.

"Er—how are you?" I said.

"How do you do?"

Her voice put the lid on it. It might have been Honoria herself talking. Honoria Glossop has a voice like a lion tamer making some authoritative announcement to one of the troupe, and so had this girl. I backed away convulsively and sprang into the air as my foot stubbed itself against something squashy. A sharp yowl rent the air, followed by an indignant cry, and I turned to see Aunt Jane on all fours, trying to put things right with the cat, which had gone to earth under the sofa. She gave me a look, and I could see that her worst fears had been realized.

At this juncture dinner was announced—not before I was ready for it.

"Jeeves," I said, when I got him alone that night, "I am no faintheart, but I am inclined to think that this binge is going to prove a shade above the odds."

"You are not enjoying your visit, sir?"

"I am not, Jeeves. Have you seen Miss Pringle?"

"Yes, sir, from a distance."

"The best way to see her. Did you observe her keenly?"

"Yes, sir."

"Did she remind you of anybody?"

"She appeared to me to bear a remarkable likeness to her cousin, Miss Glossop, sir."

"Her cousin! You don't mean to say she's Honoria Glossop's cousin!"

"Yes, sir. Mrs. Pringle was a Miss Blatherwick—the younger of two sisters, the elder of whom married Sir Roderick Glossop."

"Great Scott! That accounts for the resemblance."

"Yes, sir."

"And what a resemblance, Jeeves! She even talks like Miss Glossop."

"Indeed, sir? I have not yet heard Miss Pringle speak."

"You have missed little. And what it amounts to, Jeeves, is that, though nothing will induce me to let old Sippy down, I can see that this visit is going to try me high. At a pinch, I could stand the prof and wife. I could even make the effort of a lifetime and bear up against Aunt Jane. But to expect a man to mix daily with the girl Heloise—and to do it, what is more, on lemonade, which is all there was to drink at dinner—is to ask too much of him. What shall I do, Jeeves?"

"I think that you should avoid Miss Pringle's society as much as possible."

"The same great thought had occurred to me," I said.

It is all very well, though, to talk airily about avoiding a female's society; but when you are living in the same house with her, and she doesn't want to avoid you, it takes a bit of doing. It is a peculiar thing in life that people you most particularly want to edge away from always seem to cluster round like a poultice. I hadn't been twenty-four hours in the place before I perceived that I was going to see a lot of this pestilence.

She was one of those girls you're always meeting on the stairs and in passages. I couldn't go into a room without seeing her drift in a minute later. And if I walked in the garden she was sure to leap out at me from a laurel bush or the onion bed or something. By about the tenth day I had begun to feel absolutely haunted.

"Jeeves," I said, "I have begun to feel absolutely haunted."

"Sir?"

"This woman dogs me. I never seem to get a moment to myself. Old Sippy was supposed to come here to make a study of the Cambridge colleges, and she took me round about fifty-seven this morning. This afternoon I went to sit in the garden, and she popped up through a trap and was in my midst. This evening she cornered me in the morning room. It's getting so that, when I have a bath, I wouldn't be a bit surprised to find her nestling in the soap dish."

"Extremely trying, sir."

"Dashed so. Have you any remedy to suggest?"

"Not at the moment, sir. Miss Pringle does appear to be distinctly interested in you, sir. She was asking me questions this morning respecting your mode of life in London."

"What?"

"Yes, sir."

I stared at the man in horror. A ghastly thought had struck me. I quivered like an aspen.

At lunch that day a curious thing had happened. We had just finished mangling the cutlets and I was sitting back in my chair, taking a bit of an easy before being allotted my slab of boiled pudding, when, happening to look up, I caught the girl Heloise's eye fixed on me in what seemed to me a rather rummy manner. I didn't think much about it at the time, because boiled pudding is a thing you have to give your undivided attention to if you want to do yourself justice; but now, recalling the episode in the light of Jeeves's words, the full sinister meaning of the thing seemed to come home to me.

Even at the moment, something about that look had struck me as oddly familiar, and now I suddenly saw why. It had been the identical look which I observed in the eye of Honoria Glossop in the days immediately preceding our engagement—the look of a tigress that has marked down its prey.

"Jeeves, do you know what I think?"

"Sir?"

I gulped slightly.

"Jeeves," I said, "listen attentively. I don't want to give the impression that I consider myself one of those deadly coves who exercise an irresistible fascination over one and all and can't meet a girl without wrecking her peace of mind in the first half-minute. As a matter of fact, it's rather the other way with me, for girls on entering my presence are mostly inclined to give me the raised eyebrow and the twitching upper lip. Nobody, therefore, can say that I am a man who's likely to take alarm unnecessarily. You admit that, don't you?"

"Yes, sir."

"Nevertheless, Jeeves, it is a known scientific fact that there is a particular style of female that does seem strangely attracted to the sort of fellow I am."

"Very true, sir."

"I mean to say, I know perfectly well that I've got,

roughly speaking, half the amount of brain a normal bloke ought to possess. And when a girl comes along who has about twice the regular allowance, she too often makes a beeline for me with the love light in her eyes. I don't know how to account for it, but it is so."

"It may be Nature's provision for maintaining the balance of the species, sir."

"Very possibly. Anyway, it has happened to me over and over again. It was what happened in the case of Honoria Glossop. She was notoriously one of the brainiest women of her year at Girton, and she just gathered me in like a bull pup swallowing a piece of steak."

"Miss Pringle, I am informed, sir, was an even more brilliant scholar than Miss Glossop."

"Well, there you are! Jeeves, she looks at me."

"Yes, sir?"

"I keep meeting her on the stairs and in passages."

"Indeed, sir?"

"She recommends me books to read, to improve my mind."

"Highly suggestive, sir."

"And at breakfast this morning, when I was eating a sausage, she told me I shouldn't, as modern medical science held that a four-inch sausage contained as many germs as a dead rat. The maternal touch, you understand; fussing over my health."

"I think we may regard that, sir, as practically conclusive."

I sank into a chair, thoroughly pipped.

"What's to be done, Jeeves?"

"We must think, sir."

"You think. I haven't the machinery."

"I will most certainly devote my very best attention to the matter, sir, and will endeavor to give satisfaction."

Well, that was something. But I was ill at ease. Yes, there is no getting away from it, Bertram was ill at ease.

Next morning we visited sixty-three more Cambridge colleges, and after lunch I said I was going to my room to lie down. After staying there for half an hour to give the coast time to clear, I shoved a book and smoking materials in my pocket, and climbing out of a window, shinned down a convenient water pipe into the garden. My objective was the summerhouse, where it seemed to me that a man might put in a quiet hour or so without interruption.

It was extremely jolly in the garden. The sun was shining, the crocuses were all to the mustard, and there wasn't a sign of Heloise Pringle anywhere. The cat was fooling about on the lawn, so I chirruped to it and it gave a low gargle and came trotting up. I had just got it in my arms and was scratching it under the ear when there was a loud shriek from above, and there was Aunt Jane half out the window. Dashed disturbing.

"Oh, right-ho," I said.

I dropped the cat, which galloped off into the bushes, and dismissing the idea of bunging a brick at the aged relative, went on my way, heading for the shrubbery. Once safely hidden there, I worked round till I got to the summerhouse. And, believe me, I had hardly got my first cigarette nicely under way when a shadow fell on my book and there was young Sticketh-Closer-Than-a-Brother in person.

"So there you are," she said.

She seated herself by my side, and with a sort of gruesome playfulness jerked the gasper out of the holder and heaved it through the door.

"You're always smoking," she said, a lot too much like a lovingly chiding young bride for my comfort. "I wish you wouldn't. It's so bad for you. And you ought not to be sitting out here without your light overcoat. You want someone to look after you."

"I've got Jeeves."

She frowned a bit.

"I don't like him," she said.

"Eh? Why not?"

"I don't know. I wish you would get rid of him."

My flesh absolutely crept. And I'll tell you why. One of the first things Honoria Glossop had done after we had become engaged was to tell me she didn't like Jeeves and wanted him shot out. The realization that this girl resembled Honoria not only in body but in blackness of soul made me go all faint.

"What are you reading?"

She picked up my book and frowned again. The thing was one I had brought down from the old flat in London, to glance at in the train—a fairly zippy effort in the detective line called *The Trail of Blood*. She turned the pages with a nasty sneer.

"I can't understand you liking nonsense of this—" She stopped suddenly: "Good gracious!"

"What's the matter?"

"Do you know Bertie Wooster?"

And then I saw that my name was scrawled right across the title page, and my heart did three back somersaults.

"Oh—er—well—that is to say—well, slightly."

"He must be a perfect horror. I'm surprised that you can make a friend of him. Apart from anything else, the man is practically an imbecile. He was engaged to my Cousin Honoria at one time, and it was broken off because he was next door to insane. You should hear my Uncle Roderick talk about him!"

I wasn't keen.

"Do you see much of him?"

"A goodish bit."

"I saw in the paper the other day that he was fined for making a disgraceful disturbance in the street."

"Yes, I saw that."

She gazed at me in a foul, motherly way.

"He can't be a good influence for you," she said. "I do wish you would drop him. Will you?"

"Well—" I began. And at this point old Cuthbert, the cat, having presumably found it a bit slow by himself in the bushes, wandered in with a matey expression on his face and jumped on my lap. I welcomed him with a good deal of cordiality. Though but a cat, he did make a sort of third at this party; and he afforded a good excuse for changing the conversation.

"Jolly birds, cats," I said.

She wasn't having any.

"Will you drop Bertie Wooster?" she said, absolutely ignoring the cat motif.

"It would be so difficult."

"Nonsense! It only needs a little willpower. The man surely can't be so interesting a companion as all that. Uncle Roderick says he is an inveterate waster."

I could have mentioned a few things that I thought Uncle Roderick was, but my lips were sealed, so to speak.

"You have changed a great deal since we last met," said the Pringle disease reproachfully. She bent forward and began to scratch the cat under the ear. "Do you remember, when we were children together, you used to say that you would do anything for me?"

"Did I?"

"I remember once you cried because I was cross and wouldn't let you kiss me."

I didn't believe it at the time, and I don't believe it now. Sippy is in many ways a good deal of a chump, but surely even at the age of ten he cannot have been such a priceless ass as that. I think the girl was lying, but that didn't make the position of affairs any better. I edged away a couple of inches and sat staring before me, the old brow beginning to get slightly bedewed.

And then suddenly—well, you know how it is, I mean. I suppose everyone has had that ghastly feeling at one time or another of being urged by some overwhelming force to do some absolutely blithering act. You get it every now and then when you're in a crowded theater and something seems to be egging you on to shout "Fire!" and see what happens. Or you're talking to someone and all at once you feel, "Now, suppose I suddenly biffed this bird in the eye!"

Well, what I'm driving at is this, at this juncture, with her shoulder squashing against mine and her back hair tickling my nose, a perfectly loony impulse came sweeping over me to kiss her.

"No, really?" I croaked.

"Have you forgotten?"

She lifted the old onion and her eyes looked straight

into mine. I could feel myself skidding. I shut my eyes. And then from the doorway there spoke the most beautiful voice I had ever heard in my life:

"Give me that cat!"

I opened my eyes. There was good old Aunt Jane, that queen of her sex, standing before me, glaring at me as if I were a vivisectionist and she had surprised me in the middle of an experiment. How this pearl among women had tracked me down I don't know, but there she stood, bless her dear, intelligent old soul, like the rescue party in the last reel of a motion picture.

I didn't wait. The spell was broken and I legged it. As I went, I heard that lovely voice again.

"He shot arrows at my Tibby from a bow," said this most deserving and excellent octogenarian.

For the next few days all was peace. I saw comparatively little of Heloise. I found the strategic value of that water pipe outside my window beyond praise. I seldom left the house now by any other route. It seemed to me that, if only the luck held like this, I might after all be able to stick this visit out for the full term of the sentence.

But meanwhile, as they used to say in the movies—

The whole family appeared to be present and correct as I came down to the drawing room a couple of nights later. The Prof, Mrs. Prof, the two Exhibits, and the girl Heloise were scattered about at intervals. The cat slept on the rug, the canary in its cage. There was nothing, in short, to indicate that this was not just one of our ordinary evenings.

"Well, well, well!" I said cheerily. "Hullo-ullo-ullo!"

I always like to make something in the nature of an entrance speech, it seeming to me to lend a chummy tone to the proceedings.

The girl Heloise looked at me reproachfully.

"Where have you been all day?" she asked.

"I went to my room after lunch."

"You weren't there at five."

"No. After putting in a spell of work on the good old

colleges I went for a stroll. Fellow must have exercise if he means to keep fit."

"*Mens sana in corpore sano,*" observed the prof.

"I shouldn't wonder," I said cordially.

At this point, when everything was going as sweet as a nut and I was feeling on top of my form, Mrs. Pringle suddenly soaked me on the base of the skull with a sandbag. Not actually, I don't mean. No, no. I speak figuratively, as it were.

"Roderick is very late," she said.

You may think it strange that the sound of that name should have sloshed into my nerve centers like a halfbrick. But, take it from me, to a man who has had any dealings with Sir Roderick Glossop there is only one Roderick in the world—and that is one too many.

"Roderick?" I gurgled.

"My brother-in-law, Sir Roderick Glossop, comes to Cambridge tonight," said the prof. "He lectures at St. Luke's tomorrow. He is coming here to dinner."

And while I stood there, feeling like the hero when he discovers that he is trapped in the den of the Secret Nine, the door opened.

"Sir Roderick Glossop," announced the maid or some such person, and in he came.

One of the things that get this old crumb so generally disliked among the better element of the community is the fact that he has a head like the dome of St. Paul's and eyebrows that want bobbing or shingling to reduce them to anything like reasonable size. It is a nasty experience to see this bald and bushy bloke advancing on you when you haven't prepared the strategic railways in your rear.

As he came into the room I backed behind a sofa and commended my soul to God. I didn't need to have my hand read to know that trouble was coming to me through a dark man.

He didn't spot me at first. He shook hands with the prof and wife, kissed Heloise, and waggled his head at the Exhibits.

"I fear I am somewhat late," he said. "A slight ac-

cident on the road, affecting what my chauffeur termed
the—"

And then he saw me lurking on the outskirts and gave
a startled grunt, as if I hurt him a good deal internally.

"This—" began the prof, waving in my direction.

"I am already acquainted with Mr. Wooster."

"This," went on the prof, "is Miss Sipperley's
nephew, Oliver. You remember Miss Sipperley?"

"What do you mean?" barked Sir Roderick. Having
had so much to do with loonies has given him a rather
sharp and authoritative manner on occasion. "This is
that wretched young man, Bertram Wooster. What is all
this nonsense about Olivers and Sipperleys?"

The prof was eyeing me with some natural surprise.
So were the others. I beamed a bit weakly.

"Well, as a matter of fact—" I said.

The prof was wrestling with the situation. You could
hear his brain buzzing.

"He said he was Oliver Sipperley," he moaned.

"Come here!" bellowed Sir Roderick. "Am I to understand
that you have inflicted yourself on this household
under the pretense of being the nephew of an old
friend?"

It seemed a pretty accurate description of the facts.

"Well—er—yes," I said.

Sir Roderick shot an eye at me. It entered the body
somewhere about the top stud, roamed around inside for
a bit, and went out at the back.

"Insane! Quite insane, as I knew from the first moment
I saw him."

"What did he say?" asked Aunt Jane. "Roderick says
this young man is insane," roared the prof.

"Ah!" said Aunt Jane, nodding. "I thought so. He
climbs down waterpipes."

"Does what?"

"I've seen him—ah, many a time!"

Sir Roderick snorted violently.

"He ought to be under proper restraint. It is abominable
that a person in his mental condition should be

permitted to roam the world at large. The next stage may quite easily be homicidal."

It seemed to me that, even at the expense of giving old Sippy away, I must be cleared of this frightful charge. After all, Sippy's number was up anyway.

"Let me explain," I said. "Sippy asked me to come here."

"What do you mean?"

"He couldn't come himself, because he was jugged for biffing a cop on Boat-Race Night."

Well, it wasn't easy to make them get the hang of the story, and even when I'd done it it didn't seem to make them any chummier towards me. A certain coldness about expresses it, and when dinner was announced I counted myself out and pushed off rapidly to my room. I could have done with a bit of dinner, but the atmosphere didn't seem just right.

"Jeeves," I said, having shot in and pressed the bell, "we're sunk."

"Sir?"

"Hell's foundations are quivering and the game is up."

He listened attentively.

"The contingency was one always to have been anticipated as a possibility, sir. It only remains to take the obvious step."

"What's that?"

"Go and see Miss Sipperley, sir."

"What on earth for?"

"I think it would be judicious to apprise her of the facts yourself, sir, instead of allowing her to hear of them through the medium of a letter from Professor Pringle. That is to say, if you are still anxious to do all in your power to assist Mr. Sipperley."

"I can't let Sippy down. If you think it's any good—"

"We can but try, sir. I have an idea, sir, that we may find Miss Sipperley disposed to look leniently upon Mr. Sipperley's misdemeanor."

"What makes you think that?"

"It's just a feeling that I have, sir."

"Well, if you think it would be worth trying— How do we get there?"

"The distance is about a hundred and fifty miles, sir. Our best plan would be to hire a car."

"Get it at once," I said.

The idea of being a hundred and fifty miles away from Heloise Pringle, not to mention Aunt Jane and Sir Roderick Glossop, sounded as good to me as anything I had ever heard.

The Paddock, Beckley-on-the-Moor, was about a couple of parasangs from the village, and I set out for it next morning, after partaking of a hearty breakfast at the local inn, practically without a tremor. I suppose when a fellow has been through it as I had in the last two weeks his system becomes hardened. After all, I felt, whatever this aunt of Sippy's might be like, she wasn't Sir Roderick Glossop, so I was that much on velvet from the start.

The Paddock was one of those medium-sized houses with a goodish bit of very tidy garden and a carefully rolled gravel drive curving past a shrubbery that looked as if it had just come back from the dry cleaner—the sort of house you take one look at and say to yourself, "Somebody's aunt lives there." I pushed on up the drive, and as I turned the bend I observed in the middle distance a woman messing about by a flower bed with a trowel in her hand. If this wasn't the female I was after, I was very much mistaken, so I halted, cleared the throat, and gave tongue.

"Miss Sipperley?"

She had had her back to me, and at the sound of my voice she executed a sort of leap, or bound, not unlike a barefoot dancer who steps on a tin tack halfway through the Vision of Salome. She came to earth and goggled at me in a rather goofy manner. A large, stout female with a reddish face.

"Hope I didn't startle you," I said.

"Who are you?"

"My name's Wooster. I'm a pal of your nephew Oliver."

Her breathing had become more regular.

"Oh?" she said. "When I heard your voice I thought you were someone else."

"No, that's who I am. I came up here to tell you about Oliver."

"What about him?"

I hesitated. Now that we were approaching what you might call the nub, or crux, of the situation, a good deal of my breezy confidence seemed to have slipped from me.

"Well, it's rather a painful tale, I must warn you."

"Oliver isn't ill? He hasn't had an accident?"

She spoke anxiously, and I was pleased at this evidence of human feeling. I decided to shoot the works with no more delay.

"Oh, no, he isn't ill," I said; "and as regards having accidents, it depends on what you call an accident. He's in chokey."

"In what?"

"In prison."

"In prison!"

"It was entirely my fault. We were strolling along on Boat-Race Night and I advised him to pinch a policeman's helmet."

"I don't understand."

"Well, he seemed depressed, don't you know; and rightly or wrongly, I thought it might cheer him up if he stepped across the street and collared a policeman's helmet. He thought it a good idea, too, so he started doing it, and the man made a fuss and Oliver sloshed him."

"Sloshed him?"

"Biffed him—smote him a blow—in the stomach."

"My nephew Oliver hit a policeman in the stomach?"

"Absolutely in the stomach. And the next morning the beak sent him to the bastille for thirty days without the option."

I was looking at her a bit anxiously all this while to see how she was taking the thing, and at this moment her face seemed suddenly to split in half. For an instant she appeared to be all mouth, and then she was staggering about the grass, shouting with laughter and waving the trowel madly.

It seemed to me a bit of luck for her that Sir Roderick Glossop wasn't on the spot. He would have been calling for the strait-waistcoat in the first half-minute.

"You aren't annoyed?" I said.

"Annoyed?" She chuckled happily. "I've never heard such a splendid thing in my life."

I was pleased and relieved. I had hoped the news wouldn't upset her too much, but I had never expected it to go with such a roar as this.

"I'm proud of him," she said.

"That's fine."

"If every young man in England went about hitting policemen in the stomach, it would be a better country to live in."

I couldn't follow her reasoning, but everything seemed to be all right; so after a few more cheery words I said good-bye and legged it.

"Jeeves," I said when I got back to the inn, "everything's fine. But I am far from understanding why."

"What actually occurred when you met Miss Sipperley, sir?"

"I told her Sippy was in the jug for assaulting the police. Upon which she burst into hearty laughter, waved her trowel in a pleased manner, and said she was proud of him."

"I think I can explain her apparently eccentric behavior, sir. I am informed that Miss Sipperley has had a good deal of annoyance at the hands of the local constable during the past two weeks. This has doubtless resulted in a prejudice on her part against the force as a whole."

"Really? How was that?"

"The constable has been somewhat overzealous in the performance of his duties, sir. On no fewer than three occasions in the last ten days he has served summonses upon Miss Sipperley—for exceeding the speed limit in her car; for allowing her dog to appear in public without a collar; and for failing to abate a smoky chimney. Being in the nature of an autocrat, if I may use the term, in the village, Miss Sipperley has been accustomed to do these things in the past with impunity, and the constable's unexpected zeal has made her somewhat ill disposed to policemen as a class and consequently disposed to look upon such assaults as Mr. Sipperley's in a kindly and broadminded spirit."

I saw his point.

"What an amazing bit of luck, Jeeves!"

"Yes, sir."

"Where did you hear all this?"

"My informant was the constable himself, sir. He is my cousin."

I gaped at the man. I saw, so to speak, all.

"Good Lord, Jeeves! You didn't bribe him?"

"Oh, no, sir. But it was his birthday last week, and I gave him a little present. I have always been fond of Egbert, sir."

"How much?"

"A matter of five pounds, sir."

I felt in my pocket.

"Here you are," I said. "And another fiver for luck."

"Thank you very much, sir."

"Jeeves," I said, "you move in a mysterious way your wonders to perform. You don't mind if I sing a bit, do you?"

"Not at all, sir," said Jeeves.